But What Do I Know?
[Vol. 1]

A COMPILATION OF NEWSPAPER
COLUMNS OF THE SAME NAME

WRITTEN BY COLUMNIST

Tom Treece

PROVERBS 3:5-6

But What Do I Know? [Vol. 1]
by Tom Treece

Printed in the United States of America

ISBN 978-1-60477-342-2

Unless otherwise indicated, Bible quotations are taken from King James Version and/or New International Version.

Typesetting and layout design by Crysti Esper, Monroe, MI

www.xulonpress.com

TABLE OF CONTENTS

*Pages 129-482 Were Reprinted By Permission From
The Monroe Evening News*

DEDICATIONS

There's a method to my madness: up at five for coffee, then daily devotion from "My Utmost for His Highest" by Oswald Chambers, followed by spirit-led scripture reading and then quiet time listening to The God of Abraham. Once those are complete I counsel with Him, passing along my prayers and petitions for personal guidance, for family, friends, leaders, mankind.

When I need one it's during this time I ask Him to "give me a column." When prayers are over I sit for a while contemplating, and then my fingers find the keyboard and I begin to write. What lies within these pages is what comes from those sessions.

Once completed there is one final, important task to accomplish: I call my soundboard, my soul mate, the other half of the one that we are, my wonderful wife, Renee, and read her my rendering. Once I have her approval I know the work is ready for my publisher, and, ultimately, you.

Therefore, I wish to dedicate this collection of columns to my main inspirations: my Heavenly Father, who created me, reclaimed me and keeps me, and the love of my life, my sweet Renee, both of who rescued me from my lowest ebb of life.

Also to the family, friends and foes who makeup the myriad of memories and experiences you are about to read.

Special thanks to my editors along the way - Cindy Trudeau of LZ 142, Mike Schaffer of *The Monroe Guardian* and Deborah Saul of *The Monroe Evening News* – for believing in me enough to include my work in their publications. To graphics guru Jim Dombrowski of MP Design for fantastic covers for all my work. To Bryan Bosch of *The Monroe Evening News* for his work on this book's back cover photo, Dave Eby for providing me with much needed photos, and to the endless copy editors along the way who have interceded for me each time it was obvious I hadn't been listening or learning during English class.

Also, Monroe Bank & Trust, to whom the last chapter of this book is dedicated, and especially to mine and Renee's special friend for believing that these stories should be read more than just once each week; you know who you are.

Finally, to all American patriots who have served our great country - especially during time of war – protecting the freedom we all love so very much that allows us to openly express opinions such as are found in this book. I especially honor ones who gave the ultimate sacrifice, specifically a few of my closest, personal friends killed during the Vietnam War, all of whom you will read of in this book: Rodney Vore, Richard Gilbert, Lenny Liparato and Vince LaRocca. Rest in peace, my brothers.

FORWARD

While I've always loved to write, what has evolved into this book started from me being a member of the staff of LZ 142, the monthly newsletter of my local Chapter 142 of Vietnam Veterans of America in my hometown of Monroe, Michigan.

One evening while discussing our latest edition with Editor, Cindy Trudeau, I suggested we add an opinion column to our publication in order to discuss important issues affecting veterans.

"Great idea," she said before adding, "You write it!"

I agreed and began adding one for each issue; later I decided the column needed a moniker.

Like most folks I have always had an opinion and was never shy in sharing it. Whether asked or simply offering, I would detail my position about the subject matter as in-depth and eloquently as possible before always adding one final statement at the end in order to qualify my position; that statement was, "But what do I know?"

While I have always had a strong belief system, likewise I have always believed that everyone on the planet thinks and sees things differently. We all see the world through our own eyes and create our values, morals and judgments based upon that personal vision. As a result, everyone thinks they are right about what they think, say and do.

I am no different; I too think I am right. However, knowing no one is always right and no one is always wrong, I simply qualify myself and my opinion at the end by saying, "But what do I know?"

What this does is tell the reader that I know I am just another one of the many scratching and clawing their way through this life, and, as a result, don't consider myself to have any special insight to life.

If you read something in this book that you agree with and it helps you get along a little easier through your life as a result, great! If you think I am the biggest raving lunatic you've ever read, great!

I decided that "But What Do I Know?" was the name I wanted for the column.

In addition to addressing veteran's issues in those early columns I began writing what I call an "Obitorial," a combination of an obituary (for when someone unique to the chapter had died) coupled with an editorial about their life. I continue to write those to this day.

A call came one day from Mike Schaffer - then-editor of the *Monroe Guardian* weekly newspaper who knew I was involved in veteran's issues - asking if I would write a story for a special Memorial Day section he was putting together, which I did.

Not long after, he heard about my columns and asked if I would like to submit one every now and then for publication; before long I was a weekly feature. While I wasn't being paid for my work, I was happy to have an outlet for my writing.

One day Mike called me into his office and said, "Love your columns but you've got to cool the "God stuff." I was a bit shocked at feeling like I had done something wrong; I assured him I would comply.

There was only one problem. The next time I began to write a column, nearing completion I realized I was heading back into the "God Stuff" so I trashed it.

The next week was the same; each time I would get into the meat of the column the "God Stuff" would flow in and I would have to stop and toss the idea.

After the third week, Mike called questioning why I had not submitted a column. I explained, "Every time I start to write I always end up coming back to the "God Stuff" because that's what I'm all about, so I guess I just can't write for the paper anymore."

Turned out readers had been calling wondering why my columns had disappeared. Mike assured me he wanted me to continue writing for the paper and that perhaps I could just cool the "God Stuff" a bit. I went back to writing as I always had and never gave it another thought and never had another problem.

After a couple of years Mike called me into his office one day and informed me the paper had been sold and there would no longer be room for my column. I thanked him for the opportunity he had afforded me and started to leave.

"That's it?" he asked. "I've been putting off telling you this because I thought you would be upset considering how passionate you are about your column!"

I assured him my hope was in my personal relationship with Jesus Christ and not in the column and that God was simply closing this door in order to open another.

Three weeks later my phone rang again; this time it was *Monroe Evening News* Editor and long time friend, Deborah Saul.

After a bit of small talk she asked, "Do you intend to continue writing your column?" to which I responded, "Well, I'd like to but, unfortunately, I don't have a venue for it."

"How would you like to write for the Monroe News?" she asked.

Excitement shot through my veins at the very thought of writing for the newspaper that had been such an icon in my life. Not only had I always read it religiously, but my mother and brother had previously worked there and my first job had been as one of their paperboys.

Suddenly I remembered the "God stuff" problem with the *Guardian* which tempered my joy so I backed down a bit.

"Well, that depends on a few things," I answered.

Somehow she must have known I had been working for free as her response was, "Oh don't worry, we'll pay you!"

"I'm not talking about money," I called back before adding, "I write a lot about my faith and if that going to be a problem – as it has in the past – then I'm not interested.

"No problem!" she insisted.

"What about politics; I get political sometimes and might have an opposing opinion to the paper's; any problem with that?" I asked.

Again her answer was, "No problem!"

"Are you willing to put that in writing?" I asked finally.

"Absolutely," was her reply.

We worked out the remuneration and contract details and on October 27, 2003, I wrote my first column for the Monroe News titled, "From Carrier to Columnist," and my career as a columnist was launched.

I'm not sure how people perceive me. Personally I think I am "either, or, but never maybe," meaning they either love me or hate me. One thing for sure is, writing this column has certainly changed my life.

What you have before you is a compilation of weekly essays that translate into my opinion about what was going on around me during the times of these writings. If you don't know me personally or if you're not a native of the Monroe, Michigan area, there will undoubtedly be many things in this book that will make no sense to you.

On the other hand, I believe there is an underlying philosophy exhibited in these writings that are a bit of a throw-back to days gone by when men meant what they said, discipline was paramount, value systems were in place and nobody was unscrupulously trying to get ahead of you in line.

If you think those things are out of style, you probably won't like this book. On the other hand, if you do, I expect you will.

Personally, I think these stories are fun and interesting and can be an inspiration to some who may be struggling while trying to make sense of their life.

But what do I know?

OBITORIAL – ADMIRAL
ELMO ZUMWALT, JR.

J A N U A R Y, 2 0 0 0

The commander of U.S. Navy forces in Vietnam from 1968-70 is dead at the age of 79. Credited as the architect of the modern Navy and being widely revered as one whom genuinely cared for the soldiers under his command, Zumwalt relaxed Navy standards to allow properly maintained beards and longer hair, as well as relaxed in-port dress standards, making the Navy more attractive to potential enlistees. He dealt with military downsizing by incorporating more sophisticated weaponry, a practice still in effect today some 30 years later.

Perhaps we best know Zumwalt as the man who ordered the spraying of the Vietnam jungles with Agent Orange, the chemical defoliant containing dioxin. Zumwalt's son, Elmo Zumwalt III, served under his father's command and later died from lymphatic cancer in 1988, leaving the father to believe that he had inadvertently been responsible for his own son's death.

Zumwalt began to lead efforts to study the deadly effects of the chemical on the people and the land upon which it rained down, obviously to the dismay of the US military. "No one has done more to face the consequences of Agent Orange and provide benefits to sick vets," said President Boy Muller of the VVA Foundation in Washington, D.C.

We obitorial Admiral Zumwalt today as a man who, in spite of achieving tremendous success due to his gifted vision, organization and insight, had the courage and conviction to stand in the face of the military machine he once commanded and say, "We made a mistake…. we need to fix it!" And, while his words have fallen on deaf ears (as ours continue to do) we salute him today for being a man of courage who at least made an attempt to do what was right.

We are reminded of the recently released, formerly secret-taped telephone recordings of President Lyndon Johnson wherein he admits our involvement in Vietnam "Is a mistake!" As we see it he never had the courage to openly admit that mistake or try to correct it. Worse, we shudder to think that ones - such as former Defense Secretary McNamara, who in writing a book 30 years later, would acknowledge that same mistake yet act shocked when Vietnam veterans called for his head – might still be in positions of power today.

I guess to Johnson, McNamara and the local draft board member (whose two sons somehow never got drafted), it really didn't matter as long as it didn't affect them. But to Elmo Zumwalt, as soon as that mistake drifted through HIS from door and into the lymph nodes of HIS son, things were entirely different. Too bad something like that has to "come home" before action is taken.

We are thankful for men of courage in positions of leadership who are willing to acknowledge, and then correct, mistakes!

A WOMAN WANTS TO BE CHERISHED

FEBRUARY, 2000

"A woman wants to be cherished and a man wants to be understood." I don't have a clue who made that statement but somewhere along the line I heard it and have never forgotten it; I also believe there is great truth in that statement. Women want to be cherished and men want to be understood.

I knew a Vietnam veteran once whose wife used to adamantly say every time he would mention what happened to him in the war, "I don't want to hear any of this Vietnam crap; it's just a crutch and you ain't getting any sympathy from me!" As a matter of fact, I knew that guy extremely well. Fortunately for him he isn't married to her anymore. Besides, I'm sure he was as much of a jerk to her as she was to him.

It reminded me of this month's assignment from our newsletter editor to share some stories about the impact that our spouses have had on our lives as Vietnam veterans. I can't gush enough about my lovely Renee! She has been exactly the opposite of the aforementioned. She has never been too busy or not wanted to hear what I have needed to express, especially about our "run through the jungle."

There have been so many times that I have gotten so frustrated with my life for seemingly no apparent reason. I call it, "The Scalding." It's like when you turn on the shower and jump in; not realizing the water is so hot that you scald yourself. You slap the showerhead away and adjust the water to where it doesn't hurt and then climb back under the water. Soon you realize you turned it down too much so you increase the hot again. This continues to happen until - if you stayed in long enough - you would actually return the water to the original scalding temperature. Once you've been in that trauma, sooner or later anything less just won't satisfy you anymore.

That has always been difficult for me to explain. It is an analogy I use for the scalding we suffered from being plucked out of life and sent 14,000 miles from home and loved ones, given automatic weapons and told to go kill people about whom we knew nothing. As most of you know, finding someone to hear that and truly understand has been difficult at best. That is, for me, until Renee!

She has been there for me at every step of the way. She shuts everything down until she knows what I mean or am thinking. She holds me, assures me that everything will be all right, that I will find another job and that we will have enough money and that no matter what the dragon is that stands in the way of today...we will slay it together. She buys my clothes because she knows I hate to shop; she nurses me when I'm sick, she launders my clothes because she wants to, not because we can't afford dry cleaning. She always finds time to meet my every need and usually starts each day asking if there is anything she can do for me. She is the love of my life and I thank God for sending her to me because without her, I'm sure that the scalding would eventually kill me.

I want her to know that she is the only one for me and that I would die for her and that my job in life is to make her life as happy as it can possibly be.

There's a Dan Fogelberg song that says, "There's a song in the heart of a woman that only the truest of loves can reveal." I want her to sing that song every day because she knows she has that in me!

I want her to know that I cherish her because I believe without a doubt that she wants to understand me.

But what do I know?

A NEW HEART
MARCH, 2000

Yesterday I received two phone calls. The first came from our editor, Cindy Trudeau, advising me that one of our beloved members – Ed Tolen – had been called to Ann Arbor to receive...a new heart! Everyone knows that Ed has a big heart, but he also has a deep history of heart trouble, which has included quadruple bypass surgery twice. Recently he was placed on high priority to receive the next available donor heart; the call came yesterday in the early morning hours.

After I received the call, I made a call to my constant companion, the One who advises and leads me: The Great Physician, The King of the Universe...Jesus Christ! I asked Him to lead the team of surgeons and for His will to be done in Ed's life. Then, I stopped worrying about Ed.

Last evening, after returning from a late night of work in the office, the answering machine relayed many different concerned members' updates on my lifelong friend informing me he was out of surgery and resting comfortably and that so far there was no rejection of the new heart by his body.

I thanked God for the good news and started thinking about sharing with you the two issues that kept crossing over from each other in my thoughts and I realized I needed to write about...a new heart.

As I finger these keys I have no idea what the final outcome of Ed's surgery will be. Even though heart transplants have become somewhat of a common occurrence, it still remains an extremely dangerous procedure. However, the prognosis for complete recovery and an even better life than ever before is a distinct reality with new medical technology.

Let's face it; we can't live without our heart. We can live without a hand or fingers, legs, eyesight or hearing, but not without that heart. Until late this century the heart was irreplaceable. Now, however, a team of doctors can take the heart of one person and place it in another, returning him to restored health, which in turn gives that person a new spirit and lease on life.

God has been performing that same operation since time began; maybe not in the physical sense, but certainly in the spiritual sense. We say, "Have a heart!" "Don't lose heart!" "Believe in your heart!" or, "He's got a big heart!" to each other. Those aren't physical requests or statements; they are spiritual!

God spoke through the prophet Ezekiel in 36:26a (NIV) and said, "I will give you a new heart and put a new spirit in you." God has promised that He will transform your mind and heart and bring about a change in any that choose to accept and follow Him.

I gave my heart to Jesus Christ January 16, 1991, moments after falling on the floor while reaching for a shotgun in the closet. I ended up on my knees, and instead of taking a similar avenue of suicide many Vietnam veterans have taken since returning from war, I called out to Him and asked Him to come into my heart and transform my life, and that's exactly what He did!

I can still be as big of a jerk as anyone else and I still sin and make mistakes like everyone else, but now I have a Guide that I didn't before. He is my Heavenly Father and I talk with Him constantly; He is always by my side.

Like my earthly father who whipped my butt when I needed it and then showed me love and forgiveness after, God corrects and forgives me along the way. He never goes on vacation, never gets sick, never takes a day off or turns on the answering machine. He is always there when I call and I have learned to trust Him completely.

I know in my heart of hearts that as long as my life is centered on Him and His restored gospel, nothing can ever go permanently wrong. On the other hand, if my life is not, then I believe nothing will ever go permanently right.

I thank Him today for giving me a new heart, and I also want to thank Him for making a way for Ed to get a new heart.

He can give YOU a new heart! All you have to do is, "Ask and it will be given to you, seek and you will find, knock and the door will be opened to you. For everyone who asks receives; he who seeks finds; and to him who knocks, the door will be opened." (Matthew 7:7-8)

If you need someone to personally introduce you, I would be honored to be that person. I love introducing my friends to important people that I know, and believe me, there is nobody more important than Him!

But what do I know?

WHY A MINORITY AFFAIRS COMMITTEE?

FEBRUARY, 2001

With God as my witness and absolutely no offense intended toward anyone who is or has been chairperson of Chapter 142's Minority Affairs Committee...

As we have focused this month's newsletter on Minority Affairs and specifically how it conjuncts with Black History Month, I couldn't help myself from over and over asking these questions: Why do we even have a Minority Affairs Committee?

In my mind I searched the hundreds of pages of chapter minutes that I have personally and officially recorded through the years. For the life of me I could not recall even one verbal or written Minority Affairs report given at a chapter meeting, in spite of the fact that I'm sure there have been some.

It seems that as long as we see a chairperson's name listed behind the committee when we see it printed we can feel ok about ourselves and that we are properly dealing with this organizational issue as a chapter. (Just so you know this is not meant to indict anyone, let me remind all that this includes the one year that I led the chapter as president!).

The truth is that we have never taken action on this issue and in defense of the chapter and VVA, I don't' even know what we are supposed to do. I always thought the intent of the issue was to try and recruit minorities into the chapter, but with Monroe County listed as 97% white, that makes it extremely difficult.

The newsletter committee even struggled with the concept as we identified the issue months ago as one we wanted to target for this edition. We asked ourselves why we wanted to do it, and then we asked ourselves how we were going to do it. It was almost as if we agreed to do it because we believed it was important, but we didn't really know why and were uncomfortable with it as a result.

I rolled it over in my mind. My pastor gave me insight as I remembered a sermon he had delivered about how Jesus was no respecter of persons and how people of this world look on the outside but that He looks on the inside to see a man's heart.

I thought of Dr. King's famous words about his hope for the day when a man will be judged by "the content of his character instead of the color of his skin (I would add, "or the amount of money he has in the bank!").

I thought about the interview with chapter member Larry Gregory (in this issue) where he told about his father insisting he "never forget this act of kindness" shown to his family by a white family when he was a young boy and how he reciprocated that kindness every year since.

I wondered personally how this mountain of a man with such a sweet spirit must have felt when a southern redneck adamantly opposed having to sleep in the same foxhole with him during a Vietnam combat situation. And then I wondered how it would have felt had that been me instead of Larry.

I spoke with VVA State President Lupe Alviar – himself a minority – who assured me that the issue is not about recruiting but simply about recognizing minorities and their accomplishments. He shared that most minorities have developed a complex due to the repression they have lived with for so long, and, as a result, choose to hang out with their own kind rather than associate with the majority.

I have no idea of what direction we should head in order to make this committee work in the manner for which it was intended. I believe that by the very action your newsletter staff has taken by concentrating this edition on this issue is at least a proper and honorable step in the right direction. (By the way, part of next issue's focus will be women veterans and specifically the women of Chapter 142)

As Mr. Gregory said, rejection and repression due to the color of a man's skin has gone on long enough; it's time to correct that problem. And, even though when you watch the evening news it seems insurmountable, the truth is that it must begin one heart at a time.

With God as my witness I hereby pledge to begin this action within my very own heart, and I ask that each of you do the same to examine if there is intolerance, racism or attitudes of injustice lurking in the depths. If so, please join me in removing it for the sake of the future of this great country and the planet. If not, prepare for trouble like you have never seen that will be nothing compared to what I believe that final day of judgment will be when you will give anything to have made that change as I believe God will ultimately be YOUR witness!

But what do I know?

AMERICA CAN'T GET IT RIGHT FOR VETERANS

J U L Y , 2 0 0 1

We just can't seem to get it right here in America, especially with veterans.

Some three months ago I found scrawled on the weather-beaten pages of the Monroe County Vietnam Veterans Memorial Guest Log at Heck Park four messages complimenting Chapter 142 on our park while also extolling the virtues and patriotism of a group of WWII veterans who had visited who were known as the "Navaho Code Talkers."

With interest I watched yesterday's news as President Bush welcomed to a special White House ceremony four of five living Navaho Code Talkers who represented the original 29 Navaho veterans of WWII. It seems that during the desperate hour of war these men used their precious and sacred language – older than the US Constitution – as the only military code the Japanese could not break which saved countless American lives and enabled the Marines to prevail during an island-hopping campaign across the South Pacific.

Mr. Bush bestowed the highest civilian honor Congress affords on these men some 50+ years after their heroic service to our country. This, of course, is the same country that slaughtered their people some 150 years earlier in the name of civilization and then honored the men who led the charges across the west with statues like the one of General Custer that stands mightily in downtown Monroe. This same general is now the object of much hate and criticism and I wonder if the same treatment will be awaiting Generals Swartzkoff and Powell in another 150 years?

The attitude of the American government and people toward the returning Vietnam War veteran is well documented. We suffered the effects of the chemical defoliant Agent Orange but Congress assured us there was no link to our cancers.

All the people who were 100% behind the war effort in the beginning suddenly disappeared and were replaced by the ones who thought we should have never been there in the first place.

I remember what a joke my promise for a VA loan upon my return turned out to be.

Then came Desert Storm and out came the American flags, "Pray for Peace" bumper stickers and Support the Troops rallies that all disappeared three months later as it was back to business as usual.

The City of Monroe threw huge, city-wide parties and parades for the returning veterans who arched their eyebrows in wonder at all the attention as they knew they had watched the three month war on video screens from safe distances just like all the American people did in their living rooms.

So much attention for what they didn't do was just as detrimental as so little attention for what the Vietnam veteran did do!

Ah, and then they started getting sick. "Gulf War Syndrome," they call it, but once again Congress assures us that there couldn't possibly be a link to their service in the Persian Gulf!

The people I'm talking about won't want to read this "whining" from one who "can't let go of the past." Actually it is nothing more than hands thrust into the air in an attempt to stop the American way of calling on our young men (and now women) to fight our wars, then abandoning them and their maladies once the need has passed.

Reading the plight of the Navaho Code Talkers makes me realize that even though I'm thrilled they have finally been recognized, the truth is that we just can't seem to get it right here in America when it comes to our veterans.

But what do I know?

OBITORIAL — ED TOLEN:
GOODBYE LLOYD

A P R I L ,   2 0 0 2

"Hi Lloyd!" is how we used to greet each other in high school. You see, there was this wild and crazy man in the neighborhood that we all loved who used to call everyone "Lloyd," the name of an even crazier guy in the neighborhood. For some reason all the guys in the neighborhood started doing the same by calling each other "Lloyd."

Our friendship started in church as our parents were strict Southern Baptist and we were there religiously. That friendship maintained itself easily as we went to school together, fished, hunted and camped together, were both sports nuts and lived in closely bordered neighborhoods.

As soon as we could drive we ganged the guys together and cruised Monroe Street between Park 'N Snack and the Dixie Drive In, singing to the top of our lungs and cooling out only to ogle the finest babes or hottest machines.

One day one of the guys on our varsity basketball team – David Gilliland – tried to say his last name and instead called him, "Total Loss." It was a time of nicknames and this one stuck, mainly because Ed seemed to like it for some reason.

He was a wizard at shortstop or second base and even though he wasn't a power hitter, he knew how to hit the ball where the other team's players weren't. I remember him scoring 40 points the day our VVA team lost by one to the Sheriff Department during a benefit basketball game fundraiser for the We Care Telethon.

Even though he enlisted and I got drafted we both ended up at Kentucky's Ft. Knox Army base for basic training. We would meet at the service club and play pool. In later years he would rub it in as when we got to 'Nam, despite the fact that he was a clerk and I had "gone Airborne," he ended up with the 82nd Airborne and I ended up with the 11th Infantry. He loved that!

Yesterday morning I hand-fed 200 pound Gulf of Mexico stingrays on a gorgeous 85 degree day off the coast of Grand Cayman Island and yesterday afternoon Renee and I dined on filet mignon and lobster and celebrated our anniversary. Then, last night Vice President Warner called to share the sad news that Ed had finally lost his struggle with life. Isn't it strange how the day's events can change great joy into sadness in a single moment's notice?

I lay there in bed silently staring out over the Caribbean and thought about my friend and all the great times we have shared. I though of how he turned our Product Sales into such a viable entity that not only made money but plastered our name with class over the entire community and I wondered who would do that now.

I wondered who would run the golf tournament, the euchre tournament; who would sit and sweat for six days managing our booth at the Monroe Count Fair?

You were a good man, Ed Tolen! I don't for a moment think that you had a malicious bone in your body. I also don't think you had any idea what cool dude you really were.

And as I gazed up at the ocean of stars in the heavens last night I looked beyond and saw you there in God's choir of angels. Warm up the band and save us a seat, my brother, as I'm sure it won't' be long before some more of us old soldiers will be coming to join you. Till then....Goodbye Lloyd!

Tom and dear friend, Ed Tolen, playing pool at Ft. Knox KY, 1968

OBITORIAL— GRANT KOSINO
NO WHEELCHAIRS IN HEAVEN

A P R I L ,   2 0 0 2

The look on his face always gave him away. Some days it was the sly grin and the look in his eyes as he was about to pull one over on you. Other times it was the arched eyebrows and the wrinkled forehead that preceded a strong opinion.

Today it was the tight lips of determination and the focused eyes of concentration as he maneuvered the little blue Jimmy into the parking space. I sat in my car and watched as he struggled to open the door and pull his hand bag into position for easy retrieval once he had cleared the vehicle. I had offered to carry him into the meeting on numerous occasions; he would have none of it.

He reached down and grabbed his own thigh, lifted and spun it through the opening. Reaching back he did the same to the other, positioning the lifeless limbs in just the right spot for balance. He reached back for the aluminum cane that would allow him to keep that balance once upright, and the handbag of papers he would need for the meeting. The steering wheel made for leverage as he slowly spun and slithered his way out the door.

With the hurdle of exiting the vehicle behind, he eyed the next: the curb. My brain tells my leg to step up and over an insignificant barricade such as this and I'm gone in two seconds. Grant Kosino's brain had to tell his arms and hands (during this time   when they were still working...somewhat) to again physically lift his leg over the curb and position the cane in just the right spot for leverage. Then, with a combination of stabilization from the cane and a push off from the open car door, he dragged the other leg up and over the curb. The next task was to prepare a proper backswing with the door to ensure it latched the first time; otherwise it would be another ten minutes to turn around and secure the door.

Bag in hand and vehicle secured, he began his slow trek across the width of the sidewalk to the door that would lead him into the meeting of the board of directors of Vietnam Veterans of America, Monroe County Chapter 142, of which he was an extremely proud member!

I won't bore you with the details of him trying to open the door the times when a member wasn't available to hold it for him. In fact, I expect many are kind of bored with these details of his typical trip to chapter meetings...when he could still come.

Grant Kosino was always great inspiration for me. I always thought of him when I heard the excuses of those elected to chapter positions for not being able to make meetings and perform their duties. It was an honor for Grant. He would arrive at 8:00 AM for an 8:30 meeting just to begin the aforementioned procedure. Proud, resolved, determined, responsible...Grant Kosino! I wish I could have seen him dance!

The Vietnam War couldn't get him, Multiple Sclerosis couldn't get him, but cancer finally did April 11, 2002.

Because you should know...Grant was born June 5, 1950 (a kid to us old guys) in Monroe. The dad and mom responsible for teaching him to be the man he was were Byron and Eunice. The woman with whom he fell in love and married September 16, 1972 in Vidalia, Louisiana was Josephine ("Jodi" to those who know and love her) Corley. This woman would go on to show the same grit and determination in her attempts to save Grant that Forrest Gump did trying to save Bubba, only over an extremely long period of time.

Grant was a self-employed carpenter, working in the Kosino Woodworking business with his father. If you have any wonder whatsoever as to his woodworking skills, PLEASE take time at the next meeting to get a good look at the chapter podium he built; it is a masterpiece...a prized possession! What it will not show is the fact that he built it from his wheelchair!

Grant graduated from Jefferson High School in 1968 and enlisted in the Air Force and served from 1968-1972, earning the National Service, Vietnam Service and Republic of Vietnam Campaign Medals. He was a member of VFW Monroe Post 1138 and served Chapter 142 on its board of directors as well as chairing its Memorial Site Additions committee. He was also instrumental in bringing the highly successful annual circus fundraiser to the chapter.

In addition to Jodi, Grant is survived by son Ryon of Newport, daughters Brandi of Osan Air Base in South Korea and Kelly of Baltimore, Sister Daryl Nels of Dayton and brother Mark of Monroe.

Just like the curb in front of the chapter meeting room, Grant was perhaps seemingly insignificant to many in this life. But, just as the curb was a huge hurdle to him, to those of us who knew and loved him, his presence was just as huge and significant in our lives. I wouldn't trade my private times with Grant for anything, and I will always hold dear to my heart certain memories, such as Santa Larry Richter sitting on Grant's lap at Christmas, or the realization that State Representative Randy Richardville would come all the way from Lansing just to be at his birthday party!

Let us keep Grant tucked close inside the front door of our memory banks where we can be quickly reminded of one who...even though he had every reason to complain, rarely did...when we, who have virtually no reason to do so...do!

There'll be no wheelchairs in Heaven, Grant. Can't wait to see you dance!

OBITORIAL — JERRY C. BARTNIK: FLY FREE

APRIL, 2002

Missing from Jerry's obituary – born June 27, 1943 and died April 8, 2001 from the cancer that claimed his life – was the fact that he was a member of Chapter 142.

Jerry was a veteran but not a Vietnam veteran and I think he tired of explaining to others that he was an Associate Member.

I also think that worrying about keeping his membership up while he was worrying about keeping his life up wasn't something he was worrying about, and at this moment I'm worrying that we let him slip through the cracks and didn't keep it up for him!

I also think we have a tendency to bring flowers to one's funeral instead of giving them to them personally while they are alive!

What many people didn't know, which I expect includes many of you, is what an important part Jerry played in the chapter, especially during the early stages of Heck Park.

Jerry's career took him from political life in Bedford to the floor of the state legislature as our representative, and it was during this time he assisted us with his influence. The next time you are in a chapter meeting at VFW Post 1138, take a closer look at the oversized $35,000 check on the wall and you'll find Jerry's signature at the bottom. That state grant – thanks to Jerry – opened donation floodgates and gave validity to the initial building stages of the Monroe County Vietnam Veterans Memorial and Heck Park!

Once the memorial was built I remember telling Jerry how unsightly the park looked from the highway due to the tiny telephone poles that had huge strands of cables draping from one to another. In his cocky style he said, "No problem, I'll take care of it!" and by golly, two months later the poles were pulled and the cables run underground and Detroit Edison's power lines were rerouted across the street.

I approached him again when we dedicated the Huey helicopter and told him we wanted something dramatic for the ceremony to depict the plight of the Prisoners of War and Missing in Action. He said, "Let me think about it," and then called a week later with a solution.

On dedication day he came onstage with a Harrier Hawk that had previously been wounded and nursed back to health. He explained to the audience that the bird had been kept in the cage against its will and with the same resolve to see our POW/MIA's released we would set the bird free, which we did. It couldn't have been better!

As Heck Park continues its saga of growth and reconfiguration, I thought it important that we pause and remember one whose help and dedication was so very critical to the elementary success of what has turned out to be a primary focus of our chapter.

Thanks, Jerry, rest in peace dear friend! You were a tough old bird who loved that freedom yourself, and I expect that all the cancer that brought your death actually did was open the door of your cage so you too could fly free.

But what do I know?

WHY I FEED THE BIRDS

J A N U A R Y   4 ,   2 0 0 2

I froze as I caught movement in the tree. My eyes searched the branches for my prey. More movement from a slight turn of his head allowed me to lock my vision onto him. Slowly I shouldered my weapon and squared him in my sights. I gently squeezed the trigger and heard the gun spit the projectile.

"Yes!" I called out as the bird fell lifelessly from the tree.

The 12 year old boy was on his way to becoming the 'great white hunter', hopefully in the eyes of his family.

I had heard the stories of what a great hunter my father had been, especially the one about how he and his dog had killed 13 quail with just two shots from my grandfather's double-barreled, 12 gauge shotgun when he was a boy like me. Putting food on the table was the concern of each day as he grew up in the hills of Tennessee...a mighty important concern considering there were 12 mouths to feed.

And although times had changed and it was no longer necessary to hunt for food, the importance of being a "good shot" was still an underlying importance in my family.

Dad had reluctantly allowed me to buy a BB gun; my practice was on neighborhood birds. I loved to hunt, longed to win the approval of my father and older brother and for the day I would be finally old enough to join them on the hunt.

On this day I raced around the bush from behind which I had been hiding and dashed into our neighbor's yard to retrieve my kill. I took three steps...then stopped dead in my tracks.

The bird had fallen at his feet. The shoes were heavy old brogan work boots and the milk-white hair whispered his age. Both arms draped disappointedly at his side and for the longest time he simply stood and stared at the fallen bird. Finally, Mr. Lictfeldt raised his head and turned to look at me.

His face was smooth and silky. Wild, bushy eyebrows perched atop the soft, blue windows to his soul. I waited for him to start screaming at me. He did not.

Instead, after a long pause and in a soft and gentle voice, he called out to me… "Tommy, please don't kill my birds!"

I noticed the feeder hanging from one of the tree's low limbs just before I muttered, "Oh…uh…sorry!" and ran back into my yard. He was attracting the birds to his yard with the feeder which was just perfect for me.

I expect my thoughts at the time were about how the old man just didn't want us kids to have any fun, or something similar. I didn't give it much thought and simply went on with my hunting. I figured if he complained to my dad I would for sure lose my gun so I steered clear of his yard.

Years later, after being drafted into the United States Army and sent to fight in Vietnam, those years of handling weapons and being a good shot worked to my distinct advantage, but there was a tradeoff.

Once I had returned to the states, the sheer joy of hunting was no longer in my heart. No longer did I have a desire to kill anything. No longer did I even want to touch or own the guns I once worked so hard to purchase and proudly own.

So much was this new attitude that to this day I will grab a dishrag and capture a wasp or bee that has unintentionally become trapped inside my house, releasing it back to the world of which it simply wants to be a part…as opposed to killing it.

I had forgotten all about the incident with Mr. Lictfeldt; he and his wife had moved years ago.

I remember standing behind that same bush not too long after returning, gazing at the very spot the incident had taken place. I could see those soft eyes crying out to me, and once again I could hear him say, "Please don't kill my birds".

My nose tingled and the knot came in my throat as the wisdom of war and the maturity of those few years humbled me at the remembrance.

The next day I found his new address, chose a card and personalized it. I told Mr. Lictfeldt how sorry I was that I had killed his birds as a boy. I told him how my life had changed because of war and of the joy the birds now brought to my life with their singing and beauty.

Then I told him, "Mr. Lictfeldt, I promise you that as long as I live...I will continue to feed your birds!"

What I didn't know was that when he received that card he was nearing his appointment with death.

A few weeks later I read his obituary in the newspaper and went to the funeral home to pay my respects. I had to remind his wife just who I was, but when she made the connection she gasped and took me by the shoulders. "Oh Tommy", she said as she began to cry, "When Edward read your card...he wept!"

I stopped by ACO this morning after an early appointment. I was in a bit of a hurry to get back to work but I had run out of birdseed and wanted to re-supply. It was 8:50 and they didn't open until 9:00. I thought about waiting until next week to get the seed, but that would have meant Mr. Lictfeldt's birds would have gone without for a few extra days.

I waited the 10 minutes until the store opened, then bought an extra 20 pound bag. I think Mr. Lictfeldt has lots of birds in Luna Pier!

But what do I know?

THE DAY I HIT THE WALL

MARCH 21, 2002

I saw daylight from an opening between the two vehicles in front of me. In less than a blink of an eye, I made the decision and slammed the accelerator to the floor.

The engine roared in response and the car rocketed forward, into and through the opening ... but not without a price.

My heart pounded as the engine raced and that priceless feeling of euphoric uncertainty that only comes from dancing on the edge of fear and danger flooded my being.

I jerked my foot from the accelerator to slow the car; braking surely would have sent me into the concrete barrier looming to my right.

It wouldn't matter as I would make that visit soon enough.

Out the other side of the opening the car began to spin, ever so slightly at first, then almost sideways. The tires screamed and surrendered shredded bits of rubber as they tried to grip the smoking asphalt and respond to the commands of the steering wheel.

In that moment I found myself going forward, skidding sideways, with the car bouncing up and down on the tires trying to straighten it.

In another moment the car straightened and I was in the lead!

I could almost hear Momma's words in my ears: "Now, son, don't do anything stupid."

I couldn't help it.

There has always been something inside wanting to push the accelerator to the floor, from jumping out of airplanes to rappelling the Niagara gorge to driving my motorcycle at 140 mph or climbing to the very peak of Diamond Head.

So when the call came a few years ago from the Automobile Racing Club of America's Flat Rock Speedway to be a participant in a special "media race" at the track, of course I said an emphatic "yes."

My big brother had always been a racing enthusiast and dragged me along in my youth to various events.

Later, I sponsored a racecar through my business and was a regular attendee every Saturday night at the quarter-mile oval at Flat Rock, where you can still get one of the best bangs for your buck in entertainment.

While I can't remember all who participated in that day's race, the one I do remember is my boss here at The *Guardian*, Editor Mike Schaffer.

He was in the lead car that I tried to fly by that day. As a matter of fact, to this day he still calls me "Crash," and here's why.

I have always felt there are two positions where you can finish in sports: first and last. Being a typical male who hates to lose, I was not happy simply circling the short track that day in fourth (last) place.

So, when I saw daylight between those two lead cars, it was like an invitation to come and dine at the euphoric table of life and I accepted.

These were "street-stock" automobiles, meaning they virtually have nothing in them but a high performance engine and safety-reinforced bodies — no glass, no cushy seats, no air conditioning. From the racing fan's perspective they do not appear to travel at a high rate of speed.

Changing the perspective to staring through the windshield over white knuckles clenched around the steering wheel, it seems more like 120 mph!

The truth is probably somewhere between 50 and 60 mph.

I was quite shocked by the speedway's adamant attention to detail regarding the safety of the drivers.

It took some time, but a fire suit to fit my 6-foot-5-inch, 260-pound frame finally was found and borrowed.

The next task was to find a car with a driver's seat wide enough to accommodate my rear end. Helmet, safety goggles and fire-resistant driving gloves were next.

Climbing through the window and getting comfortable in the seat was no easy task but was finally completed. Then the straps: right leg, left leg, around the waist, over both shoulders, all winched to the point

I expected circulation to stop.

"I can hardly move!" I complained to one of the regular drivers assisting me.

"You hit that wall doing 60 and you'll understand why we do this," he said.

I was minutes away from finding out exactly to what he was referring.

All I needed now was a steering wheel. They handed it through the open window and I secured it firmly in place. I was ready to race!

I fingered the key and twisted it to the right. The engine groaned as it turned, then exploded in great power and noise as the cylinders fired and it roared to life.

Wow! The car trembled and shook and I thought about the difference between my nonchalant perceptions of the drivers while sitting in the grandstand to the reality of the moment sitting there in the hot seat.

Out pit road and through the gate and suddenly I was on the track. I teased the gas and felt the surge as the car lurched forward. This definitely wasn't my father's Buick!

I pulled the wheel hard from left to right to zigzag the car as I had seen drivers do countless times before to warm up the tires for the contest.

I wanted all watching to think I knew what I was doing. (As I write this, what comes to mind is the saying, "If you can't dazzle them with brilliance, then baffle them with BS").

As we slowly circled the track to get the feel of the cars, the flagman positioned us and gave the white flag, alerting us that after one more time around it was Showtime.

We bunched the cars together and built our speed down the backstretch. Out of turn four we saw "The Green." I floored it and almost hit the car in front of me.

"Be patient!" I told myself.

"Patience?" I responded, "There are only four laps to this race!" I knew I had to make a move soon and in turn one of the second lap I saw that daylight and made my move to take the lead from "Parnelli" Schaffer.

As I mentioned earlier, I executed the move successfully: into and through the opening, making the necessary corrections then into the lead. I remember saying, "Yes!" and feeling safe — just before the first impact.

Someone behind had followed my lead. As I straightened the car, I was hit from behind. The car lurched to the right and in a freeze-frame moment I saw the wall looming ahead.

In all my born days I have never stopped what I was doing faster than I did that day. One moment I was flying along and the next I was dead in my tracks.

I had hit the wall head-on. There was no recoil or bounce.

The shock of the collision had me reeling. I remember wondering if I was dead, or perhaps dreaming. I heard a spectator on the other side of the wall call out, "He's moving," and I realized he was talking about me and that I was definitely alive.

The words of the driver who assisted me into the safety harness rang in my ears like a church bell. He was right!

I looked down at my arms, hands and legs and wiggled everything to see if all my parts still worked. I could not believe I had gone through the trauma of that collision and not received the slightest scratch.

Suddenly, all of the extra effort and adamant enforcement of safety issues by ARCA made a lot more sense to me, and as they pulled me from the twisted wreckage of that vehicle I remember clamoring about how incredibly safe that car turned out to be.

The rites of spring include the openings soon of Flat Rock and Toledo speedways, and once again, I am excited.

There is something so special about man and machine pitted against each other in a contest in spite of the danger. And even though there are a few racing ladies out there each week, for the most part, I think it's a guy-thing.

Oh, by the way, I conveniently forgot to tell you that my boss won the race that day. I wonder if he was the one who hit me in the butt and sent me into the wall. Probably not. And besides, if it were him, I wouldn't accuse him. He'd just use that as a reason to get rid of me again!

But what do I know?

NO MIDEAST PEACE

A P R I L 1 8 , 2 0 0 2

There will never be peace in the Mideast.

Oh, perhaps there will be little pacts and temporary agreements here and there, but never real peace.

I first realized this January 16, 1991. The U.S.-led coalition attacked Baghdad that evening at 7:00 P.M. to begin a three-month assault that would drive Sadaam Hussein's insurgents out of neighboring Kuwait and dismantle much of his country's offensive weaponry.

Endless waves of aircraft and Tomahawk missiles pounded his Republican Guard and destroyed power and communications systems, resulting in his rapid retreat and virtual surrender.

There were over 50 countries allied against Iraq that evening; Israel was not one of them. However, Sadaam immediately did something I thought quite strange: he fired a Scud Missile at Israel, one of the few countries not attacking him.

I wondered why anyone with enough power and might to assemble the fourth-largest army in the history of the world would make that his first retaliatory move.

Then it hit me.

His whole purpose was to try and draw Israel into the conflict so the rest of the Arab nations would enter the foray based upon their burning hatred of the Jewish people and their sole desire to see them exterminated.

Does that thought remind you of anyone else?

Yes, Hitler's goal, masqueraded as world domination, was also to exterminate the Jewish people.

Why? What makes Jews such a target? Here's what I think.

Israel became an official state recognized by the rest of the world in 1948. Their claim to the land is backed by the Holy Bible, which historically states that God promised and gave this "land of milk and honey" to the Jewish people (and actually punished them, including

Moses, for not taking it after it had been given).

In my opinion, Abraham, the Jewish father of Israel, started this whole mess by not believing God would provide him an heir, also as promised.

As a result, he fathered a child by his wife's slave, Hagar, an Egyptian Arab. Later, his wife, Sarah, also a Jew, delivered the son God had promised, and the two children, Ishmael, the Arab, and Isaac, the Jew, would begin what I believe was a birthright fight that continues in the streets of Bethlehem today.

Read it for yourselves in the 16th and 17th chapters of Genesis.

Genesis 16:12 describing Ishmael, says, "And he will be a wild man; his hand will be against every man, and every man's hand against him; and he shall dwell in the presence of all his brethren."

Matthew Henry's Commentary suggests "That he should live in strife and in a state of war: His hand against every man — this is his sin; and every man's hand against him — this is his punishment."

After Isaac was born, Abraham asked God not to forget Ishmael. God responded that Ishmael would be prosperous, multiply and hold his own against the rest of the world, which is certainly true of the Arab world today.

The difference between the two is that God, for whatever reason, decided to covenant with Isaac and not Ishmael (Genesis 17:19-21).

Again, from Matthew Henry, "Many that are children of godly parents have, for their sakes, a very large share of outward common blessings, though, like Ishmael, they are not taken into covenant: many are multiplied that are not sanctified."

God chooses with whom He will covenant. (Is it coincidence that America, once an "In God We Trust" nation, has prospered to be what seems to be the only superpower/ country in the world to which people of all nations desire to come to live ... especially including Muslims?)

As Mideast bloodshed rages out of control, can you hear the "brethren" calling out to President Bush to "get over here and do something with these two before they kill each other and we all get into it!"

I believe what the Bible states: the land in question belongs to Israel.

However, as Heaven is intended to be an eternal place for all who would believe in the God of Abraham, I would love for Isaac (Israel) to find it in his heart to be forgiving and share the land with Ishmael (Palestine).

It won't happen.

First, because Israel knows Palestine would use the opportunity to move in their Trojan horse to complete the mission of the Arab: the complete destruction of the Jew. Second, and more important, is simply because God gave that land to Isaac (Israel).

My father gave my older brother, Hal, our old family stand-up radio. I loved that radio and have such fond memories of sitting on my father's knee listening to The Lone Ranger and other early radio favorites.

Considering that I went on to a 20-year radio career, it seemed only fitting that I should have had that heirloom and symbol of my industry. The only problem was that my father made a covenant (a binding agreement) with Hal for the radio, not me.

I guess I could go kill him and take the radio, but that would break the covenant I have made with God to love my brother as myself. Therefore, I must respect the decision made by my father, not only because I loved and respected him, but simply because I knew him personally and that it that was his radio to give!

If you believe the Koran, I expect you believe Mohammed is the Messiah who came from the lineage of Abraham and Hagar. If you believe the Holy Bible, then Jesus is the Messiah who came from the lineage of Abraham and Sarah. Perhaps you believe in the "Big Bang Theory" or that man evolved from apes or crawled out of the ocean.

I guess it all comes down to what you believe, or, perhaps more specifically, with whom you covenant.

The only Arab leader who ever had the true concept of peace in his mind was former Egyptian president Anwar Sadat, who walked onto Israeli soil and signed a covenant of peace with the Jewish people. A short time later he was machine-gunned to death by his own people.

In my opinion, the only peace the Arabs will consider is when Israel is exterminated and Palestine owns the land. And, according to The Book in which I believe...that will never happen!

But what do I know?

"Sunshine Coordinator," Mom (Pearl), 1997

REMEMBERING MOTHER

MAY 19, 2002

As crazy as this sounds …

A toothpick is walking down the main street of a deserted town. The sky has turned dark and ominous. The toothpick sees mountains towering over the walls of the town. Suddenly they begin to rumble and break loose from the earth and fly through the air towards the now-trembling toothpick to crush it.

At this point I cried out in the night, "Momma, Momma…"

In an instant she was there at my bedside, brushing the covers aside to pull me to her breast. She would cradle me in her arms and begin to rock me, softly assuring that it was only a bad dream and that momma was here to take care of me. She would gently sing until the tears were gone and then she would pray and ask God to watch over and protect me.

Funny how I can still remember the bizarre-yet-vivid details of a recurring nightmare from the earliest days of my life; mother always came to my rescue.

Almost 50 years later, ravaged by war, divorce, insecurity and no sense of purpose, I found myself once again calling out to mother.

I had gone for a ride with no specific destination in mind. My life was miserable and all I knew was that I couldn't sit still for another moment. Suddenly I saw the familiar sights of my childhood and realized my instincts were taking me back home to mother.

It was summertime. I pulled into the driveway and walked onto that old porch I had painted many times in the past. I peered through the screen door to see mother sitting in her rocking chair. Her face lit up when she realized it was one of her children and she called out the phrase that will ring in my ears forever, "Hi, Buddy!"

She named me 'Thomas' and called me 'Tommy Joe,' but the name she used for me I now cherish most was 'Buddy.' She was my buddy. She was my first friend. She was my first girlfriend. She was my first teacher. She taught me unconditional love and on this day that was exactly what I needed.

Before she could get out of that rocker I pulled open the door and bolted across the living room and fell in the floor at her feet. My emotions exploded and tears poured from my eyes as once again I cried out, "Momma!" I had no specific request but simply said, "Momma, will you pray for me?"

Once again, joyfully, she reached forward and cradled me in her arms and pulled me to her breast. 50 years ago I was less than a laundry basket to handle; this day I was 6 feet 5 inches tall and 260 pounds. It didn't matter, as I was still her "little boy."

She proceeded to pray a prayer to God I shall never forget, once again asking Him to watch over and protect me as she had all those years ago. My life changed that day and everything that was upside down turned right-side up, all with the help and the love of a mother

It's nice to have a special day to honor our mothers, and Sunday, like you I hope, I'll be remembering "momma."

And, if there is anyone out there who will read this and think of me as a "sentimental sap," let me say to you right now …

But what do you know?

WAR GAMES

MAY 23, 2002

"Got room for two more?" called one of the two first lieutenants walking our way. Their clean, fresh, not-yet-faded-from-the-Vietnam-sun uniforms gave them away as new guys who had just arrived in the country.

Rivers of sweat poured from my pores as 110 degrees from the midday sun baked the two teams of soldiers from the Americal Division's 11th Light Infantry Brigade.

"Sure," I called back as I welcomed the break to catch my breath.

We were in base camp at Landing Zone Bronco, Duc Pho, Republic of South Vietnam, welcoming a timeout from the war to enjoy a spirited game of basketball. A metal ring from a crate of nails was our rim; a piece of plywood stolen from the motor pool was our backboard. Both were mounted on a utility pole whose main purpose was to thrust the base's command bunker antennae high into the sky.

The "first louie's" told us their names; we took one per side and resumed the game. An hour later, drenched and drained, we slapped high-fives, shared home towns, lives and loves and hooted about how great it felt to forget the war — still just yards away outside the camp's concertina wire — for even just a short while.

We had to stop the game so the lieutenants could catch a convoy from L.Z. Bronco going north to their new home for the next 365 days at L.Z. Liz. I waved goodbye to these two likable fellows and worried about them as I knew the stretch of dirt road they were about to cross was notorious for having booby traps planted by the Viet Cong.

Some two hours later a call came over the radio asking if anyone from Bronco, who might have met two first lieutenants who had just arrived in the country, could come to brigade headquarters and identify their bodies! I closed my eyes and gritted my teeth; my mind cried, "Please don't let it be them!"

The battalion executive officer, remembering our basketball game, instructed me to go. I jumped into his Jeep and maneuvered the mile to headquarters, where I was instructed to go to a side room that served as a morgue. I will spare you something I can never spare myself: the image of both lieutenants lying on the floor, lifeless.

I just stood and stared at them. The friendly, talkative one ... Hollywood handsome, blond hair, blue bedroom eyes that saw no more now glazed in death. The other ... quiet, strong, sensitive, who had told of his great love for the wife and daughters waiting at home with whom he would never share love again.

One moment ... so alive and happy ... even in a hostile land, playing a game. The next, stripped of life by the powerful force of a land mine explosion that turned the vehicle that gave them their last ride on earth into a twisted, unrecognizable pile of scrap.

For the life of me ... I couldn't tell you either of their names or from what cities or states they came. Neither can I tell you exactly why they came to my mind as I asked God to direct me to write a special column for next week's special holiday.

I expect, for whatever reason, they needed to be remembered as we prepare Monday to remember all who have died serving this great country during times of war.

This year will be unique in that a new classification of veteran has emerged from a new type of war. Firefighters and police officers, dying trying to rescue thousands killed by crumbling buildings bombed by insurgents commandeering American aircraft-as-weapons in a completely unconventional war ... have given birth to a strange new Memorial Day focus.

Let me take this moment and say a special thank you to all who will visit a cemetery, decorate a grave, fly the flag, or simply take a few moments to bring their world to rest Monday to honor the memory of any or all who died trying to preserve this worldwide-envied American way of life.

Let me also ask that we carefully continue to guard this freedom we hold dear to our hearts as it can be taken from us. There is half a world out there that would love nothing more than to do exactly that, people who already are dedicated to our virtual elimination from the planet. And, as terrible as 9-11 was, it could turn out to be nothing more than the opening volley of war yet to come to our hallowed land.

We must not allow ourselves to be lulled back into the complacency of 9-10, and we must firmly but fairly give anything that even resembles a threat to the democratic infrastructure of our country - if nothing more - the harsh glare of examination!

But what do I know?

INMATES CELEBRATE STANLEY CUP

JUNE 6, 2002

It turns out just about everyone was going cup crazy last week.

Fans packed local bars and restaurants to watch the deciding game of the Stanley Cup finals while friends and family members sat around television sets to cheer on the Red Wings.

And, at the Monroe County Inmate Dormitory Facility, inmates donned red-and-white jumpsuits as they supported their Hockey town heroes.

The photo I saw recently capturing the image of these prisoners cheering on the Wings caught my attention.

Unmistakable by Sheriff Tillman Crutchfield's courageous order that inmates must wear "prison stripes", the "residents" were doing the exact same thing I was Thursday evening: rooting and hooting for our NHL hockey champion Detroit Red Wings.

At first glance, I was happy for them as all who share in a common victory. It was the second glance that got me thinking.

A closer look at the picture showed the following: The 29 pictured residents sat or stood lounging around game-board tables set up on a polished cafeteria floor watching a wall-mounted television in a large, likely air-conditioned room.

Beverage cups sat on the tables and one resident's hand was crammed into what looked like a bag of potato chips. In the background was a convenience/condiment table that featured a microwave oven and beverage containers.

What's wrong with this picture?

First, let's eliminate the political correctness of America 2002 and call a spade a spade: instead of "dormitory residents" these were "inmates, jailbirds, prisoners" who were in jail because they obviously had broken the laws of our country and who are supposedly being punished!

These guys looked like they were having the time of their lives and I imagine the only punishment they were experiencing was being deprived of being able to do the exact same thing they were doing at a local watering hole instead of this "terrible" dormitory.

It is my intent to be as kind and compassionate in this life as I can possibly be, and I certainly believe in rehabilitation. That second glance, however, left me shaking my head about the distance between what I was seeing and the concept of "cruel and unusual punishment."

The last (and only) time I was in jail (for littering — I promise to share that story with you soon), I had a steel slab with silver-dollar-sized holes in it for a mattress, a toilet in the corner of a 6-by-6 steel-barred cell and the privilege of making that "one phone call."

The experience made me want to make sure I never went back!

The homeless veteran I met some years ago, who was living underneath the Monroe Street bridge, would have loved to have been sharing punishment with these guys.

There, he could have had a bed and mattress; three squares a day, beverages, chips, air conditioning, fresh clothing, hot showers, free haircuts, color television ...

But instead of that terrible punishment he only had to deal with the nightmares of what happened to him after he was ordered to go to Vietnam and kill other people for some political purpose ... or go to jail!

Too bad he couldn't have waited 30 years to have that option; he could have told Uncle Sam to go fly a kite and been watching the Stanley Cup Finals in the care and comfort of the Monroe County Jail ... err, Dormitory.

But what do I know?

DAD LOVED MY LEFT EAR

J U N E   1 3 ,   2 0 0 2

Dad loved my left ear!

I can still hear the dreaded words from one of the neighborhood kids: "Hey, Treece, here comes your dad!"

Usually, I was locked into the emotional embrace of the thrill of a simple baseball game on the old lot across the street from the house where I grew up.

His instruction that day, as the result of something I had previously done wrong, was clear as a bell: "DON'T go out of the yard!"

There was another thing about dad that anyone who knew him knew — he always meant exactly what he said!

I can remember standing in the corner of the yard watching all the other guys as they "picked up teams" and would each call out, "I'm Mays, I'm Mantle, I'm Hank Aaron."

My hands would be crammed deep in my pockets as the game would start; I would fidget and shift back and forth just dying to be across that street.

I could almost look down and see a chalk-line barrier on the edge of our property that served as the perimeter of my cell.

Suddenly, one of the guys would have to go home, leaving one team one man, err ... "kid," short.

"C'mon Treece," they would call, "just one inning. Your dad's not home yet. He'll never know!"

That moment of decision, for which I would soon be learning a painful lesson about making wrong choices, was a no-brainer!

"I'm Al Kaline," I screamed joyfully and bounded across that barrier and into the flow of one of the favorite thrills of my youth.

The problem, of course, was that one inning led to two, then three, and soon, dad's instruction was the furthest thing from my mind, that is until I heard those dreaded words.

My heart froze and I stopped what I was doing and looked toward center field, the direction of home, and saw his massive frame coming for me.

The sight of Germans marching on Paris could not have been a more fearful sight. His arms swung in heavy rhythm as he walked. Each plant of his feet seemed to shake the whole world.

The frown on his face left no doubt about his intent and his eyes were fixed on me like a hungry, charging lion's on a trembling, fleeing gazelle. The only difference was that a gazelle would have run for his life — I knew better than to do something that foolish!

Needless to say, the game came to a complete stop and all the other kids scrambled to get out of his way.

He never said a word. He just walked up, grabbed me by the left ear and turned toward center field, pulling me alongside.

Now if you've never had a 6-foot-3-inch, 260-pound man grab you by the ear to irreverently take you for a walk, then you do not know true pain. The pain, however, was the easiest part, and dad knew.

The hardest part, you see, was the embarrassment! Having your dad come and lead you away by the ear in front of all your coolest buddies, neighborhood mothers' eyes peering out kitchen windows as well as surely the entire rest of the world, was the worst punishment he could have given.

Unfortunately, that was just his appetizer before the main course: a belt soufflé.

The best part, however, would always come a half hour after being whipped and sent to my room.

He would come to my room and say, "I know you probably hate me right now, but I just want you to know that I have done what I have done because I love you, and one of these days you will understand."

With eyes still spilling with tears I would usually look at him and think, "Yeah, right!"

Today, some 45 years later, it is with great love and admiration that I share this memory with you in tribute to my father, Homer Treece. How right he was!

How wonderful to know he was willing to rob himself of being my best friend in order to straighten this sapling being bent by the winds of life in order for it to grow tall and straight when old.

All those disciplines I couldn't wait to get out from under helped keep me alive through the jungles of Vietnam and my early, wild American life. All those times of him making me go to church to learn about God ended up steadying my ship during the storms of my life.

And the discipline I hated then, I so appreciate now. It is, I think, something dreadfully missing from most American families today.

But what do I know?

WHY THE COLUMN?

JUNE 27, 2002

I love being wrong! Ok, not really, but, like everybody else on the planet, I would like to be right about everything in my life.

I believe that everything you find in life that is false only leads you to what is true (which is not to say that everything that is true is right). It's just that when you discover where you've been wrong, you can make corrections and then be right.

I also believe it is the nature of humans to think they are right about everything, but, of course, we know that nobody is right all the time. I certainly am no different.

I have always had an opinion about almost everything, and sharing that opinion with anyone who wanted to hear it was something about which I was never too shy.

It has gotten me into trouble on occasion and I expect it will do so again somewhere down the line.

The only thing that qualifies me to write this column is the self-realization that I am just another one of the many scratching and clawing his way through this life in a simple attempt to be happy.

I don't pretend to have all the answers or any special powers and I don't believe I have ever tried to force my beliefs on anyone. I do have that opinion, however, and it has led me into many deep debates that have mostly been enjoyable…as long as everyone understood that it was only my opinion.

Through the years I developed a certain habit when sharing that opinion. After I would finish verbalizing my thoughts I would end them with the phrase, "But what do I know?"

It was a way for me to qualify what I was saying as being nothing more than an opinion. I encourage whomever I am speaking with to take what I am saying with however many grains of salt they choose.

When The *Guardian* asked me last fall to start sharing those opinions on a regular basis I was hesitant and avoided it for months.

I have found that the best way to stay out of trouble is to keep your mouth shut. And besides, who cares what I think?

I finally decided to give it a try and I have enjoyed it, so far. I guess I've been mentally flinching from the anticipation of someone outraged and offended by my column to write and say, "Just who do you think you are?"

And that is precisely the point of this column, and specifically its name.

You see, everybody sees the world through their own eyes and makes judgments based upon their own moral and ethical belief systems. As a result, everybody pretty much thinks they are right about everything.

Who's right? Who knows?

I once heard a line in a movie that said, "There is no right or wrong, just opinion." So...what do you think? Is that right...or wrong?

I know that there is wrong, because I know that there is right. In fact, I believe the biggest problem in America today is that everybody is concerned about "rights" and nobody is concerned about "right."

I think I'm right about that....

But what do I know?

JUDGE MISSED MARK
ON PLEDGE RULING

JULY 7, 2002

You must have been visiting another planet last week if you are not aware of the firestorm kicked up by San Francisco Circuit Judge Alfred Goodwin's order that the phrase "under God" in our "Pledge of Allegiance" is unconstitutional.

The country's overwhelming negative response to this order pleasantly surprised even me. I'm sure you're probably tired of hearing about it by now, but you know I couldn't let this subject go by without a comment.

You also already know I don't believe this life we live "just happened" and that I do believe life as we know it was created by God.

Every morning at 5:15 I get up, go to my desk and through prayer address Whom I believe to be the King of the entire universe: God. And even though I consider myself a poor example of what one who follows Him should be like, the truth is that I choose to place my life under God.

I also believe that the true essence of democracy (men with evil intent can derail any purpose) comes originally from the freedom found in following God's instructions, like the Ten Commandments. I believe that is why we chisel "In God We Trust" into the walls of our judicial institutions and print it on our money.

The incredible prosperity and world rank America has enjoyed for so long didn't just happen either; it has come, in my opinion, from following those instructions. In addition, a peek at the document which proclaims the reason America celebrates tomorrow provides obvious hints as to the Founding Fathers guidance in forming the government of our country. Consider the Declaration of Independence.

Let's start with, "We hold these truths to be self-evident." In my simple understanding that means whatever the author is about to say is a no-brainer or perhaps that it doesn't take a rocket scientist to figure out.

Next comes, "that all men are created equal," certainly one of the most important statements ever made. Read the Bible and you will find that God "is no respecter of persons" and simply looks at each of us in the exact same manner (could that be where their idea came from?)

Here is what stumps me regarding Goodwin's decision. The next line reads, "That they are endowed by their Creator with certain inalienable rights." Hmmm.

Now who do you think the Founding Fathers were identifying when they used the word, "Creator?" Here's another thought: Whoever they were identifying was obviously not considered an equal, but above them.

One of those authors, Benjamin Franklin, in addressing the president of the Constitutional Convention, suggests that the reason they were "groping as it were in the dark to find political truth" was because they weren't having the "daily prayer" that had saved them in the "contest with Great Britain."

He also made the following statement: "Sir, a long time, and the longer I live, the more convincing proofs I see of this truth that God governs in the affairs of men."

How ironic that just a few days short of exactly 226 years later we have a judge who renders a legal decision suggesting he knows more about the intentions of the original constructors of our government.

Goodwin needs to read on in the declaration where it says, "Governments are instituted among men, deriving their just powers from the consent of the governed!"

This issue speaks to us of the importance of choosing wisely the judges we allow to interpret our law. The biggest failure President Bush has experienced so far has been his inability to have his judicial appointments confirmed. (We are most fortunate to have a great roster of judges here in Monroe County.)

The last-mentioned of those inalienable rights the Creator has given us equals, (according to the framers of our constitution) is "the pursuit of happiness."

I hope you intoxicate yourselves with that pursuit this weekend and have a fabulous time celebrating the independence of our great nation. Come on out to Luna Pier Saturday and see our fireworks display; it's the best one in Monroe County!

But what do I know?

VOTE YOUR CONSCIENCE

J U L Y   2 5 ,   2 0 0 2

Several years ago, then Democratic Monroe County Commissioner Randy Ansel and I were standing on a downtown street talking about issues when we were interrupted by one of his constituents.

"Hey, Ansel" the guy began, "Why the heck did you vote for Dale Zorn for Chairman of the Board of Commissioners?"

Randy turned to the man, paused a moment, then said, "Because I thought he was the best man for the job."

"Yeah, but he's a Republican and you're a Democrat!" the man responded emphatically.

"So?" was Randy's reply.

I can't tell you how much I loved that response!

That board of commissioners went on to accomplish as much as any board I've seen during my lifetime and I believe it was because they worked together in a non-partisan manner.

That also was the beginning of the end of the terms of Ansel and fellow commissioner David Roberts. They weren't re-elected because they were bad commissioners — they weren't re-elected because they didn't vote the way their party had wanted them to vote.

I have never been a "party" voter. Once, inside one of the old voting machines, upon reviewing my vote I discovered all the candidates for which I had voted were Democrats, but I had made that vote person-by-person and not by pulling the master lever.

I love our way of life but believe the process by which we elect our leaders is flawed. We should not allow political parties, action committees, big business or powerful people to pump cash into candidate campaigns.

As soon as they do, the candidate is then "on the line" to vote as the donor wishes instead of the way he or she believes. That is, of course (as in the cases of Ansel and Roberts), if they want to get re-elected.

Candidates should be judged solely upon their records and character. While we all have made mistakes along the way, I still believe that the greatest indicator of future performance is past performance.

Here are some examples: I have known Sheriff Tilman Crutchfield, a Democrat, most of my life and know him to be a man of great integrity. When first-time Commissioner Jerry Oley, whom I do not know personally, recently questioned the sheriff's integrity, it only made me question Oley (who, incidentally, was the Democratic Party's choice to succeed Roberts on the board).

I have watched Zorn, a Republican, burn the midnight oil and take action to get policies implemented that has made Monroe County a much better place for all to live; few have performed better. Running against him this year is a friend of mine. I believe my friend could do a good job, but I know from past performance that Zorn is the one I want on that board.

The point is that it has nothing to do with political affiliation and everything to do with personal character and past performance.

As primary election day approaches (Aug. 6) I trust you will take advantage of one of the most important rights you have as an American: helping choose who will make law and policy and help steer our government into the future.

When you do, try not to be influenced by all the big-money advertisements you'll see floating all over the place. Instead, find out about the person's character and past performance, and then vote your conscience.

It's the right thing to do.

But what do I know?

WHAT COMES FROM THE HEART...

JULY 25, 2002

I have a friend who is black.

His name is Rev. Al Overstreet, and I mention his ethnicity because I want to write today about boundaries and how they can be rendered irrelevant by the heart.

I met Al years ago when I was a member of the Monroe YMCA. I was singing "Amazing Grace" while getting dressed for a workout one day when this man peeked around the corner.

He smiled at me and said, "I had to come and see who was singing boldly about my Savior!"

We became instant friends and have been ever since. He is the kind of friend who, if I didn't see him for 10 years and he called out of the blue and asked for anything, I would respond. We call each other "Brotherman."

He shared a favorite saying with me that has become one of my favorites. Al says, "What comes from the heart, reaches the heart."

I didn't think much of it at first, but the older and wiser I become the more I realize the truth of these words.

People are not as stupid as some would have us believe. God gives all of us certain gifts, one of which is discernment. If you listen with your heart and not your head or fleshly desires, you can pretty much tell when someone is sincere or not.

The heart speaks its own language that only another heart can hear and discern.

The head is capable of speaking truckloads of intellect, and while the heart may respect and be impressed with the work involved in learning, it really doesn't hear that language.

The smartest or richest person in the world is still going to experience pain and anguish at some point, and when it strikes deep personally — like losing a child, spouse or lover — intellect or money becomes useless.

It takes the heart of another to come and wrap its arms around you to bear your burden, to understand the pain and offer comfort and support in the time of trial.

The heart reaches across boundaries. This white man would do anything for my black friend; the color boundary — that has been so infectious in America for so long — is non-existent between us.

Another thing I discovered years ago during a stint as a scrub nurse in Mercy Memorial Hospital's operating room was that the heart of a black man doesn't look any different than the heart of a white man.

A few summers ago during a mission trip to Vietnam, my wife, Renee, and I sat for hours conversing with Vietnamese families. Because of the language barrier, neither side could understand the other.

We did, however, communicate beautifully, because, through our gestures, charades and desire to communicate, what was coming from each side was coming from the heart — and it was reaching the heart.

These exchanges were not just across ethnic boundaries but across oceans and the borders of a communist country.

I have heard many excellent musicians in my time who structurally knew every in-and-out of their instrument. While I appreciated their talent they could not move me because what was coming to me was intellectually from their head and not soulfully from their heart.

I have also heard an untrained musician hammering away on a dime-store guitar who has stirred my heart to unbelievable heights, because what was coming to me was coming from the heart.

I love to sing! I love to throw my head back and simply let out what is inside of me through song. I have no training and can't even read music, but that doesn't stop me from being king-of-the-mountain when I am singing.

It's a feeling that can't be purchased for any amount of money, and it doesn't really matter how good you are either, it just has to come from the heart!

It's funny how we label certain people by their hearts: cold heart, hard heart, good heart, kind heart, big heart.

Cold hearts seem lifeless and distrustful, hard hearts seem

wicked and unyielding, good hearts are fun to be around, kind hearts are always a blessing, and big hearts are loved by all.

So, what kind of heart would your friends say you have? I hope it's big or good or kind. I don't like being around the negative ones. You can always tell which ones are which, you know, simply by listening to them with your heart.

But what do I know?

JOHN DINGELL: PUBLIC SERVANT

AUGUST 1, 2002

In the mid-1980s I was general manager of Monroe's WTWR, Tower 98, radio station. Lake Erie water levels were at an all-time high and were threatening to destroy the station's transmitter, located 200 yards inland at the Toledo Beach Marina.

I had petitioned the Federal Communications Commission with a request to move the facility, but was informed by my Washington, D.C., attorney that the request was buried under paperwork and that it would probably be a year before approval or denial.

This left my business in trouble (and Monroe County in peril as Tower 98 is the county's only 24-hour emergency broadcast facility).

I did what each of you can do when you get in trouble: I called Congressman John Dingell.

Two days later he was sitting in my office listening to my dilemma. Two days after that I received a call from the attorney informing me that for some strange reason the FCC had cut through the paperwork and had approved my petition. The difference was John Dingell.

In the early 1990s I was an officer with Vietnam Veterans of America's Monroe Chapter 142. We had constructed a memorial at Heck Park and were searching for a decommissioned helicopter to mount alongside for static display. Over a three-year period I had written 130 letters in conjunction with the search.

After all that work we were elated to finally hear that we were getting our "bird." As we prepared to send a semi to Massachusetts to pick up the aircraft we received a call telling us that a high-ranking military officer had seen our plans and decided to commandeer the aircraft for his hometown.

I knew how to handle this situation; I didn't call Ghostbusters, I called John Dingell. Two days later his office called me and said, "Go get our helicopter!"

Now, fast-forward to spring 2002 and the turn of a new century.

This time, as the administrator for the city of Luna Pier, I was in heavy meetings with the Army Corps of Engineers. We were seeking solutions for offshore soil erosion and dike repair in preparation for the inevitable return of those same Lake Erie high waters.

The meeting was completed and as the mayor and I were saying our goodbyes to the corps I thanked them specifically for what seemed to me to be their special dedication to the project.

"Don't thank us," one of them began, "be thankful you have John Dingell as your congressman. We're only here because of him!"

I returned to my office and sat for a moment thinking about the impact this remarkable man has had on our community, and, specifically, on projects with which I have been involved.

Three times over three decades he had met my need: first for my business, second for my veterans' civic group, and now for my local municipality. What a debt I (we) owe to this dedicated public servant!

I'd like to share one final note regarding the integrity of Dingell. When the radio tower had been moved and business was back to normal, I shook the congressman's hand and assured him that it could not have been done without him. I also said, "It's not much, but in appreciation I would like for you to have this Tower 98 coffee mug."

The congressman smiled at me, shook my hand and said, "Please don't be offended when I don't accept this gift. I hope you can understand that it wouldn't be right to take a gift for simply doing my job." He closed by saying, "All I want is for you to be my friend."

A week after witnessing the joke of the exit from Congress of Ohio's convicted felon, James Traficant, it is heart-warming to fondly remember that little exchange.

No matter whether you are a Republican or Democrat, if you live in Monroe County you have to know how very fortunate we are to have John Dingell representing us in Congress. If, for some reason (thanks to Michigan's Republican redistricting fiasco) Dingell would not be re-elected, it would be one of the darkest days in the history of Monroe County.

We cannot let this man go until he is ready to let go. That's what I think...

But what do I know?

SILLY SAYONARA

AUGUST 29, 2002

Before you go there are a few things I want to say.

I know this is something you have to do, but I want you to know how it crushes my spirit when you leave. You do this to me on a regular basis. Yet, in spite of how you always leave me hurting, when you come back I forget my pain and welcome you with open arms.

It wasn't always this way. A younger man, looking over his shoulder, I found your leaving bittersweet as I hated to see you go, yet still had eyes for one I knew was waiting ahead for me. I frolicked with her for years until her cold embrace began to methodically leave me with a constant longing for you.

Now, it hurts even more when you go, as I know I must deal with her again soon. Perhaps it is a matter of age and maturity. All those years ago I was carefree and simply carried on with whomever was waiting around the next corner.

Now, older and wiser, I long to be near you every hour of every day. The heat of my love for you, even when it inconveniences me, is something of which I can no longer get enough. Even when you scorch me and the world I live in, it is still sweeter than the draft of the evenings that reminds me of her.

I suppose, like so many others, I will one day resolve to make the sacrifice of turning my back on my family and friends and the home that I love and come to you, just for the glory of being able to stay warm by your fire all year long.

I hate the thought of making that sacrifice. A lifetime of love and relationships make it seem unconscionable to leave. Conversely, the joy that floods my heart when you come is undeniable, and the only sorrow I feel is from the unsuccessful attempts to cram all the delicious delights you offer into your short visit.

Let me just say that I know God's plan for this world is perfect, so I cannot deny her importance in that plan. It's just that ... I don't love her anymore.

So, go on, run to your lovers in the south, who, as I will be in about six months, are grinning in the anticipation of your return to them.

I'll reluctantly pull on socks, jeans and a sweater and enjoy the beauty and bounty of fall, then prepare the shovel and salt for the time I have to spend with her again.

I know it has to be this way, at least for now. It's just that it's so difficult to have to spend such quality days of your life with one you no longer desire.

See you next summer ... summer.

Some readers may snicker at my silly sayonara. Passion runs deep, however, and deep love affairs often cause men to do silly things.

But what do I know?

UNCONVENTIONAL WARFARE

S E P T E M B E R 5 , 2 0 0 2

After failing at trying to start this week's column with various subjects I eventually want to share with you, I finally realize I am resigned to talking about what everyone else in America will be talking about in the next two weeks: 9-11.

Six days from today's date marks the one-year anniversary of what I believe to be the greatest tragedy in American history. And, while it kills me to admit this, from a military strategist's point of view, it was a thing of beauty!

Now, before you call for my head based upon the seeming insensitivity of that statement, hear all I have to say, please!

Almost one year later I continue to shake my head in amazement at what has happened to us. How in this world — considering our superior weaponry, technological know-how and sophisticated satellite and intelligence-gathering spy systems — could a handful of Arab insurgents come to our country (and have us teach them how to fly jumbo airplanes), then commandeer (with razorblades) four, wisely-chosen aircraft laden with fuel and passengers, and, with almost-pinpoint accuracy, fly them as bombs into the American icons of finance, military and (purportedly) administration, killing nearly 3,000 citizens and paralyzing our economy to the extent that one year later a $127 billion surplus is reduced to a projected $157 billion deficit?

Like I said, it throws a moldy, wet blanket on my spirit to have to admit that this was a tactical masterpiece of war. What hurts most is that it was enacted against the country that I love.

However, it also reminds me of another brilliant military strategy in American history, one from which we need to learn a lesson.

The American colonists, burdened by King George's excessive "taxation without representation," revolted, causing the good king to send the likes of General Cornwallis and his army to put down the revolution.

In traditional military fashion and procedure of the time, the "redcoats" flanked and marched in straight lines and were making quick work of those untraditional early American veterans.

I don't believe history records the name of the brilliant strategist who realized it wouldn't take long for the superior training and weaponry of the British to end their dream of freedom. (Hollywood identifies him as the character Mel Gibson plays in a great movie called "The Patriot")

Whoever he was, he taught the unconventional concept of hiding behind the rocks and trees and picking off the redcoats one-by-one instead of traditional straight-line fighting. It was a beautiful tactical concept and helped win the Revolutionary War.

September 11 was simply the opening volley of a war like we have never seen or considered in this country. It's all about the ongoing historical attempts to eliminate the Jews from existence; America just always happens to get in the way each time an attempt is made.

So, a brilliant strategist (bin Laden?), knowing there is no chance to match the superiority of American firepower, masterminds something so simple yet so powerfully effective in an attempt to begin the process of finally removing the Jewish junkyard dog.

One more thing: An operation of this magnitude obviously had to be heavily financed. It is certain that bin Laden has tons of money at his disposal. However, in my opinion, the true financiers of this war on us ... are us, and we send a new payment every time we stick that gas nozzle into the tanks of our vehicles.

But what do I know?

9-11: ONE YEAR LATER

SEPTEMBER 12, 2002

By the time you read this, the first "9-11" anniversary will have come and gone. It will be wonderful to not have to read (or write) about this terrible event for a while, but, as I noticed through the years with our older generation who lived through the similar attack on Pearl Harbor, it will never go away. Nor should it!

We can never allow ourselves to forget what happened that day, and we must remember that those who fail to learn from mistakes of the past are prone to repeating them.

As war veterans know, we must also remember that freedom is not just a right, but it is a responsibility to be passionately protected as well as enjoyed.

I used to wonder about what exactly it was that caused Cubans to gamble their lives by climbing onto rickety, makeshift rafts (with which I wouldn't even venture onto Lake Erie) and attempt to cross 90 miles of treacherous, shark-infested Gulf of Mexico waters to come to America (Elian Gonzales' mother even took her child).

The same thing amazes me now when I visit a Vietnamese-American friend who weeps when he recants his ordeal of being one of the original "boat people" who left communist Vietnam in a rusty, overloaded boat and crossed the Pacific in search of that same liberty.

I'm also amazed that there are so many people in the world who absolutely hate America, yet many of them want to come here so badly they do desperate things like these to make that happen.

Obviously, the opportunities offered by Western civilization cause outsiders to become as children, hating (and wanting to hurt) anyone who has something they do not have or cannot afford. With children the difference is determined by the ones who teach them.

In regards to the perpetrators of 9-11 (Arab Muslim extremists), it's not just a matter of hate; they simply, as Hitler did, want to remove ones who do not think and act as they do from the face of the Earth. And that's where things get sticky.

I want to be as forgiving, tolerant and understanding as I can possibly be, mainly because those are the instructions of the one I choose to follow (Christ). On the other hand, I am more than prepared to rise up against any enemy who even threatens to try and crush this democratic philosophy we love in America. My prayer is that the multitude of Americans feels the same way; otherwise, I fear for our immediate future and, specifically, the lives of our children.

As much as we would like to think that the bashing we gave the mountains of Afghanistan has countered 9-11 and that we will soon be able to get back to the party, it ain't so! We are at war, and the calm assurance of everyday life Americans have enjoyed for so many years … is over.

Fear is the essence of terrorism. We may be able to escape it for little snippets of R & R during movies, sporting events or the like, but it will be in the back of each and every one of our minds, reappearing in a consistent manner.

In the meantime I continue to be perplexed by the people of Arab descent and the Muslim faith, specifically the ones living in America. I haven't seen them rushing to the defense of the democracy that now protects and provides for them.

I haven't heard adamant, vocal outcry in admonishment of one of their own, as you would from me if Christians were indiscriminately killing Arabs in 9-11 fashion.

I need to ask them the question President Woodrow Wilson asked Germany in his Fourteen Points speech to the Congress of 1918 when he said, "It is necessary as a preliminary to any intelligent dealings with her on our part, that we should know whom her spokesmen speak for when they speak to us."

Until that time I have no choice but to be wary of anyone who even resembles in sight, thought or action one of those murderers of one year ago yesterday.

That philosophy may not be politically correct or even right, but like I said, I'm ready to do whatever to protect this democracy.

That's my opinion.

But what do I know?

AMERICAN YOUTH PARALLEL VIEW

SEPTEMBER 19, 2002

In the past few weeks, I had two separate observances of today's American youth that left me with quite different reactions.

The first came after watching the MTV Video Music Awards Show on television; the second after participating in a 9-11 memorial service with the students of Mason Consolidated Schools.

I've always considered myself a rather contemporary individual willing to stretch his boundaries of tolerance. Those boundaries, however, were put to the test while watching the awards show.

I can't tell you how many times — in shock of what I was seeing — I wanted to turn the show off. I forced myself to watch, as I wanted to know what our children were watching and to whom they were looking up.

Body piercings, tattoos, wild hair and various extreme stages of undress were the major opportunities these "winners" used in their attempts to out-outrageous each other.

My wife kept asking, "Do we really have to watch this?" Probably the most disturbing moment for me came when one particular category winner, stepping to the podium on national TV to accept her award for outstanding achievement, shared with the audience that she was "drunker than Pink," referencing an earlier award-winner who had detailed to that same audience the stage of her intoxication.

As some of you probably remember, I've been no angel in my lifetime, but I can't tell you how stunned I was at this entire show. It dulled my senses and I went to bed praying for America's youth. I remember thinking to myself: "No wonder the Arabs hate us. They're probably afraid this crap might come to their country!"

Ah, but hope springs eternal in the hearts of man, especially this one, after being able to observe the students of Mason schools.

My boss, city of Luna Pier Mayor Jerry Welton, informed me that the school had called and asked for us to participate in a special 9-11 memorial service in the Eagles football stadium; he would speak and I would sing.

Fall was evident as the sun began its climb into the September sky the morning of 9-11. I sat and watched as the entire student body of the school system filed quietly and orderly into the stadium seats.

The superintendent welcomed the students and introduced the guests on the stage. I was impressed that each member of the school board had attended, but what impressed me most were the kids!

While they were excited and antsy anticipating this out-of-the-norm event, they were on their very best behavior. They cheered wildly as each of their principals or administrators were introduced, and they were courteous, reverent and attentive as each speaker took his or her turn at the microphone.

I can't tell you how it moved me to hear that multitude of students, in perfect unison, pledging their allegiance to the flag, so loud that it seemed like you should have heard it all the way in Monroe.

The shock I felt at observing this event was from hearing all those kids joining one of their fellow students in belting out "The Star-Spangled Banner" at the top of their lungs.

There were no catcalls. There were no attention-drawing interruptions. There were no looks on student faces of disgust at "having to attend some stupid ceremony."

As the service wound down, the sun warmed most of my body from the early morning chill, but it was the students who warmed my heart. I basked in a glow of satisfaction at being able to see firsthand, that, in spite of the fear I felt after witnessing the American youth on the MTV show, the future of our country is in good hands if the students of Mason Consolidated Schools are the ones who will be in charge.

I guess the difference between the two events is motivation. Mason schools have dedicated, professional educators concerned about delivering intelligent, responsible adults to the world, while MTV seems only to be concerned with how much the cash drawer jingles at the end of the day.

But what do I know?

DEAR MR. PRESIDENT

OCTOBER 3, 2002

Dear Mr. President,

I am but one of the millions of Americans, most of who undoubtedly have an opinion of how our country should be run, that you represent.

I first want you to know I am a member of the Presidential Prayer Team and pray regularly for the one from whom I seek daily guidance to also daily guide your hand.

On Friday, a man for whom I have great admiration came to our city to ask for input and opinion from our citizens. U.S. Rep. John Dingell's action reflected his great wisdom as he too sought guidance for the important vote he must soon cast.

That vote will or will not give official authorization for you to wage war on Saddam Hussein and Iraq. The majority of those citizens in attendance urged him not to give you that vote.

Last year, from my bedroom window, I watched as a hawk "came from nowhere" (just like the 9-11 terrorists) and dived onto a timid, peaceful and unsuspecting dove. I watched the dove slowly die in the inescapable grip of the hawk's talons, and then become his dinner. How ironic that both birds were the very political symbols of world leaders who seek either war or peace.

While I have no desire whatsoever to destroy others for personal gain or motivation, neither do I have desire to sit by and do nothing when I know there are those in our world who have designs to do exactly as the hawk.

Thirty-two years ago I was called from service to my infantry unit during the Vietnam War to personally escort the remains of my best friend, who had been killed in action, home to the United States and his parents.

I flew from Vietnam to Oakland and saluted as the casket containing Rodney Vore of Maybee was slowly delivered down the conveyor belt from the airplane; I did the same after we landed in Detroit.

Earle Little Funeral Home Director Dick Cavanaugh met us and brought us back to Monroe where two things happened that shall be forever etched on my heart.

The first came as I stood in my dress uniform at the foot of Rodney's casket later that evening at the funeral home. The door opened and as the family entered the room I snapped hard to "Attention." Rodney's father took one look at his son and completely broke down emotionally. As hard as I tried not to, I did the same.

Later, after regaining his composure, Mr. Vore would give me my first political lesson and vision of what was wrong with our involvement in that war.

The second came a few days later. Rodney's funeral was conducted at the old Holy Ghost Lutheran Church in Maybee.

After the service we carried Rod across the road to the local cemetery for interment. When the committal service was completed, I slowly and meticulously folded The Stars and Stripes draping his casket into the ceremonial triangle, then walked to his mother and presented to her all that seemed left of her son. She looked at the flag, then at me.

The emptiness on her face reflected how her spirit had been emotionally stripped. I shall never forget that look, and, though I know it will not happen, I would hope there will never be another mother who must go through that experience; neither, another soldier.

As a former soldier, sir, who answered the call of his country at a time when it was unpopular to do so, I must tell you that I am greatly concerned for what lies ahead. I don't want to be the "sitting duck" dove who expects the rest of the world to be as peaceful and timid as she, and I don't want to be the careless, unforgiving hawk obeying his own laws and taking what he wants whenever he needs to feed his hunger.

More so, I don't want to see another 15-year war costing another 58,000 Rodney Vore's for a political battle that has no objectives or redeeming grace.

Therefore, Mr. President, I ask that you take the advice of one who sat in that office before you who said, "Speak softly, but carry a big stick." I believe following the guidelines of the United Nations, just as in 1991, is the proper course of action to resolve this conflict.

If you have smoking gun proof that Saddam was behind 9-11 or has developed weapons of mass destruction, then let's waste no more time and go get him. If you don't, then let us continue our war against terrorism, not Iraq.

You have mentioned publicly that you are a follower of Christ. Therefore, the best advice I have to offer is that you continue to seek His guidance each day for everything you do.

But what do I know?

HOWLIN' WOLF

O C T O B E R 1 0 , 2 0 0 2

The small, smoky cafe was packed with people. They sat elbow-to-elbow at a square counter surrounding a grill, two cooks and a waitress. They sat crammed into tiny tables along a larger square hugging the walls.

I excused myself through what was left of the aisle and moved to the back of the middle square. Heavy smoke choked my eyes as I joined the game of trying to get the attention of the waitress.

In a hurry, I leaned over the shoulder of a rather rotund black man sitting at the counter and snaked my arm through the opening to flag her down. The brim of his hat caught my cheek as he turned to catch a view of the intruder to his space.

"I'm sorry, sir," I said as I retreated.

He eyed me up, then turned and barked at the waitress.

"Come take care of this young squire."

She stopped what she was doing and came smiling.

"Large black coffee to go," I responded to her "What'll ya have, honey?"

It was mid-70 and I was in downtown Toronto just 20 minutes or so ahead of performing with my country-rock & blues band at a night club called the El Mocambo.

It was a time of crazy names for bands and "Brussel Sprout," while certainly not a name I cared much for, was certainly a name not easily forgotten. We had recently signed a five-year contract with MCA Records and released our first recording; I really thought I was somebody!

"So, young squire, what be the hurry?" the old gentleman asked, spinning around on his stool.

"My band is the opening act for Howlin' Wolf at the El Mocambo next door," I started babbling to him. "Have you ever heard of him?" I asked. Not waiting for a reply I continued to tell him what a fabulous bluesman he was and how he had influenced people like the Beatles and Rolling Stones and how we had cut a record and were trying to "make it big" in the industry and what a lucky break it was for us to do this show.

"Here's your coffee," the waitress called to me, much to the obvious delight of the old black man chuckling at my elongated enthusiasm.

"I always drink hot coffee before I sing," I told him as I paid her and grabbed the Styrofoam. "It loosens my vocal chords. You should come next door and catch the show," I called to him over my shoulder as I headed back through the crowd; he grinned and nodded good-bye.

Brussel Sprout took the stage and gave the crowd an energetic set of music. They liked this American band with a new hit record, but the cover charge they surrendered at the door was not for us, but for the Wolf man himself.

I quickly put my guitars away after the performance and hustled into the audience and scooted onto the floor in front of the stage: I wanted to be in the front row!

Howlin' Wolf's band took the stage and broke into a hot blues tune that got everybody groovin' to the music. Five minutes into the song the band lowered the volume and the guitar player grabbed the microphone.

"Ladies and gentlemen," he began, "please put your hands together and give a warm Toronto welcome to the king of the blues himself, Mr. Howlin' Wolf!"

The audience exploded in thunderous applause as the curtain behind the stage parted, and out strolled ... the old black gentleman from the coffee shop!

I had stood there encroaching on the space and conversation of the blues legend himself, and didn't even know it.

He strolled to the front of the stage and eased into the awaiting chair. The music blasted back to full volume as he smiled and waved to his adoring fans.

My mouth was still open when he turned his head in my direction, smiled and winked at me. I gave him a huge smile back that I'm sure was saying, "I feel like an idiot!"

That night gave me a great lesson in humility. When you're nobody you have to tell everybody you're somebody. When you're somebody, you don't have to say a word.

But what do I know?

BUZZARDS

O C T O B E R   2 4 ,   2 0 0 2

The first thing that must have told everyone within earshot that something was dreadfully wrong was the unmistakable screaming of tires on pavement. The truck's 18 wheels locked up and tried to stop the inertial movement of tons of coils of crushing steel.

I expect the heart of the truck driver leaped into his throat to instantly choke him as he realized an unthinkable fear was only moments away: a child-laden school bus had pulled into his path and he was about to broadside it at 55 mph.

Dear God, please assure me those precious children were happily playing, anticipating their minutes-away school outing to the Erie Orchard & Cider Mill, and did not see this steel monster racing to devour them. If they did, they will continue to see it, forever.

And God, I pray for the bus driver, whose only probable assurance for the rest of her life will be that none of the children have died.

My boss, Luna Pier Mayor and Fire Chief Jerry Welton, Building Inspector and Erie Fire Chief Michael Demski, were two of the first ones on the scene of Oct. 10's crash. The next day they submerged themselves in great discussion of this truck/bus crash, so horrific that it made world headlines.

They raved about how much all their mock-disaster drill training had paid off. They raved about the overall cooperation of everyone involved, from volunteer firemen to first responders to passers-by to neighbors to Mason Schools personnel to the bar owner on the crash corner.

"I didn't see anyone there that I wouldn't say that I was proud to be associated with," remarked Welton.

There was one he must have overlooked, however, even as he donned the cap of an air traffic controller and repeatedly looked skyward to successfully guide multiple life-flight helicopters to the scene.

Circling, too, overhead was a buzzard, waiting for his opportunity to take advantage of yet another tragedy. A few days later, he swooped onto the scene to methodically begin to pick the bones clean.

That buzzard was lawyer Geoffrey Fieger.

The ink wasn't even dry on the accident report.

While I'm no legal analyst, I expect there is a strong element of liability involved in this matter. However, no one on the planet is going to convince me that anyone involved in the tragedy that day wanted it to happen; it was an accident, and accidents happen to everybody.

Capitalistic America is out of control with lawsuits. I believe that the right or wrong of anything you do depends on the attitude and motivation of why you do what you do.

In this instance, naming the seemingly innocent truck driver as a plaintiff in the million dollar lawsuit filed by Fieger, tells me that greed is the why in this case.

Speaking as one who has them, there is no amount of money that will ever erase horrible memories from the minds of those who have suffered trauma; in this case, the truck driver, the bus driver, the children and the rescuer's of that day's real-life drama. Unless the victims have no means to pay for medical treatments, having to live with those memories should be enough.

I guess it's no wonder why you hear so many "lawyer-jokes" these days.

But what do I know?

THE CLOCK: FRIEND OR FOE

D E C E M B E R   5 ,   2 0 0 2

One of my priceless, prized possessions is a friend and a foe.

It is a clock and it sits on the mantle over the fireplace in the great room of our home. It is the heartbeat of the great room, which is also where I have my office and where I write.

The old, wind-up Seth Thomas has a curved-glass face cover that swings open for winding and setting. On the hour it chimes the number of whatever hour of the day it is; on the half hour it chimes once.

While it is somewhat valuable as an antique, my description of it as priceless is due to the fact that it was my father's wedding gift to my mother, meaning it is a family heirloom and will never be for sale.

Recently, I took it to my good friend, Dariel Loop (aka "The Clock Man"), as it was losing time dramatically and in obvious need of a tune-up.

The Clock Man worked his magic and, when I picked it up, told me, "That's the loudest-ticking clock I have ever heard!"

I was fortunate to have Thanksgiving's four days off from work. Each of those mornings I arose at 5 a.m., made a steaming cup of cappuccino and sat at my desk to write, or, at least, to make an attempt to do so.

As I've told you before, my method of operation for writing is to sit at my desk and ask God to tell me something about which to write. The first three of those days the only thing I heard was the constant "tick-tock-tick-tock" of the clock and its half hour updates. It is frustrating when nothing comes to me, as I feel like I am just wasting time.

Sunday morning, as I repeated the process and the clock reminded me at 7 a.m. that I had already lost two hours, it hit me how quickly time slips away from us.

I thought of my youth, when I couldn't wait for time to pass so I could finally be a teenager, drive, vote, be an adult and on my own.

My how quickly the time has flown. Suddenly, I am a senior citizen in need of the hot tub, not for relaxation, but for relief from an aching back.

Suddenly, I realize that all the things I have wanted to do in my life that I have not yet done are in jeopardy of not being done unless I prioritize my time left on the clock.

It made me think of football. Late in the game when one team is ahead of the other, it's not the opposing team that is the enemy; it's the clock! The object is to stay ahead in the game before time runs out and the game is over.

Staying ahead in the game used to mean being successful and making money. As the clock continues to wind down my game plan has changed.

Now, the most important things in my life are spending as many of the remaining ticks on that clock that I can with the woman that I love, and being there for anyone who may need help along these roads of life. (There are two, you know: one wide, one narrow. Each tick of that clock reminds me of the importance of being on the narrow.)

With eight chimes, the clock just yelled at me that it's time to get ready for church. I love it as it helps keep me on track. I hate it as it reminds me how quickly time disappears. I revere it because it respects and waits for no one.

Like this special clock of mine that keeps it for me, time is one of the most important things in my life; there's just never enough of it to satisfy me.

But what do I know?

NO TIME FOR CHRISTMAS

DECEMBER 19, 2002

Yesterday, from out of the attic, I finally opened the box containing my 50 or 60 Christmas CDs.

I pulled out my favorite - Trans-Siberian Orchestra - pushed it into the player, leaned back in my chair and began to enjoy my holiday music.

My wife's voice interrupted the solitude with, "Honey, we'd better leave if you want to be on time."

I sat up in the chair, gave her a questioning frown, and then confirmed by my watch that she was right: I had an engagement that meant the music and solitude was over before they had even begun.

Today, I woke early, emptied the contents of the same box and chose 37 of the CDs I wanted to make sure I took the time to hear. Then it dawned on me that, based on the schedule I have with less than a week until Christmas, there is no way I will find time to listen to all that music.

There just isn't enough time!

Out loud I asked myself, "And whose fault is that?"

I thought about how Renee and I had taken our tree down from the attic the day after Thanksgiving but had been too busy to put it up until now.

About how we had missed our time-honored tradition of — together — opening, remembering, then hanging each individual ornament because I had a meeting and she had to do it by herself.

About how I had not yet sat in silence by the fireplace on a cold winter's night to watch the lights wink at me from the tree.

I called to Renee and said, "Perhaps we shouldn't even bother putting up a tree or buying presents anymore," which, of course, stopped her in her tracks.

"Are you crazy?" she asked.

"Yes," I answered, "crazy because I have come to the conclusion that we don't have time for Christmas anymore!"

As I sit here realizing that this is the fourth or fifth column I have written this year about time, or, more specifically, the lack of it, I'm wondering if this is just a barnacle that has attached itself to my trunk. More so, I hope it isn't growing!

Og Mandino says that only a fool turns over in the sand and goes back to sleep after noticing the tide approaching. So, I must do something about this problem...now!

My lovely and I have decided that, in spite of the fact that New Year's resolutions are still weeks away, we are starting them now!

Next year the tree will be down from the attic, unpacked, conjointly decorated and, along with the rest of the house, ready for the season Thanksgiving Saturday. Any unnecessary December committees, meetings or events are history!

Christmas is too important to bog down with irrelevant details.

And speaking of important, I'd like to take this moment to wish you and all those you love the very happiest of holiday greetings.

I would also like to tell you that, regardless of all the political correctness and atheists in the world, Christmas, plain and simple, is the celebration of the birth of the Savior of the World, Jesus Christ. O come let us adore him.

Now, if you will excuse me while I hit the play button, I'm leaning back in the chair to enjoy "Boney James' Funky Christmas" while I urge you to make sure and take time to enjoy Christmas!

But what do I know?

NEW YEAR'S INTERNAL REVIEW

DECEMBER 26, 2002

In the movie, "Forrest Gump," Forrest is in the New York apartment of Lieutenant Dan during a New Year's Eve celebration.

One of two visiting young ladies utters the line, "It's New Year's; everybody gets to start over."

While the statement isn't totally accurate, it does reflect a great opportunity for all of us.

Christmas has always been the most special time of the year for me. Christmas is about love, giving and getting. We give gifts as tokens of our love to each other, just as Christ was God's gift to us, which is the very reason we celebrate the holiday.

But, when Christmas is behind us, as it is today, it's time to move on.

When I was a child, I begged my father to keep the Christmas tree on display for as long as possible. I remember one year when he let us keep it up until January 10.

Times change, as today the tree is down, packed away and back in the attic; it's time to move on, which brings us to, first, the end of the year, and second, the New Year.

It is said that in life, everything you find that is false only leads you to what is true. The end of the year is the perfect time to closely examine all that is happening in your life in order to decide what is working and what isn't.

You have to do that with your "stuff" every now and then, too. Things I wouldn't have even considered getting rid of just a few years ago get a quick thumb's down these days.

Priorities, along with the times, also change. So many things in my life that, for whatever reason, were so important just a few years ago are no longer.

Once again, finding the time for that introspection is critical; the process won't work without the review. The week between Christmas and New Year, however, is usually a bit of down time, and if you look closely, you will find the time you need.

After the internal review, it's time to resolve (analyze) in order to make necessary changes, become resolute (firmly determined in purpose), then make resolutions (a formal statement expressing intent) regarding the new direction you want to take.

I think most people make New Year's resolutions each year, but I don't expect the rate of success is too high. Old habits are hard to break, especially the older you get.

So, my plan this week is to review my life in 2002 and recommend changes for myself for 2003. Perhaps I'll share some of them with you next week. Perhaps you'd like to share some of yours with me?

I would love that. In fact, I would love to hear from any of you who read this column regularly. Do you like the column? Do you hate it? Do you wish it would go away?

I could use the input as I review my first full year and begin my second of writing this column for The *Guardian*. And please, be honest. I want to know what you think!

And besides, who cares if I don't like what you have to say. All I have to do is say...

But what do you know?"

NO MORE LEFTOVERS

JANUARY 9, 2003

Summer before last, my wife, Renee, and I sat enjoying the afterglow of dinner on our deck.

The sinking sun reflected off low-hanging clouds, guiding Lake Erie through its afternoon, chameleon ritual of segueing mauve to lavender to pink to purple.

Great blue herons waded in the water spear fishing for supper. Flocks of Canada geese sailed out of the sky and skidded onto the water for landing.

The fragrance of honeysuckle drifted into our noses and fired our senses as we glided to the groove of the stereo's smooth jazz.

We marveled at the miracle of flight as a hummingbird, seemingly suspended in mid-air, sucked sugar-water from his feeder while goldfinches hung upside down pecking thistle from theirs.

The hibiscus blazed red with nine fabulous flowers as huge as my hand.

Renee caught my glance from across the table.

"This is fabulous," she whispered as she squeezed my hand. "It doesn't get any better than this."

She was right.

We had worked hard the last five years to build our little Luna Pier castle overlooking Lake Erie. There was only one problem: this was one the few nights we had time to enjoy it. (Might as well start the New Year with my favorite whine!)

I looked her in the eye and began:

"You know, I've been thinking. We kiss each other goodbye every morning at 7:30. I head for Toledo and you for Monroe. We go to our jobs and spend the best of our day giving the best we have to other people.

"Then we return each night at nine or ten to give each other whatever we have left over of ourselves. I don't want to do that anymore; I want you to have the best of me!"

"Then let's do something about it!," was her reply.

And we have.

Doing something about it, however, hasn't been easy considering my job, her job, three businesses, our home, all the related bills, and all the different involvements of which she and I always seem to find ourselves in the middle.

We prayed and asked God to guide us as he is the most important thing in our lives. We decided to give more time to him and to each other.

I have since walked away from a 20-year career that paid me handsomely and of which I was in the hierarchy. God filled my laundry list to the letter and gave me a new, hometown career that I love.

He brought a buyer for our Monroe business in the middle of tough economic times, which has allowed Renee to run the business we built and named for her, also in our hometown.

Now, I can't wait for summer. I expect we will watch that hummingbird every day on the deck instead of every now and then.

Our new word for 2003 is "downsize." Our new phrase is "No More Leftovers." Our description for success is, "God is good!"

But what do I know?

JEALOUS OF THE SPARROW

JANUARY 12, 2003

It was a bad day to overfill my Zippo as the leaking fluid burned through the lining of my pants and felt hot on my thigh. The straps, winched so tight across my groins and shoulders that I had to sit fetal just to keep circulation, refused my attempts to reposition the lighter.

Rivers of sweat flushed my face and then dripped - methodically, rhythmically - onto the floor below. Every few seconds I reached up to poke the horn-rimmed glasses back onto the bridge of my nose in response to their endless slide. I couldn't wait to go out the door!

The noise was deafening and I envisioned being inside a tin can in a wind tunnel while people on the outside beat it with baseball bats. I expected the rivets to pop and the craft to come apart at any second.

I don't know if it was the weight of all the paratroopers crammed like sardines into the plane or the antiquated aerodynamics of the old C-119 "flying boxcar" that caused it to sway like a car on ice you have to turn into the spin to keep straight.

The jumpmaster jerked open the back doors of the aircraft and stood defiantly in the door; a single parachute with no reserve. Tattoos decorated his arms like postcards from different world theatres in which he had served.

Holding handles on each side of the door, he stuck his head out and looked for our drop zone. I remember being shocked as I watched the force of the wind slashing by the plane pull the skin off his face and flap it alongside his face like a flag in a gale. It pulled his skin so tight you could virtually see his skull.

He pulled himself back into the aircraft and gave us rookies a look as if to say, "What'd ya think about that?"

I thought he was nuts! Then again, I wondered if I was nuts for being up there with him!

Suddenly he barked out a command: "Stand up!"

The bulky parachutes on my back and belly made it difficult to do anything.

"Hook up!" he screamed over the roar of the plane.

I snapped the metal clip I had been clutching in my hand onto the steel static line that stretched the length of the ceiling.

Again he barked, "Stand in the door!" The command caused the "stick" of soldiers to shuffle like a herd of cattle toward the opening. Sunlight streamed through that opening and I knew cold-air relief from the sauna was only moments away.

And then, show time!

"Go!" he screamed and one by one we leaped into the wild blue yonder to experience one of the greatest thrills man has ever known.

I thought of those days this morning and was jealous as I lay in bed and watched a sparrow leap from his treetop perch and float down to the birdfeeder I had earlier loaded up for him outside my window.

Then I remembered the verse that says, "To every thing there is a season," and realized that my season of soaring had come and gone … and I was okay with that.

"Stand in the door!" Paratrooper School, 1968.

Then I looked at the gorgeous woman lying warm beside me and figured … maybe he was jealous of me!

But what do I know?

CHAOS AT MONROE HIGH?

J A N U A R Y 1 6 , 2 0 0 3

The quiet, personal-conversation murmurs I've been hearing for the past few months regarding student security at Monroe High School has elevated itself into a hot local topic with letters to the editor and front page headlines of local newspapers.

At issue is whether or not students are safe to attend classes, as there have been reported gang-style beatings in recent months. In addition, an underlying theme seems to question the current administration's ability to deal with the issue as well as legitimate concern for proper policing of what some consider criminal-style activity.

While I wouldn't know the school's principal if he walked up to me on the street, I do know current Monroe Public Schools Supt. David Taylor and have always held him in the highest esteem and am quite certain that he has nothing but the very best of interests and intentions for all students.

However, I did have an experience a few years ago with the school, virtually unrelated to this issue that has burned in my belly since it happened.

The person in charge of a local event, of which I was asked to be master of ceremonies and about which I needed to speak with her, worked at the high school as a security guard. I secured permission to enter the school and found her serving as a hall monitor.

Classes were still in session and we spoke quietly in the hallway about the details I needed regarding the event.

Suddenly the bell rang and the hallways filled with students cruising to their next classes. I grinned as I watched them and for the moment fondly remembered my days of doing the same.

I was jarred back to reality as one young man walked by my friend and said, "Hey, bitch!" (Forgive my use of that word; it is important for this story).

My eyes and my mouth popped open simultaneously in disbelief of what I had just heard. I turned and watched the punk walk on down the hall. He kept looking back at me as to say, "And what are you gonna do about it?"

I did want to do something about it, but turned instead to my friend and said, "I can't believe he called you that name!"

"That's nothing," was her reply.

She was right.

For the next three minutes I heard students call her names that not only would I not repeat to you in this column but ones that also made me want to grab them by the collar and knock a couple of teeth loose.

They called her vulgar, nasty, degrading names that I would never stand by and allow anyone to call a friend of mine, especially a woman old enough to be their mother.

"I can't believe you let them get away with this!" I exclaimed.

"What do you expect me to do?" she questioned. "If I lay a hand on them, I'm going to jail. If I respond verbally, that just agitates them and my car gets keyed."

I couldn't believe the attitudes of the children (?) in the hallways of my alma mater. Unfortunately, I don't think this behavior was unique to just their school. I think it is happening all over our country as respect for elders and authority daily becomes nothing more than a faded memory of how life used to be during the education process.

"Tom," my friend began again, "there is one name they can't call me."

"And what is that?" I asked.

"God," was her answer.

That hit me like a ton of bricks.

In spite of the fact that the framers of the Constitution prayed asking God to guide them as they wrote the very foundation of our system of government, His name is the one name that cannot be spoken without penalty in our school system.

Any son of mine I heard using that kind of language on a person of authority, as in this case, would have received what my father would have given me in that situation: a bar of Irish Spring crammed into his mouth. It's difficult to talk at all when that happens.

I wonder these days if it's too late to try to correct the situation. I wonder if our way of life is headed for the trash heap, as that's what usually happens to things that receive no respect.

Not only is there allegedly chaos at Monroe High School, but there is chaos all over America. Unless parents begin to understand the concept of "train up a child in the way that he should go" and start teaching the reality of the Ten Commandments instead of bowing to the power of political correctness, things will get much worse before they ever get better, if they ever do.

But what do I know?

THE FINAL FRONTIER

JANUARY 23, 2003

All my life I've heard it said that "space is the final frontier." I disagree. I believe the subconscious state of man is the final frontier.

It doesn't matter who you are, what color you are, from what country you come or religion you represent, there is one specific thing that links all human beings together. It is something that you must do whether you like it or not: sleep.

Some people need very little, some people need much, some can go for days without it, but eventually, everybody must sleep.

You've seen or heard of people falling asleep in church, at work, on a park bench or even while they are actually driving a vehicle.

Some time ago, I noticed a gentleman slumped over the wheel of his vehicle parked on the side of the road. Fearing he was in distress, I pulled alongside and tapped on the window to wake him. He informed me he was a private investigator staking out a house. I don't expect I'll ever hire him.

So, where do we go when we sleep?

I don't think most people give it a second thought. They simply believe our bodies were created to replenish themselves by returning on a daily basis to a subconscious state for rest and recharging.

I'm sure this is true; at least it's what we've been taught. I'm also sure, however, that there is something deeper attached to that daily journey into the subconscious.

My theory is that it has something to do with the spirit world. Perhaps God programmed us when he created us to go into daily life, and then return to him regularly for some purpose.

What about dreams?

What got me thinking about this subject was a dream that woke me at 2:30 a.m. on a recent Sunday. In the dream, I was trimming trees as part of a work crew. At the end of the day, when I tried to return my trimmers to the work truck, it pulled away and deliberately left me.

The driver watched me in the rear-view mirror and waved goodbye, knowing I was trying to return the trimmers.

The driver in the dream was, in real life, an employee I had hired a few months prior under a special agreement: She was in need of a place to work and I was in need of some assistance.

We made a deal and all was fine — until she reneged on the agreement. I confronted her and our relationship soured, although I allowed her to continue to work.

A few weeks later, I had the dream. That afternoon, I went to the place where she worked for me and found that she obviously sneaked in after hours, took all her things and left me only a note in an attempt to justify her actions.

I jumped for joy! I was so excited I could hardly speak. In spite of the fact this employee left me feeling that I had been used, I believed that, just like He did to the Wise Men of the Christmas story, God had warned me of the situation in my dream.

Suddenly, my issue regarding the employee was trivial. I realized it had turned trouble into great triumph for me as I believed in my heart that the King of the Universe had specifically spoken to me as a result.

Man has been dealing with sleep and dreams since his beginning. And, in spite of all we know about the state that induces them, I'm sure we know virtually nothing about the subconscious state of man.

The technology that produced the international space station, the shuttle and Hubble telescope has certainly opened up the frontier of space. In spite of these innovations, I fear man hasn't even scratched the surface of being able to see what's really out there.

And besides, what are we looking for with these innovations in the first place? Other planets? Other life forms? The meaning of life? God?

If your answer is either of the last two, then I believe you are looking in the wrong frontier. The true meaning of life is found when one finds God, and to find him you have to look in, not out.

And guess what? You don't even need a space shuttle or a telescope. All you need is to believe He is exactly who He says He is.

But what do I know?

WE CARE: MAKING A DIFFERENCE

FEBRUARY 6, 2003

I found the remote and turned up the sound on the TV. It was terrible.

I groaned and shook my head in disgust, chastising myself for agreeing to perform on this live TV program without considering the quality of the production.

"Grin and bear it, kid," I told myself as the childhood image came into my head of my father pointing his long-since-gone finger at me and saying, "You told them you'd be there and your word is your bond!"

I had been asked by Mary Jo Steinman, co-founder of "St. Michael's We Care," a local fund-raising organization, to sing a couple of songs for their annual February cablecast telethon, to which I had agreed.

I fumbled again for the remote to turn off the program. I had seen enough to convince me that no matter how well I performed a few hours later on the show, the sound was going to be terrible.

Suddenly, just as my finger pressed the off button and the screen went black, something caught my eye. I pushed the button again and the distance shot of the stage at the old Monroe High School, now Monroe Junior High School, came back into focus.

Former Detroit Tiger pitching great Denny McClain was hosting the show and had just begun to introduce his backstage helpers.

"Wow, what a hottie!" I thought to myself as my eyes focused on the beautiful young woman he had just introduced who had caught my eye.

Empty, alone, still stinging from a painful divorce and in desperate need of a valentine, I sat back down and continued to watch just for the occasional background glimpse as she would sashay on and off the screen to help stage each act that performed.

"Hmm," I thought to myself, "Maybe this won't be as painful as I thought," as I realized that in a few hours I would be on that same stage and this gorgeous woman would be helping me.

I was right. And she did.

And today, some 10 years later, she looks a million times more beautiful than then as she lies sleeping beside me.

It took a few years for us to come together, but thanks to that performance I really didn't want to do for "We Care," I found, and married, the most wonderful woman on the planet.

Saturday, alongside dear friend Gary Vancena, aka local disc jockey legend "Daddy G. Knight" (who will keep me laughing from start to finish), I will once again perform at the St. Michael's telethon. Gary and I will open the show at noon as the first of many local masters of ceremony and close the telethon from 9 p.m. until midnight.

Along with local celebrities in the phone room, we will be taking calls from those, who, even in economically distressed times, know how blessed they are to have good health, as well as have children and grandchildren free from the debilitating diseases and maladies suffered by ones for whom we will be raising money.

In His word, God tells us that it is more blessed to give than receive. I believe that. Just as I believe that you can selfishly eat or horde a single grain of corn, or you can have the faith to believe that if you give that grain away by sowing it into the ground, it will multiply into thousands of grains of corn.

Almost regretfully, I performed for the St. Michael's "We Care" telethon all those years ago and have sung and hosted it ever since. Little did I know I would reap a field of dreams that would include, other than my relationship with Christ, the most wonderful thing that has ever happened in my life.

The telethon will come to your living room live on your local cable TV station from noon to midnight Saturday. I urge you to turn us on.

I also urge you to consider an amount you can pledge to give to help those less fortunate than we. Then pick up that telephone and make that call.

Now I'm not guaranteeing that you will find a wife or the valentine of your dreams like I did, but I do guarantee that if you call and pledge, God will bless you in a most special way.

And besides, you can't buy the feeling you get when you know you've made a difference in someone else's life.

But what do I know?

WINTER: PART OF THE PLAN

FEBRUARY 27, 2003

Each morning, after I return from my nightly journey into the subconscious, the first thing I do is pray. I ask God for His divine guidance for my life, my wife, our children, our businesses, my job, our president, our country, those who are burdened by trouble or affliction, etc.

I begin my prayer with praise and thanksgiving for Him. (It may not always show, and for that I apologize, but God is at the center of my life). I don't ever pre-plan what that praise will be; I just open my mouth and out it comes.

What came out yesterday was so odd and foreign it started me laughing during the prayer.

I said, "Lord, I want to thank and praise you for the ice and the snow and cold we've been locked under for the past two months."

I stopped my prayer in shock. My mouth and eyes all popped open in amazement as I realized I had said words that would never normally come out of my mouth.

Why? Because I hate snow and ice and cold and frozen tundra and cars that won't start and dripping noses, frozen toes and the 40 pounds of clothes you have to wear, and —pardon me while I catch my breath, because, trust me, there's much more.

I thanked God for those things because, even though I hate them, I know they are part of His divine plan for life on this planet.

I will listen to no one who tells me that life as we know it "just happened," "evolved from apes," "crawled out of the sea," or is the result of the "big bang theory."

Times like these, when our portion of the Earth tilts away from the sun and we get so cold we think we are going to freeze to death — but never do — makes me realize that there is master control.

In just a few months, when we will have traded the burden of coats, hats, boots and mittens for bathing suits as we try to escape summer's searing heat that comes, when, once again, our portion of the Earth rotates so close to the sun that we think we are going to burn to death, I will think the same.

My spirit is dying for spring! I expect I am longing for warm weather more than any time in memory because of the brutality of this winter.

I need to be awakened and welcomed to each new morning by the unchained melodies of songbirds singing to me through the same window that brings the billowing breeze barging into my bedroom.

I need to inhale the freshness of the dew's overnight delivery.

I need to playfully push open the door to the world and feel the tickle and coolness of the grass between my toes as I lovingly bathe and quench the thirst of my plant children.

I need to sprawl in the sun and feel the burn on my belly as the wind whips through what hair I have left.

I need to prepare gourmet food on the grill and fine-dine on the deck with the woman I love and just sit and marvel at the place to which we have been deposited by His divine plan.

So, until then, here's how I am coping: we only have to deal with 11 more days of February, and then we hunker down for the Ides of March, and then celebrate the coming green of spring by partying with St. Patty. Four days later, presto, it's Showtime!

OK, I do have an ace up my sleeve. Just to make sure I get my heart jump-started in case Puxatawney Phil was kidding, the next day I'm flying with my lovely to the Yucatan Peninsula for a week on the sun-drenched shores of the Island of Cozumel.

Then, when I get back, the flowers should be in full bloom and I can become intoxicated with the glory of spring.

However, speaking of jump-starting, right now I have to go out into nine degrees and deal with the too-cold-to-cooperate carburetor on Renee's car and try to get it running for the first time in three days.

Did I tell you that I hate winter?

Thank God he has a perfect plan for it. Otherwise, I think I'd just go lay my head on the railroad tracks.

But what do I know?

FROG LEG INN: THE SECRET IS OUT

MARCH 6, 2003

To those of you who have never been there, I'm not sure I should share with you one of my very favorite places on the planet. I would hate for the day to come when it became so popular I couldn't get in.

The truth, however, is that I love to share wonderful things I have found with those I know who appreciate an experience that leaves them with a feeling of pleasure and satisfaction.

To describe it, let me first tell you that I spent most of my life fending off jokes about my weight — or, should I say, lack of it! I was skinny as a bean pole.

Then when God took away — cold turkey — that nasty tobacco habit I had, I suddenly discovered the incredible wonder of the taste of food —— and the ramifications of higher intake.

In my wild and crazy days, I occasionally frequented a beer and pizza joint in southeastern Monroe County's tiny town of Erie: the Frog Leg Inn.

I was excited when dear friends Tad and Katherine Cousino purchased the establishment some years ago and have marveled at how that old just-another-smoky-bar stigma has deliquesced into the magnificent, fine-dining experience it is today.

Katherine, or Katrina as I call her (you have to roll the "R"), will meet you at the door. You are charmed from the moment she greets you in her heavy French accent and guides you to your seat.

The ambiance alone is worth my trip as I love to commandeer a quaint, quiet corner table-for-two and savor precious moments with the woman I love. Candlelight dances across the table and into her eyes as the worry and woe of the day evaporates underneath small whispers of love. This is heaven for hopeless romantics!

As wonderful as the atmosphere is, I wouldn't be going if it weren't for the bottom line — the food. Chef Tad is definitely from that fabled line of Cousino cooks and I am amazed at how he continually strives to take his taste creations to a higher level.

Last Friday night, I sat before a 2-inch-thick Delmonico steak cooked to perfection. I guided the first bite into my mouth then closed my eyes and shook my head in ecstasy as the flavors exploded into great satisfaction about which you want to tell someone else.

Clumsily I dropped my steak knife. Instead of requesting another I picked up my butter knife and effortlessly sliced through the prime piece of bovine.

Perhaps Tad's finest creations are his sauces, which have become so legendary they will soon be bottled and marketed to a much wider group of consumers.

There is a down side. With food this fabulous one must burn an extra mile or two on the treadmill, but it's worth it!

The secret is definitely out that the Frog Leg Inn is — without a doubt — one of the finest places to eat in Monroe County or Toledo.

But what do I know?

NO FUNERAL FLOWERS

MARCH 13, 2003

Thirty-two years ago this month I sat alongside my grieving mother trying my best to think of something I could do or say that might make her feel better. There was nothing, as a few feet away in his casket lay my father, her husband of 35 years.

I remember sitting there watching wave after wave of friends and loved ones passing by to extend their condolences.

I remember their comments: "He was such a good man," "He was so much fun," and my favorite, "He would give you the shirt off his back if he thought you needed it, but don't be stupid enough to try to take it!"

There was another common comment I kept hearing, one that sank deep into my heart. It was a thin thread of sorrow from many who would regretfully say, "I wish I would have told him — while he was alive — how much he meant to me."

I made a decision that day, sitting on the couch of the Earle Little Funeral Home, to use that thread to knit together a philosophy for my life: I will never bring

Two of my three fathers: Grandpaw Moses and Dad (Homer), 1957.

flowers to a funeral unless I could not give them to the person while they were alive.

I'm not talking about the kind of flowers we hope to see poking their heads out of the ground in a few weeks. Rather, the kind of flowers that make another person smile and feel good about themselves, like a helping hand, or a friendly, "Good morning!"

I'm talking about going to another before it is too late and telling them exactly what they have meant to you, how they have influenced or motivated you.

I'm talking about a boss telling his employee what a great job they are doing instead of just thinking it or assuming they know it.

About a husband telling his wife how much he appreciates what a great mother and wife she is — in a day and age of so many bad ones!

Of reaching across the fence to shake the hand of your neighbor to make sure he or she knows how much you appreciate the tolerance of close proximities.

Of calling or visiting your mother or father you haven't had time for because of all the real important things in your life!

My father once said to me, "Oh, what I would give if I could have back the one moment that I sassed my mother!"

I remember thinking that was one of the craziest things I ever heard!

He had "talked back" to his mother one time and was regretting it? Unbelievable! I had done it to my mother many times and didn't think it was too big of a deal, then.

Now, five years after she left to go live with Jesus and I find myself wishing I could pick up the phone, call her and hear that enthusiastic, "Hi Buddy!" on the other end of the line, I find myself thinking, "Oh what I'd give if I could have back every moment that I..."

Every now and then, instead of just giving you a regular opinion with this column, I think I'll write a letter to someone I want to send flowers to while they are alive.

I know it sounds so ... flowery ... but just think of what a nice world it would be if everybody gave flowers to somebody else every day! Gosh, what a concept!

But what do I know?

FLOWERS FOR THE CHAMP

M A R C H 2 0 , 2 0 0 3

Dear Champ,

Last week in this column I told my readers of my philosophy of not bringing flowers to the funeral of a person who has meant a lot to me; rather, it is my intent to bring them while they are alive.

I have some flowers for you.

I remember watching you sitting in the balcony at church when you were a kid. Even then, in spite of being a normal, "Gee-Dad- do-I-have-to-go-to-church?" kid, you had a reverence about you.

I remember following your career in the beginning: Amateur Athletic Union, Golden Gloves; that's when I first started calling you, "Champ," because I knew one day you would be one.

Then you turned professional and started making a name for yourself.

I must tell you that I have always thought of boxing as such a brutal sport. Watching two guys try to pound each other into oblivion is not my idea of fun or sport. On the other hand, fighting is probably the oldest and most elementary engagement known to man as even the Bible records the fight between Cain and his brother Abel.

I'll never forget two moments when you won your first world championship. The first was the moment you popped Santos Cardona; there was no faking as he staggered and unceremoniously hit the canvas – lights out.

The other was when they shoved the microphone in your face after placing that gaudy, glittering world- championship belt around your waist. I, along with millions of other people around the world, waited to hear what you had to say.

I remember grinning and shaking my head at your fortitude as you opened your mouth and said, "Thank you, Jesus."

Why? Because when you had the greatest moment of glory in your life you attributed your success to your Savior. Let me tell you brother, even those who believe in Christ don't always want to hear or speak His name openly these days because it's too controversial and certainly not politically correct. You were bold as a lion!

I remember thinking about how, with two seconds and three words, you told more people about your love for Christ than all the pastors in Monroe County had collectively in their entire careers.

Even now, only someone who knows Christ personally and can testify to the dramatic change He brings to his or her life can know the importance of which I speak. To those who don't, the entire concept of The Man is foolishness.

I know you haven't gotten rich off boxing, yet at your final fight with Winky you declined thousands of dollars to wear a temporary tattoo on your back to advertise a casino because it wouldn't be a good example for one who teaches children's church.

There's another thing, Champ. I know, like me and everybody else in the world, you've made your share of mistakes. It used to cut to my heart to hear people trash-talk about you — only because you were the champ. You see, people don't want to talk about a nobody, only a somebody, like you. I guess it makes them feel like they are somebody.

And, when you profess to follow Christ, everyone watches your every move and considers you a phony if you do make a mistake. Thank God for redeeming grace.

What a thrill it is for me these days to see how God has rewarded your faith by blessing your life. He has given you the finest of gifts in your gorgeous wife, Brandi, and those precious children, Whitleigh, Banyon and Brooklyn.

Considering that today is the anniversary of the day God brought you to this planet, I guess it's a good day to give you this bouquet of flowers.

Thank you for your great friendship. Thank you for your great faith and witness. Thank you for the great husband, father, son and American I know you to be.

May God continue to bless you in the finest of ways, and may He help me find a recipe with which I can wrestle the Brotherman Rib Cooking King Award away from you this summer. You're the best, Champ!

But what do I know?

TYRONE SHOELACES

MARCH 27, 2003

Everything was perfect: guacamole, chips, soda and a roaring fireplace keeping the great room toasty while the north wind whipped against the outside of the house.

Renee and I snuggled deep into the couch and prepared to do what millions of other people were preparing to do that day: watch Super Bowl XXXVII, which, by the way, would keep my record intact of never missing one since Super Bowl I.

Even though I had recently retired from a career in advertising, I was still extremely interested in the manner with which corporations and businesses would be presenting their messages regarding the benefits of their products and services to this massive, captive audience.

In short, I was there for the commercials and could have cared less who won the game.

With just minutes left before the coin toss, Bill Romanowski, linebacker for the Oakland Raiders and featured in one of the pre-game commercials, came onto the screen carrying a goldfish in a fishbowl.

Instantly, chips went flying as Renee jumped to her feet and screamed at the top of her lungs, "Oh dear God, Tyrone!" and went racing out of the room.

I heard her little feet hit every third step as she bolted down the stairs. I heard the garage door open, the car start and the engine race as she gunned it out of the driveway.

I stood in the window, mouth open, guacamole dripping from a chip waiting to be devoured, and watched her go, wondering what the heck had come over this woman who shares my world.

And then I remembered.

For her recent January birthday, our god-daughters, Kate and Betsy Friend, had given her a beautiful plant growing out of a large vase of water; swimming inside under the roots of that plant was a gorgeous exotic, Asian Siamese beta fighting fish.

Renee loves her goddaughters and loved her gift, and, since she had received it at the beauty salon we own, she decided to keep the fish there and on display so our customers also could enjoy it.

"There are two things you need to know," began Lisa, Kate and Betsy's mother, that day. "His name is Tyrone Shoelaces and don't forget to buy him some food."

It must have been the innocence and simplicity of the moniker the girls had picked out for the fish because we laughed and laughed at it — and completely forgot about the food!

Now, four days later, thanks to a Super Bowl commercial, Renee was jolted back to reality and launched off into the night in search of fish food instead of relaxing with the game.

"What am I going to tell Tyrone?" she barked at the Kroger stock boy who informed her they didn't carry fish food. "Perhaps you could try Rite-Aid down the street," he correctly advised her before adding, "And tell Tyrone we're sorry."

Tyrone Shoelaces now sits on the snack bar of our kitchen so when we eat, he eats. I'm shocked he survived four days without food as the boy definitely likes to eat.

Last night, as we watched him ravenously nail the floating, freeze-dried bloodworms he loves so dearly, we laughed once again at the disaster averted by the Super Bowl commercial.

I looked across the table and into the eyes of Miss Compassion and thought of the recent story of a mother charged with starving her child to death and thought about the incredible distance there is between both women.

But what do I know?

SNOWBIRDS HAVE IT FIGURED OUT

M A R C H   3 0 ,   2 0 0 3

I can see for miles!

It's pretty easy when you're cruising at 29,000 feet above Earth on a clear day. I expect by now we are somewhere over northern Florida. It's amazing how symmetrical and perfectly plotted the land is below.

I decided to take advantage of my advantages — two airline ticket-gifts from a friend, the free use of an oceanfront, Pompano Beach condo from another, and the paid, extra-day-to-the-weekend Martin Luther King holiday (I love working for the government!) — to take my lovely wife for a weekend getaway for her birthday.

We landed at West Palm Beach Friday night, caught a ride to the condo and immediately paid a visit to the sea.

Tiny ripples, building momentum, transformed into giant waves and raced to the edge of the ocean to crescendo-crash on the sand with a thunderous roar as night birds flew by the light of the moon.

Unfortunately, the jet stream had turned into a bully and pushed deep into the South, plunging the normal, southern Florida 70s into the low 40s.

I shivered and pulled Renee closer to me.

The cold was irrelevant. What was relevant was that I had left 8 degrees and my normal routine behind in Michigan and had come to visit one of the most beautiful places in America. Best of all, I had the woman of my dreams by my side!

Saturday morning we had a blast as we spent the day bargain hunting at the giant, Fort Lauderdale flea market. (I hate shopping, unless I get to do it with my wife.) Price and selection were probably the best I have found anywhere and we certainly took advantage of the opportunity.

Before we left the market, we stopped by the fresh fish stand and bought 30 or so fat, juicy shrimp to complement the steaks I cooked on the barbie later that evening.

Sunday morning, after our own private church service where we thanked God for his marvelous blessings in our lives, we donned our swimsuits and parked our bods on the beach for the duration of daylight. Thankfully, it had warmed to 68 degrees, which allowed us to cook inside the cabana that sheltered us from the Canadian hawk's rare visit to this far south.

I wandered down to the ocean and searched the seashore for shells and then shared my treasures with Renee. She smiled with that "whatever makes you happy makes me happy" look on her tanned face.

I finally cornered the courage to get wet. My first step into the icy Atlantic sent a bevy of goose bumps across my body. Slowly my skin became acclimated to the water's cold and I enjoyed a heart-shocking, short-lived plunge; it was refreshing.

Sunday evening we flicked the remote between football and the Golden Globe Awards. We had no favorites in either and commented only on great plays on the gridiron and which of the stars looked fabulous or ridiculous. (I won't even begin to share my disgust with the award show's hosts, the Osbournes!)

This morning, awestruck, we thanked God for our eyesight as we watched a searing sunrise set the sky on fire over the Atlantic. We power-walked the beach one last time, then said, "See you in March," to the ocean and walked slowly back to the condo.

After bacon and eggs, we showered, packed the luggage, caught a ride back to the airport, breezed (amazingly) through security and launched into the pale-blue yonder and headed back to the frozen tundra.

We passed over what looked like Tennessee's Cumberland Mountains about a half- hour ago, and now the only thing visible below is a huge comforter of billowing cotton clouds.

In spite of even being cold in Florida, it's been great to get away. There's something about breaking up the regular routine that refreshes one's spirit.

The stewardess just told us to return our chairs to the upright position as we were beginning our descent into the Detroit metropolitan area. Going home sounded exciting — until she told us it was 4 degrees on the ground!

Snowbirds have it all figured out: winter in Florida, summer in Michigan. Can't wait to get my wings!

But what do I know?

TEMPERED VACATION

A P R I L   3 ,   2 0 0 3

I believe that life must go on.

However, as I write this from Mexico's paradise city of Isla de Cozumel and immersed in one of the most pleasurable vacations I've ever had, there is a part of me deep inside that cannot quite let go to have the wonderful time I have been anticipating for the past six months.

One of the slogans Renee and I live our lives by is, "Work hard, play hard;" it is an accurate description.

The first day of our vacation was somewhat overcast so we went to town and shopped till we dropped.

The second day was absolutely gorgeous and we plopped down in the sun and just lay there and soaked it up. Later, Renee would say, "I can already feel my batteries recharging."

Wednesday, we took the ferry to the city of Playa Del Carmen on the mainland and traveled 300 miles inland through the jungle to visit and climb the ancient Mayan Indian pyramid ruins at Chichen Itza. It was a tremendous experience I will never forget and I will tell you more about that another day.

Thursday, we rented a jeep and explored the beautiful island of Cozumel.

Friday, we spent our last day in the sun simply baking our bellies, and then later took a taxi to town for our anniversary dinner at a quaint little open-air restaurant.

After dinner, I ushered Renee from shop to shop until I found the perfect anniversary gift to remind her of my great love for her and the importance to me of this day.

I tell you all this because I want you to know that, as always, I am trying to have fun and enjoy the vacation we've worked hard to earn.

The problem is this: Thirty-five years ago I was in a situation similar to the one our American soldiers are in today — thousands of miles away from home in a life-and-death struggle of war for our country.

Other than trying to make sure I didn't get killed or maimed — like many of my friends — the main problem I had was that while I was in that life-or-death struggle, back in the states life was going on as normal, and that was something I couldn't keep myself from resenting.

I craved letters from home with news of what was happening socially with my friends, but when they came, they unintentionally pierced my heart.

I couldn't help but feel — like in days gone by — that if our country was at war, the whole country should be at war, not just the ones unlucky enough to have been drafted.

It killed my spirit to think that while my brothers-in-arms were dying all around me, by buddies back home were cruising Monroe Street looking for "chicks" without a care in the world.

Perhaps the difference is that in today's war, there is no draft. The soldiers fighting at this moment in Iraq and Afghanistan are there because they have chosen that profession as opposed to being told to go fight or go to jail, as was in the case of my generation.

As I stated before, I know that life must go on. Still, with a quick glance at the "United We Stand, Divided We Fall" sign, I can't help but feel a little guilty at my week of leisure during our soldier's struggles for survival. Just like I wanted loved ones at home feeling for me then, I cannot help but feeling for them now.

I have enjoyed my vacation, but it has been tempered daily by my thoughts and prayers for our soldiers. For their sake, and for the sake of the future of our country, I only hope that every American feels a little bit of their pain.

But what do I know?

HONORING A FALLEN SOLDIER

A P R I L   2 4 ,   2 0 0 3

As I pulled open the front door of the Pawlak Funeral Home in Temperance last Thursday, I greeted Toledo Mayor Jack Ford on his way out.

Dignitaries would not be the only ones paying their respects this Easter weekend.

As any former drill sergeant would, I checked my pockets to insure that each button was buttoned on the camouflage military uniform that felt like it had shrunk since I last wore it.

A mirror in the foyer confirmed that my beret was on straight and I was publicly presentable.

I noticed a gathering of others wearing the same uniform and I quietly glided through the crowd of whispering people to join them.

By the 7:30 p.m. start of the honor service more than 20 members of Monroe County Chapter 142, Vietnam Veterans of America, had joined the gathering. We formed a straight line and came to attention.

One by one we marched to the front of the funeral home and came to rest in front of the closed coffin of Marine PFC. Juan Guadalupe Garza Jr.

A Baghdad sniper's bullet had ended the life of this 20-year-old Summerfield High School graduate and Iraqi War soldier nine days earlier.

One by one, fellow soldiers from a war 35 years prior paused in front of this fallen comrade to render a final, slow-motion salute of honor.

We then took one step backward and snapped a salute of honor and loyalty to the flag of the United States of America that hung proudly above the casket, then turned to quickly, reverently, exit the room.

I couldn't have stood there for more than 20 seconds, yet in that short span of time, thoughts and memories flooded my mind.

For some reason, the sweet, pungent aroma seeping from the hundreds of flowers that choked the room caught my attention and I wondered why funeral homes have a different smell from a bouquet on the kitchen table.

The flag-draped coffin reminded me of a 34-year-old moment in another funeral home when I stood military honor guard at the feet of best friend Rodney Vore of Maybee, who was killed in action in Vietnam.

I wondered about the emotion that inevitably causes the lump to find its way into my throat to choke me during times like these.

But, most of all, I thought of the person behind the face that stared back at me from the 8 x 10 color photograph of the proudly dressed Marine that sat on the closed coffin.

In that moment of time I thought about how I wouldn't have known him from Adam had he walked up to me on the street two weeks ago.

Yet, here I was, on an evening I would rather be relaxing with my family —after finding and polishing my old combat boots and squeezing into my uniform— being so emotionally moved by honoring one about whom I knew absolutely nothing until a newspaper story of a few days ago.

It is a silent, unspoken bond that exists among defenders of the flag of freedom of our United States.

It is recognition of sacrifice from one to another, and, in the case of PFC. Garza, the supreme sacrifice. It is the reality that, but, for the grace of God, it could have been this soldier lying in that casket.

And, speaking of God and supreme sacrifices, on this Good Friday eve I thought of John 15:13 that says, "Greater love hath no man than this that a man lay down his life for his friends."

As Christians around the world celebrate the resurrection of Christ, I thought about how the day will come when I will meet Pfc. Garza face-to-face.

You see, he too was a follower of Jesus and had given his life so that others might live in freedom.

It was my distinct honor, as it was for Chapter 142, to honor him on this day.

But what do I know?

CONNER PETERSON: HUMAN BEING

MAY 1, 2003

The phone rang in the middle of the night. The frantic, labored voice on the other end of the line was a dear friend, six months pregnant with her first - and only - child.

Having pregnancy complications and driving herself to a Toledo hospital, the unwed mother-to-be asked if my wife and I would meet her there.

We threw on our clothes and dashed into the dark of the night. I set the cruise control on 90 mph as we raced down I-75.

Anxious hours crawled by in the quiet morning of the obstetrics waiting room. Finally, the door swung open and a tired doctor came through, pulling the surgical cap from his head.

We sat on the edge of anticipation for his words: "Mom and baby … are fine."

Our exhaled sighs of relief echoed around the room as three-hour frowns were eclipsed by ear-to-ear grins.

"Wait till you see that little boy," the doctor continued, "And I do mean little!"

Another few hours and we were peering through the glass at the premature baby boy who had come into our world three months early. The nurse had placed a tiny, blue stocking cap on his head.

I was awestruck at seeing this unbelievable miniature human being lying there in the incubator. He was 2 pounds, 2 ounces — and in critical condition.

That was one long night — 14 years ago.

Today, that child, who made such a fragile and dangerous entry into the world, is a typical teenage boy who is wild about sports.

The reason I mention this young man is because I thought of him today after reading about Conner Peterson. It is difficult to talk properly about Conner because, by law, I guess he's not really a person.

Conner Peterson is, or was, the unborn son of Scott and Laci Peterson. Laci and Conner washed up onshore off the San Francisco coast a few weeks ago. Scott has been charged in the murders of them both.

The question, of course, will be whether or not Conner can actually be considered a "person," since the last time anyone knew anything about him he was still inside his mother's womb.

According to many in this country, as well as interpretation of the law, if he had not come out for air on his own, he was 'nothing more than' a fetus and could not be considered a human being with rights to life.

Because of early complications 14 years ago, my friend brought a wonderful son into our world after only six months in her womb.

Because he was not given a chance to come from his mother's womb, Conner Peterson, even though he was two months older that my friend's son, not only will not know the joys of life but will not even legally be considered a human being.

Roe vs. Wade, prepare for another harsh glare of examination, if nothing more!

And, if Scott Peterson is guilty of this horrendous crime, I'll trust American justice to give him what he's got coming; I know God ultimately will.

However, I expect he might just simply be a player in a greater drama getting ready for the American stage where the abortion issue will be the important issue on trial instead of him. It will be a volatile issue whose time has come, and rightfully so.

Conner Peterson was a human being who deserved a chance, and right, to live and pursue happiness, in spite of what the courts dictate.

But what do I know?

REMEMBERING RICHARD

M A Y   2 2 ,   2 0 0 3

I was fifth in line for the only telephone booth on the company street of my Paratrooper Training facility in Fort Benning, Ga. It was May, 1968 and the night before I was to make my very first parachute jump.

The line inched along until it was my turn to hear the "ding" of my dime falling into the coin slot; soon the sweet voice of my mother was on the other end of the line.

We exchanged our greetings of love and updated each other on all that was happening. I was so excited about being on the eve of the most incredible thing that I had ever done and I detailed that excitement to her.

Through it all I could tell from her voice that she was only trying to be excited for me. Finally I asked, "Momma, is everything OK?"

She paused a moment, then, dealing with the truth, said, "No, son, everything is not OK. We just got word that Richard Gilbert was killed in Vietnam."

Silence screamed in my ears. It seemed as though someone had hit the pause button on my life and I stood frozen to that phone booth from the words I had just heard.

I shook my head as if coming out of a dream; surely this couldn't be true. I started to say, "Mom, you're kidding me," but I knew that about something like this she would never kid, especially with me only months away from going to the same theater.

Richard Gilbert was one of my best friends. We had grown up together, gone to church together, gone to school together, gone to jail together!

Yes, Richard was with me the night we were fingerprinted, booked, charged with "littering" and sent to jail for toilet-papering General Custer's statue in downtown Monroe.

Richard and I became extremely close through church. We were both members of the Royal Ambassadors for Christ youth group and spent many summer weekends having a blast on camping and fishing excursions.

We both loved to sing and always tried to sit next to each other in church so we could harmonize on the old gospel favorites. During the weekends, we would borrow one of our dad's cars and cruise Monroe Street singing at the top of our lungs with the songs on the radio.

Dear Friend, Richard Gilbert,
KIA Vietnam, 1969.

As I think back on that night, we reminded me of the Bible's Paul and Silas as I remember sitting in that jail cell singing songs about Jesus. The difference was that Paul and Silas were praising God for the freedom they had in their hearts, even, and especially, during incarceration.

I expect we were trying to get on the good side of Jesus, hoping He would intercede so our fathers wouldn't beat our butts — as we knew they were going to!

"Son, are you OK?" called that sweet voice on the other end of the line.

There were no words to say. Tomorrow's excitement had been crushed by the thought that my dear friend and I would never again sing together — at least not in this life.

Three weeks later, after graduating from "jump school," I flew home for a 30-day furlough before heading for a war on the other side of the planet in a country I could hardly find on a map. I did not get home in time for Richard's funeral.

A few days after arriving home, a letter came in the mail for me. The return address said, "Richard Gilbert, Vietnam." I tore the letter open and out popped a picture. The beautiful smile of my dear friend flooded the photograph as he posed with two of his Vietnamese friends.

His letter told me that everything was fine, in spite of the heavy action, and that he was simply counting the days until he could be home again with his loved ones.

I winced at the words, knowing, now, that would not be happening.

Suddenly I noticed the date of his letter.

"Mom," I asked, "what day was Richard killed?"

"May 14th," was her answer.

The date on the letter was May 14, 1968. Only hours before his life was taken away by war, my dear friend had written me a letter.

I guess I have a soft heart, because, 35 years later as I write this, I cannot stop the soft swell of tears slowly seeping into my eyes as I sit here remembering my friend.

On Monday, Americans will celebrate Memorial Day and I will once again go hang out with my friends: Richard Gilbert at Roselawn Memorial Park Cemetery, Lenny Liparato at St. Joseph Cemetery and Rodney Vore in Maybee's Holy Ghost Lutheran Church Cemetery, to name a special few. There are more.

Please take, if nothing more, a moment to remember them and all the others who gave their lives in service to our great country. It is the very least we can do to honor their sacrifice.

It will also go a long way in helping re-weave the state of the ragged patriotic fabric of our nation, which, sadly, we have allowed to regress.

But what do I know?

DOMINO THEORY

J U L Y   1 0 ,   2 0 0 3

Two of my very favorite teachers from school were Tolbert and Mary Sandlin. They helped me grow and learn in so many ways and I recognized that even then.

That's why when Mrs. Sandlin called me about a month ago asking for a favor, my response was, "Name it!" even before she got specific.

Her request was for her granddaughter, Whitney LaBeau, who needed to interview a Vietnam veteran for a school assignment. I was happy to oblige and we set the day and time.

When the day came it was a treat to see Mrs. Sandlin again and meet her beautiful granddaughter. After an exchange of pleasantries, Whitney, articulate and well prepared, began with her questions.

It was her first, simple, elementary question that staggered me a bit and has had me thinking about it ever since.

Basically, she asked me why America fought in Vietnam.

I just stared at her for a few moments, and then started stammering as I tried to collect my thoughts.

I told her how the oppressive, Communist government of the North was trying to exact their will on the people of the South and how the Americans came as liberators.

Then I told her about the Domino Theory. She asked what that was and I shared that America believed – in those days – that Communism was spreading throughout Asia and the rest of the world in the same manner as dominos-on-end: when you push the first one over, it falls into and pushes over the second one, then the third, and on and on until they all fall in rapid succession.

I hadn't thought of that theory in some time and as I was explaining it to her, the morning's lead news story was ringing in my head.

The Iraq War had ended and President Bush was rattling his saber at Iran, warning them about harboring terrorists or possessing weapons of mass destruction.

Pro-democracy demonstrations had already started in the streets of Tehran and I expect the Iranian government was in fear that America might just decide to push across the Iraqi border into Iran.

It hit me at that moment. As I was telling Whitney about the Domino Theory, I wondered if, somewhere, someone in the world might be warning of a Capitalistic Domino Theory when they consider...Afghanistan, Iraq, and Iran.

And now, Liberia?

Sunday, President Bush ordered the president of that African nation to step down and leave his civil war-torn country or risk American troops coming to do it for him.

Now, thanks to the inquisitive mind of a young lady working on a homework assignment, my thoughts about world politics have been thrown back into the mental washing machine.

I guess it all comes back to how everybody in the world thinks they are right.

I think America is right – if nothing more by insuring that the world keeps repressive regimes – like the Taliban – at bay, along with mass murderers – like Sadaam Hussein – eliminated, one way or the other.

But what do I know?

MINI LIFETIMES

J U L Y 1 7 , 2 0 0 3

This morning as I was praying and thanking God for this new day and asking for his guidance, I thought about how I have come to view each new day as a mini-lifetime.

When I was young I had the carefree attitude that I had my whole life ahead of me. Now, at 55 (wondering where the years have gone), wiser and much less naïve, I have learned to not think or worry too much about tomorrow as it is not promised.

Instead, I have learned to take each day as it comes and consider it as possibly my very last.

It's like I am re-born every morning and I begin my life anew. I first spend my time with God, thanking him and seeking his guidance.

This equates to infancy and childhood as we are taught through those stages of life by the ones who physically birth us, our parents.

They teach us (hopefully) right from wrong and are always there for us to lean on, find comfort from during difficult times, and love us even when no one else will.

In the mini-lifetime, God provides all that for each day during my personal time with him.

Then, it's off to my job, where, in exchange for a paycheck, I use my personal skills to help the entity for which I am working provide a greater service or product to a greater number of people in exchange for profit or satisfaction (non-profit).

At the end of the workday I say goodbye to everybody and go home to my wife and spend the rest of the day doing what we want to do.

This equates to my lifetime of employment, and then retirement. While we may love our work, I expect the ultimate goal of most people is to get to that stage of life where you work at things you want to and spend time with the people with whom you want to spend time.

I don't expect there are not too many more wonderful sounds in life than the five o'clock whistle! Why? Because that means you are retired for the day and get to go home.

As the evening gets late eyes get tired and you start to yawn. Movements slow down and you don't feel like getting up and doing anything else. Content just to sit and watch TV or read a book, muscles atrophy and soon you have only enough energy to climb into bed and turn out the light on this day's mini-lifetime.

Sleep, which is something we all must do, equates to something else we all must eventually do: die. The Bible even refers to death as falling asleep.

Fortunately, in this life of ours, we sleep, and then we wake for a new day. As a Christian, I believe that after I die God will wake me for a new day, forever.

Till then, I just take each day as it comes. I try to deal with each person I come into contact with as if this will be the last time I will ever see them, especially my wife.

I want her to know how very much I love her and appreciate what an excellent mate she has been — just in case I never get another chance to tell her personally.

I want to take the time to glory in each breath-taking sunset and marvel at every color of each new rainbow. I want to make sure the ones I love know that I love them, not wonder. I want to live each moment like it is my last, because, one day, it will.

I hope you enjoy the rest of today's mini-lifetime. You never know when it will be the last one you get.

But what do I know?

THREE TIME LOSER

JULY 23, 2003

I'm still crushed!

It's taken a whole month for me to recover and draw enough strength to write this column.

You have to understand that I've always considered myself to be a pretty good cook. I do most all of the cooking in our house. I grow and use my own herbs and spices to exact just the right taste in the food we eat.

I can't remember specifically how it all started. Seems to me that while hanging with two of my best friends — Rev. Al Overstreet and boxing great Bronco McKart — talk turned to who could cook the best ribs.

You've read of each of these brothers of mine in recent columns I've written. We call ourselves "Brothermen" because in addition to being great friends, we are Christian brothers.

The problem is that each of us is highly competitive at virtually anything we do. So, when talk turned to who could cook the best ribs, the only answer was to have a competition.

Thus, on the first Saturday of Spring, we conducted a "rib-off" with the Annual Brotherman Rib King Award "trophy" going to the winner. (The trophy is a walnut plaque with a mounted, scorched rib with each year's winner's name engraved under it).

Our rib-off has turned into quite a festive occasion as we meet at my house and grill our ribs simultaneously on the deck overlooking Lake Erie. Bronco brings wife Brandy and their kids, Al brings his Dana, and, of course, I have Renee to cheer me on.

We slap the ribs on the grills and begin hammering each other with catcalls.

"You boys might just as well turn your grills off and come watch the master chef at work," calls Al.

"Are you kidding," returns Bronco, "I'll bet the dog won't even eat your ribs."

And so it goes for the next few hours as the children squeal with delight dancing on the deck while the wives just look at us, smile and shake their heads at all their kids.

When the ribs are done we each choose a section we're sure will be the winner and place it on one of three paper plates, the bottoms of which are numbered 1, 2 and 3.

The ladies take them into the kitchen where an impartial judge, kept carefully and fairly segregated from the cooking process, takes his time to taste each entrée.

The first year the winner was....Bronco.

The second year the winner was...Bronco!

Determined that this was going to be my year, I concocted my special sauce and even parboiled my ribs for extra tenderness. I had my fire just right, and, without a doubt, cooked the best ribs I've ever cooked.

The judge was another good friend, Brian Hall of Luna Pier, who was a last minute replacement for Vietnam veteran-friend, Clifford Trudeau, judge of the first two years' competition.

The three "Brothermen" stood by with baited breath as Judge Hall moved from plate-to-plate, savoring the spicy sweetness of each slab selection. Then, in typical rib-eating fashion, he licked his fingers dry, gave each plate one more look, then pointed to the plate in the middle and said, "This one!"

Did I mention that I was crushed?

Well, I wasn't alone as Bronco began to wail like a dog when you step on his tail. I swear that Bronco whined more over losing his Rib King title than either one of his World Boxing Championships!

But that was nothing!

Reverend Overstreet — whose ribs were on plate No. 2 — threw his hands into the air as if he had just scored the winning touchdown at the Super Bowl and began to strut his stuff all over the kitchen.

For the next hour Bronco and I were addressed as, "My royal subjects."

And, needless to say, one month later it has not let up. (By the way, if you know Brother Al, next time you see him, address him as "Your Royal Highness" or "Rib King," then get ready to hear the story from beginning to end!).

Oh well, back to the mixing bowl for a new sauce recipe for next year.

What great fun! And, what great brotherhood!

A few weeks ago I told you about Al's "What comes from the heart, reaches the heart" saying. One of his favorite scriptures is the first verse of Psalm 133 that reads, "Behold, how good and how pleasant it is for brethren to dwell together in unity."

He's right. Our bond of brotherhood is something you cannot buy, but is available for free. It's the love God gives us from, and for, Him and for each other.

Even when one of those brothers is a three-time-loser!

But what do I know?

FAIR MEMORIES

J U L Y   3 1 ,   2 0 0 3

Anticipating the annual visit of the Monroe County Fair was paramount in my spring and summer when I was a boy.

I mowed lawns, washed cars and picked up returnable pop bottles to earn and save money for what was always the best time of summer. During almost 50 of those visits that I can remember there were many memorable events that stand out in my mind.

I remember receiving my first advertising lesson. I didn't know it then, but it was one that I ended up teaching to my sales staff through 20-some subsequent years of radio management.

My father pulled our old '53 Pontiac alongside one of a couple hundred other cars already filling the old parking field next to the fairgrounds. When we got out of the car, dad pulled out his old red bandana and tied it to the radio antenna. When I asked him why, he told me he would tell me later and we proceeded in to enjoy the fair.

Hours later, money and energy expended, we left and headed back into the lot. Now, instead of a couple hundred cars, there were thousands. Dad hoisted me for a better view and said, "Now, you tell me why I tied that bandana to the antenna."

I scanned the lot and instantly identified our car, as it was set apart from all the others by the bandana. During my advertising career, my goal was to always figure out a way to set my client's business apart from all the others.

(My father had to leave school in the second grade to help with chores on his father's Tennessee farm, yet somehow, he seemed to have more wisdom than most of the college graduates I've met in my time).

I remember getting older and asking whomever my love interest was at the moment to meet me at the fair and then trying to sneak a kiss on top of the Ferris wheel.

I remember one year sitting in the YMCA dunking booth and

seeing my big brother, Hal, (who was a star baseball pitcher in high school) approaching the booth. I verbally abused him, baiting him to spend his money in an attempt to try and dunk me. Thirteen consecutive bulls eyes later my catcalls turned to gurgling begs for him to quit.

I pitched a little in my day and remember one night throwing a baseball through a tiny target hole, which rang a bell and released a caged goose that came sliding down a children's slide to me.

I had no idea what to do with the goose, so I took it home and secured it in my sleeping parents' breezeway, where it proceeded to trash the place and wake up not only them, but everyone in the neighborhood.

I remember one of my first bands - Caesar and the Romans - performing at the band shell. It was the first concert I ever gave and I was hooked on playing music from that moment.

I remember being asked, as general manager of Tower 98 radio, to enter the 4-H celebrity goat milking contest, and winning. The highlight of that contest, in addition to receiving a trophy with a goat on top, was winning in spite of wasting some of my goat's milk by squirting then-State Senator Norm Shinkle--milking his goat adjacent to mine--in the back with an occasional turn of the teat.

The Monroe County Fair Association is an outstanding organization run by dedicated individuals who have done nothing but improve the quality of the fair throughout those 50-some years I've been attending.

My wife and I will again be at the corner of M-50 and Raisinville Road this week to create a few more entries for the memory bank. It's easy to do when you attend the best county fair in the entire country!

But what do I know?

MEETING DRAKE

AUGUST 28, 2003

It looked like a back massager and the technician smeared its face with lubricant before pressing it to her distended belly. Once in place, he turned to face the computer screen and pressed the button.

The screen, literally, came to life and cast its green light onto the faces of family gathered in the darkness of the ultrasound room of Mercy-Memorial Hospital's Radiology Department.

Gasps of delight filled that room as sound waves of technology painted onto the screen the outline of the tiny body of the child growing inside the womb of this beautiful, young mother-to-be.

My wife, Renee, gripped my hand tighter and I could feel her heart racing as she looked upon the image of her very first grandchild for the very first time.

The technician, extremely professional and courteous, gave us a visual tour of the newest member of our family as he carefully slid the magic wand around her belly.

"Here are the eyes," he began. "Here's the nose and mouth."

Even after 56 years — which included a stint as an operating room technician early in my career who helped deliver babies in this very hospital's Surgery Department — I still stood spellbound and in complete awe of the initial stages of this miracle of life.

He slid the wand off to the side and said, "There's the spine."

A series of symmetrically sequenced slivers ran horizontally from the base of the head to bottom of the baby's butt, and we could actually see the tiny spine shift ever-so-slightly as the baby moved in the womb.

I wondered what the fetus was feeling as the steady stream of sound encroached on his, or her, sanctuary.

Curiosity conquered the unspoken suspense as the question finally spilled out.

"Can we see if it is a boy or a girl?"

As I said, the technician proved his professionalism and courtesy as he responded with, "That's completely up to Karie."

I looked down upon the face of my beautiful daughter-in-law as she grinned back at the family of faces gathered to share this glorious moment.

I remember thinking that the two years that had passed since I had the honor of singing at the wedding of Karie Bolicki to our youngest son, Nathan Carr, seemed like only months ago.

I swelled with joy as I thought about how this new wife had recently called, crying, because she and Nathan had been desperately, unsuccessfully, trying to conceive.

She and I became "Two or more gathered in His name" that evening, and we asked — in the name of Jesus — for God to intervene and bless her and Nathan with a child.

Now, only months later, the very fruit of that prayer, incredibly, lay peacefully protected inside her body and delightfully displayed on a computer screen!

At that moment I prayed she would never forget the power of that prayer, and, specifically, of the One who had answered it.

The technician turned to Karie, waiting while she finished sharing that precious moment through the eyes of each of us gathered to share her precious moment.

Her nod of approval sent his attention back to the screen and he launched the magic wand in search of the answer to the initial question.

Finally, he stopped, pointed to the screen and said, "Ok, see that little dot right there? And, see that other little dot right next to it?"

Our collected hearts beat even faster on the edge of the big moment.

"Looks like testicles to me," he finished.

There were two men in the room – Nathan and me – and we erupted with a simultaneous, vociferous "Yes!" followed by a spirited high-five.

I interrupted my joy to catch the reaction of the new mommy: a tear spilled from her right eye and I wondered if it was a minute disappointment that "Drake" was not going to be "Kiana," or that it was simply her joy at knowing that she was squarely in the middle of one of life's most taken-for-granted miracles.

I didn't ask.

Suddenly, the in-room chatter and excitement died as the magic wand revealed the most incredible moment of the day.

"Ah, there it is," called the technician.

There on the screen, as clear and distinct as the sun beating down from a cloudless sky, was a tiny heart beating out to the new world he was about to enter.

I gasped and caught my breath, then finally spoke out loud: "How is it possible that anyone could see that and say that this is not a life?"

I want to say a special "thank you" to Nathan, and especially, Karie, for granting me the privilege of sharing this special event with them, and for giving me permission to share what I witnessed that day with you.

I would also ask those of you who know and trust in the One who sent this child to us here on earth to lift this mother and child up in prayer.

And, maybe more importantly, I ask you to pray for all the misguided souls, who, unlike this grateful mother, would consider the beating heart inside their womb nothing more than a tumor and make the decision to terminate that life!

Abortion is the greatest crime against humanity, yet most easily hidden.

But what do I know?

THE NEED TO REMEMBER

SEPTEMBER 11, 2003

Finding myself between the desires of not wanting to be too predictable, juxtaposed with the desire to be timely and effective, I want to address, again, 9-11.

For some reason, in my head I keep hearing the second verse from the country hit song by Darryl Worley, "Have Your Forgotten," which says, "They took all the footage off my T.V., Said it's too disturbing for you and me. It'll just breed anger that's what the experts say. If it was up to me I'd show it everyday."

I am not a sensationalist or someone who craves gory details, but I miss not seeing those airplanes flying into the World Trade Centers on a regular basis.

I try to put myself in the place of one who lost a specific loved one that day to see how I might feel seeing it over and over knowing that my loved one was on that plane or in that building.

Even then, I still feel that the need of the country to see those attacks and be reminded of the motivations behind them is even more important than what I expect the personal tragic reminder might be.

It reminds me of how, in the Bible, the Apostle Paul asks God three times to "take this thorn from my side," and how God answers and says, "My grace is sufficient for thee."

Paul has, I assume, an affliction of the flesh for which he repeatedly asks God to remove. (I note that in describing the thorn Paul uses the words, "A messenger of Satan.") God chooses not to remove the "thorn," but, in my opinion, uses the thorn as a reminder to Paul that he is to seek God's counsel and guidance in order to overcome the "evil messenger."

Those hijacked aircraft two years ago were "Messengers of Satan" sent to try to destroy the good for which this country has stood for over 200 years.

The message was clear: two aircraft sent to bring down the towers:

the symbol of capitalism, one to smash the symbol of our power: the Pentagon, and the other, though not clearly identified, thought to be either for the White House or Capital building, symbols of our administration and government.

It is the essence of evil to make you want to destroy the good that is in front of you that you don't have! It is the nature of evil to hate and try to destroy anyone who doesn't think like you.

So many people around the world hate America, but, they all want to come here to live and bring their families!

When you are on top of the pile very few are happy for you, but, more often than not, very many want to knock you off or see you get knocked off!

And I don't care what anybody says, read your history and you will see that the forgers of the Constitution sought the counsel of God in shaping the laws and way of life of our country. I also believe that – as He has me personally – God has blessed this country as no other in history in reward of that belief in Him.

And that is why America is the greatest country on the planet, not because we have great gold or oil resources, smarter people or sophisticated weaponry.

I want to see those airplanes smashing into the WTC to constantly remind me that the forces of evil will always be out there like a roaring lion seeking whom he may devour.

I want to be reminded that, just like that traumatic life and death drama we lived through two years ago today, life is not really about us, but about God and Satan and the struggle between the forces of good and evil.

As we stand on the edge of seeing the vestiges of any references to the One who made this nation great slowly disappear, I prepare for the ridicule and chastisement from the atheists and agnostics, who used to be few, to the finger-pointing, political correctness of the "let's not offend anyone" crowd, who now are many.

I have not forgotten, nor will I.

I want to be reminded of the great pain I felt that day as a thorn in my side, reminding me that in spite of how great the country is in which I live, things are not ok and that Messengers of Satan are plotting even as I write to bring it to its knees.

But, in order to deal with the thorn, I will humble myself and seek God's sufficient grace. The problem, of course, comes when we turn from being "One nation under God" to virtually kicking Him out of our lives and society to make sure we are politically correct and don't offend anyone.

I can't imagine Him blessing anyone with that kind of attitude.

But what do I know?

TOMATO TRIGGERED MEMORY

SEPTEMBER 18, 2003

I could smell it as soon as I walked into the kitchen.

There on the counter sat at least 25 tomatoes that different friends had brought, sharing the great success of this year's growing season with Renee and me.

Big, beautiful, rich-looking tomatoes, but that smell told me that one of them had been here too long.

I scanned each until the look of one in particular jumped out at me. The touch of his skin told me I had the culprit, and the juice that streamed as I moved him out of formation and into the sink confirmed his condition.

It's funny how smell can trigger memory.

Just before I fed him to the garbage disposal the smell of that very ripe tomato instantly shot my mind back to my boyhood home.

My gaze went out the kitchen window but in my mind's eye my older brother, Hal Dean, and I were in our family garden picking tomatoes.

My father was the world's greatest gardener and he grew the biggest, juiciest, sweetest tomatoes I ever tasted. We had a huge garden and it was our job, along with our sister, Janet, to tend to it.

I remember long hours of planting, watering, weeding and hoeing. The reward was great bounty in the summer and fall, and mom religiously canned that bounty and we ate our provision for the next year until it was time to do it all over again.

Hal Dean would make me hold the basket while he waded through the tomato plants looking for the ripe ones, which he would pick and hand to me.

On this particular day the sight of him all spread out in the garden, bent over at the waist with his big butt sticking up in the air – for some reason – was just too tempting of a target to ignore.

I eased the basket to the ground and selected a nice, baseball-sized tomato, silently glided backward to prepare for my getaway, then wound up and blasted him with the tomato.

Crime and punishment were real in my family so I knew that retribution would be inevitable, but, on this day, I was full of you-know-what and vinegar.

I heard him yelp as the tomato disintegrated on his butt and back, but I was gone, tearing through tomato plants, crashing through corn, racing through the radishes and headed for the safe haven of our garage.

The movie I watched in my head as I gazed out that kitchen window was running in slow motion, even after all these years.

I chuckled as I watched the laughter on my face as I ran out of that garden, knowing I had blasted big brother and was getting away with it.

I guess it's here I should probably tell you that Hal was a star baseball pitcher for Monroe High School. He was my idol and I used to go to each of his games. He had also inherited a special skill from my father: accuracy. My father used to take two rocks, throw one into the air and then hit it with the other rock while it was still in the air.

It was a good 40 yards from where I had smacked Hal with my cowardly assault to the safety of the garage, and now I was just steps away.

I slowed my run, reached out for the edge of the garage and turned to see his reaction, give a haughty laugh and gloat.

His timing was perfect.

Just as I turned to look the biggest, ripest, rankest, smelliest tomato that used to be in the garden smacked me in the side of the face and knocked me down.

The air was unceremoniously sucked from the sails of my ship.

Worse than that, you would have thought he had just thrown a no-hitter to win the World Series as he screamed, pumped both fists into the air and jumped up and down at his triumph.

We didn't have a shower in those days, but I took baths for three straight days and still couldn't get the smell of that rotten tomato off me.

It's funny. Yesterday I couldn't even remember my cell phone number, and today, the aroma of a ripe tomato triggers a 45-year-old memory that warms my heart and lovingly gives me the pleasure of a mental visit with my dear brother and the mischievous shenanigans we used to pull on each other when life was simple.

What an incredible thing is the mind. No matter how much money I could pay to purchase the most sophisticated computer known to man, it couldn't do for me what this simple brain God assigned me 56 years ago did for me today...and all because of a rotten tomato on the counter.

Ode to Renee: "Big bang theory...yeah, right!"

But what does she know?

MUHAMMAD ALI: FRIEND OR FOE?

S E P T E M B E R   2 5 ,   2 0 0 3

Last week I took my lovely wife to the West Indies for a fabulous week of vacation on the gorgeous tropical island of Antigua. We almost cancelled the vacation due to Hurricane Isabel and I'm glad we didn't as we had a wonderful week of weather!

There was something that happened on our way home that intrigued me, however, and I wanted to share it with you.

We had "puddle-jumped" from Antigua to San Juan, Puerto Rico, then had a direct flight to Pittsburgh for an hour layover before the last leg of the flight to Detroit.

As we sat in the airport I looked a few feet seats away from us and noticed this man sitting there.

"Honey," I interrupted Renee's reading, "that looks like Muhammad Ali."

The man looked pretty feeble and I soon dismissed him as a "look-alike"…until he got up to move to another chair. It was then I recognized the unmistakable effects of a disease that had left one of history's most charismatic and greatest-known sports icons in one of the most helpless and heartbreaking conditions known to man: Parkinson's Disease.

Never one to hide my enthusiasm or emotions much, I leaped to my feet and bolted over to him, stuck out my hand and blurted out my favorite Bronco McKart moniker: "Champ!" I addressed him.

Have you ever seen someone completely change the expression on their face -without ever moving their mouth — by smiling with their eyes?

The former heavyweight boxing champion of the world never said a word and never cracked a smile, but his eyes told me how happy he was to be thousands of miles beyond the roar of the crowd — and his prime — and still be recognized by a fan in an airport.

"Could I have my picture taken with you?" I asked, hoping not to be intrusive. He immediately began a struggle to stand and I reached down and wrapped my arms around him to help him to his feet.

At that moment I thought of how many would-be-champs with both their energy and one-shot-at-fame gone who had draped their arms around this man trying to hang on after being pummeled.

I slid my right arm around his waist and turned toward Renee, who by now had dug the camera out of our carry-on and was already focused on this historic moment.

"Give him the right hook," she called out to the champ, who instinctively raised that famous fist to my chin.

The moment was frozen in time, both on the film and in my memory.

I turned, looked into his eyes and grabbed that fist with both hands and converted it into a handshake.

It was that moment that blew me away and has kept my head spinning ever since.

In that moment his eyes thanked me for remembering him and wanting to share a moment of his being.

In that moment I looked deep into those eyes and saw the young and pompous Cassius Clay claiming his ticket to glory with an Olympic championship in Rome, who would later ride in a Louisville-hometown parade in his honor, then be refused service in a restaurant because of the color of his skin.

In those eyes I saw the "Float like a butterfly, sting like a bee" poet predicting which round he would knock out challengers to his throne, and I remembered being one of the millions tuned in to see if he was prophetic.

I saw eyes that could no longer glare at opponents or steer the body to climb the ropes and scream, "I am the greatest!" to the crowd he had whipped into a frenzy.

I saw the jokester pulling the wig off the head of Howard Cosell, his greatest promoter of all.

There was no time, but also in that moment I saw the draft dodger who refused to answer his country's call for military service in Vietnam and I wanted to talk to him about it from the perspective of one who did.

Muhammad Ali and Tom, Pittsburgh Airport, 2003

I saw the man who would be one of the first to convert to Islam, take a Muslim name and denounce white-America, and I wanted to ask what he thought personally about 9-11, terrorism and the state of our country and the world.

I found myself in the bittersweet moment of holding the hand of a man who had thrilled millions and made millions, yet who also in another day and time would have been hung for treason.

Those eyes hinted to me that while he took turns in the ring of life as a great sports figure, politician, minister, cultural icon and leader of his people, the bottom line was that he had been an entertainer, and now the show was over.

After I took pictures of him hugging Renee I noticed a crowd had recognized the celebrity and begun to gather. I felt a bit of guilt for creating this intrusion into his life and quickly said, "God bless you, champ," and we walked off to catch our plane.

Today I'm trying to figure out if I had a glorious opportunity to meet one of the greatest men in the history of our country, or, as crazy as it sounds, had been fraternizing with one who could turn out to be one of the architects that brought it down.

But what do I know?

*"From Carrier to Columnist," Tom delivers
The Monroe Evening News, 1963.*

FROM CARRIER TO COLUMNIST

OCTOBER 27, 2003

I'm guessing I was about 10 years old when I got my first job.

I remember being excited about it because my mother and brother both had worked there before me.

Through the years I always felt as though I would go back there one day, and now, 46 years later, here I am.

I've always had an opinion and I've always loved to write, so, years ago, I started writing a column for my Vietnam veterans' chapter newsletter.

I finally decided I needed a name for the column and thought about how, through the years, I had always been more than willing to share my thoughts and opinions with others about almost anything.

However, when I would get to the end of the opinion, I would always say, "But what do I know?" which was my way of qualifying that opinion.

In other words, who cares what I think! I'm just another slug scratching and clawing his way through life like everybody else on the planet and everything that comes out of my mouth is nothing more than ... my opinion.

Everybody sees the world through their own eyes and makes their values and judgments based upon their own moral and ethical belief system (or lack of one!). As a result, everybody thinks he is right about what he thinks and does; I'm no different..

But, we all know that nobody is right all the time (except my wife, of course).

So, the column was named and I enjoyed writing it.

A couple of years ago an invitation came for me to write the column for the *Monroe Guardian*. I jumped at the opportunity and wrote it weekly, until recently, when the format changed and I was informed there would no longer be room for the column.

Though disappointed, I had learned long ago that God only closes doors in order to open others, and, sure enough, a few weeks later, one of my favorite columnists, Editor Deb Saul, called with the offer to join the staff here at *The Monroe Evening News.*

I was thrilled, to say the least, at being able to continue the column. Perhaps more so to be able to associate myself alongside some of the great writers employed here.

For this first offering I thought it best to give you a little history about how the column has transpired.

Perhaps I should warn you that I am a born-again Christian who is undoubtedly not a good reflection of Christ's light but wants to be. While I don't consider myself a "religious fanatic," you will read few of my columns where I don't refer to the Bible or Christ Himself.

That is because I have been through the storms of life, like war, divorce, heartbreak, job termination, to name a few. And, speaking of termination, like Arnold, there have been times when I have behaved badly along the way.

However, when I asked Christ to come into my heart and take over my life, everything changed for the better, and I have no choice but to give Him the credit for that change.

And now things have come full circle. At 10 years old I was delivering papers, with opinions, for *The Monroe Evening News.* Today, I'm delivering an opinion in the same paper, only another 10-year-old is bringing it to your door.

I once heard a line that said, "There is no right or wrong, only opinion."

So what do you think? Is that right … or wrong?

I know it's wrong because I know there is right. In fact, I believe the biggest problem in America today is that everybody is concerned about "rights" while nobody is concerned about "right."

But what do I know?

THE FLAVOR OF FREEDOM'S FABRIC

N O V E M B E R   1 0 ,   2 0 0 3

The engine growled with determination as the Jeep tackled each new incline. White knuckles gripped the steering wheel as I tried to stay in the driver's seat while the bucking-bronco mountain road tried to eject me.

Finally at the top, I found my favorite spot, killed the engine and climbed onto the hood of the Jeep.

I stripped off the soaked, olive drab T-shirt and closed my eyes for a moment of enjoyment as the cool breeze toweled away the swirls of sweat generated by the sweltering Southeast Asian sun on this 100-plus degree afternoon.

As often as I could, I would borrow a Jeep from the base camp motor pool and make the climb to this majestic vantage point where I could see for miles and miles.

I spent hours on that mountaintop, thinking, praying, crying, but mostly longing for home and the family and friends I missed so desperately.

The year was 1968 and the place was a hamlet called Duc Pho, South Vietnam.

Just six months earlier I had been a student in the very first class of the not-yet-built Monroe Community College, playing on a championship basketball team, cruising Monroe St. and thinking about marrying this little hottie from Petersburg named "Joyce." Now I was 14,000 miles away from all that, mired in the middle of the Vietnam War with the United States Army's 11th Light Infantry Brigade.

Today I still see that mountaintop view in my mind's eye. Looking due east, there was a valley between two smaller mountains. Across that valley was the South China Sea, and I would sit for hours dreaming of what was waiting for me on the other side.

This morning as I prayed for our soldiers facing daily death in Iraq, I wondered how many of them had a vantage point where they could sit and dream of what lay beyond their direction of home.

I thought about the ribbon of love and understanding that weaves together the hearts of former soldiers with current soldiers.

Today my heart hurts for the hurts in their hearts because I know exactly how that ache feels.

Scrawled on a mess hall wall during my Vietnam service was a phrase that said, "Freedom has a flavor the protected will never know." I believe that is the fabric of which that ribbon is made.

It's the same flavor featured in the picture currently circulating on the internet of the disabled veteran who has climbed out of his wheelchair and placed his hand over his heart to be the only one of the parade throng standing as the Stars & Stripes passes by.

It's the same flavor exhibited by the guards at the Tomb of the Unknown Soldier, who, hours before September's Hurricane Isabel ripped through Arlington, refused the offer to be excused to go home and stay safe and dry ... leaving the tomb of their fallen comrades unguarded.

Whether you think they should be there or not, tomorrow, would you ask God to protect our soldiers in Iraq and around the world? Also, if you know a veteran who has already given that service, wish them a good day. In my opinion, it's because of them that you can have a good day.

But what do I know?

ANNE MURRAY AND ME - IN MY DREAMS!

NOVEMBER 17, 2003

Monroe's little-known jewel, the River Raisin Centre for the Arts, was packed to the gills with many faces I knew and many I didn't as I peeked through the thick, heavy curtain separating me from the buzzing, pre-show audience.

It had been my life long dream, even before it changed from a movie house to a concert theater, to perform here.

I remembered sitting in the balcony waiting for "The Poseidon Adventure" to begin its opening film credits and dreaming of being on this very stage playing my screaming guitar and singing for hometown friends.

Now, 30-some years later - minus the guitar and all the energy it took to drive it - I was about to live that dream.

I took a moment to glance up at all the renovations and improvements the facility had received since those early days when Joe Sterling replaced an old broom shop with a then-state-of-the-art concrete building to show "movie pictures."

"Monrovians," as I often call us, used to stand in two lines to get tickets: one going south past the old post office - now a museum - and the other north to First St. past the old Silver Dollar Bar, now a parking lot.

I thought of how the Downtown Kiwanis Club, along with Monroe Bank & Trust, had ventured initial seed money back in 1987 for a local group of visionaries to purchase the building and save it from the scheduled wrecking ball.

Tonight, Canadian songstress Anne Murray was the headliner and I had been asked to join her in a duet for her Grammy-winning hit, "Could I Have This Dance."

The concert was wonderful and when it came time for the song, Anne introduced me and I joined her onstage.

The music began and I grinned as that incredible voice glided through the first verse. Recognizing my cue I took her hand to join her in what should have been the chorus of, "Could I have this dance for the rest of my life." Unfortunately, that's not what came out.

I frowned, shot her a quick look, and then panicked as I realized … I had forgotten the words!

Anne's first look at me was as if to say, "What the heck's the matter?" As I struggled to remember the words I began to sing whatever was in my mind, which sounded like I was singing a totally different song than she.

Her second look was as if to say, "Who hired this bozo?"

Her third look was as if to say, "Get this clown off the stage" as I continued to sing what sounded like the Chinese version of the song.

I assume it was the trauma of knowing I was embarrassing this international star, my hometown and especially myself that caused me to wake up.

I sat up in bed and looked over at Anne Murray to apologize. Fortunately, it wasn't Anne Murray lying there sleeping beside me, but my wife, Renee, instead.

It was 5 a.m. and obvious to me there was no way I would be going back to sleep after that fiasco, so, I got up and came to my computer to tell you about the dream before I forgot it.

Dreams. What a weird thing!

But what do I know?

SUPPORT THESE SOLDIERS

N O V E M B E R 2 4 , 2 0 0 3

With hands stuffed deep into his pockets and head hung low, he made his way across the parking lot and headed for the door. Looking somewhat disheveled and as if he had not one friend in the world, he stood out from the other happy shoppers like a scarecrow in a cornfield.

Snowflakes danced in the air around me as I stood by the Wal-Mart doorway and shifted back and forth from one leg to the other in an attempt to keep warm. It was so cold I couldn't feel the bell that would occasionally escape the frozen grasp of my fingers and clang to the pavement.

As he came near, the look on his face told me something was dreadfully wrong in his world. With a quick motion I pointed my bell at him and began to sing, "We wish you a Merry Christmas and a Happy New Year!"

Startled and bewildered by me singling him out, the gentleman stopped dead in his tracks and stood there staring at me. After the song I just smiled and returned to ringing my bell. I have no idea what the hurt in his heart was, but, my season's greeting pulled him away from it, if nothing more than for the moment.

And, in that moment, giving - the true spirit of Christmas - was exchanged as a smile finally chased the burden from his face and he pulled one of those hands out of his pocket clutching a crumpled, one dollar bill which he pushed into the slot of my kettle.

"He's paying you not to sing!" came a catcall from one of my fellow bell-ringing Vietnam Veterans Chapter members.

"Thank you, sir," I told the giver with my mouth.

"No, thank you!" he told me with his eyes as he passed and walked on into the store.

Last Friday night's Loranger Square Tree Lighting Ceremony kicked off the Salvation Army's annual Christmas Kettle Drive. It is my distinct honor to have been chosen to chair this most important fundraiser for this season. We have an ambitious goal of $95,000 for the kettles and $100,000 for direct mail.

Yes, yes, I know, times are tough and everybody's hurting; it's no different at the Treece household. And, I must tell you that if it's going to put a true burden on you or your family to give this year, by all means, don't!

The blessing is in giving what you can. If everyone gives what they can, we will have no trouble meeting this important goal and all the services for which it provides.

Money is not the only thing you can give; we need bell ringers! The experience of standing on a corner greeting friends and strangers in the spirit of the season - and helping those less fortunate in the process - is something my wife and I love doing!

Please consider making a donation when you see the soldiers of this army ringing the bells this season.

Please also consider that the greatest man that ever walked on this planet said, "Unto the least of these, what you do for them … you also do for me."

Oh, one more thing. That Wal-Mart giver came back out 15 minutes later and put a $100 bill in my kettle. I know God blessed him real good for that act of kindness!

But what do I know?

YOUR OLD MEN
WILL DREAM DREAMS

D E C E M B E R 1 , 2 0 0 3

The anguish and agony on my brother's face was virtually tearing out my heart. I could hardly stand to look at him and couldn't imagine what he must be going through.

A month-long, continuous headache had taken his normal robust body and life and crumpled it like an unwanted piece of tin foil. The fear on his face told me he expected that wad to be tossed into the trash at any moment.

We've all had headaches; fortunately, for most, two or three Excedrin kills the pain. This was obviously the mother of all headaches and we began a suicide watch on my brother as he inched closer to the edge of desperation to escape the 24/7 torment.

Tom with big brother, Hal, 1994.

I recently shared a lighthearted story with you of a dream I had about singing with Anne Murray. You will hear more from me about dreams as I find them not only fascinating and indiscriminate, but, as in the story I'm about to share with you, prophetic.

My brother, Hal, had been to many doctors, none of whom could give him relief. We prayed with and for him daily, asking God to intervene; that is exactly what He did.

Uncle Albert was my father's brother who lived in Tennessee.

One day, during the height of Hal's misery, the telephone rang with Uncle Albert on the other end of the line.

"Hal Dean," he began, "I had a dream last night and the Lord told me to tell you that your problem is your teeth!"

Through the pain of simply sitting upright and talking on the telephone, Hal was kind and considerate to our elderly uncle and thanked him for his advice and concern. Later he would share with me, "I didn't have the heart to tell him I have false teeth ... There's no way they could be the problem!" and pain continued to rule his world.

The wisdom of wonderful wives always seems to come into play eventually, as was the case for Hal. A few weeks later, his incredibly strong Christian wife said, "Perhaps you should take Uncle Albert's advice more seriously and go see the dentist." Desperate for relief, he took her advice.

I remember him telling me about struggling into the chair and sharing with the dentist his uncle's silly dream.

After thoroughly examining my brother and his partial plates, the dentist, at the very last moment, discovered that "his bite" was just a bit uneven and made a tiny adjustment to the plates.

The rigors of the dental process itself had caused Hal's head to throb worse than ever and he staggered his way out and to the parking lot. Opening the door to his truck, he collapsed across the seat and fell asleep.

When he awoke, he sat up, started the truck and headed home. It took a couple of blocks before he became fully awake and the reality hit him that - for the first time in months - his headache was gone! I might add that it never returned.

We laugh about it now but it wasn't funny then. We also thank God for His Word that says, "and your old men will dream dreams," and specifically for the prophetic one He sent Uncle Albert.

But what do I know?

BOTH SIDES OF THE HUNTING ISSUE

D E C E M B E R 8 , 2 0 0 3

Two weeks ago our editor, Deb Saul, wrote a tongue-in-cheek column calling on deer-hunting widows to unite and "invent something equivalent to deer hunting." She added her take on the idea of hunting and the entire concept of "chasing down and killing graceful woodland creatures."

Last week's column shared that she had been taking heat from hunters over her views.

At the risk of alienating my hunting friends, and, worse yet, suffering the obvious brown-nose accusations from fellow columnist Ray Kisonas, I'll toss my two cents into the foray.

Like the philosophy I shared in my initial column, Deb, like you and me and everybody else on the planet, sees the world through her own eyes and simply related how she felt about this behavior. To those with similar vision, hunting is barbaric at best.

I have been on both sides of the issue.

I grew up at the tail end of family generations where hunting was an extremely important activity.

One of 10 children, my father "had" to quit school after the second grade to help with chores on the farm; they grew and hunted their food. With great pride he would recount a time he and his dog went hunting, flushed a covey of quail and killed 13 with two shots from his shotgun. That evening he was the family hero as each member had his or her own fine feast of fowl for supper.

In our generation, my brother and I continued the hunt to put food on the table, even though it wasn't necessary. In hindsight, I can see how "the need to hunt" slowly turned into "the desire to hunt," and, somehow, coming home empty handed seemed to become an issue of manhood.

As a teenager I loved to hunt and couldn't wait for the season.

Once it arrived I hunted before and after school every day. I loved being in the woods and testing my skills against my prey. I loved hunting with my father and brother and the interaction we shared in those family moments.

And then ... I got drafted into the United States Army, explicitly trained in the art of killing another human being and sent to a Vietnam War infantry unit.

It was like being fed into a machine with a 19-year, programmed state-of-mind, then being spit out the other side two years later as a completely different person.

I came home from war, sold all my guns (other than one my father gave me) and have virtually never picked up another in the 35 years since.

Other than "for sport," I don't condemn hunting, but for me, I will never kill another living thing unless it is important or necessary.

If putting food on the table ever again becomes necessary, it would be no problem. If I thought someone was trying to kill me or a loved one, even though I wouldn't like it, I would certainly do whatever was necessary.

While I'm happy to be rid of it, I have never been able to replace that great love for hunting I had in my youth.

To me, it always comes down to why you do what you do. That, at least through my eyes, always makes the difference as to whether it is right or wrong.

But what do I know?

PUTTING THE 'X' IN CHRISTMAS

D E C E M B E R   1 5 ,   2 0 0 3

I am a huge fan of the Internet and the technological advances in communications, like cell phones, instant messages and e-mail.

I have specifically enjoyed the various Christmas e-mails circulating now, many which warm the heart, and others that tingle noses, lump throats and flush eyes.

Trying to be a follower of Christ, it's hard to sit back and watch as references to Him, or, more generally, God, are slowly being taken out of the traditions of American daily life, including government and even Christmas. It's only a matter of time until there will be no mention at all of The One who has blessed this great nation so abundantly for 228 years.

I specifically loved the e-mail about the lady who, frustrated by the pressure of shopping and keeping up with all the Christmas activity, crams herself into the crowded elevator and says, "Whoever started this Christmas thing ought to be strung up and shot!"

A voice then calls out from the back of the elevator, "Don't worry, we already crucified Him."

Today, however, I got one that bugged me.

The subject line showed that this was the fifth time the e-mail had been forwarded. I downloaded the attachment and began to read the poem.

"T'was the night before Christmas and all through the town, not a sign of Baby Jesus was anywhere to be found."

The poem went on to share the now-familiar Christian-cry of how the holidays are consumed with Santa, presents, shopping and parties and that we just can't seem to find time to include "The Reason for the Season."

While agreeing with the argument but not overly impressed with the poem, I began to close the attachment and hit the delete button when, once again, the subject line caught my attention. For some reason I hadn't noticed it before, but now the two words behind the five forward abbreviations screamed at me for inspection.

"X-mas Poem," it read.

I couldn't believe my eyes.

With respect to my friend who had simply, and, I trust, innocently, hit the forward button with a desire to share a subject he correctly felt was dear to my heart, he had become the very essence of the focus of the poem by replacing Christ with an X.

For starters, the term, "X-mas" has always rubbed me wrong, simply because for me Christmas is all about Christ and His coming to earth. (Advertisers, if you want to keep me out of your store, use this term!)

We celebrate the days that Washington, Lincoln, Martin Luther King, our moms and dads and friends and neighbors "came to earth," but the overwhelming majority of Americans have celebrated a complete season and intricate tradition all these years for only one: Jesus Christ.

Unfortunately, there is a groundswell flooding the very foundation of belief in America today that scoffs at our history and perceives Christ (and God) to be nothing more than fictional characters that need to be removed from that belief system. That philosophy comes from another biblical character, and he's not fictional either!

Christians, for the sake of saving a fraction of time or space, amplify that philosophy every time they use that "X."

But what do I know?

MY TWO MOST PRECIOUS PRESENTS

D E C E M B E R 2 2 , 2 0 0 3

Sitting in the quiet stillness of early morning and my favorite time of day with only the soft beauty of winking tree lights illuminating the darkness, I'm thinking about ... presents.

I have been so blessed in my life, mainly to have been raised by humble parents who couldn't buy me fancy presents, but who taught me important instructions that ultimately saved me when later storms of life crushed my lifeboat on the rocks.

It's only natural to think of presents at this "most wonderful time of the year," and I, like you I expect, have been making sure everyone's name is scratched off my list.

This morning, however, after reflecting on presents I have received through the years, I'm overwhelmed with joy as I consider the two most precious gifts I have ever been given, and both came from the same giver.

The second-most precious gift came some eight years ago. After multiple failed relationships, I made a covenant with God that even if I never had another relationship with a woman for as long as I lived, I had made the decision to put Him first in my life. The very next day ... I met Renee. What a coincidence!

I can't tell you how she has changed my life. She's my best friend, lover, encourager, confidant, sounding board, helpmate, inspiration and, without a doubt, the most beautiful woman in the world! I am so grateful for the precious gift of my wife.

But, as wonderful as she is, there is even one gift more precious gift that He gave me and you 2003 years ago, according to the way man has recorded time on earth. I don't expect Renee cost God a great deal as He knew exactly what I needed and had already created her. The cost of this gift, however, was a different story!

It took me a long time to fully accept this gift, as I, being a man of logic and reason, had a hard time putting faith in the biblical concept of a Supreme Being sending his Son to earth — via immaculate conception — to teach man how to live by making Him the central focus of their lives.

Unfortunately, because of my need for logic, God had to take me through the heartbreaks of life — to the very edge of suicide — before I broke down and decided - with faith the size of a mustard seed - to accept and embrace His Christmas present.

That was the day my life changed and every day just keeps getting better. The personal relationship I have with The One who came to earth that night totally eclipses anything I have ever done or been given.

The best part is that God didn't give Him to just me; He is there for everybody, only most people refuse the gift because of one simple fact: They don't believe.

Knowing what I know now, it grieves me sometimes to think of how this "Doubting Thomas" had to go to a similar extreme of needing to put his finger in the nail hole. On the other hand, perhaps that was God's plan all along in order that one like me might urge one like you to accept and open that precious gift that is greater and more important than all the others you will receive in your entire lifetime.

But what do I know?

ENDINGS ARE BEGINNINGS

DECEMBER 29, 2003

I used to hate endings! The end of a favorite movie, the baseball season and especially the end of Christmas, were seemingly traumatic things during the early years of my life.

I remember begging Dad to let us keep the tree up still in January; even then, I hated to see it come down.

My how things change.

As much as I have loved having our beautiful tree displayed the last month, I can't wait to take it down! Normally it doesn't stay past Christmas Day, but we have had out-of-town guests through today and kept it up. As soon as they go, so does the tree!

It's just that my focus has changed through the years. Now I can't wait to get Christmas behind me and move - excitedly - into the New Year to see what new things God has in store for me.

It's like having a program director for your life, and, every day, you get up and talk to Him and He sends you on a thrilling new adventure.

And, just like when your favorite team loses or something bad happens in your life, not every day is rosy. That, however, is part of the history pages of your life and, no matter how difficult, you learn to accept it go on; it's part of the plan!

Also, if you believe in that program director, you believe His words from Romans 8:28 which say, "All things work together for good to them that love God, to them who are called according to His purpose."

I can tell you with certainty ... now... that most of the worst things that ever happened to me turned out to be the best things that ever happened to me.

It just takes a little time (and maturity) to look backward to see that the bad actually led me to good. Spankings a child receives are simple course corrections, but try telling that to the screaming child. Plus, everything you find in life that is false only leads you to what is true (if truth is what you seek).

So, Christmas, 2003, is over. Hopefully, we will keep the spirit of giving in our hearts through the coming year. That would be a wonderful goal for us to set for ourselves.

Speaking of goals, I love to set them. I'm not a fan of "New Year's Resolutions" as they resemble cut Christmas trees: on display for the season but dumped soon after alongside other curbside trash.

I begin on my goals Christmas Day and finish New Year's Day. I write them out, file them and then pull them out next New Year's Day to see how I fared.

I've done that with my wife and sons and it's fun to look back to see how their lives - and goals - have changed through the years.

Well, I see that I've come to the end of my column for today.

I'm excited; now I can end Christmas and New Year subjects and start writing some of the other stuff bouncing off the walls of my mind and heart.

One thing that does not end is God's love and His command that we share it with one another.

There probably isn't a more important goal you could set for 2004!

But what do I know?

WELCOME, DRAKE!

J A N U A R Y   5 ,   2 0 0 4

It was exactly 11 minutes after 10 on the very first morning of this New Year. I was standing just outside your mom's room and had my foot between the door and the frame, leaving it open just enough so I could hear all the exciting things happening inside.

I heard my wife call out, "There he is!" followed by, "Wow, he already needs a haircut!"

And then, the precious sound that marks the incredible miracle of birth ... you screaming at the top of your little lungs!

Welcome to earth ... and to our family, Drake Boyer Carr, 21½ inches long, 8 pounds, 3 ounces!

We actually got to see you, sort of, last August. Your mom had graciously allowed your grandmother, Renee, and me (along with others who love you and can't wait to meet you) into the room during what's called an ultrasound. There, on a computer screen, we saw your tiny body growing in your momma's womb. We knew you were going to be "Drake," and not "Kiana," because of two little dots we saw on that screen, which caused great celebration between your dad and me!

Let me warn you about your grandmother, Renee. She is my wife and the coolest person on the planet and she is going to spoil you rotten! Ever since you came she has been soaring up in the stratosphere like an eagle (it's a big bird; you have so much cool stuff to learn!).

Anyway, she's soaring because of something called "pride," but don't worry, she'll come back to earth, especially when it's her turn to "keep you." She hopes you call her "Nonnie," but will love whatever you call her.

Nathan and Karie, your mom and dad, have been working hard getting ready for you to join them in their life together. You have no idea of the impact you will have on these two wonderful people. Neither do they!

You and I are going to have lots of fun. I'll teach you how to bait your hook, how to lay off the high fastballs, how to bring what you feel in your soul out through the strings of your guitar, how it's not a good idea to try to baptize the cat, how to honor your mother and all women, and I'll tell you how my grampaw taught me how to become "an old rat from the barn!"

And, even though you won't remember Him, I'll teach you about the One who sent you to us in the first place. You see, about 11 months ago your mother came to me crying, because, in spite of how much she and your dad wanted a baby, things just weren't working out for them. So, together, through something called prayer, we asked Him to send you to us. Two months later, He answered that prayer and began sending signs to your mother that you were coming!

I can't tell you how excited we all are that you're here. You'll find that this is a tough world, but, surrounded by our love, you'll do great!

God is so good, Drake. I can't believe … that out of all the grandfathers there are out there in the world, he picked me to have the coolest grandson of them all!

But what do I know?

HONORING DR. KING
WITH MOTHER'S MEMORY

J A N U A R Y 1 9 , 2 0 0 4

Tears streamed down the cheeks of my dear mother's face and she stared out the window and sobbed like a heartbroken child. She lay in bed, days away from taking her last breath and achieving her lifelong goal of going to Heaven. It broke my heart to see her weep.

"What's the matter, Momma?" I asked in an attempt to comfort.

She turned toward me, and, after a while, began to tell me a story.

"I was a little girl and on recess at school," she began. "The teacher had us hold hands and make a circle to play Ring-Around-The-Rosie. ..."

She stopped the story for more sobbing and I sat there trying to imagine what sort of grade-school experience could have brought her to this emotional state. Her eyes looked at me expectantly as if I would condemn her for what she was about to share. Finally, she began again.

"There was a little black girl standing next to me and I wouldn't hold her hand because I thought her color would rub off on me; I can't imagine how she must have felt."

My 82-year-old mother, with cancer coming quickly to claim her life, was heartbroken and grieving at wronging a schoolmate 75 years prior because of nothing more than the color of her skin.

I had never heard that story until that day.

It seems strange now to tell you that I remember things like ... separate drinking fountains: one for whites and one for "coloreds."

I also remember growing up in a white world. I lived on the west side of Monroe and really didn't come into contact with any referred to as a "Negro" until I got to Monroe High (even saying that word is uncomfortable as it is the root word of the horrible slang responsible for so much hatred!). There I made many black friends - especially competing together in sports - and I remember wondering what all the fuss was about.

That sweet mother was always quoting Bible scriptures to me, including the one that says that "man looks on the outward appearance, but God looks at the heart."

Today we honor the memory and legacy of Dr. Martin Luther King Jr. I remember from my youth how white people were scared of him, how they thought he was a revolutionist come to tear apart our country. They were half right.

To this day I continue to be moved by the speech this revolutionary messenger from God gave so appropriately in the shadow of the Lincoln Memorial.

Specifically, "I have a dream that my four children will one day live in a nation where they will not be judged by the color of their skin but by the content of their character."

And, in the case of my mother, "where little (black boys and) black girls will be able to join hands with little (white boys and) white girls and walk together as sisters (and brothers)."

I am grateful to have the precious memory of my mother grieving over her elementary philosophy. I am also encouraged at the thought that perhaps she and that little black girl are now laughing at the incident in a place where there are no tears, grieving, cancer - and most certainly - no racism!

But what do I know?

FRUITS OF THE SPIRIT

JANUARY 26, 2004

Love is the single most positive, active agent known to man; more powerful than any weapon, more important than any possession, more fruitful than any planting. Man has been commanded that - alongside putting God first in our lives - the most important thing we can do in this life is share this agent with one another.

Joy is a feeling that invades your heart and makes everything wonderful in your world, even when everything seems to be wrong. It makes you want to hug the sunshine streaming in your window, even on a cold winter day. It is a feeling of happiness that comes from a sense of believing that everything is wonderful in your world.

Peace is something you would give anything for ... if you didn't have it. I remember once not having it in my heart and the only relief I found was sleep. I couldn't wait to go to sleep and it grieved me when I awoke; it was not a fun time. Peace, with your conscience, your neighbor, boss, family, in the world, in your heart ... is priceless!

Patience might be better served without an endorsement from me, but I'm trying to improve. Learning to be content with trials or injury and deferring anger when things don't go my way has been one of the most difficult areas of my life.

Kindness is one of the most important characteristics a person can possess. People may forget what you say or do, but they will never forget the way you made them feel.

Goodness is the positive side of one's actions. Every day, in virtually everything we do, we have the choice to do good or bad, right or wrong, help or hinder; results of these choices determines and defines character.

Faithfulness is the glue that keeps things all together. The quality of life flourishes with fidelity, justice and honesty and implodes with infidelity, injustice and dishonesty. Too bad it takes so long to learn this lesson.

Gentleness, first cousin to patience and kindness, causes us to be in control of our passions and emotions, not easily provoked and slow to anger. While I believe myself kind and am practicing patience, I believe I need to learn to moderate myself more as I have a tendency to get loud and boisterous, especially when I am quick to anger. (Sigh)

Self control stands right behind faithfulness in the importance line. Obviously, the prisons of America are choked with ones, who, at some point in their life, possessed no power to restrain or regulate themselves. Every time I try to button my britches I realize that, when it comes to food, this is another area in my life that needs more discipline.

These characteristics, better known as the Fruits of the Spirit, are outlined in the fifth chapter of the Apostle Paul's letter to the Galatians.

To me, while eliminating evil from the world is paramount, simply not doing evil is not enough. Working constantly on the quality of our character is a prerequisite for a happy life and peaceful world.

And, while I have come to this revelation, making it work in my life is another issue. I just keep trying to do what my friend, the Rev. Overstreet, says, and that is to try to make sure that "my good ... outweighs my bad."

But what do I know?

OUTRAGEOUS SUPER BOWL SHOW

F E B R U A R Y   2 ,   2 0 0 4

Every day that goes by I realize that - like it or not - I am becoming a relic. I wonder if it's just a matter of age. Is it maturity? And, does one come with the other?

Yesterday I was talking with a friend about how - now - we think back to all the dumb things we did when we were younger and wonder why we did them. And, was I - then - as outrageous to the adults as some of the youth are to me today?

"Outrageous," that's the key word I'm looking for today. You see, last night I watched - along with probably most of you - the most exciting Super Bowl ever, and I think I've seen every one of them.

And, having spent a career in advertising, I recognize the hype of this day and the fact that football is a mere sidebar to what is really happening: for great amounts of money, messages are sent ... specifically to Americans.

For the most part we think about the commercials that run in the game, but last night I received a different message and it has been running over and over in my mind ever since.

Never mind that I was mildly disappointed at the lineup of entertainment for the MTV-produced pre-game and halftime shows. Never mind the scantily clad women onstage whose choreographed dance lines were so sexually suggestive. Never mind all the times Nelly grabbed his crotch. Never mind that I tried my best not to judge P. Diddy by his previous gun-toting run-in with the NYPD, or Janet Jackson because of the if-nothing-more strange behavior of her brother she so vehemently defends.

At the conclusion of the Jackson/Justin Timberlake performance (which coincidently ended the show), Timberlake reached over and pulled off a part of the out-of-breath Jackson's outfit (that coincidentally happened to not be attached, even after all that dancing!) exposing her breast for millions to see.

Today's news will offer denial after denial that it was an accident and unplanned. Balderdash! As I said, "outrageous" is the word.

After last year's MTV Awards show, the winners were irrelevant. Nobody stood around the water cooler the next day talking about them; the news programs didn't show them either. That's because they were all talking about the outrageous display of affection (?) from Britney Spears kissing Madonna. (Madonna then kissed Christina Aguilera but the camera had cut away (coincidentally poised to record the reaction of Timberlake, Spears' former boyfriend); Aguilera was furious because she received none of the publicity).

Today will be the same. The most exciting Super Bowl ever will be background fodder for the halftime "accident," while Jackson and Timberlake get the lead news stories and become legends in the mind of our young people.

Years from now no one will talk about who won the MTV awards or yesterday's game, but they will still be talking about "the kiss" and the exposed breast.

Neither of these incidents were coincidence or accidental; they were carefully choreographed by the babysitter of American youth: MTV. I wonder what's coming next?

Put a frog in boiling water and he will jump out. Put a frog in cold water and slowly turn up the heat and he's cooked before he knows it. Unless something changes, American youth await the same fate.

No wonder the Muslims hate us.

But what do I know?

READERS REACT TO
SUPER BOWL COMMENTS

FEBRUARY 9, 2004

Last week's column about the Super Bowl halftime show debacle elicited much e-mail response, most of which were agreeable with my take on the issue.

One exception, however, was from (I expect a young) J.H. of Monroe who suggested I return to being a newspaper carrier instead of columnist. He informed me that "times have changed" and that "old farts" like me should "go back to listening to WJR and watching re-runs of Leave it to Beaver if a two second shot of a woman's breast gets you that upset."

J.H., I almost fell in the floor laughing over your honest and heart-felt comments, which I actually appreciate more than you know. I was honest with you - I am an old fart - and you were honest with me.

While, thankfully, you weren't vicious, you were a perfect example - in my opinion - of the direction and attitude of today's MTV-influenced youth.

Seeking an unbiased, middle-of-the-road opinion, I forwarded my column and your response to a much-heralded, younger-than-me professional journalist, who shared, "What grinds me is people like J.H. who can't just disagree but have to be sarcastic and insulting about it."

Now I'm sure you have no idea what I'm talking about, because, as Sparky of Monroe reminded me, "How many kids today have to go get their own switch off the tree, knowing what's coming after?" (Thanks, Sparky, for the painful-but-appreciative reminder of my father!)

Sparky went on to say that, "Technology has taken our children into a time warp that knows no boundaries. If I'd spoken to either of my parents like kids today I would have had dentures long before I needed them!"

Unfortunately, or, perhaps ... fortunately, Sparky triggered another thought pattern.

Regarding my comment about "scantily clad-sexually suggestive" dancers, she reminded me of the many years during which I performed as an entertainer that women did pretty much the same thing to the music I was making. While I don't remember them quite like what I saw in that half-time show, she was right.

So, was it okay for me then but not okay for them now? Do I (and other "old farts"), with age, simply become intolerant of behavior outside the parameters of my morality meter reading?

For me, thanks now to my relationship with Christ, I'm not the same person I was back then and I have no choice but to reflect that change. And I'm certainly not a prude; I just believe there's a time and place for all things.

However, Sparky zinged me with, "You can't write one week about being a Christian and then the next week put down people we don't know." Hmmm, I need to think about that one as I don't want my shortcomings and sins being held against Christ.

One last thing for J.H: I wonder if you have enough fortitude to mail these last two columns to yourself and not open them for 30 years or until you have children of your own at least 5 years old?

Believe it or not, J.H., one of these days ... you are going to be an "old fart," too, and it will be interesting to see how your attitude has changed. The problem is that by that time the things you thought and did in your youth will seem pretty tame, too!

But what do I know?

JUDGE JUDGES JUDICIOUSLY

F E B R U A R Y 1 6 , 2 0 0 4

Thrilled is how I recently felt after reading of longtime and dear friend Michael Weipert's decision to run for circuit court judge for Monroe County.

Thrilled for him because I know it has been his lifelong dream to sit behind the same bench that has been so traditionally linked to the Weipert name.

Thrilled for our citizens, because, if we choose him, we will be getting one who possesses the unique combination of education, even temperament and unprejudiced thinking, coupled with the willingness to be strict or sympathetic in rendering proper adjudication.

Monroe County is blessed with a bevy of good judges ... and I wouldn't want to be in any of their shoes!

I can't imagine, day-in and day-out, having to sit in judgment of others. I have a hard enough time just throwing out my opinion of what I think here in this column, let alone arbitrating two sides then deciding who I thought was right. Having a personal opinion is one thing; rendering decisions that affect lives is another.

Yet, those positions - and, more specifically, ones even higher on federal levels - are the defining and clarifying signposts pointing the way for the current and future direction of our country.

Suddenly, it seems virtually everything we have believed in throughout the history of this country is being challenged, and the determination of whether it is right or wrong usually falls on one or a few persons ... judges!

As we saw in our last presidential election, our country is split right down the middle and it's the various issues - reduced to final interpretation by judges - that have been the greatest contributors to that split. There is no better example than abortion. To many of us, the very sanctity of life is at stake and there is no higher law than God's, which we interpret through the Bible. To others, eliminating the life growing within them "ain't nobody's business" but theirs and the law-of-the-land ... interpreted by a handful of judges ... says so.

What cranked me onto this issue in the first place was the outrage I had to try to quell in my own heart after suffering through yet another national abduction/murder of a young girl by an older man. We all watched the car-wash security camera capture the image of convicted felon (and scumbag) Joe Smith as he led 11-year-old Carlie Brucia of Florida away to her death (and who knows what other nightmares before).

Was that bad enough? Oh, no, now we have to hear that Smith had been arrested 13 times in Florida since 1993, and, despite violating his probation three times since New Year's Day, 2003, was not re-incarcerated by Judge Harry Rapkin. Huh?

I know the only way to maintain order in society is with law and that man must make and interpret that law. However, law is worthless if there is no recrimination and punishment as consequence for breaking law. I would think applying "common sense" to judgments would be commensurate to drawing from education and experience.

Had Judge Rapkin used some common sense Carlie would still be laughing and loving and dreaming of having babies of her own some day.

Whether by election or appointment, few civil actions in life are more important than ensuring we put the right people in these positions. When it comes time to vote, judge judge candidates judiciously!

But what do I know?

FROM CARTWHEEL
TO CHIROPRACTOR

F E B R U A R Y   2 3 ,   2 0 0 4

With my wonderful wife under my right shoulder for support, I snailed over the curb and into the front door of Dr. Dennis Warner's Temperance Chiropractic Clinic. Extreme agony accompanied every movement of my body.

It took the good doctor months to undo what I had done in seconds a couple of nights earlier.

I've always been a daredevil of sorts, but for these kids, anything goes, or at least it used to.

The pledge card read, "I'll give $50.00 if Tom Treece will do a cartwheel on TV." I laid the microphone down and sent my tuxedo-clad bod into a 360-degree spin via my hands across the phone room floor of the St. Michael's We Care Telethon.

I didn't need the microphone for everyone to hear the wail I let out as the pain shot up my back. I finished the show, but the next morning … I was incapacitated.

I don't do cartwheels anymore, but I'm usually game for most anything when it comes to the telethon, which comes again Saturday from noon till midnight on your local cable TV channel.

One of the "funnest" and funniest guys I know - Gary Vancena, aka "Daddy G. Knight," and I will kick off the telethon as MC's at noon, and then return from nine till midnight to close the event. In between will be myriad local hosts and hostesses reading your pledges from the telephone bank being answered by your friends and neighbors.

Local talent will perform live for the cameras from the Cantrick Middle School stage and the school at Riverview and Maywood will become a beehive of activity as our community comes together to make a difference in the lives of others. Chapter 142, Vietnam Veterans of America, will sell "Love Pops" from downtown street corners.

I offer a debt of gratitude to retired founding members Hank and Betty Jo Steinman, (who recently sent best wishes for a successful telethon) as well as to the memory of another founder, Deacon Al

Gary Vancena and Tom hosting We Care Telethon.

Hoffman. The third founder, friend Greg DuShane, will - in spite of the multiple sclerosis that continues to constrict his body - make an appearance to open the show.

Nineteen years after these wonderful people formed this group, cries for help from friends and neighbors who have children with debilitating diseases (that insensitive insurance companies refuse to cover) no longer fall on deaf ears.

Despite stellar efforts, we have lost some along the way. We have, however, been able to make the difference in the lives of others, and to see them on the occasion of "normal" daily life is exhilarating.

Saturday, we will call to you from your TV to ask you to call us with a donation to make a difference in the lives of those less fortunate than we. The only thing I ask is that you consider how you would want everyone to react if your beloved child was teetering on the edge of death because of a reason as stupid as no money for a life-saving procedure.

Call us at 242-1002 and share your blessings with "the least of these." And, while I don't think there will ever be anymore cartwheels, you never know what Daddy G. and I will get into on live TV, especially now that we're both grandfathers!

But what do I know?

E.C. PETERS: COUNSELOR, TEACHER, FRIEND

MARCH 15, 2004

We waited until we heard him snoring before we crept under the blanket of darkness to his tent. Fading flickers of light cast by the dying campfire helped us identify the object of our mission: his pants or, "britches" as the good ol' southern boy who wore them called them.

Quickly, quietly, I grabbed the jeans and backed away. Giggling like the bunch of teenage boys that we were, we darted across the campsite to the flagpole where we buckled the britches to the line and, with great glee, ceremoniously hoisted them to the top.

The next morning we were up early and waiting when we heard him bellow through the campsite, "Dad Jim you boys, who took my britches!"

We covered our mouths and tried to suppress uncontrollable laughter coming from the satisfaction of knowing we had pulled one over on our counselor.

Peeking through our tent flaps we watched him crawl from his and look for the guilty. Suddenly, his britches, billowing boldly in the breeze like a banner blazing over the campsite of the Monroe Missionary Baptist Church's Royal Ambassador's youth group, caught his attention.

In my mind's eye I can still see him and those lily-white legs dashing to the flagpole - clad only in his underwear - to retrieve his modesty.

He took us camping more times than I can remember, along with trips fishing, to baseball games and the like. Even though he had a family of his own at home, he had a call on his life to mentor the young boys of his church, and he thoroughly believed in the group's motto that "It is better to build boys than to mend men." He loved to laugh and we kidded him mercilessly, and, thank God, the turtle we slipped into his sleeping bag during one trip didn't bite him!

He's been gone for a couple of months now; I had the honor of singing for his funeral. I must tell you that I believe in a place called Heaven, and I also believe if anybody from earth is there, E.C. Peters is there!

In spite of knowing him my entire life, I have no idea what "E.C." stood for. The moniker didn't matter, however, as it was the heart of this man that was the attraction.

He was always ready to lend a hand to another in need, and he loved his church, his wife and family, his fellow man, and - most of all - The One who created it all. Through all the fun, personal attention and care he administered, there was always an underlying theme he projected, and that was his love for God and his desire to see that we knew right from wrong and followed God's instructions for how to live our lives.

We were buds from the start and the fact that we had both served our country during different times of war only cemented our hearts more tightly together.

I hope more like him are coming, not only as fathers, but ones who will prominently stand for what they believe is right no matter what the cost, for I see a terrible storm on the horizon for which our children and grandchildren will need men of courage and integrity to lead and teach them in order to survive.

But what do I know?

MY COLUMN:
JUST WHAT DO I KNOW?

MARCH 22, 2004

Reflecting the views of several others, reader J. Salter writes, "I think your closing line, which appears in all columns, detracts from the overall seriousness and theme of your writing. Sometimes it seems appropriate if the topic is light-hearted but when the nature is serious it adds an air of flippancy that detracts from what was just read. The fact is, you DO KNOW about certain things."

That closing line to which Mr. Salter refers says, "But what do I know?" and is also the name of my column.

Some at *The Monroe Evening News*, who possess great wisdom from years of experience and a much greater writing ability than mine, have shared similar opinions. To their credit (and my delight), their suggestions were to eliminate the line, but, that it was up to me. (Freedom is a wonderful thing!)

Allow me to re-state my reason for the title (as I did in my very first News column).

I, like most of you, have always had an opinion, and, when asked, love to share it. I have, however, no desire to push my opinion on anyone else.

Everyone sees the world through their own eyes and they make judgments and decisions - about life, what it's all about and how to live their lives - based on that vision.

Everybody thinks they are right, including me! It's true; otherwise they wouldn't do what they do. Some people do wrong knowing it's wrong, but it's right for them as long as they think they can get away with it. Some people ask, "Who determines what is wrong or right?" Good question! It all comes down to in what - or whom - you believe.

I have a dear friend who rejects Christianity because "If you'd been born in China you'd be a Buddhist." He's probably right, but that doesn't change the fact that - because I know Him personally and have asked Him to order my steps - I am a follower of Christ.

Personally, I believe I'm right about that, but that doesn't mean I want to sit in an ivory tower and look down on those who don't agree, which brings me to why I chose the column cognomen.

While I adamantly believe in what I believe, I don't particularly like people who believe their way is the only way, in spite of the fact that - like everybody else - I think I'm right!

My attitude is that I'm just another one of the many who scratch and claw everyday at life trying to make a living for my family and do what I can to help others along the way. And, if the ideas and ideals I share through this column mean something to you or you agree with ... wonderful! If not, wonderful! I don't want you to think that I think I know it all; I certainly don't.

On the other hand (as I will soon share from a previous column), my goal in life is to become an "Old Rat from the Barn," which, translated, means, my desire is to become a man of great wisdom based on 56 years of experience on this planet.

So, when I say, "But what do I know?" it's only meant to qualify my opinion and urge you to take what I say with however many grains of salt you choose.

I think I'm right.

But what do I know?

TRYING NEW THINGS

MARCH 29, 2004

I can still see him sitting in his brown La-Z-Boy, making a face and sticking out his tongue to visually tell us he'd rather eat dirt than what we were trying to get him to eat.

"C'mon, Dad, it's really good! It's the latest thing," we would say in futile attempts to get him to try it. Nothing worked.

"I can't believe any kids of mine would eat something that stinks up the house so bad!" he would say.

It was the late '50's and "the latest thing" in food ... was pizza. If my memory serves me correct it was Chef Boyardee pizza and came in a yellow box.

My sister, Janet, the one in the family who was always trying new things, brought a box home one day. Everyone loved it ... except Dad, of course. He wouldn't even try it.

He wouldn't even let her make it for supper when he had to eat at the same table, so, she would serve it up as a late-evening snack. I remember watching her wait for the yeast to rise, grease the pan and knead the dough into the corners, spread the sauce that came in a little can, sprinkle on the cheese, add pepperoni slices then pop it in the oven.

Soon the smell of what was about to become one of the most popular food items in America drifted from the kitchen to tickle the taste buds of our nostrils. All but dad's, that is. As soon as he caught a whiff...there would come "that look."

Years went by, and one day a friend stopped by...with a pizza. Due to the growing popularity of this new Italian specialty, pizzerias were popping up all around town.

All those years of family begging had failed, but something this visitor said shredded his defense. We held our breath as Dad - reluctantly - took his first bite of pizza.

His eyes darted around the room at each of us as he savored the combination of ingredients. When he finished chewing he swallowed the bite and then looked down to contemplate a response. Finally, he looked up, smiled almost grudgingly and said, "Not bad!"

"Not bad" turned out to be a pretty indifferent response for someone who, from that point on, started bugging Janet every other night to make pizza. Then he discovered the Golden Drumstick pizzeria and would drive from our west side home to the corner of Eastchester and Third for one of their fabulous pizzas.

I loved my father dearly and am so grateful for all he taught me. Oddly enough, that story taught me a different lesson.

I thought of all the years he denied himself what turned out to be one of his favorite things ... only because he wouldn't "try" something new. I made up my mind right then that I would at least try everything new that I could during my short stay on this planet, and I have done exactly that.

How about you? Do you try new things, or are you locked into everyday routines? Have you tried Rollerblades? Do you order the same thing from the menu every time? If so, you may have no idea of what you are missing and how much more exciting your life could be!

But what do I know?

PASSION OF THE CHRIST

APRIL 1, 2004

They kicked him, beat him, spat on him and struck him on the head, even though they didn't know him. As he lay bleeding in the street, a man - brick in hand - danced forward and in a calculated manner smashed the brick into the side of his head, igniting thunderous applause from bystanders.

As I sat glued to my cinema seat watching "The Passion of the Christ," I couldn't help but wince at each blow Jesus endured. And, I must admit that as the beatings continued, I wanted to jump to my feat and scream, "Enough!"

How fitting that Mel Gibson is being vilified for this epic film, as Jesus told His followers that just as He would be persecuted, so would they. Gibson didn't write this story, that, in my opinion, is the virtual play-by-play and ... blow-by-blow ... account told in the Holy Bible.

Hollywood meticulously grinds out trash movies daily and no one says a word; Gibson tells the simple story of Jesus' murder and everybody's up in arms.

Personally, my spirit soared in the cinema in spite of the gruesome account of what Jesus willingly endured to show us what life is truly about (Him), because I know He did it for me. And, that's why - when I took this job as columnist -I did so only with the agreement that I could freely write about my belief in Him and our relationship; I owe Him that ... and more!

Do I think the film is anti-Semitic? Absolutely not, in spite of believing Jesus' own people - the Jews - provoked Pontius Pilate into allowing Christ to be killed (Don't get mad at me; I didn't write it either). That, however, was part of God's redemptive plan, and the truth - starting with Adam and Eve - is that we all are responsible for Jesus' death, a fact symbolically and heroically heralded by Gibson's use of his own hand to deliver the film's nail into Jesus' hand.

And while I'm not a fan of violence, I'm also not a fan of political correctness or telling-it-like-it-wasn't in order to not offend. Depictions of Jesus with trickles of blood coming from the crown of thorns neatly placed on His head or from the clean little wound in His side are ridiculous.

Are we capable of such mob-mentality behavior today? Certainly. While you may have thought I was describing Jesus in the opening of this column, instead I described another innocent, Reginald Denny, who was pulled from the cab of his truck and savagely beaten live on TV during the 1992 Los Angeles riots. I thought of him during the movie as Jesus was being beaten on the Via Delarosa.

The irony? Like Jesus, who urges disciples to love their enemies, Reginald Denny asked people to forgive the brick-thrower who almost killed him.

In a powerful line from the film, Jesus asks, "What credit is it to only love those who love you?"

It always comes down to personal agendas. If you know and believe in Christ, this film is monumental. If you don't, it's a perfect opportunity to throw a brick.

But what do I know?

BLAME GAME

APRIL 12, 2004

"Where are you; why are you hiding?" called the father.

"I did something you told me not to do," was the son's response.

"Why?" the father inquired.

Pointing to the woman beside him he cried out, "She made me do it!"

And so began the blame game. If you want the details or the actual account, read the third chapter of Genesis; the players are Adam, Eve and, of course, God.

If it's true that character traits - just like looks and actions - get passed along from generation to generation, then all humans on the planet are inflicted with the character flaw of blaming others. And, while I haven't lived close enough to all the people of the world to make a certain determination, I'd still say that Americans are the worst!

How refreshing is the rare occasion when someone - who has done something wrong - steps forward to say, "Yep, I did that and I was wrong. I made a bad decision and I take full responsibility for my actions."

It's not in our general nature.

I remember - as a child - doing something I had seen my brother do that we both knew our father would kill us for if he ever found out. The only problem for me was that I was the one who got caught. Then, in typical human fashion, I pointed my finger at my brother and bellowed, "He did it too!"

I thought of the blame game as I watched National Security Adviser Condoleezza Rice getting grilled by the Sept. 11 Commission on TV. Just like you and me, everybody in that room had a personal agenda.

Democrats blamed the Bush Administration. Re-publicans blamed the Clinton Administration. I think families of the 9-11 victims simply wanted anybody to blame in order to make themselves feel better.

Regarding 9-11, I'd say we are all to blame. Why? For starters, we've turned our backs on The One who has blessed this nation for 228 years and I envision Him retracting that blessing and protection. Slowly but surely we are kicking him out of our schools, our courts, our homes and our way of thinking.

In exchange we have be-come a throw-away society that sanctions the butchering of our babies before they even breathe. The "If it feels good, do it" (even if it's wrong) mentality is old hat these days.

Sex, God's wedding gift to man and woman, has degenerated into a simple recreational activity. And, I expect the day will come when one will murder another and be acquitted by the oncoming liberal courts because it will be a right of expression.

As I write this on Good Friday I'm reminded of the recent uproar about "Who killed Jesus?" from Mel Gibson's "Passion of the Christ."

Jews pointed the finger at Gibson because they felt he was pointing the finger at them, and, I expect many Christians were doing just that.

I agree with Gibson's assessment that we are all to blame. Everybody makes mistakes and nobody is right all the time. Why is it so hard for us to accept our part of responsibility?

In the case of the 9-11 blame game, it's important to learn the truth to insure this never happens again.

In the case of "Who killed Jesus?" it's irrelevant, because Jesus isn't dead; I spoke to Him just this morning!

But what do I know?

GOD FIRST, BE THE BEST

A P R I L   2 6 ,   2 0 0 4

Many years ago, as I was trying to rise from the ashes of divorce, a beautiful young lady invited me to dinner for my birthday. She labored over a seven-course meal and meticulously made sure each napkin and fork was perfectly placed.

With a smile of pride stretching ear-to-ear she called me to the table. Steam swirled from the piping-hot food. I was humbled by the sight and by the obvious labor of love on my behalf.

"This looks delicious!" I remarked and slid into the guest of honor seat just as the telephone rang; it was for me.

From the earpiece came the frantic voice of the daughter of one of my best friends, "Mother needs you ... right now!"

I didn't need details to know something was dreadfully wrong. I turned for another look at the table - and the woman - both waiting just for me.

"I'll be right there," I answered and hung up the phone.

I turned to my friend. Hands were on hips and the ear-to-ear smile was replaced with a, "Don't even think about leaving!" look.

"I'm sorry, I have to go!" I told her.

"I won't be here when you get back!" she answered.

"Do what you have to do," I responded, "I'm doing what I have to do!" I closed the door behind me and bolted for my vehicle.

I raced to my friend's house and was greeted at the door by the daughter, who took me to her grieving mother. One look at her face told me she was "hanging on for dear life"...to her life.

This friend, who had been like a sister for most of my life, was going through what I had recently gone through: a terrible divorce. Without a doubt, I believe she might even have taken her own life to escape her misery had her faith in God not been so strong.

I held her hand and did my best to console.

Suddenly, she gripped my hand and pulled me close. Her eyes pierced mine and stabbed deep into my soul.

"Tommy, I have a message for you...God first, be the best!"

I was taken aback by her statement and said, "Pardon me?"

"God first, be the best!" she repeated.

I did my best to comfort her that day, then drove back to see if dinner - and the woman - would still be waiting, which they were.

The woman turned out to be a good friend, and good friends understand the importance of prioritization, especially when a life is on the line.

The irony of the incident is that a few days later it hit me that what truly happened that evening was...that instead of sending me to help her, God had sent her to help me! It was a time in my life when - while I believed in Him - I was not putting Him first in my life. Not long after I made the decision to do just that, and that's when everything started to work for me.

From that birthday incident I learned an important lesson from my dear friend: When you put God first in your life ... you can be the very best at anything you want to do or be.

But what do I know?

B R E A K A L E G, R O N!

A P R I L 2 9 , 2 0 0 4

Yesterday as I was reading my *Monroe Evening News*, I turned the page and found a large picture of Sports Editor Ron Montri smiling back at me.

The picture was part of a new advertisement informing that - beginning Wednesday and then running every Wednesday - Ron will be our newest columnist sharing his opinions.

Sounds strange considering he has been with The News for a gazillion years already (Sorry, Ron, don't mean to make you sound old!).

I thought of how - for years - I have been amused while reading his sports columns and observing him struggling - in my opinion - to somehow keep sports as the underlying theme.

Ultimately, I loved watching him weave his perspectives on the fabric of life and how it covered - or exposed - the true attitudes of the ones who play the games or compete in the events and make that the focus of the columns.

What I love most about Ron is he realizes that sports are down on the list of importance in life. I love how he takes incredibly talented athletes, to whom people bow down and worship because they can score 40 points a game or hit a baseball farther than anyone else, and expose them as the jerks they sometimes are because of their values (or lack of them), or how they treat their wives or those around them. He knows that the key word is ... attitude!

Seeing his picture also caused my mind to drift back to an important time in my life in which Ron was involved.

I have always loved to play sports; basketball was my favorite. I played for Monroe High School but was never better than being a sub off the bench. That didn't change my love for the game and I tried to be the best sub I could be for my team.

I kept abreast of all the other school teams in the county and their star players. The star at Ida High School at the time was ... Ron Montri.

A few years after high school I was asked to play on a city recreation league team. I was shocked, but excited, to learn that most of my teammates were many of those former high school stars, including ... Ron Montri.

Needless to say, we were the class of the league, hadn't lost a game and I was thrilled to be on the first championship team of my life when something happened to steal that joy: I got drafted into the Army!

After serving two years, including 13 months in the Vietnam War, I returned to Monroe and embarked on trying to forget all the bad things that had just happened to me.

One day some of those old teammates came to my door with a package; inside was a blue sports jacket with an emblem on the front that said, "Golden Drumstick - League Champions 1968."

I couldn't believe they hadn't forgotten me and for as long as I live I won't forget that wonderful gesture from Ron and the rest of those teammates.

Break a leg, Ron. Continue to "tell it like it is!" only now you won't have to try to keep a sports theme as the ultimate focus.

"People may not remember what you said or what you did, but they will always remember the way you made them feel!"

But what do I know?

OLD RAT FROM THE BARN

MAY 10, 2004

His hair was milk white and the handlebar mustache flowed off his lip to corkscrew at each side of his mouth. He would sit for hours in silence, stroking it between his thumb and forefinger and curling it when he reached the end.

His eyelid muscles had failed years ago, and, in spite of perfect vision, he had to use the palm of his hand to hold the lids open when he wanted to see.

Aptly named, "Moses" Treece was my grandfather. I remember –as a boy and long before superhighways –the fascinating 16- to 20-hour trips from Monroe to his home in Tennessee. My father was one of his 10 children.

Things were a different then. For heat in

"The Old Rat from the Barn,"
Grandpaw Moses Treece, 1940's

winter you didn't just turn up the thermostat ... you went out to the coal pile for some large chunks to stoke the potbellied stove.

Alongside that pile was another pile, only this pile had something called an "outhouse" over it where you read the Sears and Roebucks catalog while doing your business.

I loved the feather bed in the attic, especially during storms when I could fall asleep listening to rain dance on the tin roof.

*Tom with Ms. Lois Schadewald,
second grade teacher.*

"Grampaw" sat in the living room next to that potbellied stove and I would sit on his lap for hours listening to stories about life that always had positive endings, especially about trusting God.

Because he couldn't open his eyes naturally I could stare at his face and explore each feature without feeling self-conscious.

After each story I would say, "Grampaw, how do you know all those things?" He would answer, "I guess you could just say I'm an old rat from the barn."

Back in Michigan and second grade at Custer School, Miss Schadwald asked each of her students to tell what we wanted to be when we grew up; Bobby said, "Fireman," Lucy said, "Nurse," and Tommy said ... "old rat from the barn."

The class erupted in laughter.

In her infinite wisdom, Miss Schadwald calmed the class and then asked me to explain; I gave my best effort.

"I don't know what that is," I began, "but my grampaw is one of them and I want to be just like him when I get big!"

Miss Schadwald grinned and hugged me because she knew what grampaw was implying with that descriptive phrase: He had weathered the storms of life and learned from each experience.

Like an old barn rat, he had gained wisdom each time he was fast enough to escape the barn cat or owl, smart enough to resist the lure of the farmer's trap, slippery enough to keep his tail away from the farmer's wife's carving knife.

In my life's barn I've been a mechanic; car, motorcycle and radio salesman; surgery nurse; clothing store department manager; soldier; recording artist; singer; songwriter; disc jockey; radio station manager; city administrator and columnist.

Some of the many storms in that barn have been war, divorce, drugs, alcohol, the edge of suicide. ... Although I've had many jobs in my life I believe I'm still on track to achieve that vocation I shared with Miss Schadwald all those years ago.

And although I'm not on the same level with him, I'm getting closer to being - just like grampaw - an Old Rat from the Barn!

But what do I know?

JOYFUL NOISE

M A Y 1 7 , 2 0 0 4

I love to sing!

I don't know why it is, but if I had my choice to do only one thing for the rest of my life, singing would be a serious consideration for that distinction.

Can't read a note! If you hand me a songbook with all those lines and little dots with flags on top, you might as well hand me a Chinese dictionary. But, I do love to sing!

I think most people love to sing, only most people are intimidated - and don't - because they think they have a lousy voice. I admit that some voices are more pleasing than others, but there's great distance between what you sound like and how it makes you feel when you sing.

I find it interesting that the King of the Universe writes in His instruction book that we are to "Make a joyful noise" and to "come before His presence with singing."

How strange He should juxtapose those two words.

"Joyful" has to be one of everybody's favorite things to be, but, no matter how I look at it, "noise" depicts a negative connotation, which leads me to believe that God isn't concerned with how you sound when you sing, but, simply, that you sing. It's so free and easy, and, the best part is it gives me a feeling of satisfaction I can't buy for any amount of money.

The next-best thing to singing is hearing others sing, especially if that is their special gift from God. Like you, I have my favorites, and three of my favorites - Mica Estep, Chuck Estep and Barry Myers, collectively known as the group Proclaim - have learned to fuse their three distinct voices together for a single blend of harmony, which is a specific type of singing I love.

This Trinitarian triad takes the stage as broken bread and poured-out wine and then mixes their combination of voices and spirits into a jar of clay to pour out for the nourishment of others. That mixture flows off the stage and is taken in by my being where it sooths, satisfies and sears my soul like few other things in life can.

I can't explain why it feels so good. It just does!

If you've never heard Proclaim, or it you have something inside you that seeks the same satisfaction I've shared about myself, then you have an opportunity to feel it for yourself Sunday as Proclaim will appear in concert at Monroe Mission-ary Baptist Church at 6:30 p.m.

There's no admission charge but what's called a "freewill offering" will be taken. And, no, the money won't go to them or the church, but instead to benefit a local young man who has been stricken with an affliction.

This young, handsome, former Marine appears to be strong as an ox. The only problem is the marrow in his bones has been invaded by the dreaded "C" word, and the "C" word he has to consume to counter the cancer causes one to not be able to keep a job or afford insurance.

Want to do something wonderful for yourself? Come and feel the generated "joyful noise" Proclaim will bathe you with, and, help us lift up one who is down on his luck. God will bless you for it!

But what do I know?

RADICAL MUSLIMS

M A Y   2 4 ,   2 0 0 4

I think O.J. did it!

I've always believed O.J. Simpson murdered his wife and Ron Goldman, from the look in his eye when he was arrested to what I considered insurmountable evidence against him. Obviously, the jury and I disagreed.

However, since the time he was exonerated I have found a new reason to believe him guilty. Let's just say that if someone murdered my wife (even if she were estranged) and mother of my children - especially in such a brutal fashion - I would never stop looking for the killer! The only thing O.J. seems to be concerned about not stopping is playing golf. I have the idea he is not concerned with finding the killer because he already knows who the killer is and sees him every morning when he shaves.

I told you that to lead into a thought regarding America's war on terrorism.

I don't know much about Islam or Muslims and don't like talking of things about which I know little. I expect most Americans consider Muslims somewhat fanatical in their religion. Actually I'm pretty fanatical about the personal relationship I have with Jesus Christ, so in some ways I am envious of Muslim's allegiance to Islam. I happen to believe in the Holy Bible, which tells me that there is but one name under heaven by which a person can reach God ... and that name isn't Mohammed. (I'm not trying to cram my philosophy down your throat; it's just what I believe, and you know what my last line always says!)

I also understand that there will always be breakaways from groups of people who become extremists and give the rest of the group a bad name. Timothy McVeigh certainly didn't speak for me when he blew up the Murrah Federal Building, and while capital punishment is a subject for another column on another day, I was at least happy we caught and punished the perpetrator ... especially when it was one of our own!

So here's what's in my craw. Radical Muslim terrorists have been mercilessly killing people for a good portion of my life (from Olympic athletes in '72 to cutting off Nick Berg's head live on video and many in between). As they sawed off Berg's head they screamed, "God is great!" To these Muslims, Americans are infidels, or, ones who don't believe in their religion, and, as a result, we all deserve to die.

Now if I were what I expect a true worshiper of Islam should be ... I would be on the front lines trying to find this band of butchers and bring them to justice in order to protect the purity of the religion. This is exactly what America did with McVeigh and what I think one like O.J. should be doing regarding the killer of his wife!

If a rebel Christian was killing Muslims in the name of Jesus and urging others to do the same because they didn't believe in Him, I would personally be out there trying to find and stop this demoniac.

I believe in the pursuit of happiness for all people, and if Islam provides that for Muslims, great. However, until followers of Islam take a stand against these radical, murderous terrorists themselves, I can't help but feel that hidden inside is actually sympathy for the devil!

No matter what your religion ... you're either for America, or against her!

But what do I know?

TATTOO
MAY 31, 2004

There were seven of us: Tough guys, Lean, mean, fighting machines…trained killers, on our way to Vietnam.

It was June, 1968. Rodney Vore of Maybee was my best friend. We had just finished Paratrooper School and a 30-day leave visiting our folks. Rodney had seen his family for the last time.

Two innocent young men strolled the Seattle Airport trying not to be concerned that they were on their way to war. We passed a pub and Rodney gave me the wry grin that always preceded one of his profound statements. "We're not old enough to drink, but we're old enough to die for our country!" he lamented.

We caught a bus to a downtown pre-determined location where we waited for yet another bus to take us to Fort Lewis for processing. Similar military orders of fate brought the seven of us together on that street corner that day. And, as fate would have it, that bus stop was directly in front of … a tattoo shop!

"Let's all get a tattoo!" one shouted.

Soon, six of seven were in accord and in line to get a parachuting little blue devil stenciled on their left biceps; across the top read, "U.S. Para-trooper;" across the bottom read, "Republic of South Vietnam - 1968."

"What, you chicken Treece?" they catcalled.

"I'm not chicken," I responded, trying to sound like a bold infantryman on his way to war. "It's just that … my dad always told me if I ever came home with a tattoo, he would kill me!

"Son, your daddy ain't even gonna see that tattoo 'cause Charlie's gonna kill ya," called one of them.

The Communist insurgents - to whom he was referring that we were on our way to fight - were Viet Cong, more commonly referred to as "V.C.", which, phonetically, stood for "Victor Charlie," or, as in this case, just plain old "Charlie" for short.

One by one, including Rodney, they sat with their sleeves rolled and received the little blue devil.

It was one of the biggest dilemmas of my 19-year-old life. I wasn't afraid to have it done and I certainly wanted to fit in with they guys, but I just couldn't get the vision of the disappointment on my father's face when he would see it - if he would see it - out of my mind. I shuddered at both options.

"I'm still thinking about it," I kept telling the others. Finally, with no one left in line, the six, with symmetrical tattoos emblazoned on their arms, stood before me grinning like Cheshire cats. The looks on their faces were saying, "Well?" I hated having to make that choice, but perhaps they were right; perhaps my father would never see it. I sat down in the chair.

I don't remember much about the tattoo artist ... other than he obviously practiced prominently on himself and that he was happy we had made his cash register jingle so early on this morning.

He swabbed my arm with alcohol and shaved the hair. I couldn't believe I was actually getting a tattoo. I drifted off into disappointment, knowing I didn't want this, yet was relenting to simple peer pressure. I flinched as the pain of another swab of alcohol over fresh-shaved skin brought me back to reality.

Mr. Tattoo reached for his paintbrush ... the needle gun. It was shiny and silver and reminded me of my dentist. He flipped the switch and the gun whirred to life with a high-pitched squeal. There was no turning back. He rested the heel of his hand on my forearm and slowly guided the gun's needle into position.

Suddenly one of the six started screaming, "The bus is here, the bus is here."

I don't think I ever heard more welcomed words in my life. I jerked my arm off the table and said, "Sorry man, gotta go; keep the money!" and raced out to join my waiting warrior brothers.

"Man, sorry you didn't get your tattoo," called one as we dragged duffel bags onto the bus.

"Can you believe it?" I responded. "I shouldn't have taken so long to make up my mind!"

I tried to sound disappointed. The truth was I was overjoyed my stalling had paid off and I did not get the tattoo.

Seven of us walked into the tattoo shop that day; six had a devil tattooed on their arms. We all went to separate units once we got to Vietnam and it was hard to keep track of my comrades. I understand four of the seven came home in body bags, including … my best friend Rodney. A land mine took both legs at the thigh of another, and the last word I heard of the sixth was that he was a hopeless alcoholic who had been in and out of jail five times, the latest for beating his wife.

And then there is me.

Is it coincidence that six inked the devil on their arms that day … and one didn't?

I must tell you that many times in the 36 years that have wafted by since that day I've desired to find a tattoo artist, describe the tattoo and have him - finally - give it to me. The temptation is still real and I also continue to have a parallax view of the tattoo … happy, yet guilty, that I didn't get it!

Fortunately, even though he's been gone 33 years, my father's memory comes to mind each time and somehow I think he would still find a way to kick my butt, and I resist the temptation.

I'm thinking of those six soldiers … buddies … today, along with so many other friends who gave the supreme sacrifice for their country; like Lenny Liparato, one of the best musicians I ever heard, and Richard Gilbert, who sang with me like Paul & Silas in jail the night we toilet-papered General Custer's statue, and Vince (Mighty Mite) LaRocca, the best pound-for-pound athlete I ever saw.

I miss those guys today! No matter how I try I can't suppress the lump in my throat when I think about them, and, that, but for the grace of God, it could have been me those of you who truly understand why we have this day off will be memorializing today.

One more thing I want you to know: I don't believe in coincidences!

But what do I know?

BLIND HOG FINDS ACORN

J U N E 7 , 2 0 0 4

I eyed the shot. The hole was on a downhill slope. Only a perfect hit would cause it to die at the right time and drop into the hole.

I stepped to the ball, shifted my feet, loosened my grip, regained it, then took one more look at the hole before I pulled the club back and slapped the dimpled ball.

It raced across the green and started to die as gravity slowed it, pulled it down the slope, and ... right into the hole.

You would have thought I had won the Masters. I threw my hands in the air, jumped up and down and emitted strange male sounds of victory.

High-fives came from the other three in my foursome for making the 22-foot putt.

Normally it wouldn't have been such a big deal, but, considering we were playing a scrambles tournament where each team had to use at least one shot from each member, it was a big deal.

You see, I am the world's worst golfer. Oh sure, a big, fat guy like me can hit the ball a ton; the only problem is that nobody wants to play with me because it takes so long to find the right and left slices that go a couple hundred yards off course.

On this day, however, I was having a blast, mainly because I knew my team was going to win the joint Kiwanis/Exchange Clubs Golf Tournament, and that we would do so in spite of the fact that I was on the team. Why? Because fellow Kiwanian Judge Jack Vitale and Monroe High Golf Coach Lindsay Blackwell - who happen to be two of the best golfers in Monroe County - were on my team.

"Even a blind hog finds an acorn now and then!" they kidded after my putt.

They were right; that lucky shot was the only one I made for 17½ holes.

Because of Jack and Lindsay, we were the team-to-beat. Because we started last, the other players - now finished - gathered around River Raisin Golf Club's 18th hole to watch us finish.

Our next-to-last shot left us out about 125 yards.

One-by-one the others took their shot; no one made the green. It was up to me.

I felt hundreds of eyes checking me out as I lined up for the shot. I could hear their comments in my mind's ear.

"Treece any good?"

"Must be if he's playin' with those guys!"

I expected to answer their questions by busting the windshield of a southbound car on I-75, but God must have felt sorry for me that day as He gave me another acorn.

I smacked the ball and watched it sail through the air, hit just off the green and roll within three inches of the cup.

The onlookers erupted in applause as I turned to my dumbfounded teammates.

The judge just stared at me, then shook his head and turned to the others.

"Can you believe this guy? We carry him for 17 holes, but when everybody's watching ... he hits the shot of the day!"

After receiving our trophies I assured Judge Vitale he could call me any time he needed help again. That was the late 1980's ... I'm still waiting for that call. I figure he hasn't had stiff-enough competition yet to warrant calling in the big gun.

But what do I know?

COSTLY CANDY BAR

J U N E   2 1 ,   2 0 0 4

His name was Notch Petkovich and he was a skillful businessman who turned a tiny store on the corner of Dunbar and Telegraph Rds. into one of the most successful and enduring groceries in the area.

"Mr. Petkovich," my father began, "my son has something to tell you."

My 8-year-old hand was locked in the vice grip of my father's huge hand and I knew it was time to face the music.

I looked up at Mr. Petkovich with fear and trembling, hoping he would call the cops to take me to prison rather than face what I knew was waiting when all this was over and I was back home with Dad.

With my other hand I extended a half-wrapped, half-eaten candy bar and began my painful confession.

"I stole this from your store, Mr. Petkovich. I'm sorry; I didn't mean to do it!"

This, needless to say, was a lie. Of course I meant to steal it. A more honest answer would have been that I didn't mean to get caught. I had been taught that stealing was wrong, but, earlier that day - in the store with Mom while shopping - I had slipped the candy into my pocket. I knew Mom wouldn't buy it for me and I wanted it real bad.

Later, in my room and feasting on the candy, the door suddenly opened and there stood God himself, my father. When he saw the candy bar, that familiar furrowed frown filled his forehead and he glared at me.

"Where'd you get that?" he asked.

Caught in the act, I searched for an excuse.

"Uh, well, uh, I, uh," I stammered.

It was no use.

Times were tough and Dad worked hard to keep food on the table. Occasionally there was a treat, but, for the most part, candy was not part of our life growing up. He knew Mom hadn't bought it for me and that I didn't have any money, so an explanation for why I was chomping on a Mars bar in the middle of the afternoon was necessary. It was time to come clean.

"I stole it from Hi-Lite," I told him in my now-trembling voice. I began to cry hoping it would elicit some sympathy; what a stupid thought!

"Let's go!" he commanded and grabbed me by his second-favorite body part for discipline: my ear.

Out the door and down the street we went, walking all the way to the store.

Mr. Petkovich, impressed with Dad's insistence on honesty and accountability, was gracious and even said I could finish the candy; Dad would hear nothing of it.

Satisfied with my apology and Mr. Petkovich's acceptance of it, Dad paid for the candy and we left the store. On the way home he told me how disappointed he was in me, that I had been brought up better than that.

Once home I thought for a while I was off the hook, but, he called me to his room, took off his belt and used it on his first favorite part of my body for discipline.

While I'm somewhat embarrassed - for me - to share this story with you, at the same time, and in conjunction with Father's Day, I'm proud to share this story with you ... for him.

His name was Homer Treece. He loved his family dearly and believed that if you spare the rod you spoil the child. Unfortunately, there aren't too many of his kind around anymore. What a shame.

But what do I know?

THREE NUTS AND A SQUIRREL

J U N E 2 4 , 2 0 0 4

Not only was he the littlest guy on the team, he was the littlest guy in the entire Custer Little League! His nickname was "Dink," and he reminded me of Eddie Gaedel, the midget St. Louis Browns owner Bill Veeck sent to bat against the Tigers in 1951.

Later, God saw fit to bring us both back from the Vietnam War, and now – all these years later – we work together daily; he for the Luna Pier Police Department and me as the city's administrator.

Last week he walked into my office to talk at the exact moment my wife called to say, "We have an issue at home; there's a squirrel in the house!"

"I'll be right there," I told her, and then told Sergeant Darryl Ansel about the problem, to which he replied, "I'll go with you; I know about these things," and we were off to my home just minutes away.

"We'll need a broom and fishing net," he said as we walked through the door.

I grabbed a broom and said, "Sorry, no net."

Seeing nothing better, Darryl grabbed an umbrella from its stand and up the stairs we stalked like two great white hunters on safari.

There we found Renee pointing to the invader perched atop the curtain valance over the sliding door of our bedroom.

I didn't have to ask how he got in. Each morning during warm weather I crack the slider just enough to allow Zeke, our cat, to access the balcony overlooking our Lake Erie view. There he annoys the local bird and squirrel population until we bring him in, close the door and leave for work.

This morning, obviously, while Zeke had gone back inside to patrol other sectors of his kingdom, this brazen interloper ventured inside the room searching for the stash of corn and sunflower seeds I feed him and his furry friends during winter months. Once discovered by Zeke, the instinct to climb to safety sent him to the valance where he made noises that made Renee think the furnace was trying to ignite and launch into space.

I shared my strategy with Darryl.

"I'll scare him down; you make sure he doesn't get past you into the rest of the house!"

I raised the broom to the critter, which, as planned, sent him dashing down the curtain. However, instead of easy access out the door, he headed straight for Darryl.

If you could only have seen what I saw!

There danced the great, renowned hunter and lifelong public protector in full-dress uniform - including a 9mm pistol strapped to his side - pointing a now-opened, bright, yellow golf umbrella at the charging squirrel, who bounced off the umbrella and then turned and bolted out the door making Rocky the Flying Squirrel look pale by comparison as he soared off the 20-foot balcony to the grass below.

As long as I live, the image of Darryl holding off that charging squirrel will be imbedded in my mind. And that's good, because for nights like tonight, when the mayor and council and I try to balance the budget, I'll be able to occasionally rerun it on my mind's monitor as a reminder that God has a sense of humor and sends along little dramas like this now and then to help me stay focused on the fact that life...is supposed to be fun!

But what do I know?

DEAR DRAKE

JULY 12, 2004

Dear Drake,

It's hard to believe just six months ago I stood outside the cracked door of a Mercy-Memorial birthing room and heard your very first scream of life. What a thrill to have you in our life!

My dear friend, Luna Pier Treasurer Mary Larrow has been driving me crazy the past three years goo-gooing over her grandchildren.

"Just wait until your first grandchild!" she would say; "You'll see!"

And, of course, she was right; we're nuts about you Boo!

Who's Boo? That's you, little buddy. Your gramma Renee calls you "Boo Boo" and then just shortens it. Why? Don't ask me, but that's something you'll need to learn quickly about women: they don't need those things ... reasons.

And speaking of names, Renee picked out what she wants you to call us when you start talking, which shouldn't be too far away. I'll be "Poppy" and she'll be "Nonnie."

I don't think it really matters because what she wants you to call us and what you call us will probably end up two completely different things.

"Rock Star!" Drake Boyer Carr, 2004

I remember my sister and me playing "Cowboys and Indians." She was the Lone Ranger and I was his sidekick, Tonto. On the radio show (there was no TV then - can you believe it?), Tonto called the Lone Ranger, "Kemo Sabe," which, I think, means, "trusted friend." Every time I tried to call her that, what came out was, "Seebee Sobee," and 50 years later that's what I still call her.

Talking to you at this stage of your life is a gas; I had no idea I was so fluent in baby-talk. And, if you think I'm good, you should hear the conversations your Nonnie has with you.

When it comes your time to choose a wife, if you find someone who loves you half as much as Nonnie, you'll have it made, little buddy! I wish you could see and know the great love she has for you; it really is awesome.

You are such a good boy, Drake. I pray for you every day and ask God to keep His Hedge of Protection around you all the days of your life. I also ask Him to allow you to keep that sweet, sweet spirit I already discern in you. All I have to do is grin your way and your face explodes in smiles.

I can't wait to take you for long walks on the beach. I can already see us walking hand-in-hand, me answering your questions and you picking up every rock and shell that catches your eye. I'm going to teach you how to be "an old rat from the barn," just like my grandpaw taught me.

We stared deep into each other's eyes this week as I gave you a bottle of milk.

You won't remember it...but I'll never forget it. All I could think was how grateful I was your mom and dad didn't consider aborting you. I can't imagine not knowing you!

Today is Monday, I'll return to work and rave about the great time I had with you last weekend. But, then I'll have to deal with Mary, who will nod her head and say, "See, told ya!"

Get ready to hear that phrase a lot in your life, bud; it's a favorite of women!

But what do I know?

THE VISIT OF THE APOSTLE PAUL

J U L Y 2 6 , 2 0 0 4

While I certainly believe in the spirit world, I couldn't honestly tell you whether he actually came to me in that manner, whether it was a dream, a prophetic vision, delirium or simply hallucination, but it definitely was some kind of apparition.

What I know is I was sick as I've ever been in my life, but, after his visit, my fever broke instantly and I got well.

I started feeling sick while meeting with then-Ambassador "Pete" Peterson in the U.S. Embassy of Hanoi, Vietnam.

Later that afternoon we were to visit the infamous "Hanoi Hilton" prison camp just down the street where former Colonel Peterson spent seven years in the late 60's incarcerated as a prisoner of the Vietnam War; unfortunately, I would not make that visit.

Instead, I stood shivering, staring out the window of my plush, 21st floor, downtown hotel room, wondering what it must have looked like on the nights American bombers lit up this city 35 years ago.

That was the extent of my Hanoi visit as I would spend the next two days between the bed and the bathroom, where I knew the exact number of holes in each ceiling tile.

Ravaged by a blistering fever, my body accelerated between the extremes of "burning-up" and "freezing-to-death." My wife, Renee, rolled a comforter and laid it between us as a firewall on the bed in an attempt to escape the intolerable heat radiating from my body.

Not only did I think I was going to die, I was so sick I almost wanted to die. And that's when he came.

It must have been four in the morning. Renee, totally exhausted from being up and down with me for three days, had finally found sleep.

I have no idea how I knew it was him, but I knew it was him! I have no idea how I became aware of his presence in the room as he spoke not a word nor made a sound before I pulled my head up to peer at him standing at the foot of my bed.

A hood covered his head and his long, flowing robe seemed to be burlap.

"So," he spoke, "you praise God when everything is going great in your life; how about now when you are about to die?"

"Wow, this is it!" I thought to myself. I had always wondered what it would feel like to die and now I was about to find out.

I struggled up to my elbows and began singing, "Praise God, Praise God," to the tune of Amazing Grace.

Halfway through the first verse Renee awoke and asked if I was ok. I turned to look at her, then back to him...but he was gone.

"Did you see him?" I asked Renee.

"See who?" she replied.

"The Apostle Paul....he was just here!"

Later she told me she thought I was hallucinating; maybe I was. But, maybe I wasn't. Personally, I believe I met the author of much of the New Testament that morning. I also believe he was not there to "take me home," but to take me to a new level of belief. I look forward to seeing him again to ask if he was really there, and I expect he'll be grinning.

But what do I know?

M O O N W A L K

J U L Y 2 9 , 2 0 0 4

His name was Mr. Rich and he was reading a newspaper while balanced on the back legs of a chair leaning against the wall of the hotel. I nodded as I passed, entered the lobby, checked in and was shown to my room on the 14th floor.

In broken English, the bellman, who had delivered my bags to the room, bowed and asked, "Any ting else?" I thanked him, slapped a dollar in his palm, closed the door behind him and turned to sprawl spread-eagle on a real bed.

I remember thinking, "Seven days! I can't believe it!"

I showered away the funk of the long flight, changed clothes, splashed on some Jade East and headed back down to the lobby to inquire about a cab for the evening.

"Ah, Mr. Rich," the clerk advised me and summoned the man from his leaning post.

"Twenty dollars for the whole week?" I asked incredulously.

That was correct. For the entire seven days I spent in Bangkok, Thailand, Mr. Rich was at my beckoned call. He would sit outside leaning against the wall until I came down to say, "Let's go for a ride!" and would we ever!

Downtown Bangkok had a four-lane highway running through its center. The vehicles were about half the size of American cars, which meant they could turn the four lanes into eight lanes, which they did.

Once he discovered what a thrill seeker I was, Mr. Rich - along with all the other Thai cab drivers - drove at breakneck speeds and would dive into impossible holes in traffic. I loved it!

I took in the sights that week as we visited the Floating Markets, the 5½-ton gold Buddha; I bought a tailor-made, shark-skin suit and a pair of prescription sunglasses. I dickered with a clerk for two hours before buying a set of silverware for my mother. I bought gorgeous silk kimonos and pajamas and shipped them home for my entire family.

Thirty five years ago tomorrow … I took Mr. Rich with me to see a movie. Everyone stood prior to the beginning when a picture of the king of Thailand came on the screen and the audience sang the Thai national anthem.

I don't remember the movie, but what I do remember is that the screen suddenly went dark and a man came onto the stage announcing something I couldn't understand. Mr. Rich, my translator, mumbled something like, "Proud day for America!" and then turned his attention back to the stage where the screen had once again come alive.

Neil Armstrong crawled out of Apollo 11, inched his way down that ladder and hopped off to plant the very first footprints of man on the moon. The crowd erupted in applause and many, recognizing me as an American, turned to applaud in my direction as if I had something to do with this historic mission.

For the next few days, every business in Bangkok had a TV in the front window showing the live black-and-white feed of Americans on the moon. I, along with all the other soldiers enjoying that week of R&R from the Vietnam War, were celebrities everywhere we went.

"All in world look up to America," Mr. Rich shared in our goodbye.

My, how things can change in 35 years!

But what do I know?

SUNSHINE COORDINATOR

AUGUST 2, 2004

I grinned to myself as I concentrated on removing the tiny strands of silk.

"If you're going to do a job, do it right!" she used to tell me.

I had shucked corn for dinner and the thrilling task of "silking" it triggered my memory.

Dad always told me that after she was gone, times would come frequently when I would regret every little thing I did that displeased her; one of those times had arrived.

I remembered summers when I wanted to play ball and she would say, "You can go after you gather me a dozen 'roasting ears' out of the garden; be sure to silk them real good!"

My "real good" and her "real good" were a long way away from each other, and I remember finishing the task, dumping the corn on the table, racing to my room to grab my bat and glove, and then - out of the corner of my eye as I flew by - seeing her re-silking the corn.

Today, knowing she always forgave me, I could manage the grin, yet deep in my heart I felt that pain of regret Dad had promised.

He left in 1971 and for the next 10 years or so, Mother wouldn't even look at another man. She finally started dating a little but I don't think she ever seriously considered getting remarried.

In those days, raising your kids was your career if you were a wife. After my brother, sister and I all left the nest and Dad had passed, she lived alone until it was her turn to leave in 1998.

I worried about how she would occupy herself during those lonely years, but God always meets the needs of believers, and to meet hers He sent a flock of angels.

I will be eternally grateful to my dear friend, Aaron Simonton, executive director of the Monroe Senior Citizens Center, and all of his angels for the way he, and they, took my mother in and gave her a brand new purpose for her life.

"Sunshine Coordinator" became her title and she would visit anyone sick or downtrodden to lift them up.

Suddenly she was no longer sitting at home staring out the window dreaming of days gone by but had a renewed sense of purpose that not only occupied her mind but filled her heart with joy and contentment.

Every day she couldn't wait to get to the Center to perform her duties and socialize with friends.

Occasionally she would ask me to bring my guitar to sing and provide special entertainment for special recognition services. I was so proud ... because she was so proud.

I can't imagine what her quality of life would have been during those later years had it not been for the Monroe Senior Citizens Center and all the wonderful people who work there and use it.

Tuesday we vote for various issues on the ballot, one of which is a renewal - not an increase - for the Monroe County senior citizens millage. I urge you to vote yes, in memory of Pearl Treece and in support of all our parents whose lives are refurbished - after we leave them to start our own lives - by this most important element of our society.

Besides, we need to keep the program in good shape as we'll be needing it ourselves someday!

But what do I know?

"I AM NOT A CROOK"

A U G U S T 9 , 2 0 0 4

"Look at him sweat!" I told my mother. "Can't you tell he's lying through his teeth?"

"Son!" she replied incredulously, "he's our president! He wouldn't lie to us! Besides, he goes to church every Sunday!"

I remember the exchange like it was yesterday instead of 30 years ago. Mother and I sat watching then-President Richard Nixon assure us - and the rest of the world, live on television - that he had no part in a cover-up of the Watergate break-in and that the soon-to-be-famous White House Tapes would absolve him. (It was the same evening he would utter his famous, "I am not a crook!" line.)

Several months later, I read transcripts of the tapes to her from the newspaper that sounded something like this: "If that (expletive deleted) Liddy doesn't (expletive deleted) tell that (expletive deleted) judge anything, I expect this whole (expletive deleted) mess will go away."

I can still hear her in my mind's ear saying, "Son, what does 'expletive deleted' mean?"

"It's a profanity, mother." I explained to her. "He's swearing."

"I don't understand," she would say and then repeat again, "he goes to church!"

She was probably more shocked and saddened by that revelation than she was that the tapes also revealed Nixon had obstructed justice, ordered "hush money" paid, counseled perjury, planned to offer clemency for perjured testimony and tampered with grand jury proceedings.

He obviously was also more concerned with his image - in the eyes of ones like my mother - than he was with his felonious behavior as he had the profanities edited out of the transcripts while leaving the "smoking guns" intact.

If my memory serves me correctly, 30 years ago last night I stood on the stage of the Welland Hotel in Welland, Ontario, performing the first set of an evening concert with fellow members of the rock and roll band with whom I was touring at the time.

Life-long friend and fellow band member Roger Manning grabbed the microphone at 8:55 p.m. and shared with the audience, "We're going to take a little break right now to watch the TV as the president of our country is about to resign."

I remember gathering around that TV and hearing his resignation speech. As an angry young man just a few years after returning from 13 months in the Vietnam War - of which Mr. Nixon was a central figure - I was anxious for his resignation.

However, once he had resigned and we had returned to the stage to finish our concert, there was great sadness in my heart as I realized our country had sunk to such a depth that, for the first time in history, an American president had resigned in disgrace.

On this 30th anniversary of the Nixon resignation I remember how crushed mother was with his deception, both as president and as a man-of-God.

Unfortunately, it would not be the last time our president would look into the eyes of the nation ... and lie through his teeth!

With the intent of the Iraq War being the most hotly debated issue on the lips of America today, let's just hope that pattern of presidential behavior isn't continuing with Mr. Bush, both as our president, and ... even more importantly to me ... as a man of God!

But what do I know.

MOTHER'S MIDNIGHT ROSE

A U G U S T   1 6 ,   2 0 0 4

I picked my way through the bramble. The full moon - the reason I had been able to make such good time on this hot summer night - had virtually disappeared in the darkness of the choked thicket.

Suddenly, I saw a light ahead and pressed toward it. I pulled aside the last branch to reveal the light ... and the magnificent sign God gave me that night.

A hole in the top of this thicket, anchored deep in the sweltering swamps of southern Georgia, had allowed a single beam of moonlight to penetrate - and illuminate - the most beautiful rose I had ever seen.

"Look at this!" I exclaimed to the others in my squad as we admired this unexpected sight.

"It's a sign!" I told them, then picked the flower and gently slid it into the pocket of my fatigue shirt.

"I'll take this to mother!" I told them and then returned to blazing a trail through the thicket.

At dark that night, all of us vying to become Airborne Rangers were trucked miles through the night to a secret location. Gathered into groups of four, we were given a compass, destination point grid coordinates and instructions to be there by sunrise or fail the course and have no chance of attaining the coveted "Airborne" status for which we were enduring all the torture, sacrifice and pain required to have silver wings pinned to our chests.

When it came time to pick a team leader, I shared with the others, "I don't know about you guys, but I'm going to be the first one back! My mother is having surgery tomorrow and if I make it back by 4 a.m., I get to go home."

They handed me the compass. I opened it, found my direction, shot an azimuth on the farthest, tallest, illuminated-by-the-light-of-the-moon-tree in that direction, closed the compass and broke into a dead run toward that tree; my buddies were in hot pursuit.

In addition to rivers and streams we had to ford, sentries were setup along the way waiting to capture the careless, which dictated snaking silently across that swamp.

Determined to not be deterred by any of these dangers, driven by the desire to go home, encouraged by the sign God gave me, and covered with dirt, scratches and cuts from the journey, we emerged from the early-morning darkness to the roaring fire marking the destination point ... the first ones back!

There, as promised, was the Jeep waiting to take me to the base airport where I hopped a military flight to Detroit.

The next day, showered, shaved, out of Army fatigues and into civilian clothes and with scratches still on my face, I walked into the hospital room, sat down beside my dear mother, laid the still-fragrant flower on her lap and told the story how God had revealed the rose to tell me she would be all right and I would make it home in time.

Now, older, wiser, I appreciate that memory more as I realize she was thrilled not as much by the rose as the fact her son was learning to recognize the little signs and gifts God places before us to help and guide us along this path of life. Unfortunately, most not only miss those signs, some step on and crush them as they go by.

But what do I know?

ONE MAN'S TRASH...

AUGUST 23, 2004

"Mr. Treece, there's a young man here to see you," interrupted my secretary via intercom. I was extremely busy signing affidavits certifying that commercials listed on the forms had indeed run on the air during the time periods listed.

"Did he say what he wants?" I inquired, not wanting to stop my work unless it was important.

"Something about a ball glove?" was her reply.

My heart leaped, causing me to leap off my chair and bolt for the office door. I opened it and peered around the corner at the young man waiting in the vestibule of what was then the downtown Monroe facility of Tower 98 radio.

The young man stood there holding a plastic bag as if it contained something he didn't particularly want to touch.

"Hello!" I called to him.

"Are you the guy who lost the ball glove?" he asked.

"Yes I am," I answered, "Please come in!"

I shut the door behind us, moved around my desk and gazed with great anticipation at the bag he held. Sadly, my excitement was such that I don't know that I even asked his name

"I found it at Cairns Field," he began to explain. "Later on I saw one of the fliers you plastered all over town. I figured if this was it and you went to all that trouble, you must have wanted it back awful bad!"

"It's ... an emotional thing," I tried to explain and shifted my gaze back on the bag.

Finally, he opened it, gently slid his hand in, grabbed the glove and pulled it out. My eyes lit up and my face exploded in a euphoric, ear-to-ear smile.

"Is this it?" he asked and handed it across the desk to me, still dangling it between his thumb and forefinger as if the old piece of leather had cooties.

"Oh, thank you!" I exclaimed...over and over.

I slid my left hand into the glove and gave it a fist-pound with my right.

Former St. Louis Cardinal's Hall of Fame outfielder Lou Brock would have been proud to know that this ragged old piece of leather with his name seared into the little finger meant so very much to this aging has-been who would soon be barely able run to first base anymore.

"You have no idea what this means to me!" I shared as I ran my hands across the tattered cowhide, once golden-brown-new, now dark red from hundreds of oiling's. Plastic ties - clipped-at-their-catch - held the back of the hand and the length of the little finger together, replacing rotted rawhide repaired years ago.

"My father bought this for me when I pitched for Monroe High!" I shared with him. I took off the glove and reached deep in my pocket, pulled out my cash, stripped a twenty and handed it to the young man.

"Is this enough?" I asked.

He looked at the twenty, then back at me and said, "Mister, I hate to tell you this. I was going to pitch it 'cause that glove ain't worth twenty dollars!"

"It is to me!" I assured him as he took the reward and left.

I sat in my chair and cradled the glove like a lost puppy finally come home and thought of how the old adage is true: One man's trash is another man's treasure.

But what do I know.

DO YOU BELIEVE ME?

A U G U S T 3 0 , 2 0 0 4

Andrew is a friend of mine. He and his gorgeous wife are from New Zealand and live in Madison, Wis., with their three wonderful and incredibly talented children. Andrew is a world-class violinist, pianist ... and person!

Do you believe me?

Seriously, stop right now and answer the question: Do you believe me?

I trust those of you who know me would answer, "Sure." The reason, in spite of you not knowing him personally, is because you believe in me.

Those of you who don't know me might say something like, "If you weren't credible, this paper obviously wouldn't print your column, so ... If you say so, or, better yet, until you give me a reason not to ... I'll believe you."

Those who attended my Put-In-Bay performance with the Toledo Symphony Orchestra some years ago would say, "Sure, Andrew was the conductor."

Those reading online from Madison would say, "Andrew? Sure, he conduct's the Wisconsin Chamber Orchestra and Treece performed a Fourth of July concert with them on the steps of the capitol building a few years ago."

Where am I going with this?

I have another Friend. He is the most wonderful person I have ever met. He is my constant companion. I am more in love with Him than I am with the incredibly wonderful woman He brought me for a wife and I can't believe I can love someone more than her!

I meet with Him every morning and then we talk throughout the day. He encourages me to bring my problems to Him, and - in His time - He works them out for my good. He never goes on vacation, never turns on the answering machine, He's never sick, too busy or too tired to talk with me.

I met Him as a 10-year-old boy but never truly believed in Him. He believed in me, fortunately, and kept me safe through my trips through the jungles of Vietnam and America. Finally, in desperation and the basement of 204 Riverview Ave. on the morning of Jan. 16, 1991, moments before intending to end my own trashed life, with faith the size of a mustard seed (I cried out, "Lord, if you're there!") I asked this Friend to come into my heart, change and direct my life ... and that's exactly what He did.

Do you believe me?

There were two letters to the editor in last week's News related to this subject that got me thinking; one said emphatically, "There is no god!" while the other virtually said, "I don't think there is a god."

The point I'm trying to make is this: The issue is whether or not you believe that the persons of Andrew - and Jesus Christ - are real, and the only way you can know for sure is for you to meet them personally.

If you've never met Andrew - or Christ - you can't know for sure if either of them truly exists. If you have - as I have - then you have a personal relationship with them and nobody can convince you that they don't exist!

And, while I hope both letter writers have the opportunity to meet each of my friends some day, the truth is I respect their right to their opinion. I would only hope they would consider qualifying that opinion by saying something like ...

But what do I know?

MRS. KACKMEISTER'S GRADE CARD

SEPTEMBER 2, 2004

As I do every day, I came home from work, grabbed the paper on the way in, dropped my keys on the snack bar, went upstairs to my office, laid my things on the desk and hit the blinking button on the answering machine.

"Tom, this is Lanie Kackmeister," the voice began.

I froze and stared into the face of the machine as if the voice belonged to it.

"I'm long overdue to compliment you on your outstanding column. I am so proud of your writing and the subjects that you pick and the Christianity you portray so openly and wonderfully."

I slowly sank into my office chair as the sweet voice of my high school journalism teacher finished her message. There were others on the machine but I didn't hear them as I was basking in the glow of unexpected approval from one who - 40 years earlier - had taught me how to do what I'm right now doing.

I sat and let my mind drift back to the Monroe High sophomore without a clue as to where he wanted to go in life. I remembered being bonkers over Beatles, basketball and a blonde bombshell by the name of ... Mrs. Kackmeister!

I loved her class because she made me think. More importantly, she encouraged me to not only bring those thoughts out of my head, but also out of my heart. While she taught me that being factually correct was at the root of basic structural writing, she also encouraged me to inject how I felt into what I was conveying.

The problem I had with her was that she made it difficult to concentrate on journalism. Mrs. Kackmeister was probably the most beautiful teacher I ever had, and, easing into "girls" at 15, it was hard to take my eyes off her.

I ran into her about a year ago; she is definitely still a hottie, and I share that perception with tempered fear and trepidation. Why?

Because as I stand at 6-foot-5, 260 pounds, Mr. Kackmeister makes me look like a boy!

I just thought about how much we value money in this life, and yet, Mrs. Kackmeister couldn't have given me $1,000 and made me feel better than how I felt at that moment, realizing I had received approval from one who helped launch me on this mission of sharing my opinions and life stories with all of you!

I wondered how it must feel for her - and teachers in general - who dedicate their lives to instruction of others. She shared her pride in seeing success in a former student in whom she had invested some of her life's work.

I wondered if the opposite was true when they see one maligned and mired in the muck of malevolence or malignancy.

I hope Mrs. Kackmeister hasn't minded me sharing her personal message and I ask your forgiveness for sharing what is seemingly a self-serving story. I do so not to blow my horn but to share my joy as well as reverberating a message my editor shared in her column some time ago about the joy of receiving approval from teachers past and the simple-but-critical importance of the role they play in our lives.

I can't remember what final grade Mrs. Kackmeister gave me in high school, but I think I got an "A" on her report card of my life.

But what do I know?

10 BELLS RING TERROR

S E P E M B E R 1 3 , 2 0 0 4

"Ding, ding, ding, ding, ding, ding, ding, ding, ding, ding!"

I frowned and looked up from my Sunday paper and wondered if the Associated Press teletype machine was having a meltdown or something big was happening; I had never before heard the Tower 98 news ticker ring ten bells.

It was 6:30 Sunday morning, October 23, 1983. On the downside of a musical career that had me performing six nights a week with a rock & roll band, I would pull a Saturday all-nighter and go directly to my 6 a.m. till noon DJ shift; staying awake was the most difficult part of the job.

The bell would ring each time stories came across the wire. The more bells, the greater importance; 10 was the max.

I left the tiny studio of the then-downtown Monroe radio station and walked to the machine now making noises that always made me expect to see Walter Cronkite looking up from behind horn-rimmed glasses.

When it stopped I ripped off the paper to read that over 200 Marines had been killed in their sleep by a powerful car bomb in Lebanon.

I interrupted programming and announced the tragedy over the airwaves, proud that I was "on top of the story."

Twenty one years later, ramifications of those bells ring much louder in my ears.

Previously I hadn't put much stock in what had been going on in the world, like Israeli athletes brutally killed during the '72 Munich Olympics or Iran's takeover of the U.S. Embassy in '79.

Today I think of the Jew in the wheelchair, murdered and thrown overboard during the 1985 Achille Lauro hijacking, and the American Navy diver murdered during the '87 TWA hijacking in Athens. I think of the hundreds who endured horrible deaths falling from the bombed

Pan Am flight over Lockerbie in '88.

I think of how we yawned and rolled over when the World Trade Center was bombed the first time in '93, followed by the Khobar Towers in '96 and our Kenyan and Tanzanian Embassies in '98. I think of the USS Cole almost destroyed in 2000 by a little, explosive-laden rubber boat. All these with virtually no retaliation.

And then, as we remembered Saturday: 9-11.

Last week ten bells rang in my head again as I watched Russians wrap up their 9-11: two aircraft bombings and the schoolchildren/ hostage crisis leaving almost 500 dead. I wondered how anyone could be so heartless, gutless, cowardly, than to use - and then murder - .children for their cause.

It was the same feeling I had when I forced myself to watch the videos of the Nicholas Berg and Paul Johnson beheadings by face-covered cowards. America needs to get serious about who we are dealing with, especially the fact that the intent of these evil persons is simply to destroy us and our way of life!

Just like Spain's train bombings, this Russian episode was the latest terrorist attempt to influence elections; I expect something similar before November 2! And anyone who thinks a more "sensitive war" on our part will get the job done is fooling themselves as well as all who believe them.

We are at war...unlike any we have ever known, and I believe these historical bells that have been ringing are warnings of what's coming to a street near you.

But what do I know?

WHO WAS THE BIGGEST JERK?

SEPTEMBER 27, 2004

My wife, Renee, never one to mince words, turned to me and said, "Personally, I think he was a bit of a jerk!" I started wondering right then who the bigger jerk was: him or me.

We had hopped a big ol' jet airliner out of Detroit and flown to Baltimore to begin a Caribbean cruise. Unfortunately, Hurricane Jeanne was churning toward the Florida coast, which meant our ports-of-call were about to receive a drastic makeover.

Having stayed up most of the previous night with last-minute packing, we dozed on the airplane; the jolt of tires greeting the tarmac woke us up. We grabbed carry-on luggage and, like cattle, followed the path to the pond out of the plane, through the motor-driven hallway-on-wheels and into the terminal.

Ahead of us walked our oldest son, John, and his wife, Kelli, who had invited us to accompany them on this cruise.

As we turned the corner and headed for baggage claim, I spotted him. Without thinking, I barked out his name, "Kirk!" and extended my hand.

My family was trying to figure out how I knew someone in Baltimore; I introduced each of them. "I'm sorry, you probably get this all the time," I told him. "I just couldn't walk on by ... you've given me so many thrills in my lifetime!"

It was odd to me that although he stood among hundreds of people, no one recognized this man who had provided at least two of the most thrilling moments in baseball history.

It was easy for me as for years I had his poster hanging on my office wall. In that instant I saw it in my mind's eye, mighty warrior, arms flexed over his head in triumphant victory after drilling a Goose Gossage fastball into Tiger Stadium's upper deck during the 1984 World Series.

Though still thin and trim, gone were the long, free-flowing blond locks that flew wildly each time he stole second.

"We're playing the Orioles tonight," the now-Tiger bench coach explained, seemingly a little put out at having to talk to us while he waited for a friend. "It's nice to see you, and thanks for the thrills!" I shared before we walked on.

While waiting for the women after a bathroom break, suddenly, there he was again passing us in the hall.

I timidly held up my camera and asked, "Picture?" He winced, then grudgingly said, "If you hurry!" I took one of my trademark "You 'n' Me" pictures of him and me, thanked him again and heard him reply as he left, "It's a bit obnoxious!"

Later, relaxing on board the Grandeur of the Seas as we cruised out into the Atlantic and set a course for Bermuda - well away from Jeanne - I questioned my family as to who was the biggest jerk. Was it former Michigan State University, Detroit Tiger and L.A. Dodger superstar Kirk Gibson, who, to me, was definitely a bit of a jerk, or the airport pest who recognized and invaded his space for a piece of his time.

For me, I hadn't really thought about it as I felt I had known him for years and simply couldn't pass him by. But, for him, I'm sure there was no question as to which one of us was the jerk!

But what do I know?

Kirk Gibson and Tom, Baltimore Airport, 2004

BEHEADINGS (WWIII)

OCTOBER 4, 2004

A couple of weeks ago in my "Ten Bells" column I shared that I had "forced myself" to watch videos of terrorist beheadings. Recently I repeated that sad, grisly, infuriating commentary with the latest round of this most-effective form of terror.

I am a man who has seen much in the way of terrible things human beings do to each other, mostly from 13 months of Vietnam War. I must tell those of you who have not seen these videos, it is one of the most sadistic and gruesome experiences I have ever witnessed! It's so hard to believe that there are people (?) in the world - no matter what the cause - who would actually perform such heinous acts on another; it was almost more than I could stand.

Perhaps you wonder why I share this, or, more so, why I would even want to watch these videos. I am not a barbarian. I believe every adult American should be forced to watch. Ten Bells chastised us for yawning and going back to sleep through four decades of "subtle" terrorism coming at us like rust. When you see these videos, you will realize that word is obsolete now.

I also thought about how I would react if I were the one making decisions for our country. My two answers, juxtaposed, caused me great concern in my own life.

My first reaction would be to make my own video and say, "Unlike the cowards that you are, my face is uncovered! Okay, you wanted Muslim prisoners released or you would cut off the heads of the Americans, which you have already done."

Then I would say, "No problem, bring in Dr. Germ."

Dr. Germ is the Iraqi female who knows exactly how to construct germ warfare programs with which to kill mass volumes of people, as she has already done. I trust readers understand that purpose is exactly why terrorists want her released.

Once Dr. Germ was brought into the room, live on video, I would throw her to the floor, take a dull knife and saw her head off and then ceremoniously hold it up for the camera to record. Then I would say, "You want her, you got her; just tell me where to send the box!"

Can't believe you're hearing this from me? Me neither. BUT ... I tell you, this is what the human side of Tom Treece would like to do. I'm afraid that fighting fire with fire is the only thing evil persons will understand.

Unfortunately, the word "evil" shakes me back to reality and thought No. 2 ... my Christianity. My Christian instructions are to "turn the other cheek," and "do not repay evil with evil."

How do I do that?

I have two stepsons. Even though they are not even my flesh and blood, there is no way I would allow them to suffer such a horrible death as Christ's, especially in exchange for a scumbag like al-Zarqawi or bin Laden.

This tells me that while I have great joy in being a Christian, I'm obviously, certainly, not where God wants me to be.

I am also not a barbarian, but, after watching these videos, and in spite of my Christianity ... just for a moment ... I'd really like to be.

But what do I know?

SPOILED AMERICANS

OCTOBER 11, 2004

I was lost in watching bubbles form in my omelet when she broke the trance.

"Where's my cook!" she demanded. "Is he on break or something?"

We were standing in separate lines waiting for the cruise ship breakfast cooks to complete our orders. I had noticed earlier that her cook had run out of eggs and had returned to the kitchen for more, leaving this blue-haired, very-proper-lady-in-her-own-mind waiting for a good five minutes.

She shifted from foot-to-foot with hands on hips and dagger-looks directed at anyone willing to sympathize with her great despair.

Finally the cook returned to "It's about time!"

He gave her a puzzled look and began assembling her omelet as I turned to the young lady standing next to me who had observed the same as me.

"We just came from islands where people were fighting each other for food and this lady's complaining about having to wait five minutes for someone to cook her omelet!" I whispered in her ear.

"Can you believe some people?" she answered.

"Welcome to America," I finished.

A few days earlier we had anchored off the coast of Haiti, ferried ashore to frolic in the sun and surf of Labadie and dine like kings and queens on the fabulous buffet provided by our Royal Caribbean hosts.

It was a paradise on Earth! The water was cobalt blue, the sand was littered pink with crushed-coral-washed-ashore and the cool Caribbean breeze comfortably countered the 87 degrees.

Renee and I have a favorite saying we live by: "Work hard, play hard!" and, after working extra hard this spring and summer we had been anticipating this trip immensely.

Original cruise plans called for visits to Key West, Cozumel, Coco cay, Belize and Grand Bahama Island. The last of the season's plague of hurricanes changed those plans.

With Hurricane Jeanne intersecting our path to the Gulf on launch day, RC rerouted us into the Bermuda Triangle, which was a brilliant move. Instead of wicked, the weather was wonderful as we sailed to Bermuda, then down to Haiti where we then followed the storm instead of fighting it.

There was only one problem for me.

As I lay lounging with my love on Labadie, I couldn't stop glancing at our mountain backdrop. A newshound, I had been keeping up with the death and destruction Jeanne had left in her wake, and from pictures painted in my mind by newspaper and TV accounts I had devoured, I knew what was on the other side.

Those pictures were of Haitians tearing at each other, fighting for food being distributed by humanitarian organizations; they were starving.

I thought of that at lunch while watching fat Americans pile their plates, gorge themselves, and then mindlessly dump untouched food in the trash.

I had a difficult time trying to enjoy my food knowing that just over that peak people were burying 2,000 of their drowned nation while I relaxed in the lap of luxury of this carefree cruise.

I know I can't save the world and can't restrict my life because of sufferings that will always be happening.

It just bothers me that we are so spoiled. We take freedom for granted and demand that someone cook our eggs right and on time instead of being humble and grateful for the incredible luck of being born in this great country!

But what do I know?

RECEPTION STILL STINGS

OCTOBER 18, 2004

Downtown Monroe had angle parking in 1969 and I steered my new Dodge Charger into one in front of what was then Baskin Robbins. There hadn't been any ice cream in the jungle or the freedom to stroll down to the local store for a cone so I was eager to lick into one again.

I got out of my car and walked toward the door just as it opened. Out came a lifelong friend, his wife and their two young daughters I hadn't seen in two years and I threw my arms open to greet them.

My friend forced a smile, uttered a few, "Nice to see you; glad you're back," phony-sounding-phrases, cradled his brood and steered them around me and down the street.

Stunned, mouth agape, I watched them go.

That morning I had finished the final leg of a 14,000 mile journey from a South Vietnam hamlet on the other side of the world to the little white house on Evergreen Acres' Cedar St. where I was born and raised.

Foolishly, I expected everything to be the same and that I could slip back into the hometown slot I had occupied for 19 years just 19 months earlier. The rude awakening was only beginning.

On August 11, 1969, an assault rifle was an extension of my right hand. Two days later I was sitting in Moore's Restaurant on Monroe St., smoking cigarettes, drinking coffee and hoping my hair would grow soon so I could fit in with local styles; out of one world and into another with no buffer or deprogramming.

I wondered why this family, who lovingly embraced me just two years earlier, now treated me as though I had the plague.

While I don't blame John Kerry for this instance as it was before he made his now-infamous testimony before Congress, I hold him in-part responsible for the overall treatment of Vietnam veterans since that time, thanks to him labeling all of us as barbarians who routinely, "cut off ears, cut off heads"... (you've heard the rest).

Did these things happen? Yes. As routine as he reported? Not a chance. Did it cause prisoners of war to be treated more harshly? Absolutely! (I've spoken with some.) Did it help or harm those who returned? See parallel above.

It's taken a lifetime to overcome stigmatisms pervaded by the likes of Kerry, who, in my opinion, used his war-quarter to launch a political career on the backs of American 19-year-olds, freaked out and frightened from being forced into physical and emotional trauma because they didn't have rich daddies who could steer them into the National Guard like you know who!

It's tough enough trying to deal with war memories that never go away, but to be labeled the way we were was inexcusable. It's like having your loved ones watch what the likes of Charles Manson and Ted Bundy did and then label you the same!

It has been unpleasant sharing these feelings with you; I have done so because many of you asked me to.

Long ago I gave forgiveness to my friend - who never asked for it - and to this day has no idea that, or how, he hurt me that night. And, in spite of it being my Christian obligation to do so, I'm having a much more difficult time forgiving Mr. Kerry!

But what do I know?

"IT'S NOT THE ECONOMY, STUPID!"

OCTOBER 25, 2004

I remember wondering how the elder President Bush, after crushing Saddam's army during the '91 Gulf War - which gave him the highest presidential rating in history - could then lose the presidency to Bill Clinton just seven months later.

The now-famous answer was found on the blackboard of a Clinton campaign office: "It's the economy, stupid!"

Whoever wrote that was right! Even though America had a great military victory, the economy was in the toilet, so instead we elected Clinton, who gave us what we wanted: money!

The economy flourished and nobody cared if the leader of the free world had an affair with an intern nearly the age of his daughter. Nobody cared that he then looked us all in the eye, told us he hadn't, was impeached for lying to a grand jury and then still was able to complete his term in office. Why? Because we all had lots of money!

Nobody cared when our warships or foreign embassies got blown up, and Clinton - in futility - launched $100M worth of Tomahawk Missiles into some mountain range to satisfy us because...we all had lots of money.

Thanks to term limits the younger Bush was elected and nine months later the most devastating attack on our homeland brought our country to its' economic knees.

Bush declared war on terror and immediately dismantled the terrorist-based Taliban government of Afghanistan, where, two years later, women previously beaten for speaking without being spoken to who could only view the world through 2-by-4 inch mesh, abandoned their Burkas and had their voices heard with their votes.

Next Bush goes after Saddam and takes down his evil empire and we watch as people dance in the streets and spit on the dictator's picture. In horror we watch as body parts fall from giant crane shovels scooping out his mass graves. I contend that any Bush hater would be kissing his boots had those body parts come from their father, mother, sister, brother, wife, husband or children! But, like the starving Haitians I wrote about a few weeks ago, it's not happening to us so we don't care!

Now we watch Jordanian al-Zarquai, openly pledged to bin Laden, kidnap Americans and cut off their heads as they beg for their lives while bound and blindfolded. Does anyone truly believe he's in Iraq because he feels sorry for Saddam? Please! Iraq is and always has been a haven for terrorists and we finally have a president willing to find the rat's nests and clean them out.

The problem - like Desert Storm - it takes money to fund a war. We'd like for oppressed people on the other side of the world to be free, just not at our expense.

I know the honeymoon's over as I've just alienated half of you, but, for me, the slogan for this election is reversed: It's not the economy, stupid, it's terrorism, and if it continues unchecked like the Clinton years, we won't have to worry about jobs or anything else. Am I trying to scare you? You bet!

I also believe the greatest indicator of future performance is past performance. After 20 years in the Senate, I can't name one thing John Kerry has done. He says he will hunt down and kill terrorists. Really? How? Given his voting record, if he wins, I expect we'll be fighting it - as Zell Miller suggests - with spitballs!

But what do I know?

KRUSHCHEV'S CAVEAT

N O V E M B E R   1 ,   2 0 0 4

Am I out of touch with America … or has America lost her focus? As a boy, Communism was the threat to America. I remember asking my father what Communism was; his answer, "They don't believe in God!"

Then - before being old enough to vote - I was sent to war in Vietnam, the purpose of which was to stop the flow of Communism. The "Domino Theory" projected that Communism, purveyed by China and Russia, was taking over the world through the one-by-one overthrow of small, third world countries, like …Vietnam!

Some will remember Russian Premier Khrushchev pounding his shoe on the U.N. table vowing to bury America from within "without firing a shot!"

When the Russian empire fell along with the Berlin Wall, I laughed at Nikita's tirade and prediction; today I'm wondering if he will get the last laugh!

You see, I thought Khrushchev's plan was for the Russian military to come and physically overthrow America to force Communism. Instead - like rust that never sleeps - it's been a slow and methodical philosophic invasion.

As my father correctly described, atheism - along with basic socialist principles - is a principal component of Communism. You could be blind and still see America rushing to throw God out of our country!

Khrushchev's words hit me like a brick, and, I must say, I have John Kerry to thank.

Like wondering how Clinton could stay in office after impeachment, I had a similar question about Kerry/America. How could a man who did something (privately negotiate with America's enemy during a time of war) that would have gotten him shot for treason 100 years ago even have the opportunity to become our next president?

At a friend's urging I went to the American Communist Party's Web site (www.cpusa.org) where I found vehement Bush bashing and obvious Kerry endorsement. That didn't shock me, but what did was how similar their 10-point philosophical platform was to the Democratic National Committee's.

That's when Khrushchev's caveat hit me!

Put a frog in boiling water and he'll jump out; put him in cold water, slowly turn up the heat and he's cooked before he realizes and can't jump out!

America became the greatest country on Earth as "One Nation Under God!" Those days are over and I fear never to return.

I also fear that no matter who wins tomorrow's election, our country is headed for a state where buses and bars will soon be blowing up not from foreign terrorists, but from American anarchists! The Right won't continue to look the other way to butchered babies and anything-goes lifestyles just because people think it's their rights, and the Left will be toothpaste that won't go back in the tube.

While I have never considered myself a Democrat or Republican I have voted Democratic 95 percent of my life, but I will definitely be voting for George Bush tomorrow!

I'm not trying to "bully" you as I have been accused. This column is just my opinion; if you agree, great, and if you don't, great.

But, if you are of the mind or age to remember the foundations on which this country was built, then you can see how far from that we have faded and the potential peril we face. And, at the risk of resurrecting Tail Gunner Joe, I'd say your vote tomorrow may very well determine whether or not Nikita gets the last laugh.

But what do I know?

BEING RIGHT OR DOING RIGHT?

N O V E M B E R   8 ,   2 0 0 4

Relieved at the sight of elections in my rear-view mirror, I sit pondering lessons learned and the path before me, us. I also wonder why a multitude of encouraging calls and e-mails of approval never seems to cancel the handful that come with razors and leave you bleeding.

Most shocking were ones who had written often to gush over thoughts and ideals I've shared in my stories, only to suddenly determine that I am actually an idiot simply because I crossed their political line.

I want you to know that I am not hung up on being right. My only concern at this juncture of my life is doing right. Everybody wants to be right and I'm no different, but there's a difference in being and doing.

Example: I think voters labeled "undecided" at the election's midnight hour were actually those more concerned with being right at the contest's conclusion.

Then there's always the question, "What is right?" Who determines what is right? It's obvious that we all have different value systems, but it's also obvious that a mass of people cannot live together without an overall standard for behavior; in America it's relatively simple ... we create laws to govern that behavior.

As a Christian, I believe in the Holy Bible, which instructs that God's law is higher than man's law. (The Founding Fathers understood this, otherwise, why would they acknowledge "inalienable rights endowed by our creator" in their Declaration of Independence?)

In that book, God says that He knew us even before we were in the womb. That tells me that inception brought me (my spirit) to my mother's womb from someplace else, and I believe that spirit - the true life within this rental property I call my body - will return to God (for judgment) after this body fails me one last time.

So what happens for those who don't believe in God? How do we resolve to create law that will be satisfactory for those who believe as I, as well as for those who believe that embryonic inception is nothing more than a tumor or wart and demand the right to have it excised? As we have seen, there is tremendous distance between those two belief systems and, as we have just seen, directions of nations can be determined by majority followings of those separate belief systems.

So where do we go from here? The abortion issue is only one of many that divide us. And, as we have seen in the last two elections, that separation grows wider with each passing day, leaving one to wonder what our children and grandchildren will have to deal with in the future.

For me, trusting and believing in Who that book is all about is my refuge, which, I realize, labels me to many as a fanatic or extremist. I have no choice, however, as it was He who pulled me from the trash pile only moments before my intent to end my own life of self-driven failures.

And, as I said, I'm not as concerned with being right as I am with doing right. In spite of the name-calling and arrows slung my way in the last three weeks, as the country song says, "that's my story and I'm sticking to it!"

But what do I know?

PLEDGING OMEGA CHI

NOVEMBER 15, 2004

"Alpha, Beta, Gamma, Delta, Epsilon, Zeta, Eta, Theta, Iota, Kappa, Lambda, Mu, Nu, XI, Omicron, Pi, Rho, Sigma, Tau, Upsilon, Phi, Chi, Psi, Omega!"

I barked out the Greek alphabet again before gasping a quick breath, then one final time to complete the assignment, after which I calmly leaned forward, puckered my lips and gave a quick blow to extinguish the match only moments away from frying the flesh of my thumb and forefinger.

"Very good, Pledge!" my "big brother" called out, obviously pleased that the one he was mentoring had done his homework to be able to recite the alphabet three times before the match burned down.

It was 1965 and "Hell Week" for freshmen pledging fraternities at Harrogate, Tenn.'s Lincoln Memorial University; I had chosen Omega Chi.

"Animal House" hadn't been made yet, and while we barely resembled the craziness depicted in that movie, we were considerably close for a conservative college cuddled near the foot of the famous Gap in the Cumberland Mountains.

Every night at midnight we reported to the frat house and received assignments for the remainder of the night, err … morning. Some assignments were silly and stupid, some tough and tedious.

On Kentucky's side of Cumberland Mountain was a cross of lights that could be seen for miles. One night our assignment was to determine the wattage of the bulbs of that cross. Through the darkness we made our way up that mountain to discover the lights 50 feet up in the treetops. We were shocked to find they were only 25 watts.

I took pride in carving and painting the little paddle we had to wear on our belts during pledge week. If caught without it you received a swat from the fraternity's master paddle!

The last night of Hell Week was supposed to be the toughest. We met at midnight, were blindfolded, loaded into a car and driven for a good half-hour.

I made mental notes of turns, when the road got bumpy, etc.

Finally they stopped the car, pulled us out, removed the blindfolds and gave instructions to be back in time for morning classes or be blackballed from the fraternity.

I remember watching those taillights get smaller and smaller as they left us there in the wilderness mountains of Tennessee.

Our only choice was to follow those taillights as that obviously was the way home.

We had gone about a quarter mile when I heard a distinct sound.

"Listen!" I hushed the others. By the light of the moon I followed the sound of running water off the dirt road, across a field and to the edge of a large river. Suddenly something clicked in my memory bank.

"Hey," I began, "I know where we are! This is the Powell River; my father was raised near here!"

I got my bearings and realized a cousin lived just over the nearest mountain; we started climbing.

I gave a 3 a.m. bang on his door, explained our plight and giggled with glee as he drove us back to school where we arrived even before the ones who had dumped us.

Carefree and cocky in the fall of '65.

Trying to be more careful 40 years later and lustfully reflecting on days when my only concern was how fast I could say the Greek alphabet before a match burned down!

But what do I know?

REST IN PEACE, PFC MILLER

NOVEMBER 22, 2004

I didn't know him, but I knew him.

Had I met him on the street a few weeks ago I wouldn't have "known him from Adam," yet he was my brother.

When it came my turn, I slowly, smartly, walked to face his flag-draped casket, clicked my heels, snapped my fists to my sides, stiffened my wrist, thumb and fingers into a straight line and slowly lifted them to the edge of my right eyebrow in a regimented show of respect to him.

The military salute for a superior officer is done quickly with precision. Saluting a fallen comrade is done slowly, with dignity and honor. Friday night at Rupp Funeral Home it was my honor to attend to Pfc. Dennis Miller Jr., who was killed-in-action in the Iraq war.

Back in line, I could not stop the video that ran through my head. Just outside the little hamlet of Duc Pho, Vietnam, the base camp executive officer had summoned me.

"You know a soldier named Rodney Vore?" he began; I left my nervous answer, "Yes?" hanging in midair with fearful anticipation of what might be coming next; I wasn't wrong.

"SP4 Vore was killed in action; his family requested you be his military escort home … I'm sorry son." I was crushed by the news of my best friend.

Rodney and I had flown together numerous times; this would be our last. I found a position of honor and saluted each time his casket was moved until his flag-draped coffin rested in place at then-Earle Little Funeral Home. At the foot of that casket, I stood honor guard in the semi-relaxed position of parade-rest; when his family entered the room, I snapped to attention.

Near the end of the mind-video I saw myself - after the funeral at Maybee's old Holy Ghost Lutheran Church - leading the march across the street to the cemetery, where I triangularly folded that flag and presented it to his mother just before we committed Rodney back to the dust from which he was formed. Burned in that memory was the deep, faraway look of heartbreak in her eyes as she took the flag and clutched it to her breast as she had done so many times with her little boy twenty some years ago.

That same look was in some of the eyes at the funeral home Friday night.

Rest in peace, Pfc. Miller. Thank you for your service to our great country. We're a bit torn apart right now by the very action in which you gave your all, but that in no way diminishes the honor you deserve.

Many rest comfortably under the warm blanket of freedom for which multitudes of our comrades gave their lives. I know it's difficult to climb from under that blanket and go out into the cold to try to rescue others, but you did that ... with courage and conviction.

"Greater love hath no man than this that a man lay down his life for his friends."

The Gospel writer John recorded these words of Jesus 2000 years ago, describing what He Himself would be doing for all of mankind in just a short time.

My simple, final, hand salute - to my dear friend Rodney 35 years ago and Friday night to a young man I never knew - was nothing compared to the honor of being described in similar fashion to The Name Above All Names!

But what do I know?

MY COLUMN: MY OPINION

NOVEMBER 29, 2004

"The more you stir it ... the more it stinks!" is a philosophical statement a friend shared years ago about an offensive-smelling by-product.

In spite of believing that, this stir is an attempt to douse the firestorm created with my election-eve "Communism" column. Specifically, to correct "facts" Mr. Lamb uses in recent letters to the editor; I have no desire to debase or injure him.

My column runs Mondays and most elections are on Tuesdays. Accusing The News of loading me into that slot for political purposes was a prejudicial political statement itself. I trust most would agree had my column instead endorsed Mr. Kerry, Mr. Lamb wouldn't have cried foul for fairness. Discernment, therefore, suggests this charge as simply embellishment-gasoline for a personal, political bonfire; I understand that.

I also admit anticipating "playing with fire" in sharing the concept that inspired me to write that column. How stupid would I be to call more than half of Monroe County - including a multitude of personal friends - communists? And that's why I didn't!

What I said was ... a friend suggested I visit the American Communist Party's Web site. There I found Bush-bashing and a platform promotion that virtually said "free health care for everybody, abortion on demand, marriage rights for gay and lesbians and yes to stem cell research."

I then went to the Democratic National Committee Web site where I found similar platform elements.

Finally, I started thinking about the 58,000 soldiers killed in the Vietnam War, the purpose of which was ... to stop the flow of Communism. I then wrote the column to paint the parallel of those facts. With trepidation, I even drew an undesired, philosophic parallel of my own thinking to "Tail Gunner" Joe McCarthy!

I called no one a Communist and I publicly apologize to Mr. Lamb and all who thought otherwise. What I did was express my pain at the direction of the political party I had most related to in my lifetime and implied that if they ever wanted me back, that direction would have to change. Many post-election summations acknowledged that voter philosophy.

I also wish to add, again, that although I have been asked numerous times to change the name of my column, I refuse because of what the name implies. While I truly believe what I write, I'm not implying I have the answers or I'm right about everything. Nobody is always right and the column's cognomen alludes to that.

After Mr. Lamb wrote with his opinion of mine and Ms. Elder objected, he rushed back with a second letter to defend and clarify his opinion and what he believes are the facts. Does anyone doubt he thinks he's right?

Everybody thinks he or she is right or wouldn't do what they do or say what they say; should I not have that same privilege? Whether you agree with me or not is irrelevant; it's just my opinion.

You should also know that I didn't ask for this job; The News offered to pay me to write an opinion column every week, not be a reporter to write facts. If you think I'm an idiot or are sick of hearing me talk about my faith (as many have written to allude), do yourself a favor and don't read the column!

Finally, hopefully, other than, "one thing I do: forgetting what lies behind and straining toward what is ahead," enough said.

But what do I know?

DAVID AND GOLIATH

DECEMBER 6, 2004

I don't know if David was breaking the speed limit or not but anyone who has ever been in a vehicle with him knows he likes to go fast. For the sake of his friendship with Sheriff Tillman Crutchfield, let's just say he was going with the flow of the traffic.

It was late, dark, and not much traffic was cruising south on I-75. David had both hands on the wheel and had joined his lovely Renee in joining Nat King Cole singing about roasting nuts on an open fire when it happened.

I expect Goliath gave a token check to his mirror and noticed David coming up fast in the lane beside him. Unfortunately for David, Goliath was also coming up fast on a vehicle in front of him. So, he did what Goliath usually does these days in situations like this ... he wheeled into David's lane without any concern whatsoever that David would have to slam on his brakes to avoid hitting him. Why he bothered to activate his left turn signal after the move was beyond David; perhaps it was a self-serving semblance of consideration.

King Cole continued his song solo while David checked his pants to make sure he hadn't had an accident while avoiding one.

Today, after pondering how Goliath has changed life for the expressway Davids of the world, I have decided I might as well risk getting another segment of my readers mad at me by sharing the fact that some truckers are driving me crazy!

Let me say that one of my problems with Goliaths is actually a welcomed barometer of a booming economy, in spite of the doom and gloom picture painted during the recent election. Most days 18-wheelers are choking the expressway, meaning merchandise - and money - is moving up and down the Detroit-Toledo corridor. I guess it's the way they're moving that bugs me.

For starters, living in lovely Luna Pier leaves little leeway for leaving the city, other than I-75. Toss into the mix that all Goliaths have to decelerate to tip the scales just north of the city and you have ingredients for an entering and exiting nightmare.

When I worked in Toledo I had the option at the end of the each day of slipping into the right lane three miles south of my exit and driving 55 until I got there, or taking my life in my hands by waiting until the last minute to find a bumper-to-bumper crevice to dive into just before the exit; the opposite was true for trying to get on.

Of course, many truckers are courteous drivers. I also know it's not easy maneuvering one of those Goliaths at 80 MPH.

I can't help feeling, however, that many are like the neighborhood bully, who, because of sheer size, make their driving moves with an attitude that says, "Yeah, what you gonna do about it?"

Unfortunately, there's not much David's can do about it.

However, at the risk of stirring up a new firestorm by saying something stupid like calling all truck drivers Communists, this David will simply load his sling with 550 smooth, small, stony words and let 'em fly, hoping to smack Goliath in the forehead to, if nothing more, at least make himself feel better.

But what do I know?

HE'S NOT GOING AWAY!

D E C E M B E R   1 3 ,   2 0 0 4

Say, do or think what you want, change names, traditions, the law, ban the symbols, even steal the baby, but He's not going away.

Recently I received a jolt while reading coverage of Monroe's wonderful Holiday Parade. Probably shouldn't have as it was just another harbinger for this point in America's existence. I don't even know if "jolt" is the proper word; let's just say I felt the water around this frog getting warmer.

Years ago I served on the Chamber of Commerce's Holiday Parade Committee. We had some great ones, highlighted by the year we featured the famous Philadelphia Mummers.

An idea I brought to the table was to create a "Christmas Kid of the Year" contest where local children would write to tell us why they - or someone they nominated - wanted the honor of riding in the parade with Santa.

Good friend and fellow committee member Dr. Lee Randall and I pored over entries, laughing, sometimes crying from the words of these little ones; it was a highly successful addition to the parade that is still in place today. Except, of course, for the harbinger.

The "jolt" I had received was from reading that - like the original "Christmas" Parade - the feature had fallen to the forces of political correctness and was now the "Holiday" Kid of the Year.

I have no idea when the name changed, but I know it's just the water heating up.

Years ago a TV commercial featured a hippie mowing grass around his VW bus home. He stops the mower and says, "Ah, the '60's, a time of agonizing reappraisal!"

On the doorstep of 2005, that's exactly where America is today. Who are we? What do we believe? Will we ever again believe collectively? I thought so, patriotically, after 9-11, but in the three short years since we have dramatically divided, if not splintered.

Agonizing reappraisal in my life included everything. I was raised in a Christian home and taught that Jesus was the Son of God. The Vietnam War introduced me to extreme opposites to my world, politically, economically, ethnically, spiritually, geographically, philosophically. It also introduced me to drugs and alcohol that did extreme makeovers on my thinking and allowed me to step out of reality for the duration of their influence.

Later, personal gifts of talent and character parlayed somewhat successful careers in music and management, making me money but little headway in my quest to find my place in this world.

And, as I've shared previously, just before giving it all away I called to The One - whose name we now labor to remove from our society - to save me and give my life some purpose; He did!

Agonizing reappraisal took me back to my starting point and I found my place in my equation of the hippie's bus ... the temporary home of planet Earth.

Last week someone stole the baby Jesus bolted to the floor of my church's Nativity Scene; another attempt to take Him out of Christmas. Whoever took him, we'd like him back, but it's obvious you need Him more than we do.

They tried getting rid of Him 2,004 years ago but it didn't work then either. So, call it what you will because it won't change the fact that Christmas is simply about the birth of Jesus Christ, the Savior of the world.

But what do I know?

A GIRL?

DECEMBER 20, 2004

The glint from the shiny, new blade mirrored the gleam in my eye and reflected mesmerizing displays of color from the tree lights. New-leather fragrance floated into my nostrils and I fingered the edge of the blade for sharpness.

Weeks before, I had noticed my name on that big package under the tree and had shaken it plenty trying to guess contents.

Moments before -- much to the dismay of mother, who painstakingly peeled paper off packages to press for another day - I ripped the wrapping to get at the goodies inside.

"Thanks mom and dad!" I whooped as I ran to hug the ones who had made Christmas Eve so wonderful with the new ice skates. I couldn't wait to try them out and as soon as all presents were opened, I bundled me up, laced them up and then crawled across the carpet, out the front door, across the lawn and the street to Mr. Miller's pond.

The "pond" was actually a small strip of standing water a soaking rain had left in our neighbor's yard. Earlier that day the temperature had tanked, creating - with perfect timing - an arena for my Christmas present.

It also was the first Christmas Eve without one of our family members present, as my brother, Hal, was at the hospital awaiting the arrival of his first child.

With hockey on the verge of becoming my favorite sport I struggled to stay steady on those steel blades.

Streetlight illumination gave me just enough against the darkness of night to stay on the frozen surface and off Mr. Miller's grass.

Suddenly a car came creeping around the corner; I recognized "The Big Shaker," the name my brother gave his '60 Chevy. My heart raced my skates to the road where Hal had stopped and was rolling down the window.

"We have a girl," he called, "we named her Deana Jo!"

My racing heart sputtered, then froze….a girl??? That 14 year-old heart, set on having a nephew to hunt, fish and play ball with, was crushed.

Needless to say, while she wasn't much into worms, she turned out to be a pretty good ball player herself, and now - 43 years later - we enjoy getting together to watch her 14 year old play sports.

It was one of the most special Christmas Eves ever as that night God sent our family one of the most precious gifts we have ever received. Deana Jo Smith is a highly successful engineer at Tenneco Automotive, and - more importantly - even more successful at the most important job on the planet … being a wonderful wife to Ric and that same nurturing matronly spirit I was blessed with to her children, Lindsay and Aric.

God is like that. He sends wonderful gifts to us all the time, which reminds me of why we celebrate Christmas in the first place … God's greatest Gift of all, Jesus!

And sometimes, like the kid who years later would get his front tooth knocked out playing hockey on those Christ-mas skates, we are disappointed when the gift isn't quite what we wanted.

But, like with the gift of Deana, He never makes mistakes, and sometimes it just takes time to realize how right He was and how perfect for us the Gift was … is!

But what do I know?

PERSPECTIVE OF PAIN

DECEMBER 27, 2004

There was no mercy as the knife plunged deep into my lower back about 4 inches above my left buttock .... or so it seemed. The pain took ... takes ... my breath away. I can't remember the last time I experienced such constant misery, yet, in spite of that and the many other problems of the last few weeks, this has been a great Christmas!

The slight tightness in my back seemed insignificant a few days before Christmas, then got progressively worse day by day until Christmas Eve morning when I could no longer take the pain and called one of my redeemers, Dr. Dennis Warner, for an adjustment. And, as always, I felt worse when I left his office than when I arrived, which is the nature of the beast: no pain, no gain.

The prescription: bed and ice.

All the great plans I had were dashed: I missed Christmas Eve service at church followed by presents and prime rib in the home of one of my favorite cooks, my sister, Janet. Worst of all, I spent Christmas Day at home alone in bed while my family witnessed the wide-eyed wonder of our beautiful grandson, Drake, enjoying his first Christmas.

And yet, in spite of it being so terrible, this was a wonderful Christmas!

As I lay in agony in the bed Christmas Eve, I thought about how one of my best friends was burying her brother that very afternoon. I thought about reading in that day's paper of how other friends of Renee's and mine (also grandparents) would be burying their granddaughter - who would never witness Christmas - in the next few days.

With the pain in my back so great I couldn't even move my legs, I thought about dear friends, Tom Cousino and Greg DuShane, both of whom are chained to wheelchairs and walkers for the rest of their lives.

I thought about how fortunate all who enjoy good health are and how we take that so for granted ... until, of course, that terrible fate strikes us!

Even though he was a wonderful humanitarian and left a great legacy, I don't expect Christopher Reeve was overly concerned about spinal cord injuries in his life until he had one himself and became paralyzed.

As I write this I dare not breathe deep or twist my body because when I do, that knife gets shoved in deeper. And, while Dr. Warner assures me he will have me back on my feet in the near future (as he has done many times before), for the moment my lower extremities are virtually useless and I can't imagine going the rest of my life in this condition.

And that's why I want you to know, that in spite of everything going wrong for me this Christmas, it has been wonderful! It's been good for me to be humbled and removed from the flow of fun one expects at this time of year; to have no choice but to sit and watch festivities proceed without me and to have that frightening fear of the possibility that this pain might persist and that I could be in this condition forever.

I consider it pure joy to suffer trials in my life that test my faith and develop perseverance in my quest to be mature and complete and not lacking in anything.

But what do I know?

DRAKE'S LETTER FROM SANTA

JANUARY 3, 2005

Dear Drake,

Well, I sure hope you enjoyed all the fun presents I left for you under your tree! You really didn't ask for much but you've been such a good boy I thought you deserved a nice little haul of goodies.

I must tell you how much I appreciated your visit with me at the mall. Some of the children were scared of me, not you! You sat on my lap and checked me out big time.

When you stuck your elbow up on my chest and said, "We need to talk," I thought I would lose it. Then when your mom kept asking you to look at the camera for a picture and you said, "Uh, mom, me 'n' Santa got some serious stuff to talk about," I knew you weren't just another kid.

By the way, thanks for your concern but I didn't burn my butt coming down your chimney. And don't worry as I finally got the frames of my glasses straightened out after you had your fun with them. Also, I sure didn't mean to scare you when I yelped after you yanked my beard. As you found out, it's the real thing.

Say, your dad didn't put you up to that, did he? I have some leftover coal for him for next year if he did! But, I know you wouldn't squeal on him 'cause it was easy to see that you two are buds!

By the way, loved your matching caps and sweaters; bet your mom picked those out for "her men," eh? It was obvious your mom and dad love you, little buddy! Unfortunately, there are lots of kids in the world that never get that kind of love. You're one of the lucky ones, and you be sure to let your mom and dad know how much you appreciate the way they love and take care of you, ok?

So, did you enjoy your first Christmas? After I ate the milk and cookies you left for me - that was thoughtful, thanks - I unloaded your presents and then sat down for a rest. Your cat - Gizmo, I think he said his name was - came and sat on my lap for a while. (Got hair all over my red suit!) Nice cat though and he thinks you're pretty cool, too.

But, then he told me the exciting news ... first, that New Year's Day you would be 1 year old! Happy birthday! Also, that you're gonna have a little brother or sister come spring! I'll bet you're excited about that! And of course that means I'll have to get busy and make twice as many toys for your house next year!

Say, I was checking out some of the other presents you got from your family and friends. Like I said, you're lucky, Drake; so many people love you. I liked that new children's Bible your poppy got for you ... have Mom and Dad read those stories to you; take it from me ... good stuff!

Gotta go. Be a good boy and I'll see you next year!

Your pal,

Santa

P.S. Make sure your poppy lets you play with that remote control car he bought you. Sometimes I think grandfathers buy things for their grandsons that they really want to play with themselves.

But what do I know?

HAPPY BIRTHDAY RODNEY

J A N U A R Y 1 0 , 2 0 0 5

Dear Rodney,

Hi bud, thinkin' 'bout you today. Then again, I never let Jan. 10 pass without thinking about you.

Forgive me for sharing this letter; I'm a columnist now with the paper that used to write sports stories about you and your brothers when you ran track and cross country at Monroe High. All you Vore brothers were legendary runners. Say, do people jog in Heaven? If so, I'm sure you're one of 'em 'cause you sure loved to run!

It's hard to believe 37 years ago today we chipped ice off that bus window to wave goodbye to our parents crying and waving goodbye to us from the street. Similar goodbyes are happening today, but instead of Vietnam, it's Iraq; I expect you've already met some of those soldiers!

I was thinking about basic training at Fort Knox when they showed us the film about becoming Airborne Rangers? You were the one who said, "That's us, c'mon!" when the film ended and we went to the front of the auditorium and signed up. I had no idea we'd be running 20 miles each day, including five before breakfast, which was a piece of cake for you. Remember how I sang cadence? Every time I checked on you you'd flash that grin I miss so much.

Speaking of basic, remember Lenny Stovall, your squad leader? He contacted me recently and we've stayed in touch. I sent him pictures of us clowning in the barracks. He said he still feels guilty; he picked you for assignments because you were so easy-going you never got mad at him. He misses you, too, and we're getting together soon.

I also got an e-mail from Nancy - the girl you kept talking about - thanking me for regularly writing about you. I think she was kind of shocked as she didn't know you were sweet on her. She's married with kids now; sorry you never got to know any of that.

I'm sorrier we got separated after Chu Lai. All our time together nobody messed with you 'cause they knew they'd have to take us both on! I keep thinking had we been able to stay together I could have protected you somehow.

I sang for a funeral at your church a while back. After the service I went across the street and visited your grave; the sky wept that day, too. I try to go there each Memorial Day. A few years back your

Dear Friend, Rodney Vore, KIA Vietnam, 1969.

brother Joel was driving by and saw me standing at your grave. He stopped and we talked about you.

I miss you buddy. I'm sorry you've missed all the fun I've had during these 37 years. The book I believe tells me no man has seen or heard of the joy that awaits the one who trusts in God and makes it to Heaven; perhaps I'm the one missing the good time, eh?

Gotta go, Rod … runnin' out of space. I'll never forget you, and as long as I'm alive, those around me won't either; I won't let 'em!

One more thing: Happy Birthday! I love you buddy!

P.S. Speaking of space, save one for me as I'll be there with you again one of these days. Lots of people down here now don't believe in Heaven. Know what I say to that?

But what do they know!

NOBLE CHARACTER

J A N U A R Y 1 7 , 2 0 0 5

"Carla" was tattooed to her right bicep. Skin-tight spandex "enhanced" about 250 pounds packed on her five-foot-frame. Mousse was the obvious product she used to stand three separate tufts of short-cropped hair straight up on top of her head. She reminded me of a rooster on steroids as she strutted by our table.

I muzzled my urge to burst into laughter and looked at my wife who gave me "that look" and said, "If I ever ... shoot me!"

A few moments later a tall, skinny white guy - who obviously had never heard of sun block - strolled by with lady-friend in tow. Obviously enticed by one of the many native Nassau women who make their living braiding hair into tiny cornrows made famous by Bo Derek in the movie, "10," she was beautiful with hair impeccably done. Unfortunately, he too had been enticed, and the tiny, colored beads dangling from the ends of two-inch braids sprouting from all over his head gave him the look of a court jester. Again I choked hysteria as Renee shared sternly, "If you ever...I'll shoot you!"

We love to people-watch, and some of the best places to do that is in airports or on cruise ships. As I pondered these two incidents I realized that in spite of how I try not to be judgmental of others, I am ... and so are you!

Either of those two could have been the most kind, wonderful human beings on the planet; just because they choose to dress or follow a custom different from mine doesn't - and shouldn't - demean their character.

What an important word character is - or should be - to our world. It has been said that your character is defined by how you act when nobody is watching. In other words, who you really are as opposed to who you want others to think you are.

Webster defines it as "one of the attributes or features that make up and distinguish an individual; mental and ethical traits marking and individualizing a person."

The word "noble" is the glove for character's hand, which Webster, again, defines as "possessing, characterized by, or arising from superiority of mind or character or of ideals or morals."

Kevin Costner, in his movie "Robin Hood," states, "Nobility is not a birth right; it is defined by one's character." I love that! Neither your position - in life or on the social ladder - nor the amount of money you have will buy noble character traits; those come from choices you make in life. However, if you are of noble character, you are indeed a rich person and our world desperately needs you.

The prophet we honor with today's national holiday dreamed that our "children will one day live in a nation where they will not be judged by the color of their skin but by the content of their... character."

Renee tells me I am a great judge of character, yet I recently suffered inner circle defection by one who for three years completely fooled me into thinking they were of noble character. How disappointing ... for them!

I would rather be a pauper with noble character than the richest man or highest-ranking king ... who has no class or character. Also, those who judge others by the color of their skin or who turn out to be wolves in sheep's clothing obviously, foolishly, have no fear of the Biblical truth that one always reaps what one sows.

But what do I know?

FORGIVENESS

J A N U R A R Y   2 1 ,   2 0 0 5

It was interesting to observe the media coverage this past weekend as Vietnam celebrated the 30th anniversary of winning what we call the Vietnam War and what they call the American War.

Sometimes it's hard to believe it's actually been 36 years since I returned from that nightmare; other times it seems like it's been a couple of lifetimes, and still other times it's almost as if it was just a dream. I can't even imagine myself today as I was then. Time changes everything.

I remember hating the Vietnamese, mainly because we soldiers couldn't tell the difference between a South Vietnamese and a Viet Cong or North Vietnamese Army regular, so it was easy to just hate them all. Often we would find one - who we thought was from the south - dead in the concertina wire surrounding our base camp the next morning after a firefight.

The only thing I was concerned with was getting out of the country alive and returning home to my loved ones.

But, as I said, time changes everything, and now, all these years later, I belong to a group called the DOVE Fund, which stands for Development of Vietnam Endeavors. In the five years since our inception, we have raised more than $500,000 and with that money have built numerous schools and hospitals, dug more than 300 fresh water wells and started a micro-finance project for the poor women of Quang Tri Province.

In 2001, along with a contingency of that group, I returned to Vietnam to dedicate some of those facilities; I have since written a book about that trip called "The Ghost Closet," which this newspaper's owner, the Monroe Publishing Co., plans to publish later this year with all proceeds going to build a special school there.

During that trip I found the Vietnamese people to be some of the friendliest on the planet. I thought they would hate me; instead, they treated me like a king. One of the most important things I have ever done in my life was making that trip as a cleansing took place within my heart.

The weekend's television coverage had a couple other interesting items that got me thinking about ... forgiveness.

First was the "Runaway Bride" who got cold feet and concocted the story about being kidnapped. I wondered if her fiancé and families would forgive her. I wondered if the general public would forgive her.

Next was coverage of the Vietnam veteran who spit tobacco juice in the face of actress and Vietnam War activist Jane Fonda. I wondered if Vietnam vets would ever forgive her for fraternizing with the enemy as she did in the '60's, an action that would have gotten her shot for treason 100 years ago.

I thought of all the stuff I've done in my life for which I am not proud all these years later. Each instance that I believed I had wronged someone personally, I returned and asked for forgiveness; I have a few remaining. That attitude began when I went before God and asked Him to forgive me, which changed my life.

Forgiveness actually benefits the forgiver more than the forgivee. In "The Heart of the Matter," Don Henley wrote, "You keep carrying that anger ... it'll eat you up inside!" He's right and the way to purge that anger is to be more forgiving of one another.

But what do I know?

A TIGER WITH INTEGRITY

J A N U R A R Y   2 4 ,   2 0 0 5

One by one they all read it for me...Alan Trammel, Dan Petry, Lance Parrish, Sparky Anderson, and even the jerk...Jack Morris. All except him, that is. He wouldn't do it.

In for only a maintenance chiropractic adjustment and only after Dr. Warner had shared with me that he had enjoyed last week's column on "character" did the subject turn to "integrity," which made me think of him.

In a flash I thought of how we had at least one common trait: in spite of each of us - certainly him - having funds enough to buy new ones, we both rejected them and passionately held on to our old, ripped, ratty, ragged baseball gloves. While I was marginal at best with mine, he was a wizard with his!

I remembered all the times I'd watch him drift back near the 440 sign in center at Michigan and Trumbull, never taking his eyes off the ball, and then at the last second, somewhat similar to Willie Mays' "bread basket" style, side-catch the ball and nonchalantly whip it back into the infield.

No flash or flamboyance, no outrageous style or behavior...unless you considered head-first slides into first base and the bread-basket-catches. Otherwise, he gave plain and simple fundamental skills; blue collar, go-to-work-and-do-your-job baseball, every day!

"Remember Chet Lemon?" I asked the Doc and shared this story after his positive reply.

I was general manager of Monroe's Tower 98 radio station. Every late-winter the Detroit Tigers would conduct a press tour to promote their upcoming baseball season. They would pick a handful of current stars, load them on a bus with the managers and then make them available for interviews during tour stops in the southeastern Michigan/northern Ohio areas; I would take my sports director and attend the stop in Toledo.

I was at the height of a pretty wild and crazy time in my life and, while not corrupt by any means, I was not overly concerned with character traits like…integrity. He was!

I would take advantage of the promotional opportunities the tour presented by preparing a written statement in advance. Then, one by one I would approach each Tiger star, stick a microphone in his face and ask him to read the statement that would sound like this: "Hello, this is Alan Trammel, and whenever I'm in Monroe or Toledo I always listen to 98.3, WTWR…Tower 98!"

Like I said, they all did it…all except Chet.

I introduced myself, explained my request and waited while he read the statement in his mind, after which he looked at me and said, "I can't do this."

"Why not?" I asked.

"Because I don't listen to your station," he continued. "In fact, I've never even heard of your station!"

In an understandable effort to grease the wheels of the vehicle that carried their industry, all the others read the statement with no thoughts whatsoever as to whether or not there was any truth involved. All except Chet, that is.

Author Charles Caleb Colton wrote, "Nothing more completely baffles one who is full of tricks and duplicity than straight forward and simple integrity in another."

Chet baffled me that day by refusing my request and by simply being a man of integrity. I didn't think it was a big deal at the time, but since Christ has changed my life, I do now.

But what do I know?

FOLDED SOCKS

JANUARY 31, 2005

It was the socks that got me going. I had gone through my usual morning routine ... prayer, devotion, treadmill, shower, shave, teeth, hair ... socks.

I sat on the side of the bed, crossed my leg and massaged my foot with some icky stuff old men like me have to use to keep their feet from cracking and falling off, I guess.

I then grabbed the socks I had earlier pulled from the drawer and tossed on the bed in preparation for this moment.

This is normally no big deal as I simply pull them apart, cram my toes in the opening, pull 'em over the heel and then up over my calf. This day was different. Perhaps I noticed them because I didn't work until later and wasn't in a panic to get ready and race off as normal. What I noticed was ... the way they were folded!

This might sound crazy, but I sat there and marveled at how neatly they had been folded. They don't look like that by dragging them out of the dryer, matching tops together and simply folding them over so they stay paired. The time obviously taken to fold them was what had hooked me, and although this too sounds crazy, I took them apart and tried to re-fold them in the same manner my wonderful wife, Renee, had done but couldn't get them to look as neat as she had made them.

Why am I going on about this? I'll tell you.

Last Thursday morning's news covered the tragic train wreck in California where some idiot wanted to commit suicide by parking his SUV on the tracks but chickened out at the last minute, causing a wreck that killed 10 people.

That coverage included the rescue of a man pinned in the wreckage who was bleeding to death. Believing he was not going to make it out alive, on the wall of the trashed train - and in his own blood - he scrawled, "I love Lil." Lil was his wife, and in place of the "word" love he had drawn a heart. Beneath it he had written and drawn the same, only in place of "Lil" he had written, "my kids."

I don't know about you but for me, each day we have no assurance when we leave home in the morning that we will ever see our loved ones again. That's why I always stand in the window waving goodbye to my Renee until she's out of sight; if it's the last time she sees me, I want her to always remember my great love for her and have that last image of me waving from the window. I appreciate so very much the constant love, dedication, consideration, understanding and support I get from the one to whom God chose to give my rib.

With what little he thought he had left, that man poured out in his own blood his great love for his loved ones. Not long after I noticed the obvious love rendered by my mate in taking time to meticulously fold my socks.

Like me, I hope you take time to tell those you love that you love them and appreciate all the things they do to make your world more wonderful ... especially the little things, like ... folding your socks!

But what do I know?

IT WILL ALWAYS BE ABOUT LOVE

FEBRUARY 14, 2005

In conjunction with Valentine's Day, it will always be about love! Concerned over what would be the quality of the sound generated by local coverage of the St. Michael's We Care telethon several years ago, I turned the TV to the local channel and began to watch.

When the screen came on, the spectacled face of Major League Baseball's last 30-game winner was staring at me, introducing the next act about to take the stage in my old high school auditorium, now Monroe Junior High School.

To this day I've never figured out whether Denny McLain was paying personal penance or if he was ordered there by the court for his criminal conduct during the years since the rawhide - and the fire - came off his fastball. Either way, love him or hate him, he gave great recognition to this important annual fundraising telethon that has gone unmatched since.

I cringed as the group began to play and sing; the sound was horrible! Every singer knows that even if you were the best singer in the world, if the system projecting you is terrible, you sound terrible!

I had agreed - after being asked by two of the telethon's founding members, dear friends Hank and Betty Jo Steinman - to sing a couple of songs for that year's production. After hearing the sound I wondered why I had done so.

Sitting there dejected and depressed less than a year beyond a painful divorce, McLain later caught my attention as he called for his stage production manager. Onto my TV screen came this stunning woman; I was taken by her.

"Hmm," I thought. "Maybe this won't be so bad after all!"

Later that evening after performing, I was a bit embarrassed by my earlier attitude. I had been worried about how I was going to sound to others and had not been thinking about why I was there. Suddenly I was surrounded by numerous children in various forms of distress, most in wheelchairs or the arms of parents with drawn faces; I was moved to get involved that evening of the early 1990s.

A week from Saturday (Feb. 26), Gary (Daddy G. Knight) Vancena and I once again will open and emcee the telethon on your local cable channel from noon until 2 p.m. and then close it from 10 p.m. until midnight with tons of celebrities and entertainers in between. I'll also torture you at 9 p.m. with a couple of songs.

We'll all be there raising money to help erase those drawn faces of those kid's parents, and - more important - give those kids the chance to be able to run and jump and have fun and know life outside the prisons of leg braces, oxygen tanks and wheelchairs; I hope you'll help us!

Like I said, the telethon will always be about love. All love comes from God and He has given those of us blessed with good health and faculties the responsibility of making a difference in the lives of those less fortunate around us. He also gave me something wonderful the night of my first telethon.

Last night, candlelight illuminated the gorgeous face of my valentine over dinner ... the same beautiful face of the stunning woman introduced to me on my TV by Denny McLain all those years ago.

See? God always blesses those who reach out to help others, and He blessed me with the most wonderful woman on the planet!

But what do I know?

APPRECIATING AMERICA'S PRESIDENTS

FEBRUARY 21, 2005

As we honor American presidents today I think about the 11 who served during my lifetime. While Harry Truman was president when I was born, the first president I remember was Dwight D. Eisenhower. "Ike's" vice president was Richard Nixon, whom everybody mistakenly assumed would win the next election against the brash Irish Catholic, John Kennedy.

Kennedy made one of the most critical decisions in American history by invoking the Monroe Doctrine and backed it with a naval blockade to repel Russian ships carrying missiles to Cuba. How sad infidelity would tarnish his great legacy. Assassination would cause him to become a greater president in death than he was in life.

I didn't much care for his successor, Lyndon Johnson, in spite of his ushering in civil rights. He epitomized the "good old boy" syndrome and was a classic, "tell 'em what they want to hear" politician. I expect my distaste for him related to his Vietnam War politics, which affected my life as one of his infantry soldiers.

Nixon was an enigma; I could never figure how a vice president could lose the presidency, then the California governor's race, and then come back to win the highest office in the land.

Based on his campaign vow that "anyone who can't end this war in four years doesn't deserve to be president," Nixon wouldn't deserve victory when he succeeded Johnson in '68. Four years later - on the doorstep of the greatest landslide victory in presidential history - so paranoid was he about losing that he committed the colossal political blunder by allowing the 10-cent Watergate burglary to crash his house of cards.

His successor, Gerald Ford, will always be an insignificant president who inherited the Oval Office by agreeing to do one thing: pardon Nixon.

Watergate affected a third president as Jimmy Carter's election was compliments of the scandal. I loved him joining hands of an Arab - Egyptian President Sadat - and a Jew - Israeli Prime Minister Begin - and negotiating them to say, "Shalom" to each other. Months later Sadat lay in a pool of his own blood, murdered by the same faction as today who have no desire for peace but only want their way in the world. Carter's failure to respond militarily to end the Iran hostage crisis torpedoed his presidency and propagated Islamic militancy into the monster it is today.

The threat of "a new sheriff in town" was enough to get the hostages released by Ronald Reagan's Inauguration Day and he too would become a presidential icon by demanding that Gorbachev "tear down this wall!"

George Bush alienated me by trashing Reagan's "voodoo economics" one day, then endorsing them the next when named his vice president, then flip-flopping with his famous, "Read my lips" promise not to raise taxes … before raising taxes!

I liked Bill Clinton playing saxophone and trying to be a people's president, but, like his idol, infidelity trashed his character and legacy.

I admit not liking George W. Bush at first as he seems a bit smug and pompous. What won me over was the familiar, relatable story of how Christ had dramatically changed his life.

While no president will please all the people or be right all the time, I appreciate those who make decisions and take responsibility for their actions, epitomized by the famous quote from the president I never knew who said, "The buck stops here!"

But what do I know?

ANACONDA

FEBRUARY 28, 2005

Even though we had the powerful 60-foot anaconda by the head, it tossed us about as if we were mere matchstick men, or so it seemed.

Minutes before we had been celebrating dedication of the new multi-million dollar control room of the City of Luna Pier's patriarch business, Consumers Energy, followed by a tour of the south-county plant.

We were enjoying the spectacular view from the roof when the call came.

"I'm sorry, we've gotta go!" I told our guide and chased "Mr. Emergency," Luna Pier Mayor and Fire Chief Jerry Welton, back down through the belly of the plant.

With the chief's fire-engine-red pickup truck's emergency lights flashing and siren wailing for people to get out of the way, we raced north on I-75 for Luna Pier.

Chief Welton begged his radio for information; Central Dispatch replied: Fire at Luna Pier Housing Complex!

The chief groaned as he identified smoke in the distance and began barking commands into the handset. We arrived to find flames flaring out a second floor window and licking at the roof.

Police Chief Jerry Winkelman, also doing double duty, wheeled the city's fire truck onto the scene and began programming the complex machine to spit tons of water onto the dragon threatening the homes and lives of our citizens.

I watched the dead snake uncoil as Mayor Welton, still in dress clothes, grabbed it and raced to the fire.

Suddenly the snake came alive as a powerful surge of water pumped life into its body and the mayor wrestled for control as water gushed from its mouth.

"I need help!" he screamed over the roar of the flames and the revving truck. I turned to see who he was calling; there was no one there but me.

I raced in and grabbed the neck of the writhing snake, allowing the chief to control the blast of water into the face of the dragon. Now and again the snake would twist us and deflect the spray, hitting the siding and soaking us instead of the fire.

Soon our real firefighters - dressed for the occasion - arrived and relieved me. One climbed a ladder and stuck the head of the snake - and his oxygen-masked face - into the flaming window to deliver a knockout punch to the monster bent on destroying this abode.

The trucks of faithful backup firefighters from Erie and LaSalle howled into the parking lot. On the sidelines, soaked and shivering, I marveled at the courage of these public servants as they executed their training to control - and kill - the fire-breathing dragon that on this day would not only destroy the abode, but take with it the life of the sweet, dear lady who lived there.

Later, lifeless and limp on the lawn lay the snake awaiting an exhausted fireman's tired muscles to recoil it back into its lair for another day when its powerful dance will again be needed to douse the dragon.

I have great admiration and respect for those who - at a moment's notice - put their lives on the line to fearlessly face the dragon we all pray never visits our homes. What an honor it was to share a slivered association with this brotherhood who receive far too little pay or appreciation for the regular sacrifices they make!

But what do I know?

AMAZED AT CHILD BIRTH

MARCH 7, 2005

She extended her right hand to me and commanded, "Kelly!"

In my mind I can still see the brown latex gloves we special-ordered for her as regular ones irritated her skin.

"Kelly!" she barked again, this time more adamantly.

I was lost in the space of amazement. The most incredible thing I had ever seen in my life had just happened right before my very eyes and I was paralyzed; her patience was running thin.

"Tom," she called sternly but gently from behind the mask covering her nose and mouth, "I know this is pretty incredible for you but we must move fast for the mother."

She turned to look at me.

Dr. Jean Golden's pair of eyes peered out at me simultaneously with seriousness of purpose yet compassionate understanding before calling one more time for the Kelly Clamp she would use to block the umbilical cord flow from the young mother on the table in front of us to the brand new baby she had just rescued via Cesarean birth.

The "scrub nurse" in Mercy-Memorial Hospital's operating room was witnessing the miracle of childbirth for the first time in the fall of 1966. The time warp and emotional roller coaster - from the shock of seeing surgical "C-section" trauma to witnessing the wonder of the arrival of the world's newest citizen - was a bit much for one waiting to exit his teens.

Dr. Golden was always kind and gentle and took her time to explain each procedure to me when time afforded.

As I remember, Surital was the drug administered by the anesthetist and we had only minutes from the moment the mother was "under" enough to operate to retrieve the baby and clamp the cord before the drug ran through to the child, the consequences of which would have proved fatal.

Once mom and baby were both safely in recovery, I remember apologizing to the good doctor for allowing myself to be distracted and her laughing over my wide-eyed wonder.

The sophomore had seen the job posted on the bulletin board at Monroe County Community College, applied, was hired and immediately began on-the-job training. The first thing to learn was the name and function of each instrument ... like the Kelly Clamp.

Of all the jobs I've held during my lifetime, this was a classic! I became good friends with the surgeons and was intrigued by the different styles and attitudes of each.

Nothing, however, had prepared me for the trauma of not only watching, but assisting as the surgeon would slice a patient open to examine, excise or repair whatever ailed them.

My supervisor, Mrs. Ong, tolerated no nonsense. I remember her instructing me to lean against the wall of the OR as I became queasy watching my first operation.

"We're not hurting them, Tom;" she instructed, "we're helping them!"

She was right, and once I adjusted my attitude, not only was I fine from then on but found the job fascinating and rewarding. Gall stones intrigued me most; some were the ugliest things you've ever seen; others were absolutely gorgeous!

I wish I would have memorized the name of that Caesarean baby who would now be almost 40. How cool it would be to visit and share the moment of their first breath ... as well as the warm scolding I got from Dr. Golden as I marveled at their birth!

But what do I know?

RESPECT

M A R C H   1 4 ,   2 0 0 5

To the lady in the green Mustang ... thank you! You were the only one who cared, which, of course, was a harbinger for life in America.

Wanting to be sure about you, I kept my eye in the rear-view mirror as I drove south on Dixie Hwy., watching for the snaking processional tail to pass you. Sure enough, when it did, you pulled back onto the highway and continued on your way. You are a dying breed, girl!

My eyes went back to the taillights of the vehicle in front of me while my mind went further south to the foothills of Tennessee's Cumberland Mountains. The procession carrying my father's family's final sibling left the funeral home and headed "down the valley" to her body's final resting place, the Red Hill Baptist Church Cemetery. It was then I really started noticing it.

Fifty yards out in a field mowing grass, a farmer in faded-blue bibbed overalls stopped his tractor, climbed down, took a position of reverence beside it and pulled the sweat-stained cap from his head and placed it over his heart.

Around the next bend a husband and wife raking in their front yard stopped their work and stood with heads bowed reverently as the procession passed.

Cars coming in the opposite direction slowed, steered onto the shoulder and waited until we were by them before proceeding, just as the lady in the green Mustang had done last week.

The spirit of my aunt, Mabel Revels, had passed from this life and we were carrying what I call her "rental property" to the Roselawn Memorial Park cemetery for the final stage of "ashes to ashes and dust to dust."

Ms. Green Mustang was already at the side of the road when my section of the snake passed her; curiosity kept me watching to see if she had car trouble or was one of the few who still have respect and reverence for funeral processions.

Respect and reverence - for the dead, for life, for the elderly, for parents, for the unborn - fades further into obscurity with each passing day. The command to "Love one another" seems to only be relevant if somehow it benefits the "me" in us.

Some years ago I visually chastised a young man cutting into a funeral line; he threw up his hands as if to say, "what?" With no idea whatsoever why I was upset he then gave me a visual gesture to tell this old man what I could do with my concern.

Young parents, it starts with you! I can only relate to my own father, who, unfortunately, in today's world would have long ago been in jail for child abuse as he certainly believed in the biblical principle of "Spare the rod and spoil the child!"

If you've been reading me for a while you'll remember stories of him washing my mouth with soap for a swear word and marching me by my ear to apologize to the store owner for stealing a candy bar.

Respect for others doesn't just fly in through the window one day; it has to be taught, one way or the other. Parents trying to figure where their kids went wrong should start by looking in the mirror; I expect the parents of Ms. Green Mustang would like what they see.

But what do I know?

SCHIAVO CASE CAUSE FOR OUTRAGE

MARCH 21, 2005

I'm sure his face was all lit up as he stood at the altar and waited for her triumphal entry. One could almost imagine palm branches strewn in her path instead of the special rolled-out carpet of white.

People may have lined the sides of that entryway and craned their necks to get a view of the most important person of the hour. Their smiles likely stretched ear-to-ear as they mouthed words of approval and wonder at her beauty as she passed them by.

She was a beauty and he probably beheld her in his eyes and heart as he waited at the altar. I don't expect there was anyone there with the slightest notion that the day would come when he would crucify her in such barbaric fashion.

The Terri Schiavo case has created such a stir in America that even as I write this the United States Congress is in unprecedented special session searching for a solution to this tragic situation.

As it is with abortion, the issue is about whether or not one who has a voice and is semi or fully responsible for another whom has no voice has the right to make a decision to end that life.

With deference to those who - also tragically - have had to sit at loved ones' bedsides and suffer through their suffering - such as my wonderful wife with her dying mother - I am of the opinion that the only one who has the right to take a life ... is the Giver of Life, no matter what the circumstance.

In this case, however, I am outraged by what is happening and, specifically, by many of the facts.

I am outraged that her husband, who may have vowed to that Giver of Life to love his bride "for better or worse and in sickness and in health," has abandoned that bride like a bag of unwanted trash, ala Scott Peterson.

I'm outraged that he melted down her wedding rings to make

jewelry for himself; that he wouldn't allow a priest to administer last rites when he initially had her feeding tube removed in 2003; that he uses the $1.5 million malpractice settlement designated for her rehabilitation instead for legal fees in his fight to legally kill her, and that Judge Greer has allowed it!

I'm outraged this louche has since fathered two children with another woman and that after all this questionable, nefarious behavior, Greer continues to see no conflict of interest in him being Terri's guardian.

Greer says he's upholding the law, but does anyone believe that if the judge's son fell and broke his neck the judge would drive the speed limit on his way to the hospital?

Michael Schiavo, Scott Peterson, John Couey - and especially Greer - are making me embarrassed to be an American.

If you did to a dog what Greer has allowed Michael Schiavo to do to Terri you'd be fined $5,000 and sent to prison. How quaint that it was Hitler who started this movement by killing mentally and developmentally disabled people.

America continues down the slippery slope as "rights" trump "right" and we stand by and watch the guilty protected and the innocent condemned, just like that day 2,005 years ago we Christians will remember this Friday.

But what do I know?

THE GREAT DIVIDE

MARCH 28, 2005

Might the mighty Mississippi become the great divide? The small stream that begins in Minnesota widens as it cuts north to south through the heart of America to points where it's hard to even see across to the other side.

Yesterday Christians celebrated what we believe will be the fate of all who know and trust Jesus Christ as Savior: resurrection to life after death. Non-believers think that's a fairy tale that gets more ridiculous to fathom with each passing day. They scoff at the thought of Him being who He says He is because they've never met Him, and, as a result, don't believe in Him.

As Christians focused last weekend on The One crucified on the middle cross, I found myself thinking about the ones crucified on each side of Jesus. One mocked Him while the other, recognizing not only his guilt but Jesus' innocence, chastised the mocker and then asked Jesus for forgiveness.

It hit me that in the last 2,000 years, hair, clothing and lifestyles have changed but philosophically, not much else.

Each day I get more concerned about the split down America's middle that continues to widen. The Vietnam War began that split for me, followed by out-of-control government personified by Watergate. Other polarizing issues followed, such as abortion, women's lib, gay and lesbian lifestyles, etc.

Presidential elections used to be opposing sides that united once one won the contest; the Bush/Gore debacle changed that methodology. The attack of 9-11 temporarily reunited us but Iraq divided us and November's election re-erected a philosophical Great Wall of China between us.

Terri Schiavo unknowingly polarized us again last week with right-to-lifers combating right-to-diers while others - like this author - were looking past the distraction at one who could possibly be setting a precedent for legalized murder.

For the record, neither my wife nor I want to be kept alive via legitimate life support should we become brain dead (which neither of us believe is the case with Ms. Schiavo). And, unless there is legal proof of those wishes, another's word - regardless of relationship - should never be trusted simply because of the potential evil that lies within every man's heart.

If you celebrated Christ's resurrection yesterday then you know He allowed His crucifixion in order "to be the propitiation for our sins." In other words, God - who we believe created us - bought us back with the life of His Son, which tells me that I am not my own; I belong to Him. Therefore He decides when life ends, not me.

Please ... I'm not trying to impose my will on you! The joy of living in America is freedom to believe as you choose. And, while I realize we must have laws guaranteeing rights, sometimes they must be overridden or changed for the sake of doing what's right, and I don't care if every judge in the country says it's legal ... dehydrating and starving anyone to death is not only not right, it's barbaric!

So, the innocent Terri Schiavo hangs on her cross waiting to die while the rest of us hang on ours beside her and trade barbs back and forth as to our beliefs. Perhaps one day we will physically split our country down the middle and give the west to the liberals and the east to the conservatives and let the mighty Mississippi control the great divide.

But what do I know?

CONTENT IN ANY SITUATION?

APRIL 4, 2005

"Excuse me," said the gentleman who had walked up to me, "are you the writer?"

Startled at being asked this question because of where we were, I responded with, "Pardon me?"

He repeated his question, "Are you the writer ... from Monroe!"

I was taken aback considering that Renee and I were two of thousands of people in the Atlanta airport last Thursday.

On March 28 I had surprised her with an anniversary card that said, "Clear your schedule and pack your bloomers ... we leave Thursday for Cancun!"

Both burned out from the long, cold, gray, drab, freezing, depressing, snowy, icy (did I say depressing?) winter, I figured she needed the break and I needed refreshment to stimulate my writing so I searched the Internet until I found one we could afford.

A 7 a.m. flight had us up at 3:30 a.m. for showers, final packing and negotiation of I-75's orange barrel express en route to Detroit Metro.

Belted in our seats on the tarmac with engines humming and sunshine streaming through portholes of the plane, we groaned when the captain shared that Atlanta's severe weather would keep us grounded. Two hours later, cramped and cranky, we finally rocketed into the sky for the Georgian Cancun connection.

"My wife recognized you," the gentleman continued and gestured toward the smiling lady in the wheelchair nearby. I looked her way and she began to beam. I didn't recognize either of them and wondered if they had me confused with another writer.

"I love your column; you bless my heart," she called from the ticket counter line before adding, "But what do I know?"

Suddenly there was no doubt they had the right writer.

"We're from Rockwood and we read you every Monday," she continued.

I couldn't believe that so far from home and in the middle of a multitude, someone recognized my mug from the paper.

"You should write your column about this," Renee chimed in.

And, while it was certainly a good place to start, I couldn't possibly omit the comedy of errors that followed.

That two-hour delay caused us to miss our connecting flight, leaving us a choice of an overnight wait in the airport or a five-hour wait for a flight to Mexico City - which we chose - where we could catch a connecting flight for - finally - Cancun.

I was wishing I had taken Spanish in high school as, of course, nobody in the Mexico City airport spoke English except a young woman who directed us to our gate, which - after another hour wait - turned out to be the wrong one.

We definitely need more exercise as our midnight run from one end of the airport to the other left us wheezing and gasping for air.

Two hours after our third seat-buckling that day we landed in Cancun, only to be rewarded with ... no luggage!

At this point even the $40 cab ride to our hotel didn't hurt too bad as all we wanted was to get to our room, which, unbelievably, was ready and waiting.

Unfortunately we didn't get our luggage until two days later, which meant we sat in the hotel room watching TV the first two days of vacation ... that is ... until the cable went out!

I think it was the Apostle Paul who said, "I have learned to be content in any situation," which means he never had to fly on Delta Air Lines.

But what do I know?

ATTITUDE

A P R I L   1 1 ,   2 0 0 5

"Houston, we have a problem!"

I remembered those historic words last week as I sat in a business meeting and heard the facilitator say, "In every crisis there is an equal opportunity." I scribbled it down so I wouldn't forget it and have mulled it since.

Eventually, everyone has crisis in their lives. Pastor and author Chuck Swindoll's theory is that there is nothing you can do about what happens to you, but there is something you can do about how you react to what happens, and it's all in your attitude.

When crises come, most people get lost in personal pity-parties and "Woe is me" attitudes and miss those equal opportunities that are also presented.

Perhaps no finer paradigm exists than an event that began 35 years ago today: the great failure and success of Apollo 13, launched - strangely enough - at 1313 hours on April 11, 1970. Two days later - April 13 - an explosion rocked the spacecraft that would not only abort their lunar landing but also keep the entire world watching and waiting on the edge of their/our seats as the drama unfolded.

The explosion caused a chain reaction of problems that had to be solved by the three in the spacecraft and their ground support team. Because of their resourcefulness - and willingness to search for and find the opportunities in the crises - they were able to improvise and make Band -Aid-corrections that barely spared the lives of the astronauts and brought them home safely.

I watched director Ron Howard's brilliant movie of the same name yesterday and was moved to tears of joy, not so much by the success of the failed mission, but by the inspiration and attitude of the players in the crisis, specifically that of Gene Kranz of Mission Control, played by actor Ed Harris in the movie.

Two separate quotes he made were the epitome of why the rescue was a success. The first came as ground technicians complained they didn't have enough to work with in order to find solutions needed. Harris, under time constraint to save the astronaut's lives, screams to the team that "Failure is not an option!" I love that!

Second, and perhaps more importantly, Harris overhears his supervisor verbally wringing his hands saying, "This could be the worst disaster in NASA history." Harris turns to him and says, "With all due respect, sir, I believe this will be our finest hour!" And, of course, it was.

It was all about attitude for Kranz. The mission, which changed completely from lunar landing to finding a way to save lives, didn't fail because the players wouldn't let it fail.

I always try to take advantage of my advantages, but I also try to turn my disadvantages into advantages. And, as the facilitator said, that opportunity is always there; one just has to assume the right attitude to look for and find it.

This philosophy is sometimes related with the half-filled glass of water; your attitude is determined by whether you perceive it as half-empty or half-full. You, then, are identified as either an optimist or pessimist based upon that perception.

I don't know about you, but I always want to be identified alongside Gene Kranz, perhaps one of the greatest optimists the world has ever known.

But what do I know?

FACE IN THE DREAM

APRIL 18, 2005

I kept staring at the woman. Who was she? I knew I knew her but for some reason her face was obscured and I eventually woke from the dream still wondering about her identity.

I'm sure I dream every night, but, for the most part, I never remember them. Sometimes when I first wake up they are fresh and vivid, but they quickly leave as consciousness brooms sub consciousness during morning transition.

Occasionally a troubling dream that stays with me through the day is usually a precursor of something intense that's about to happen.

All morning at work I kept seeing the woman's face in my mind, but no matter how I tried I couldn't identify her or why this dream kept coming to mind. All I knew was that I knew her. It got frustrating as I would mentally dismiss the dream, only to have it reoccur minutes later.

After a business lunch I returned to my office but my restlessness was so unnerving I informed my secretary I was leaving again, got into my vehicle and began to drive.

Noticing the Mans Lumber Company sign ahead I wheeled into the parking lot, remembering that I needed a downspout for my garage gutter.

Taking advantage of the nice summer day was reason enough for the business to have the front door propped open and I stared through it blindly - downspout in hand - as I waited in the checkout line.

Suddenly the chilling sound of tires screaming on hot summer pavement caused me to run to the door to see an out-of-control vehicle spinning down the center of the highway; the driver was desperately trying to regain control. I watched it veer off the road, cross a ditch and slam into an embankment; eerie silence followed.

I raced out the door, across the street and was first on the scene. I pulled on the passenger door; it was jammed. With a firmer grip I gave an adrenalin yank; it opened.

The vehicle was filled with women, all in shock from collision trauma. The one in the passenger seat had a laceration on her forehead; each time her heart pumped, blood spurted as if propelled from a squirt gun. My Vietnam training took over and I stuck my finger in the dike to stop the flow.

I checked the others and tried to calm them. I checked the driver who seemed to have no serious injuries. When her eyes met mine, however, a chill ran down my spine; it was the same face from last night's dream! The trauma of the moment stopped as I stood there - arms outstretched, fingers freezing flowing blood - and stared deep into the eyes of the mother of an old girlfriend.

EMTS arrived, took over the recovery and I headed back to my vehicle with new, white "Miami Vice" jacket, pink tie and white pants now stained crimson.

If you've read me in the past you know I have great faith in dreams and I believe the troubling nature of this one was intended to deliver me to an exact location where I would be able to reach out in a timely manner to help someone in their time of need, which is something we all should be prepared to do every day of our lives.

But what do I know?

RACHAEL'S CHALLENGE

APRIL 25, 2005

The stranger calling on the phone recounted how in his dream he had seen a river of tears flowing from the daughter's eyes and asked her father if it meant anything to him; his answer was, "No." Days later, that answer changed dramatically.

She was sitting outside the school that day sunning over lunch with a friend when perhaps the worst representation of evil approached perniciously with sophisticated weaponry in hand of which no child should even have knowledge, let alone possession. They opened fire on the pair, severing the spine of her friend and shooting her in the legs and torso.

Remembering her as a believer, one of them grabbed her by the hair and asked, "Do you believe in God?"

"You know I do," was her response.

"Then go be with Him," were the final words she heard as the spineless coward shot her in the head.

Sound like a script from the latest Hollywood movie? Nope, it's testimony of events played out six years ago last Wednesday at Littleton, Colorado's Columbine High School. The young lady was Rachael Joy Scott, the first student killed by evil's malefactors that day.

I thought about her, that day's sad commentary and its association with public education last week as I read colleague Ray Kisonas' front page story in *The Evening News* about the "air of tension" and reaction to rumors of guns and a shooting at Monroe High School, which turned out to be a hoax.

Ironically, Miss Scott's father, Darrell Scott, and sister, Dana, will be in Monroe County this week sharing "Rachel's Challenge," a series of assemblies at Monroe, Mason, Jefferson, Airport and Bedford high schools.

The assemblies will reflect Rachel's philosophies - written in an essay before her death - challenging students to be kind to one another and to reach out to those hurting or being bullied. She believed that if each student followed this pattern "it could start a chain reaction."

The week's events culminate Saturday night at 6 in Monroe High School's gymnasium with a community meeting facilitated by Mr. Scott. Hopefully, he will share the story of the stranger's puzzling dream of Rachel's tears, which became shockingly poignant those few days later when police released the backpack she wore the day she died. Inside was her diary, the last page on which 30 minutes before she died she had drawn a picture of her own eyes, crying - oddly enough - 13 tears, the exact number of persons the two who do not even deserve to have their names mentioned murdered moments later!

Although it probably won't happen, I would expect that gymnasium to be choked Saturday night with every parent and student in Monroe County; I know I will be there! And while I'm overjoyed something so positive will be coming into these schools, I'm disappointed only five deemed this important enough to present to their students.

Of course, the underlying issue that keeps educators at bay these days is "the God thing," hinted at in Mr. Kisonas' coverage of the week's events with a quote from Pastor Louie Barnett, president of the assembly's sponsors, the Monroe Evangelical Association. Rev. Barnett defensively assured, "they will not be mixing religion in the schools." God forbid they should share such treacherous doctrine as 'don't lie, don't kill, don't steal and remember to love one another.'

But what do I know?

DEAR MOTHER

MAY 9, 2005

Dear Mother,

As I sit here thinking about you my first thoughts are of ... disappointment. I'm disappointed you aren't here to see the man I have become. That may not be much in the eyes of the rest of the world, but somehow I think you'd be proud.

I've never been happier in my life, mom; I just wish you knew that, and maybe you do. Renee turned out to be a million times more than I could ever have hoped for and I do cherish her. I'm also thankful Dr. Feldman suggested we move our wedding forward from September to March to insure you would be there; he was right. You were beaming in our wedding picture; I think you knew Renee was definitely the one!

While it still doesn't motivate me, you should know I am a bit more frugal with money these days. You always reminded me that "it takes money to ride the train!" I wonder where you picked up that phrase.

Speaking of phrases, you used to drive me crazy with them. "Birds of a feather flock together!" warned me when you thought I was hanging with the wrong crowd. "All that glitters is not gold!" warned me not to let my eyes deceive me.

I still use "sir," "ma'am" and "thank you" just like you insisted and I think of you in the shower sometimes when I'm washing behind my ears.

I always remember dad saying he'd give anything if he could take back the time he "sassed" his mother. I thought that was the most ridiculous thing I had ever heard, but now that you've been gone for seven years, I understand more every day about to what he was referring. My problem is that he was upset at "talking back" to his mother; I'm hurting because of times I made you cry. Yes, "times." Can't take those times back ... and that hurts!

I was thinking about the time - I think I was about 10 - you took me shopping at the supermarket. You wore this old red babushka on your head and finally I said, "Mom, you really should take that thing off!" You did, and when I saw your hair I said, "Uh, maybe you should put it back on."

I know you laughed about it later but I'm sorry about it now.

Wish you could meet grandson Drake; what a beautiful little boy. Saturday I gave him a bath and watched him splashing in the tub with his rubber duckie, just like the one you had for me. After, I wrapped him up in a big, warm towel and held him close ... just like you used to do for me.

That night he obviously had a bad dream and woke up crying. Renee dashed to his side, cradled him in her arms and shushed his crying by assuring him everything was all right ... just like you used to do for me.

I love my life, mom; I just wish you were still here to be a part of it still.

Yesterday was Mother's Day and we gathered to honor the mothers in our family, Renee and Karie. They're both great moms, mom, but I want you to know ... there'll never be another mom as great as you! And because I expect - and hope - all my readers will disagree with me, let me close this letter by saying ...

But what do I know?

THE PRODIGAL

M A Y 1 6 , 2 0 0 5

What is it in the cycle of youth that changes us from trusting parents to teach us what's right to rejecting them and their teachings and deciding we know what's best?

In early childhood we are wary of others and each time threatened run to hide behind the safety of Dad's pant leg, knowing he won't let anyone or anything harm us. By late childhood suddenly the "old man" is from the dark ages and we can't wait to get away from him to do our own thing.

Many resent Dad's wealth and possessions and expect an inheritance now, never realizing until older how hard and long Dad worked to accumulate what he lovingly shared with them during those growing-up years.

So, we go our own way convinced we know what's best. Later, storms of life come raging into our world bringing heartbreak and pain through failed marriages, businesses and various misplaced trusts. The only problem is Dad's pant leg is nowhere in sight.

There's a Proverb (22:6) that instructs parents to "Train up a child in the way he should go; and when he is old he will not depart from it." Fortunately, if the father followed this important advice, even though the son may experience those heartbreaks he later learns Dad wasn't so stupid after all, gets his life under control and lives out a happy, peaceful life. If he hasn't, heartbreak ends only with the last breath.

I know much of about what I write.

There's a story in the Bible of a prodigal son; I expect you've read or heard it. The son acts much in the same manner as described above. In the end the son realizes Dad was right, returns to the fold and is treated like a king, angering an older brother who had remained a perfect son. Dad knows everyone makes mistakes and - with unconditional love - forgives the prodigal and welcomes him home.

I have a friend named Mica Estep with whom I grew up in church. I left him - and Dad - seeking to become a rock and roll star. Fortunately, my father believed that Proverb and had taught me accordingly. Later, those storms of life ripped the sails off my ship of dreams, sunk the ship and left me clinging to the philosophical, life preserver-road map outlined in that Proverb.

At 7 p.m. Friday, Saturday and Sunday at Monroe Missionary Baptist Church, I have the honor of playing the "old man" to that prodigal son in Mica's musical and theatrical interpretation of that biblical story, fittingly titled, "The Prodigal."

Many of you know Mica as the founder, keyboardist and songwriter for Monroe's own internationally acclaimed gospel group, Proclaim. Mica, a University of Toledo graduate, has written more than 100 songs; this is the first musical he has written.

I have been somewhat successful in music during my life; I mention that only to qualify myself to judge this wonderful creation. It is fantastic! If ever there was a truly inspired, anointed musical written, this is it and you should not miss it!

Let me add that three times during last week's rehearsal I was so moved by the work I was overcome with emotion. I expect "The Prodigal" will move you, too, especially if you are - or have - a prodigal in your life!

But what do I know?

RULES

MAY 23, 2005

"You have to not be able to fit a 4-inch ball between the spindles!" he said.

Sunlight streamed through the bedroom slider I crack every morning to allow Zeke, our cat, to take a morning stroll out onto the upstairs patio of our Luna Pier lakefront home. Winter - I hope - has finally made its long-awaited exit, freeing us cold-natured folk from its icy prison.

I slipped into the closet, found a shirt for the day and came back out to find one of the greatest joys of my life - grandson Drake - missing.

"Drake?" I called without expecting an answer from this inquisitive, busier-than-normal 16-month old.

Noticing the open slider I stuck my head through to see if he may have wandered out onto the porch. My heart jumped as I saw him on all fours trying to stick his head between the spindles of the porch railing.

"Drake!" I called again only this time momentarily fearful he may be in danger. I ran to him, picked him up and scurried back inside.

That's when I heard his words in my head.

Mike Demski is the building inspector for the City of Luna Pier. Six years ago I remodeled our home and deck; naturally, it required inspection upon completion.

"These deck spindles have to come off and be put back on," he informed me after arriving for that inspection.

When I asked, "Why?" he gave me the opening line about the 4-inch ball.

"Why?" I asked again.

"To make sure a child doesn't stick his head through and get it caught or perhaps even break his neck," he replied.

"I don't have any small children," I assured him.

"Doesn't matter; it's code!" he returned.

"Whatever!" I muttered and assured him I would make the changes.

"Call me when you're done; I'll come back for the final." he instructed before leaving.

I remember thinking how trivial that sounded and wondered if he was being a bit "nit-picky." Needless to say, realizing my grandson could have been in great peril had Mike Demski not been adamant with his enforcement all those years ago gave me instant appreciation of why we have building codes.

An added irony to the story is that a few years later - after retiring from my radio career - I became Mr. Demski's boss when I took the job as Luna Pier's city administrator. I'm pretty confidant I don't have to wonder about or check on Mike to see if he's doing a good job.

What's funny is that now - on the other side of building code enforcement - I remember my own bout of attitude at being held accountable to those codes, and believe me, I was a cupcake compared to the crap he takes regularly for making sure things are done right.

After making sure he was okay and bringing Drake back inside that morning, I gave him to Renee and immediately picked up the phone and called Mike to share with him that while I didn't appreciate his attention to detail back then, I certainly did on this morning.

Why is it in our general nature to not want anyone putting restraints on us? And, as with last week's prodigal story, we always think we know what's best. I guess one never gets too old to learn!

But what do I know?

"MIGHTY MITE"

MAY 30, 2005

I stood with arms outstretched to the audience and proclaimed, "There is no greater love!"

I had just delivered those closing lines from incredibly talented friend Mica Estep's musical, "The Prodigal," at my church last weekend. The line referred to God's great love for those of us who are His children.

When the strains of the final song, "No Greater Love," had died, well-wishers and inspired attendees swarmed the stage and I basked in the warmth of the love being shared.

While returning one particular bear hug I stopped in shock as I peered over a shoulder at what had to be a ghost waiting to greet me.

I froze. It couldn't be. ...

He was just about the best I've ever seen at anything he attempted; sports were his specialty. He quarterbacked the offense and field-generaled the defense with mental and physical agility and ability. Lightning-quick carrying the football, he was by you and gone before you could lay a hand on him.

With apologies to Rosie Barnes and his Monroe High teams, he quarterbacked the best Monroe County basketball team I ever saw from his point-guard position. He could drain the three from anywhere on the court - even though there was no three-point shot back then - and was a defensive wizard.

With his speed, he was a natural star at track and field or baseball.

I was dating a little hottie in his hometown of Petersburg when a friend introduced me to ... Vince LaRocca.

"Mighty Mite," as they called him, couldn't have been much more than 5 feet and 120 soaking wet. Quiet, happy, handsome homeboy; best of all, humble.

He was leader of the Summerfield Bulldogs in the mid-to-late 1960s, and I tried not to miss any of his games as his talent was something to behold. Later I would discover the LaRocca name itself dictated great talent, based on the band of brothers, sisters, nieces and nephews that would come behind him.

We became buds, but, unfortunately, only for a short time. The next-to-last time I saw Vince was the last game we played together (with *Evening News* Sports Editor Ron Montri) on the championship Golden Drumstick recreational basketball team; I was drafted into the Army in midseason and sent to serve in the Vietnam War.

Dear Friend, Vince LaRocca, KIA Vietnam, 1969.

The last time I saw Vince was in his funeral casket. He, too, ended up being sent to Vietnam - and killed - during that same war.

I saw no ghost that night on stage. What I did see was a glimpse of what Vince would undoubtedly have looked like today had he lived as his look-alike little brother - along with another brother - stood waiting to greet me. We renewed old friendships, and I promised to come see their mother in the near future.

This morning, during my prayer time, God again brought Vince to my mind, along with the concept of "no greater love." Gospel writer John records Jesus prophetically instructing that "greater love hath no man than this that a man lay down his life for his friends."

I miss my friend on this Memorial Day. And, while I grieve that for whatever reason he did not get the chance at life I did, I'm in awe that his sacrifice categorizes him in the same manner as that of the greatest man who ever lived!

But what do I know?

ODE TO DRINKHAHN

J U N E   4 ,   2 0 0 5

I never once saw them going north, but each morning - as the first filters of light broke across the South China Sea (and the direction of home!), I would lay on my back and watch the waves of B-52 long-range bombers heading back to their home-base Island of Guam. They were so high you couldn't hear them, but if you were watching, you could see them; I wonder if he could have been piloting one?

Until I read his obituary I didn't realize the tall, handsome superstar of our 1964 Monroe High basketball team was even qualified to fly them, which speaks volumes more than the wonderful talent and personality I knew from those carefree days of ours.

This morning I attended the funeral of Retired Air Force Colonel Marc Drinkhahn and I couldn't help but doing something I seem to be doing much of these days: wondering where the years have gone.

Could it really have been 41 years ago we fought our way past the tremendously talented teams of Grosse Pointe and Highland Park to become Border Cities League Champions?

Coach Joe Kiefer had molded the starting five of Drinkhahn, Dave Gilliland, Curt Garrett, Darrell "Putt" Meyers and Helmut Jagutis into a fine-oiled machine that won the District Championship and before pulling off what I still consider the local upset of the century by knocking off Detroit Public School League Champions, Detroit Northwestern, 75-69 at Trenton High School. Can you tell I remember it like yesterday?

I was a scrub used only during blowouts, but being associated with those guys was one of the greatest thrills of my life; Drinkhahn was our leader. He was a tough-as-nails competitor who poured his heart and soul into every thing he did.

On one particular occasion of feeling like the virtual "nobody" I actually was on the team, Marc grabbed me and said, "C'mon Treece, I need someone to practice against; everybody's important on this team!" He made me feel important that day.

Our last game together was in the University of Detroit Fieldhouse for Michigan's "Sweet Sixteen" Quarterfinals where we would lose by one to Pontiac Central in spite of Marc having a fabulous game and actually outplaying future NBA star Campy Russell. Years later the memory of walking into that cavernous building would be stirred watching the movie "Hoosiers" where a little Indiana team experienced similar emotions during their run to the state championship.

Marc was another from a super-talented sports family as older brother Don was catcher for my older pitching brother, Hal, and his younger brother, Paul, was a superstar in his own right.

I knew Marc had made a career of the military even though I hadn't seen him since he graduated a year ahead of me. And today I am thrilled I actually had the courage to crash the '64 MHS Reunion last year as I got to see my old friend one last time.

And while I have always been proud of my military service, his star-studded service record reflected his continuing superstar status throughout his life.

Perhaps most important in that glowing resume to me was the fact that Marc was an Elder in his Lutheran church in Georgia, which gives me similar satisfaction as last week's column about friend Vince LaRocca, in that I'll be seeing Marc again one day.

But what do I know?

DON'T RIB BRONCO!

JUNE 25, 2005

I had refined my recipe until I knew I had the winner.

As my entry sizzled on the grill while we three cooks sizzled in the searing sun, I felt especially confident as even my competitors were virtually verbally ready to concede after tasting my sauce.

This crazy contest began years ago after meeting a man named the Rev. Al Overstreet at the Monroe YMCA. We became great friends, and, in addition to mutual faith, we shared a mutual friend: former IBA world middleweight boxing champion Bronco McKart, whom I knew from church and had followed since he was a kid in Golden Gloves.

Perhaps the most unique aspect of our friendship trinity was how - after our daily workouts - we would go into the YMCA sauna for Bible study. Other guys would walk in, see us and bolt back out the door.

We also all love to cook and were each extolling our prowess one day when "ribs" became the topic. The shucking and jiving became so intense we decided the only way to determine who cooked the best ribs was to have a "rib-off!"

And so it began.

Officially named "The Brotherman Rib-Off" we scheduled it for summer's first Saturday.

The first contest was five years ago at my home. Immediately the harassment began with comments like, "Don't let your ribs touch mine; they'll be contaminated!" and "I'll bet the dog won't even eat your ribs."

When cooking was completed, we sliced sample sections and sent them on Styrofoam plates to the waiting judge who then savored each. Finally a decision was made and the very first Rib King was Bronco McKart, who, of course, rubbed his new championship in our faces for the next year.

I saved a discarded bone and had it mounted on a plaque announcing to all who read that Bronco was the reigning "Rib King"

Tom, Rib King Bronco McKart and
Rev. Al Overstreet, 2001

for that year.

The second year, Bronco won again. The third year, Al took honors and believe me, two years of Bronco's strutting was nothing compared to his! The new king called us his "royal subjects."

This was my year and I was prepared. The last few months I bought slabs of ribs weekly, halved them and experimented with different recipes on each until I knew I had the winner for Saturday's contest. We met at noon at Bronco's and began trash-talking each other before the first slab hit the grill.

When show time came we presented our entries and three judges began their finger-licking duty. Finally there was a decision and we faced the judges, who sucked up to the two losers with comments like, "Man, this was really tough!"

Prepared to thrust my hands upward in victory and finally show them my strut, I gasped as they called out the winning name of ... Bronco McKart? I couldn't believe it.

In spite of the fact that the judges obviously screwed up, I must admit that after four wins in five years, I guess he's the undisputed Rib King ... for now!

Getting ribbed as a five-time loser rubs me wrong so I need your help. If you have a rib recipe that will dethrone the champ, please send it to me as I am desperate. So desperate that if that don't work, perhaps I'll just go beat the snot out of him and take the trophy.

Uh, then again, maybe that's not such a good idea.

But what do I know?

ICE SCRAPER

JULY 18, 2005

I jammed the gearshift into "park" and opened the door to step from air-conditioned comfort into searing summer heat.

I heard the ruckus immediately and visually followed curiosity to see whom I surmised as a man and wife arguing boisterously, vehemently, in front of their vehicle. I winced at hearing profanity-laced names they called each other and quickly determined they were in the middle of the blame-game, trying to decide whose fault it was that they were standing in 90 degree heat outside their locked, running car, the keys to which were dangling from the ignition.

I squeezed the gas pump handle to start the flow of fuel and then leaned against the side of my van to watch bystanders try to unlock the vehicle for the tussling twosome.

"Get your ice scraper and open that car!" He said.

Shocked by the internal voice I had just heard, I looked around as if to see if someone else might have heard it.

"Ice scraper? It's 90 degrees out!" I thought to myself.

I opened the door to climb back in for some cool relief when something caught my eye; lying behind my driver's seat was ... an ice scraper! I had obviously failed to remove it for summer storage and, strangely, hadn't noticed it until now.

He spoke again: "Go open that car for them."

Still in the early years of my personal relationship with God, I instinctively grabbed the ice scraper and headed for the ruckus.

The scraper had a long, black handle with a wide blade that featured a thin, metal lip for chipping ice. All in one motion I walked up to the passenger window, inserted the metal lip inside the tiny opening at the top of the door, levered the handle upward which pried the glass out, reached in, pulled the lock up, grabbed the handle and opened the door.

The gathered crowd erupted into approval but I wasn't hearing them. I turned and headed back to my van, totally freaked out by what had just happened to ... me!

Suddenly the two combatants were at each side, thanking me profusely for ending their stalemate.

As soon as I said, "You're welcome!" and continued on, He spoke again.

"I didn't tell you how to do that so you would get the credit!" He said. "Tell them about Me!"

I stopped in my tracks and turned to the pair.

"You need love in your hearts instead of the hatred you displayed back there," I began. "God sent me to open your car so I could tell you to love each other and learn to trust Him!"

I don't think telling them I had leprosy would have caused them to make a faster exit. They were happy I had delivered them from their dilemma but they didn't want to hear anything about God!

Things changed for me that day as it was the first time I clearly heard God's voice. What hasn't changed is most people still don't want to hear or talk about Him. That is so strange to me because the most important thing that ever happened to me was the day I asked Him to take control of my life. He changed me so dramatically that I can't imagine anyone not wanting to talk about something ... Someone ... so wonderful!

But what do I know?

HANDICAPPED

J U L Y 2 5 , 2 0 0 5

I wove my way slowly through the lot looking for a space close to the door; each one was full. In fact, the entire parking lot was full and I realized if I didn't find the one I was looking for it would be a long, painful walk for me.

I already felt guilty using the red tag hanging from my rear-view mirror but, under the circumstances, it was somewhat necessary.

Finally a woman came out and headed for her vehicle, slid her bag of groceries in the trunk and climbed in to prepare to leave. Already past her, I turned and circled the row of parked cars and returned down the aisle and prepared to pull into the now-empty handicapped parking space when another car dove into the spot just ahead of me.

I shrugged my shoulders at my bad timing and started to drive on to find another before hitting the brake and watching as the car's driver jumped out and ran into the supermarket.

I stopped behind his vehicle and checked the license; no handicapped plate. I then looked for his red or blue tag like mine; none there either.

"What a jerk!" I thought to myself as I finally found a place to park and limped into the market.

Surgery on my left knee left me hobbling on a cane after a few weeks on crutches. No fun! My orthopedic surgeon ordered me off my feet, to ice and elevate my leg and to get a temporary handicapped sticker. I was a good patient and everything went well until I developed an infection that slowed the healing.

On this day I had visited the doctor and then stopped by the market to fill a prescription when Mr. Inconsiderate took the handicapped spot. Although I had never parked in a handicapped place I found myself perturbed by the one who had and it got me thinking about the handicap … of being handicapped.

I guess I just never looked at things from a handicapped person's view until I was in somewhat of the same predicament; the only difference was that mine was - hopefully - temporary.

On my way home that day, I saw a sign for a corn maze and immediately thought about how I've always wanted to take Renee through one - before realizing that in my condition I wouldn't be able to go.

Soon there was another missed opportunity, then another and the next thing I knew I had a small-but-stark realization of what it must be like for the one who is in this condition every day.

Then in The Sunday News I read the heartbreaking but heartwarming story of little Jacob Brancheau, born with sacral agenesis, who wears a colostomy bag and must crawl or use a wheelchair everywhere he goes and who only has a hope of ever walking.

Dear Lord, thank You for the taste of what it must be like to not have freedoms afforded others due to a handicap. And please smack me a good one the next time You hear me complain about anything!

And one more thing ... while you're at it, give that jerk at the supermarket a good smack, too; he - and anyone else inconsiderate enough to park in a handicapped spot without having the need - needs it!

But what do I know?

GOAT MILKER

AUGUST 1, 2005

I hadn't done it since Uncle Harry Patterson taught me when I was about 8; unfortunately, I had forgotten. Considering the fun I expected to have, I sought expert instructions.

"First you circle your thumb and forefinger around it and squeeze, which pinches off what's already in there from the rest in the sack," she began. "Then bring the rest of your fingers together one-by-one in a downward, squeezing motion which forces it out and into the bucket."

"Ah, yes, I remember now!" I replied and began practicing on my finger.

The expert opinion was from then-sister-in-law and proud Ida farm girl, Jodi McClanahan, and the instructions were needed for the task at hand: the Monroe County Fair's 4-H Celebrity Goat Milking Contest.

As general manager of Monroe's "Tower 98" radio station I was asked to participate. As the fierce competitor I've always been I didn't want to look like a rookie, I wanted to win; thus the instructions.

I reported to the Goat Barn at the appointed time and joined nine other contestants waiting to do something I expect none of us had ever done.

From their pens 10 goats were paraded onto milking platforms lined all in a row as a crowd began to gather; fabulous, funny, free entertainment was only moments away.

My goat gave me what I thought was a loving look as her owner led her onto the stand. Other goats were stomping and showing signs of resistance to the process but mine was as docile and lovable as could be.

"I think she likes me!" I told the young girl who owned her.

"Look at that sack!" the girl replied, "all she wants is relief!" The comment quickly ended any thoughts of me being special to the goat.

Soon contest instructions were given along with a bucket for catching the milk. We only had a few minutes; the bucket weighing most would win.

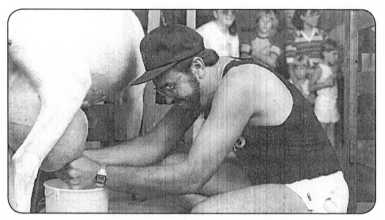

Tom milking a goat at the Monroe County Fair, 1987.

I peered under my goat to see Michigan State Senator Norman Shinkle with his back to me preparing to milk; he was a much better senator than goat-milker!

Gingerly ... I eased my hands around two of the goat's teats as we were given the "get ready!" command, and then, "Go!" I followed instructions and out jetted a white stream of milk; "Yes!" I called out to myself.

Soon I was smoking and foam began forming in my bucket from the streams of milk hitting what had already accumulated.

Every now and then the goat would turn her head around and give me what I'm sure was a smile as I was obviously giving her what the young girl said she wanted.

Suddenly an idea struck me and I weighed its consequences; while doing what I wanted might jeopardize my chance of winning, the fun was too tempting. I stopped milking and pointed the teats at Senator Shinkle and started blasting him in the back!

It turned out not to be a problem; I won with 2.2 pounds of milk, received a trophy with a goat on top and got to "milk" the senator.

I have great memories of the Monroe County Fair; perhaps none more unique and exciting than the year I milked a goat.

And, no matter how full she was, I still think she liked me!

But what do I know?

PROTECTIVE MOTHER

A U G U S T   8 ,   2 0 0 5

The front door opened and he came running out to join me on a beautiful summer evening; perfect for Frisbee. My favorite partner at the time lived next door and we played most every night.

How fascinated I was by this plastic disc! A proper flick of the wrist would send it spinning through the air to hang almost endlessly, giving the receiver time to run under and catch it after gravity compromised its flight.

Years later it would become a staple for lifelong friend and fellow rock and roll band mate, Roger Manning, and me as we crisscrossed the country on tour, playing music all night and Frisbee all day.

"Max" wasn't much at throwing the Frisbee but he never missed catching it no matter how far or hard I threw it. As fast as lightning he would race after it, anticipate its descent and then leap into the air at just the right moment to hang there himself before snatching it from flight.

He was poetry in motion and I was amazed at how - once that Frisbee was in flight - nothing deterred him from his mission of catching it! One day that passion almost caused a catastrophe!

Max was a German shepherd whose owners, Tim and Carol Towne (also lifelong friends), lived next to my mother. After my father left for Heaven, I stayed with her whenever I was in town.

God had blessed Tim and Carol with Casey, a new baby girl. During one particular evening's Frisbee session, Carol strolled out with Casey in her arms to watch Max and me play. I greeted her and instinctively tossed the Frisbee her way, never giving a single thought to Max' passion for catching the Frisbee ... no matter what!

You can imagine what happened: All 100 pounds-or-so of the dog flew through the air and met Carol and Casey at the exact moment the Frisbee arrived. Max blasted Carol broadside and sent her flying through the air and headed for the grinding gravel of the driveway.

I thought of Carol the other day as I carefully cradled brand new grandson No. 2, Gaige Braxton Carr. Renee had been hogging him - as grandmothers do - and I demanded my turn to hold him. She handed him to me and I turned to ease back to my chair when my recently operated on left knee buckled. With one arm I clutched Gaige to my chest while the other grabbed the chair back to steady myself. What if I fell?

The Carol and Casey video started playing in my mind and again I saw Max send Carol and Casey flying.

As only a loving, unselfish, protect-your-child-at-any-cost mother would do, instead of instinctively bracing herself before hitting the gravel, Carol instead instinctively wrapped Casey with her hands and arms and took the whole brunt of the fall as she slammed into the gravel. The stones cut into her flesh and she was bruised for months ... but her baby emerged without a scratch!

Today, Max and mom are both gone and Casey has turned into a beautiful, successful woman with a family of her own. She and I and my sons all share something in common: We all had mothers who would have done anything to protect their children! Hopefully, that character trait of motherhood will never go out of style, but these days ... you never know!

But what do I know?

GUIDE THE SURGEON'S HANDS

AUGUST 15, 2005

"And this form basically says I've explained the procedure and that you understand," the doctor continued before adding, "Just sign at the bottom."

Renee affixed her signature to complete the myriad paperwork required in the pre-operative meeting.

"Okay," the doctor finished. "See you Wednesday."

I stood and extended my hand to shake his before asking, "Doctor, would you mind if we prayed for you?"

He looked into my eyes and without hesitation answered, "Of course not!"

Renee and I joined hands with him and I led the circle of prayer. I thanked God for the privilege of prayer and the opportunity to pray with the surgeon who was days away from performing a complete hysterectomy on my wife.

I thanked God for the mental ability He has given man to be able to learn how to perform life-saving operations and for the time this surgeon had devoted to that study and for his devotion to his patients. I then asked God to send His Holy Spirit to guide the surgeon's hands to perform this procedure on the most important person ever to come into my life; finally I thanked Him for hearing my prayer.

Wednesday morning came and I ran my fingers through Renee's hair as she smiled back at me from pre-op's "La-La Land."

"The surgery's at 9 and should take 1½ to two hours," the doctor said. "I'll see you in the waiting room when I'm finished."

I poured a cup of waiting-room coffee, sat and began reading the morning's newspaper. I was barely through the first section when a motion caught my eye; bounding through the doorway was the doctor with an ear-to-ear grin on his face. I glanced at the clock: 9:35!

"Unbelievable!" he began, "Everything went perfect! I was able to get everything without an incision, there was minimal bleeding,

I was done in a half hour and I expect she'll be able to go home in a few days!"

He sounded like Picasso describing his latest, greatest work!

Then he thrilled me by adding, "I'll tell you ... I could feel the Holy Spirit working through my hands!"

As I write this it is "a few days" later and Renee is sleeping like a baby here at home in our bed and I just finished my prayer time, thanking God for His Guiding Hand in her, our, life.

When I shared this story with our pastor, the Rev. Roy Southerland, he just grinned and said, "Imagine what would happen if every patient prayed with their surgeon before every operation and asked God for guidance!"

Apologies to those who hate it when I write about my thrilling relationship with my Heavenly Father; I know personally what nonsense it seems to be when one does not have that relationship and reads of another's excitement that does.

On the other hand, I guess I'm like a kid with a new bike or a young man with a beautiful, new girlfriend who can't wait to "show them off." I'm excited and unashamed to share how God continues to work in my life.

I'm also thankful for the great surgery staff and nurses at Mercy Memorial Hospital who were wonderful throughout our ordeal, and I am humbled to be on the receiving end of such marvelous Blessings of life!

But what do I know?

MY HOW TIMES CHANGE

AUGUST 22, 2005

As my mother used to say, "My how times change!"

I remember from childhood how meticulously she would cut and then sew blue-jean patches onto my jeans to cover holes I had worn in them; often times even pre-washing the patch so it would blend with their already-faded color so as to not look like the jeans had been patched.

To mother, patched jeans was a sign of poverty and she didn't want anyone to know our family couldn't afford to buy new jeans when one pair got a hole. Though our family was extremely rich in love, father scratched and clawed for what he could bring home; patched jeans told the community that it wasn't much.

When I returned from the Vietnam War, I was an angry young man, for many reasons. Mainly because - unlike in today's Iraqi War - other than going to jail, I didn't have an option about going to war as I was drafted. However, I was always taught that freedom must be defended and that I had a duty to serve my country if called. So, when called - even though I didn't like it - I served.

One way that anger was vented was I stopped shaving my face and cutting my hair. The excuse I gave was, "Why spend the money on razors, blades and haircuts?" when the real reason was because - as David Crosby laments in his Crosby, Stills, Nash & Young song, "Almost Cut my Hair," I felt like "letting my freak flag fly." I was angry and wanted everyone to know it!

Another vent from that post-Vietnam culture was patched jeans. I'm not talking about trying to blend the patches either; my patches were the wildest colors and fabric I could find; the logic was, "Why toss out your favorite jeans when all you have to do is toss on another patch?" With my patches, however, my jeans were another "freak-flag."

Mother could not understand my culture and I'm sure she was grieved and even a little embarrassed over my wild display of patches.

(Today, seven years after she went to be with her Savior - and as father warned me - I grieve over all the things I did that grieved her!)

Today's mail brought an Elder-Beerman catalog that had me leafing through for no apparent reason as I'm not much of a shopper. Featured were all the latest back-to-school clothes for kids. I licked my finger and pushed pages past until pausing before one particular page of pictures.

Three or four young girls were posing in the latest style of designer jeans. What caught my eye was the fact that the jeans all had designer holes already in them! I shook my head in amazement and then thought about how culture changes from generation to generation.

Mother considered it shameful to have holes in her son's jeans and went to extreme measures so they didn't look like they did. Then I came along and had no problem with the holes and even flaunted the fact by fixing them with flamboyant patches designed to identify my anger and independence as well as cover the holes. Today's culture says, "We're not even going to buy the jeans unless they come with holes already in them!"

As mother's son says, "My how times change!"

But what do I know?

FOOL

AUGUST 27, 2005

Foolish!

I thought about using the word "idiot."

Perhaps I should have as either would describe how I'm feeling about myself at this moment.

I have done many things in life I would not do again had I the chance; I expect each of us has such a list. My list is long.

Perhaps at the top is the romance I had with ... smoking!

Growing up, no one in my family smoked. Not only was it completely discouraged, my father would have killed me had he caught me smoking. In fact, I can still hear him in my mind's ear rhyming, "Tobacco is a filthy weed, from the devil it does speed, it stains your teeth and burns your clothes and makes a chimney out of your nose!"

It was only after I left home that I took up the horrible habit. The deadly, horrible habit!

What is it about smoking that's so attractive to youth? I'm convinced that adults glamorize it and kids - who eventually desperately want to be identified as adults - start for that identification. I know I did.

Also, kids are impressionable. At one point in my smoking life I decided to quit - until I saw my favorite guitar player smoking a cigarette. Wanting to be cool like him, I went out and bought another pack.

In the Army it seemed like everybody smoked. And, with cigarettes at 20 cents a pack, affording them was no problem.

It bothers me to tell you that I loved smoking and that I would love to fire one up right now! Can't tell you why, other than that smoking was a real romance for me.

Another thing that bothers me today is how much time I spent during my life sitting in front of a cup of coffee and a smoldering cigarette, which to me epitomizes my desperate search for happiness. It seems like I was always looking for that something that would satisfy me and then allow me to toss all those temporary-pleasured bad habits for the real deal.

I have found the real deal! At this very moment of my life I believe I have found exactly what I have been searching for all these years and have unspeakable joy in my heart.

Unfortunately, I - like many others a few weeks ago - thought long and hard about all those years of smoking while watching coverage of the lung-cancer death of TV news anchor Peter Jennings.

When I was younger and deep in search of that joy, I didn't really care about myself. First of all I figured I had cheated death surviving Vietnam, but then - without that joy - I didn't feel as though I had anything that made me want to live. It sounds stupid now, but, sad to say, accurate.

What worries me now is fear that lung cancer could be days, weeks, or months away from knocking on my door, that I could be a dead man walking. I have finally found the loves of my life and my greatest fear is that the stupid, mindless habit I allowed myself to be consumed by could very well end up consuming me at the very moment I sit at the banquet table at which I have waited my whole life to sit.

I was a foolish idiot! I hope you're not.

But what do I know?

SHARING RESPONSIBILITY

S E P T E M B E R 5 , 2 0 0 5

I had a strange feeling about it when I first noticed it forming off the Bahamas. It did some damage but seemed more of a nuisance when it came ashore just north of Miami and crossed the state.

It started to make me nervous when it dipped a bit south in the Gulf before turning north and heading for our southern coast, but I became terrified for the people in its path when radar photographed it totally eclipsing the Gulf of Mexico.

Today I sit in stunned silence watching TV images of human suffering unlike any most Americans have ever witnessed and with my column deadline looming I have no idea how - or what - to share with you today.

My disdain for the human spirit vents at two types of people I watched being filmed outside an appliance store: the first the looter who came out, saw the camera and hid his face, knowing he was doing wrong. The second the looter who came out and smiled for the camera as he carried off a useless microwave oven.

My hope for the human spirit was inspired as I watched ones tirelessly trying to rescue others, of those in need of rescue themselves yet pointing rescuers to others instead, and those hungry and thirsty giving their food and water to another.

My heart is crushed as I watch tears streaming from the eyes of the thousands of heartbroken souls whose lives have been crushed by Katrina. It seems as though those who only last week had virtually nothing in their lives...have now even lost the term, "virtually."

Last evening as I clutched the hand of the woman I love and bowed my head to give thanks for the food we were about to consume I could not hold my tears as I thought of the thousands who would go through yet another night with nothing to eat or drink.

I wept for the man I had watched weeping as he told the cameraman how Katrina had ripped his wife from the clutch of his hand; how she begged him to take care of their kids just before disappearing into a grave of swirling water.

I gave thanks for the tremendous outpouring of love and support from the rest of the nation and for relief efforts under way, including many from my church and our Southern Baptist Disaster Relief Team who are on the front lines practicing what they preach. I specifically asked for protection for my older brother, Hal, currently helping feed 14,000 a day somewhere in Mississippi's devastation.

No one expected a storm of such epic proportions! No one expected that in 2005 we would sit helplessly glued to our TVs watching multitudes of Americans in such misery and hopelessness.

I hope your heart is hurting, too. I hope you have already shared something to help rebuild lives trashed by this tragedy, either through financial offering ... or that of prayer.

I also hope this tragedy inspires us to try to improve our own lives. Nobel Prize winner Marie Curie once said, "Each of us must work for our own improvement and, at the same time, share a general responsibility for all humanity, our particular duty being to aid those to whom we think we can be most useful."

Every American needs to share that general responsibility, today ... and tomorrow!

But what do I know?

THE TRIUMPH OF EVIL

S E P T E M B E R 1 2 , 2 0 0 5

Imagine if you will...that right now it is five years ago and everything you know that has happened in those five years - including 9-11 - hasn't happened. Are you with me? I'm wondering how you would react if I then told you, "Nineteen young men will come to America, totally destroy the World Trade Center, almost destroy the Pentagon and Capitol Building and in so doing kill nearly 3,000 of our citizens and virtually bring us to our knees economically!"

I don't know about you but I'm sure I would have laughed and then asked a question of my own: "Are you crazy?"

Yesterday I watched - again - National Geographic's 9-11 anniversary programming of the timetable and facts of the greatest terrorist act in the history of our country and the world as we know it, yet no matter how much time goes by I cannot seem to fathom the reality that the statement...is true!

Over and over in my mind I wonder how this could happen.

We know the perpetrators of this heinous act were extreme Muslim terrorists who did what they did - and do what they do - as an act of obedience to Allah, or God. The cockpit voice recorder of Flight 93 that crashed in the Pennsylvania field records the terrorist's last words as repeated praises to God.

I am a man of faith who believes the miracles recorded in the Bible, such as Jesus feeding 5,000 with a few fish and loaves of bread, and God parting the Red Sea to allow the children of Israel to escape before closing it on Pharaoh's army.

Perhaps it is this belief that worries me about 9-11. I just can't fathom 19 men hatching such a plan, slipping through (obviously inept) security and then commandeering four different airplanes by intimidating the multitude of passengers with box cutters and doing all they did...without some divine guidance.

Osama Bin Laden later credited God for giving them success and it kills me to even think there's a chance he could be right, yet my logical mind won't accept the possibility that - given the operation's sophistication - "luck" had anything to do with it.

Later yesterday I found a Bible scripture (Matthew 24:24) that says, "False prophets will appear and perform great signs and miracles to deceive even the elect," which made me wonder if that explains the mission's success.

The fact is Bin Laden - who openly declared war on America - and these who call themselves "holy warriors" are nothing more than evil men to be greatly feared as is anyone with no fear of death.

During an interview after the US invasion of Afghanistan Bin Laden is quoted as saying, "We love death! The US loves life; that is the difference between us."

He's right, but wrong. These evil men callously murdered thousands on 9-11 believing God will be pleased and reward them when they get to Heaven.

I can't speak for God, but I'd wager everything I own that they were all extremely disappointed when their turn came to stand before Him.

And for the rest of us, let me just say that I agree with English philosopher Edmund Burke who said, "The only thing necessary for the triumph of evil is for good men to do nothing."

But what do I know?

CRUSHED

OCTOBER 3, 2005

Almost like hair, I reached down and ran my fingers through Rosemary's and then lifted it to my nose and inhaled her unmistakable fragrance. Fortunately, she doesn't fly away for winter; I just bring her inside to stay warm.

Basil is another. I run my hands through his and he fires up the taste buds in my brain's nose.

Tarragon, dill, oregano, cilantro - to name a few of the others - all spend summer growing in my yard.

I love to cook and especially with herbs and spices. Growing my own allows me to brag of saving money, but that's the least important reason why I do. For starters, availability allows me to simply walk out in the yard each time I need a special seasoning for whatever I'm cooking.

But there's something more. There is a bonding with the good earth that my father taught me; something about fingering into the dirt to colonize seed or seedling and then watching it spring to life to ultimately meet the needs for which you have planted.

I wish I had room to grow all the wonderful vegetables he did annually; I settle for herbs and peppers in my matchbox yard.

Yesterday - in preparation to have dinner on the table for my wonderful wife's return from her day's employment toil - I strolled out to my herb garden and picked a handful of basil leaves, took them in, washed and dried them, and then crushed them for the dish I was preparing.

Later I started thinking about that last action I had taken with the basil and all the times in my life it had been done to me. Times like breaking my hand the first day of football practice, getting drafted into the Army, receiving a "Dear John" letter from my honey-at-the-time a month later, war, divorce, driven to the edge of suicide.

Each time, I was crushed.

I expect it will happen again and I will certainly be crushed if anyone from my inner circle leaves this planet before me.

However, what I have learned is that while I hated it at the time, I realize now those crushes were critical to the process of getting me to become the person I am now. And, while that isn't anything particularly special, I can't even imagine still being the person I used to be.

There are so many things that never become truly useful or valuable until they are crushed. The grain of wheat isn't very appealing in its raw form, but once crushed can be transformed into the finest of breads and pastries. Grapes are fun to plunk into your mouth for a snack, but, once crushed, can be transformed into the finest of juices or wines.

When something terrible happens that crushes, it's hard to think that it is really something wonderful, but many times - somewhere down the road - you look back and say, "That's the best thing that ever happened to me!"

It is extremely difficult to "consider it pure joy whenever you suffer trials of any kind," but the testing of your faith develops perseverance which matures and completes you, and - if you learn to accept it as the way it's supposed to be - usually ends up making you a better person in the long run.

But what do I know?

STEALING HER NUTS

OCTOBER 24, 2005

The little rodent plucked the peanut off my deck and dashed down to deposit it deep in the dirt for dinner later this winter. It reminded me of Mother.

It was a black walnut and its meat was sweet and tasty. As a boy I used the green balls hanging from our backyard tree for target practice with my slingshot. Years later - finally old enough to be trusted with the lawnmower and in too big of a hurry to go play ball to pick them up - I would run over them with the mower which launched them out into our garden as if shot from a cannon.

I remember "hulling" that soft, green cover to get at the hard shell underneath, then laying them on Dad's old iron anvil and cracking them with a hammer to get at that delicious meat. If you hit the nut too hard, you pulverized the meat. If you weren't paying close attention to what you were doing, you pulverized your finger.

I also remember unintentionally staining my palms dark brown from the juice of the hull and waiting weeks for the stains to finally dissipate.

Mother loved black walnuts and labored tirelessly to collect the meats for her family. Years later - with husband passed and children gone but not her love for those walnuts - she would gather them in her turned up apron, store them in the garage and let the hulls decay until they were ready to fall off the shell by themselves.

To eliminate hand stains and expedite the process she would sometimes spread the nuts in our graveled driveway and run over them with her car during her comings and goings, thus crushing the hulls but not the nuts. She then gathered them again and headed for the anvil on Dad's now-idle workbench to gather the meats.

A family of squirrels moved into the neighborhood and figured the walnuts were fair game. Mom didn't mind them going for the ones that fell to the ground, but she was a force to be reckoned with when they finally discovered her stash in the garage!

They would sneak in when Mom would leave the door open and gorge themselves by chewing into the walnuts, leaving the shells looking like little faces with two eyes.

Occasionally Mom would catch them in the act and would race to chase them out of the garage. On one occasion I was out in the yard when she came charging out in hot pursuit of a squirrel. After chasing him up a tree she turned and yelled to me, "He's after my nuts!"

"Uh, not so loud, mom," I called to her after seeing the neighbor raking leaves turn to give her a questioning look.

I have a love-hate relationship with this time of year. I love the concept of fall harvest and rejoice at the blessing of my eyesight each time I see the splendor of leaves changing colors, but I hate what's coming behind this change of seasons.

I wonder if animals make it to Heaven. I don't think so. But if there are and the squirrel family is there, because there'll be no enemies or confrontations, Mother is surely sharing her nuts, err, their nuts ... well, somebody's nuts ... with them.

But what do I know?

"FRIENDS ARE FRIENDS FOREVER"

OCTOBER 31, 2005

Sweetest Day had always rivaled Valentine's for one simple reason: They were in love and had been since the day he asked for her hand 52 years ago.

In days gone by dozens of radiant roses had regularly been delivered to her with his love; today she was simply satisfied to still be able to hold his hand and assure him of hers. The Tennessee day was nice enough to venture out into the back yard to enjoy what would be one of his last under God's sunshine on this earth.

"I'll go make you some tea," she said and left him alone in the garden to return to the house. That's when he spotted the prize!

He struggled with elastic straps to remove the oxygen mask from his face and forced 75-year-old legs to allow him to stand, and then slowly, faithfully, inch across the garden to retrieve his prize. When she returned, he sat there, triumphant and with a lifetime of love, holding one red rose for her.

"God knew I couldn't go get you a dozen roses," he whispered to the love of his life, "so He created one here just for me."

Tears cascaded from her eyes as she shared that story in my ear during our hug; she finished with, He had that little smirk on his face!

I turned to look down at the milk-white haired jar of clay that had housed Henry (Hank) Steinman all these years; the smirk was still there.

The first time I saw him was when she asked me to sing for them.

The last time I saw him was when she asked me to sing for him.

Later, from my lofty perch I stared down and allowed my mind to wander, and I wondered how many lives had been touched by this man whose exit from this life the world barely noticed.

And with a chorus of angels behind me I sang, "And He will bear you up on eagle's wings".

The mind wandered more as I thought of how he had requested any money intended for funeral flowers be diverted to help 2-year-old Kyle Surgo with his fight for life against a congenital disorder, about which he had read recently in The News. That was the story of the life of this one who, along with wife, Betty Jo, and friend, Greg DuShane, had created the St. Michael's We Care Telethon more than 20 years ago. And with the telethon theme song I sang, "We'll keep you close as always, it won't even seem like you've gone."

I squeezed the hand of my lovely wife as she dabbed tears from her eyes. I remembered that the day I met him was the day I met her.

And I wondered as I sang the final song, "I can only imagine what it will be like when I walk by Your side!"

Yes, this life barely noticed when Hank Steinman left it a week after offering one final rose of love to the one who called him "My Honey."

But with all my heart I believe a majestic welcome home parade and banquet was waiting when he arrived at the place reserved for those who believe that "Unto the least of these; what you do for them you also do for Me!"

But what do I know?

BUILDING A SCHOOL ONE BOOK AT A TIME

N O V E M B E R   7 ,   2 0 0 5

In battle fatigues and helmet I was on one knee with my arm around the little boy. Upside down and slung under my shoulder was my M-16 automatic weapon; we were both smiling for the camera.

As delivery date drew near, I virtually tore the house apart frantically, futilely; searching for the picture previously put in a safe place and planned for the cover of the new book just about completed.

"The subdued, upside-down weapon is a war reminder but my arm around the boy tells of my love for the children then," I shared with Monroe Publishing Co. Design Editor Jim Dombrowski. "The book tells of my love for them now," I continued.

"I'll put something together in case you don't find it," he finished.

I never found the picture but boy, did he ever put something together!

That something is the cover of my new book, "The Ghost Closet: Return to Vietnam on the Wings of D.O.V.E."

As we prepare to honor veterans Friday, I think of my own service and how it has led to my writing a book as well as the resulting project in which my wife, Renee, and I are involved; I hope you will join us!

The photograph was taken during my service in the Vietnam War. As I chronicle in the book, during that time I befriended many children, specifically at an orphanage in the hamlet of Duc Pho.

In January, 2000, I joined 20-some Toledo-based Vietnam veterans and Rotarians to form "The D.O.V.E. Fund;" D.O.V.E. is an acronym for "Development of Vietnam Endeavors." We raised funds to help the poor peoples of that Asian nation's war-torn Quang Tri Province and in that first year constructed five schools and two hospitals.

In spring, 2001, Renee joined me as I reluctantly took that 14,000 mile return trip to the "land which I swore would never see my return" to dedicate those facilities.

Catching wind of our mission trip in advance, *The Evening News* requested I keep a journal for publication upon my return. During the trip we took off and landed 24 times in 10 days; there was no time to write, but upon return I sat and wrote the basic story of "The Ghost Closet." The News published it in entirety days later.

Recently Renee and I realized we had a golden opportunity to make a difference in our world by expanding the story into a book and using it as a platform to build a school in Vietnam. I included everything there was no room for in the original script and took it to News Marketing Director Jeanine Bragg, who, along with Jim, agreed to publish the book.

"The Ghost Closet" will be on sale Sunday at the Monroe County Library System's Writers on the River series at the Ellis Reference & Information Center. I am honored and humbled to be included.

More importantly, every dime of profit from this book goes to build this school, so, when you buy the book, you are virtually buying a brick to help us build it.

While money is tight and we have glaring needs at home, this is an opportunity to bring our world a little closer together. Given today's glaring headlines, we certainly need that.

Oh, one more thing … you're gonna love the cover!

But what do I know?

COMING FULL CIRCLE

N O V E M B E R   1 4 ,   2 0 0 5

"Sproing!" was the sound made when the steel string snapped, startling me and sending me into a momentary freeze. "Wow, you're jammin man!" said good friend and bass guitar player Nep Sindel, who then gave me a high-five.

Something that had happened hundreds of times in the past had happened again; problem was it hadn't happened in almost 20 years. I had broken a string on my guitar.

Back in May I had knee surgery and developed an infection that left me immobile at home with my leg iced and elevated. Boredom had center stage ... until I remembered an old friend that had been hiding under the bed all those years.

Renee retrieved him and once in tune he was singing sweet rhythms as he had the 1971 day I bought him new. Also soon were screams from un-calloused fingertips begging me to stop the torture I was inflicting by running them across steel strings and frets.

I once carved out a meager existence touring North America strumming that guitar, writing songs and singing. Therapy for the soldier home from war that couldn't seem to keep a job turned into major marriage detraction years later; it finally got easier to leave the love of my life for the love of my wife; eventually, I lost both.

A replacement radio career was tolerable; being off the road and home in bed at night was wonderful.

The eventual emotional breakdown that took me to the edge of suicide almost ended everything, but God changed all that by changing my life forever with His special touch that day.

Eventually radio got boring and I took a government job that has been rewarding in spite of how strange bedfellows make politics so difficult.

I think everybody has a special calling in this life and we get hung up by not following that call. Many times we make decisions to please other people instead of doing what we know we were called to do; I know I did.

So 20 years later I find myself having come — as Renee suggests — full circle and back to my previous point of performing and sharing talents God gave me, only this time with His intervention in between.

Ironically, the book I've been writing just happened to be published at the same time as my return to public performing and I can present the book for sale at the same time; how convenient.

Also during my knee rehabilitation I believe God revealed to me His latest plan for my and Renee's lives; its called Guided Ministries and you can read more about it at www.tomtreece.com.

Thursday will be a special day for me as Monroe Bank & Trust, Monroe County Community College and Frog Leg Inn are sponsoring me in a concert at the college's fabulous new Meyer Center. I'll be speaking about my D.O.V.E. Fund and how and why I wrote The Ghost Closet, have questions and answers and then sign some books for those who might want to help us build this school.

I've also invited some old friends to join me on stage for an unpolished opening set of music and, I hope, I won't break a string.

Just like breaking that string, I expect it will feel strange again, but I also believe it is exactly where I am supposed to be.

But what do I know?

"IS THAT YOUR DOG?"

NOVEMBER 21, 2005

"Cats and Dogs," was how mother used to describe how it was raining that day.

The weight of the day's newspapers used the strap of the bag to cut into my shoulder and I shifted it relentlessly trying to transfer that weight. A side flap of the weatherproof bag covered and kept the papers dry and I could feel the load lighten as I methodically pulled each one from the sack and slid it into its slot along my route.

As I ambled along the road a car pulled alongside *The Monroe Evening News* paperboy servicing the Evergreen Acres subdivision.

"Hi Tommy!" he called to me.

I peered through the sheets of rain to see who was calling me.

"Hey Sock!" I called back after recognizing my neighborhood friend.

We chatted a bit as torrents of rain cascaded off the bill of the hood of my raincoat before he suddenly pointed past me and asked, "Say, is that your dog?"

I spun around in the road to look but there was no dog. I was sure my dog, Trixie, was home safe in his doghouse, but maybe he had broken loose and followed me.

"He's right there behind you!" he called out.

I spun again but still no dog.

My brother's hand-me-down raincoat was big and bulky and made it difficult for me to have much of a sight perspective in the pouring rain.

He just ran around to the other side of the car! he instructed and I raced around looking for the dog; no dog.

"He's back over here now!" he called from the drivers side; I came back around; still no dog.

He pointed down and said, "He just crawled under the car!" I got down on all fours to search for the dog; no dog.

Ill spare you the rest of the details of how Leonard (Socko) Clark virtually hung me out to dry in the rain for a good 15 minutes that day looking for a dog that never existed.

We've belly-laughed together every time we've seen each other in the 50-some years since that day; each time Sock would begin the conversation with, "Say, is that your dog?"

Last week - as we stood by his casket - the woman in the car with him that day squinted out at me through eyes swollen nearly shut from shedding tears of heartbreak as her mate had been summoned to his home in Heaven.

I coaxed a smile from Alice when I mentioned the day her husband had me hunting for that phantom dog, but the pain she smiled through stabbed my heart. Although family and friends were there heaping love and support on their mother, grandmother and friend, the reality of knowing that the one God joined her with 52 years ago would not be coming home anymore had her struggling to stay in control. I can't imagine what it must feel like losing the love of your life after all those years.

I will miss my friend, but, just like Alice, I believe I will see him again. In the meantime, to everything there is a season, a time to laugh at funny times gone by, but also a time to be there to bear each others burdens as well.

But what do I know?

"WIND BENEATH MY WINGS"

NOVEMBER 28, 2005

A faint cry so soft and subtle it's hardly audible calls through the midnight hour; two feet hit the floor.

My wife is the most amazing woman I have ever met! I hope you don't get sick of hearing about her because I can't seem to stop talking about her, mainly because as each day goes by I realize even more what a special woman with whom God has blessed me.

For starters, we share the same strong faith in The One who gave her one of my ribs, and that is the hub of our wheel.

She's also the hardest working person I've ever met. The task before her is irrelevant as all she has to give is whatever it takes to accomplish it. I've said many times that if I had a task assigned me — no matter if it was digging a ditch or building a spaceship to Mars — and could only choose one person to assist me, Renee is the one I would choose every time.

She is strong as an ox yet is reduced to tears over the slightest emotional story of a child mistreated or a kindness extended.

The song Wind Beneath My Wings should have been written for her as it is she who pushes me to push myself to showcase God-given talents or explore unexplored caverns of imagination or creative nature.

You've never read anything I've written that has not first had the litmus test: her approval. If something doesn't sound right she tells me and I lean on that approval so much that I won't let it go until I have it.

She is a drop-dead gorgeous knockout yet is the most discreet and humble person I know who without a doubt will try to talk me out of printing this!

She's a fabulous cook, yet allows me the fun and pleasure of doing all the cooking. She's an impeccable housekeeper, yet didn't scream at me last week when I turned the green towels gray with too much bleach in the wash. Her comment: I was tired of green anyway!

I always thought I was a whiz with finance until I discovered how much greater she was and quickly got out of the way. She is in charge of our business, from running the day-to-day operations to scrubbing floors when needed. She strives to meet the needs of her employees by incorporating principles taught by Christ, that if you want to be a leader, you have to be a servant.

What squeezed my heart to write this about the woman of my dreams was that cry in the night and those two feet hitting the floor moments later as Nonnie, for the fifth time that night, ran off to comfort grandsons Drake and Gaige, while Poppy continued to run the sawmill.

Our sons testify to the great mother she has been for 30 years; I testify to the great grandmother and wife she is. If all the children in the world had someone to love them like Renee we would rarely see heartbreak and sadness on their little faces.

Only when I promised God that — as instructed — I would put no one before Him in my life did he bring my second-most precious gift, the most wonderful woman on the planet! What a blessed man I am!

But what do I know?

WISE MEN STILL SEEK HIM

DECEMBER 5, 2005

How sad to see the American culture related to this time of year slowly being eliminated from our way of life.

During my entire life, "Christmas" was that most anticipated time of the entire year. There was an annual anticipatory magic about it that slowly gathered intensity like a wave on the ocean to ultimately slam itself ceremoniously onto the beach of my heart with a sensational crescendo that reverberated for months.

I hope the magic of Christmas is still there for the children; I'm not sure. As long as I live I'll not forget that Christmas morning magic of peering through the cracked bedroom door to see if Santa had come and then racing to the tree to open presents once mom and dad had given the ok.

One of my narration lines during last week's Christmas program at church addressed some folks who remember times when families weren't so well off and the gifts under the tree were nothing more than apples, oranges, pecans, walnuts or hard rock candy; I knew there were at least two of those folks there that night: my sister and me!

I also remember days later looking longingly at the glittery gifts other kids in the neighborhood had received and wishing we could have received some so expensive. I didn't realize at the time that I had received the finest of gifts, for even though they were simple nuts, fruits and candy, they were the very best that my father and mother could give at that time.

I miss having the entire family gathered together around the tree, and then around the dinner table. During these later years of my life it seems Christmas got lost in the hustle and bustle of fighting the crowds at the malls and traffic on the streets in order to get what we want and where we are going.

This year the controversy surrounds the very name of the season. We are sitting by and watching as the minority of political correctness is working overtime to totally eliminate The Reason for the Season: The birth of Christ.

Special thanks to my pastor, Roy Southerland, for reminding me yesterday that in spite of the battles over whether or not it is a Christmas tree or a holiday tree or whether the kids are on Christmas break or holiday break, nothing has changed in 2000 years.

He read to me the historical account of how "wise men" came looking for this child to worship Him and how the king of that day Herod was the very first to try to take Christ out of Christmas. And he didn't bother filing a lawsuit and taking it all the way to the Supreme Court ... he was the Supreme Court so he simply had every child in the city of Bethlehem two years old or younger... murdered.

Not a fun story to hear at this most wonderful time of year, but an important one for those concerned about whether or not there will be a successful movement to eliminate Christ from the season; there will not.

Schools can eliminate Him, malls and mega-shopping stores can eliminate Him and you can even eliminate Him from the name of your tree, but He will never be eliminated, because He is what Christmas is all about.

But what do I know?

SANTA SLEPT WITH MOM

D E C E M B E R   1 9 ,   2 0 0 5

I was thinking about Santa this morning and how everyone perceives him: red suit, fat belly, white hair and beard, glasses, black belt and boots.

Then I started thinking of how I remember Santa. He never had a red suit; in fact, he didn't like wearing suits but he did "dress up" every Sunday.

There was no fat belly; another fact is that I don't think he had an ounce of fat on him, probably because he spent virtually every day of his life doing hard, physical labor, not at the North Pole making toys but at Consolidated Paper Co. making boxes. It grieves me sometimes to remember how hard he worked just so he could be Santa to us three kids.

Those who know me know I'm a big boy: 6-foot-5, 260 pounds. Santa wasn't quite as big: 6-foot-1 and — I'm guessing — 220. Mother gave me Santa's wedding ring after he left and I used to be amazed while I sat and slipped it on and off my finger again and again. What was amazing? I could put his wedding ring on over the top of my wedding ring.

Santa was a big man! And, even though I am physically bigger than he was, I'll never be as big as he was.

Santa loved the good earth. He loved to till the soil and plant his garden. Santa was a firm believer in the concept that "you reap what you sow," whether it be in the garden or in the life that you live.

Santa loved the good guys. He loved Roy Rogers and Andy Griffith because they always stood for good and helped triumph over evil.

And here was a strange one for me: Santa also loved "Big Time Wrestling."

He couldn't wait for it to come on our old black and white TV. As the program began he would be relaxed in the chair, but as soon as Dick the Bruiser started pummeling Leaping Larry Chene his hands would grip the armrests and he would lean forward.

Soon he was on the edge of the seat in the process that would take him into the floor and in front of the set, occasionally helping Chene with a punch when he would get a staged upper hand.

Santa was one of 10 kids born in the backwoods of Tennessee's Cumberland Mountains. As the result of being forced out of school in second grade in order to help his family grow and raise the food they needed to survive, he could barely spell his name.

Santa wanted his children to have more than he had, which is why he migrated north to find work, and then — once he found it — worked like no man I have ever seen work. His work ethic was impeccable and his word was his bond.

Santa had great faith in God. He taught me that "religion" was irrelevant but that having a personal relationship with The One whose birth we celebrate in seven days was the most important thing I would ever need or do.

I miss Santa, but I will be eternally grateful for the irreplaceable gifts he gave, gifts that had nothing to do with money yet brought unmatchable joy and that have lasted a lifetime!

But what do I know?

WHO WERE THEY TALKING ABOUT?

DECEMBER 26, 2005

The most convoluted Christmas season in my life has come and gone and I'm left wondering what the future holds for Christmas — and culture — in America.

Ironically, days before the Christmas holiday, or, "Christian holy day," a judge ruled that schools cannot teach "intelligent design" (creation).

I've stayed out of this debate, mainly because I believe religion should be taught in churches.

However, since it's obvious that nobody can prove where we came from or where we're going, all possibilities within reason should be given consideration when determining curriculum for teaching our children about the origins of life.

Even without my personal relationship with God, no one will ever convince me that the incredible, intimate, intricate makeup of life results from a big bang theory or the evolution of something crawling out of an ocean on a planet in a solar system that just happened to be there. However, there's no question that some things do evolve.

What is unacceptable are judges who make arbitrary decisions determining that God has no place in our government, especially when one considers our country's origins. The question now is whether the mere mention of His name is constitutional.

My question to each of you is, to whom do you think the framers of our Constitution — and country — were referring when they wrote in our Declaration of Independence that, "We hold these truths to be self-evident, that all men are created equal, that they are endowed by their Creator with certain inalienable rights ..."

We honor the great men of wisdom who wrote these words. So why would we ignore the fact that when the Constitutional Convention turned into a "verbal brawl with little hope of compromise or progress," they called to that Creator for guidance and soon produced the finest guide for government in the history of the world?

Why would that judge — or we — ignore the fact that preambles to the constitutions of every state of this great union acknowledge God in their opening paragraphs?

Most Americans think the Constitution speaks of "freedom from religion," when — in my opinion — the intent is "freedom of religion." I think the framers believed that everybody believed in that Creator — or Authority — and what they wanted to legislate against was the possibility that someone would one day make a law dictating the specific religion of the country, such as Catholic, Baptist or Methodist.

I want everyone to believe what they want to believe, but I have no intention of sitting by and watching while our cultures — like Christmas — and other majority-accepted ways of life get trashed by those who have found the amazing tool of political correctness with which to manipulate personal agendas that will ultimately bring America to her knees.

Then again, perhaps that is exactly what it will take for us to finally find the true wisdom of our Constitutional fathers.

But what do I know?

REAR VIEW MIRROR

D E C E M B E R   3 0 ,   2 0 0 5

If you drive you use it every day. You look up and to the right and adjust it so you can simply give a quick glance to see what's behind you. If you need a closer examination of what's back there you can stare into it for extended periods of time, but it's difficult – and dangerous - to go forward during that process.

The concept of the rear-view mirror has become an important part of my life.

I have a tendency to dwell in the past, whether reveling in memories and accomplishments or grieving over failures and disappointments; I think we all do this.

It's fun to look back at good times you've had, where you've been, what you've done, but it's not fun to remember failures and disappointments.

I believe it's important to learn from where you've been but unhealthy to dwell there, either good or bad, but especially bad.

Husbands or wives who lose spouses after multiple years as one have such a difficult time trying to go forward, but go forward they must as life goes on. My own mother struggled with this for years until finally taking her eyes off that mirror and deciding to embrace today and tomorrow by getting her first job and moving forward.

I love to pull out old pictures or yearbooks and reminisce about school days and I love getting together with old band mates to retell stories of being "on the road" and laughing at the wild and crazy antics of youth.

And, while I like to do that occasionally, there are new songs to write and sing, new places visit, new friends to meet and new challenges to undertake and one cannot walk straight into today and tomorrow while looking back.

An excerpt from a letter written by a fellow whom I read regularly says, "this one thing I do: forgetting what lies behind and straining forward to what lies ahead." I don't want to forget what's behind me but the only thing that really matters is what's in front of me.

Perhaps more importantly, I don't want to dwell on the failures I have experienced. I want to turn those disadvantages into my advantage by climbing on top of them to use as a ladder get to the next plateau of my life that's ahead.

The same is true for people who hurt you, which has to be one of life's greatest disappointments. You can dwell on that and let it consume you, or you can put that – and them – behind you and strain forward to greener pastures ahead.

Renee and I "adjust our rear view mirrors" all the time. She will get bogged down with a recent hurt or one from days gone by and I stop what I'm doing, reach up and grab an imaginary rear view mirror, adjust it and say, "Yup, I see it back there!" which is usually enough to bring her two things: a smile to her face and a resolve to return her view out the front windshield of our life.

On behalf of my better half I wish you and yours a Happy New Year and hope you will use your rear view mirror to help you strain forward for what lies ahead in 2006.

But what do I know?

LOVE STUFF—HAPPY 50TH RENEE

JANUARY 15, 2006

"I've come to realize I'm in love with you, but, you're not in love with me, so I'm leaving for New York," she said with tears streaming down her cheeks.

Shocked, bewildered and somewhat defiant I responded with, "Look, I made it perfectly clear when we started dating I wasn't interested in any of this 'love stuff!'"

"I know;" she acknowledged, "it's my problem and that's why I have to do something about it; I love you; goodbye," and with that walked out my door, got into her car and drove off into the sunset.

I sat for a while in stunned silence trying to figure out what had just happened. Renee and I had been dating for almost a year and a half, and, as I said, I had told her from the outset I wasn't interested in love. She said she wasn't either and suggested we simply be friends, occasionally go to dinner and just have fun together, and that's exactly what we had been doing. That is, until she messed it all up with this 'love stuff!'

About an hour later I called her home to hear her answering machine's sweet voice say, "Hi, it's Renee, I'm out of town for a few days; call you when I get back."

"Renee, Tom," I began, "I feel bad about this but I told you from the start I wasn't interested in love! Call me when you get home," and hung up.

An hour later I called again to say, "Are you sure we can't keep this going? I mean, I don't want the love stuff but I do enjoy being with you; call me when you get this."

Just before crawling in bed I tried again; "Renee, I'm struggling with this; we need to talk! When will you be home? Call me.... please."

Over the midnight and early morning hours I must have called another seven times, until finally the answering machine was full and would take no more calls. The last one it accepted, however, had a change of tune.

"Renee, it's me and I've just realized I'm in love with you too!" I blabbered through my own emotion and tears. "I don't know where you are but I hope I haven't been a stupid fool and lost you; please call me the minute you get this; I love you Renee and I know it now!"

A month later, I led her through my house with poems giving hints as to where she could find the next hint, the last of which led to a Christmas tree ornament-bulb ring box containing the glimmering gift of my love she now wears on her left hand.

God has blessed me with the most wonderful woman on the planet, and today – on her milestone birthday – I thank Him for His immeasurable gift to me, which came all because I made a decision one Florida evening to put Him first in my life, no matter what! The very next day I flew home to Michigan…and met Renee.

If you know my Renee, email her today at tomt@monroenews. com or give her a call and wish her a happy birthday.

I may not be the smartest or best looking guy on the planet, but I certainly am one of the most blessed!

But what do I know?

TWINKLING OF AN EYE

J A N U A R Y   2 2 ,   2 0 0 6

It looked like a black lemon with a white dishrag crumpled on top; nothing has terrified me more in my life! Panic seized my heart and palpitations pounded my chest as the thought went through my head that no surgeon on earth could remove the bad from the good without messing things up for good!

In just a few seconds, my world – our world – changed forever!

I began Monday by kissing my wife and wishing, "Happy Birthday!" Little did I know it would be the tragic opposite of happy and the worst day of my life!

Renee had been lethargic for some time and recently noticed numbness in her leg and arm. Our Dr. K, concerned, ordered tests, the first of which was a 6:30 AM MRI on her birthday.

We headed for the hospital for the test and then killed time before another Dr. K appointment during which he – as professional and considerate as possible – dropped a bomb on us with, "Renee, you have a brain tumor!"

We were devastated! One moment I was the happiest, most satisfied man on the planet and the next I was gasping for air and wondering how life could have been trashed so quick and effortlessly. I didn't think she could live, which made me not want to.

We raced to Toledo where brilliant neurosurgeon Dr.

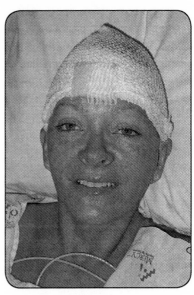

"Hi Buddy!" Renee just after brain surgery, 2006.

Lawrence crushed us even more by admitting he'd never seen anything like it and could give us no prognosis. He assured us, however, that he was the best; he was right!

With unbelievable courage and strength Renee resigned herself to what needed to be done and assured me as I wept and begged God to allow me to carry her cross that it was not mine to bear.

I called everyone I knew requesting prayers and we tried - in the short window of time we had – to get our affairs in order.

Wednesday I waved goodbye to the woman I love more than life and wondered - as she slowly slipped out of sight on her way to neurosurgery – if I had just had my last intelligent conversation – or any conversation - with the most important person in my life.

Six hours later I beat the rocket to Pluto off the launch pad after she finally opened her eyes, saw me, smiled and said, "Hi buddy!" I knew then God had answered my prayers and given me back this most precious gift.

You see, during my Tuesday prayer time God reminded me that this life is about Him, not us, and asked if I was willing – like Abraham – to give her up if that was His will. It broke my heart to answer, "Yes!" but I believe that obedience, coupled with the thousands of prayers so many of you barraged God with, caused Him to guide that surgeon's hand to do what I thought no one could do.

Renee is out of ICU but has a long recovery road ahead; I'll be with her every step. You can check her progress at www.tomtreece. com, click on "Media."

Renee and I thank God as well as those who prayed for her; please continue! We also urge you to love your loved ones more today than yesterday, as life – like ours – can be changed in the twinkling of an eye...forever!

But what do I know?

PATRICK SWAYZE WOULD
BE SO PROUD

JANUARY 29, 2006

Will you do me a favor?

Stop reading right now, look at your right index finger and concentrate on moving it just a quarter inch. Sounds silly, right?

Patrick Swayze, physically dead but spiritually alive in the movie "Ghost," tries with all his power to move a bottle cap lying on the subway station floor. Determination wrenches his face as he strains, grunts and gasps during feeble attempts to move it.

Over the past 12 days, I've watched my darling wife struggle with a similar scenario after four hours of surgery to remove two tumors from her brain left the right side of her body paralyzed.

In spite of seeing her in this heartbreaking physical condition, I was a happy man as God had answered my prayers. During prayers before surgery, I knew I had to give her back to The One who had given her to me, and -- as Christ had taught us with the Lord's Prayer -- my prayer had been "Thy will be done."

He also taught us to be specific with our prayers, so my specifics were simple: Please give her back to me alive and please let her know me and be in her right mind.

If she couldn't walk, I'd carry her. If she couldn't talk, I'd speak for her.

So, although the paralysis was hard to take, God had granted my prayer, and I was a happy man. The doctor had predicted that, as swelling decreased, pressure immobilizing motor skills on that side of her body would also dissipate. Again he was right.

the middle of last week, she suddenly could move her arm, then her leg. Thursday I asked her to shake hands, and, with a Swayze-effort, she extended the arm but had no squeeze from the hand.

Friday -- with blood veins bulging from both sides of her shaved head -- she grunted and groaned and huffed and puffed for a good three minutes until finally that right index finger moved about a quarter inch.

I screamed, threw my hands in the air and jumped up and down as if she had scored the winning touchdown in Sunday's Super Bowl game while she exhaled pent-up air and collapsed back into the bed, totally expended of all her energy.

I couldn't believe that something we all take for granted -- extremities instantly doing what the brain instructs -- had taken such a monumental effort. We have no idea how precious our health is until it is gone.

I want to take this moment to gather up all the gratitude I possibly can garner to thank all of you who were so kind to bury my Renee in the hundreds of e-mails, cards, flowers, calls, gifts of love and, most important, prayers for her during this most traumatic time of her/our life.

It would take a ton of time to try to answer each and every one, and, although I intend to try, it will be nearly impossible.

Today we expect to move Renee to a rehabilitation facility where she will need to learn to walk again. Please keep her in prayer.

Last night when I kissed her goodnight, she reached for my hand again, only this time when she grabbed it, she squeezed it. I think even Patrick Swayze would have been proud.

But what do I know?

"WASTE NO MORE TIME!"

F E B R U A R Y 6 , 2 0 0 6

Wanting desperately to return to normalcy (whatever that is) and not turn this column into the "Tom & Renee Show," although realizing the most incredible experience of my life just has occurred, I believe the story demands to be continued.

The end of the workday had come. I clicked the "start" button, then the "turn off computer" button, and pushed away from my desk. I grabbed my coat and keys to head home when, instead of turning off, my computer blinked back to life again. Puzzled, I repeated the steps, but the computer would not turn off.

The rest of the evening and into the night I repeatedly tried to shut it down to no avail. Suddenly, desperately, I realized it wasn't going to turn off no matter what I tried and, at that moment, I discerned that I was dying.

I am a dreamer. I come from a family of dreamers. During my childhood, my father had a recurring dream of a flying red horse. Every time he had the dream, the next day someone in his family died.

I don't always remember my dreams, but, when I do, they always seem to have significance. When the computer would not turn off, I finally awoke, but the dream stayed with me and I grieved as I thought perhaps the dream was prophetic.

I also believe things are not always as they seem. In my dream, the computer was my life. In normal, daily life, I turn my computer off, go home to my wife, eventually go to sleep and then get up the next day, return to work, turn the computer on again and continue my work.

This time, when the computer would not turn off, I believed it meant I was about to die and move to the next life, Heaven.

In prayer I asked God why he would take me now when my wife needed me more than ever.

You've been reading the tragic saga of how I discovered my wife,

Renee, had two brain tumors. With your prayers and God guiding the surgeon's hand, they were removed. Fortunately, she recovered her memory and mental skills. Unfortunately, her right side was virtually paralyzed.

Three weeks later, she is at St. Charles Mercy Hospital's Acute Rehabilitation Center in Toledo learning to walk all over again with the help of a walker. And, although they are 50 percent at best, she has feeling and limited use of all her extremities except for her right foot, and we are hoping that perhaps she might come home this week!

After that prayer, I had relief in my heart as I believe God showed me that not being able to turn that computer off was His signal to me that indeed I am — as we all are — dying. The significance, however, was not that it might be sooner than later, but in the meaning of four words He left me with: "Waste no more time!"

I got the message.

No more stupid e-mail jokes or mindless TV shows. I have books and songs to write and sing and a philosophy to share with those who care to hear. And, I have a dear, sweet woman to love with all my heart.

I must not waste any more time ... even by turning off the computer.

But what do I know?

HUMBLED

FEBRUARY 13, 2006

As we sit on the eve of the day dedicated to the single most important, powerful, active agent known to man, I sit and contemplate yet another word. I must admit this word is difficult for me, as I believe it is for most people.

The word describes what I believe is the most important character trait of The One whose philosophy I have chosen to follow in this life, perhaps even more than the word we celebrate tomorrow. That word is "humility."

Years ago, a popular song shared, "It's hard to be humble when you're perfect in every way." Although the song poked fun at those in love with themselves, we all love ourselves. We don't like hearing or thinking that, but it's true.

We all think we are right about most everything. We think our philosophy is right, our religion — or lack of one — is right, the clothes we wear are cool — as is the way we wear our hair. We think what's going on in our lives is much more important than what's going on in someone else's, and we think our opinions are right, right?

Life has a way of humbling us, no matter who you are, the wealth you have or your position in life. Sooner or later, some situation sends the message that everything you think important in life isn't. Our message came four weeks ago today.

I hope today is the last installment of that message because as the one taking the brunt of the situation — my wife, Renee — says, "It's time to get on with life!"

She's right.

Yesterday, I brought home from the hospital my object of tomorrow's affection. Last night — after four weeks that felt like four years — I finally felt again her silky skin against mine as we lay in bed together and she shared, "There really is no place like home!"

We lay and talked about the emotional storm on the sea of our life from which we just had disembarked. Guess what word kept coming up? Humbled.

Each day, I would bring the rubber-band-bound stack of cards and letters from all of you and countless others from across the country — many of whom we don't even know — to her bedside, slit them open and proceed to read every line to her. Virtually all had heartfelt, handwritten messages; virtually all reduced us to tears.

If we could have separated the salt from our tears, we wouldn't have needed water to drink or flavor for food! We have never been so humbled in life.

We are humbled that people loved us so much that, in four weeks, she received more than 300 cards, more than 500 e-mails, 40 flower arrangements, gifts, food, money, love! We were humbled by Mr. Zarb's tribute in Saturday's paper; thank you all!

I don't believe humility is a natural agent of human makeup, as I think we have a tendency to aggrandize ourselves. I think those who have that trait must work for it.

With every passing day, I find myself wanting to be more meek and lowly instead of high and mighty. Given the glitter and rouge passed along by the high and mighty of our society, meek and lowly is exactly where I want to be.

But what do I know?

EVERYDAY STUFF FOR THE MIRACLE WORKER

MARCH 6, 2006

Has there ever been anyone in your life who you absolutely hated and then turned their life around, becoming someone you absolutely loved?

I hated this guy! He was nothing but a big thug. He was about the biggest, meanest, toughest guy I ever saw in my life. A scowl seemed to be tattooed to his face, and he was one of those guys who — just because they just happened to be physical specimens — think that beating the crap out of someone somehow suggested superiority.

He was a heavyweight boxer who went on to become world champion. In truth, he really wasn't much of a boxer; he simply was a brute with so much power that one right or left hook meant lights out.

I remember watching in 1975 when he fought five different guys in one event and pummeled each without mercy. He seemed to enjoy physically destroying them.

Without a doubt in my mind, Muhammed Ali was the greatest heavyweight boxer of all time because he was smart and always seemed to find a way to win. But also without a doubt, young George Foreman was the "baddest" of them all, and I hated him!

Saturday's mail brought Casual Male Big & Tall's latest catalog, and this big and tall male fingered through the first few pages before stopping on a page that featured the company's latest celebrity model. Yup, Big George!

I pondered him for a bit and couldn't help myself from breaking into a grin just from looking at his big smile.

I thought about how magnetic a smile is on anyone, but the smile coming from the face of the guy I described above just amazed me.

How could anyone go from being one of the biggest jerks on the planet to one of the most loved?

The former Olympic champion had turned pro and made a name for himself by destroying Joe Frazier for the title and then other notables such as Ken Norton. Not long after, however, he was outwitted for the title by Ali's "Rope-A-Dope" tactic during their "Rumble in the Jungle" fight in Zaire, Africa. Soon after, Foreman's career was over, and, for me, it was good riddance.

But then something happened. After one of his later fights, Foreman had a near-death experience and shared that he had called out to God to change his life. Obviously, He did.

Suddenly the big pouting jerk was gone and in his place was a warm, funny, happy-go-lucky guy who started doing things to help others. He went back into the ring, worked his way back to a title fight and then — at the age of 45 — became the oldest fighter to win the heavyweight championship 20 years after losing it the first time.

After soon retiring, he became a TV pitchman for everything from mufflers to his famous George Foreman grills (I love mine), from which he has made more money than he ever did from his entire boxing career.

Before, there was nothing about him I could stand. Now there's not much about him I don't adore. I used to think that was amazing, but after having my own life dramatically changed in similar fashion, I now realize that it's everyday stuff for the Miracle Worker.

But what do I know?

NEW TRICKS FOR AN OLD DOG

M A R C H 2 0, 2 0 0 6

There's truth in the old saying, "It's hard to teach an old dog new tricks." I know — because I'm getting to be an old dog who finds it harder to learn new things.

The object of today's bemoan is computers. Thank God for laptops as my personal computer either is being fickle or has crashed.

Too bad our kids are grown and gone, as it usually takes one to show me how to work the VCR, DVD player or, in this case, computer.

Fortunately, years ago my job required I learn computers, and I am thrilled at my level of advancement. Unfortunately, compared to today's rate of technological advancement, I feel like I'm still in grade school.

Without a doubt, the computer is one of history's most important inventions, right alongside electricity, airplanes and the automobile.

I've always been super active, but one of my favorite things to do is "surf" on my computer. Within heartbeats, I can go virtually anywhere in the world. In the last few days, I've watched the techno-360 degree view from atop both Mount Everest and the Eiffel Tower simply by clicking on a Web site.

I remember as a kid a traveling encyclopedia salesman came to our door. Father, wanting his kids to have the education he didn't, made the purchase. I remember being amazed leafing through those pages and seeing the wonders of the world.

Today, instead of encyclopedias, I simply go to the browser and type in whatever I'm looking for, push the magic button and there it is. Sports, history, geography, dictionary, TV listings, addresses, anything — you name it, it's there.

Unfortunately — as with anything else — it also has easy access for evil. I love the ease of paying bills online and yet am terrified to see daily evidence of computer hacking, fraud and identity theft.

I also remember once trying to find the address of the White House and instead getting a pornographic Web site that kept reconnecting itself to my computer even when I tried to leave. I saw things there that made even this old dog gulp, and I couldn't imagine my grandkids having free access to that. I must admit that I love e-mail. What a wonderful communication tool! I find myself using it to talk to the people in our office even though, proximity-wise, we are all within 30 feet of one another. I also hear regularly from many of you who wouldn't take the time to snail-mail me (as I probably wouldn't, either).

Oddly enough, as incredibly intricate and complex as it is, the computer still is no match for the brain God gives us. The brain built the computer in the first place.

I'm performing in a musical drama this and next weekend ("The Prodigal" at First Baptist Church in Temperance) that calls for pages of memorization I learned a year ago that has been a snap to recall. I'm also amazed I can remember some things that happened more than 50 years ago and seem like they were yesterday.

Now, if my brain only had the power to fix my computer, I'd be set. Instead, I'll have to call some kid who's a computer geek fix it since one thing is for sure: I don't think this old dog will ever learn that trick!

But what do I know?

SO BLESSED

M A R C H   2 7 ,   2 0 0 6

It was midnight one cold winter night years ago. Renee and I successfully had fought off the regiment of sleep soldiers trying to drag us off to wherever they drag us off to each night about this time in order to finish the movie we had been watching.

It was a favorite time of day. Because she worked later than me, I had dinner on the table waiting when she walked through the door. Over dinner, we updated each other on all the exciting things that had happened that day. Sitting down to dinner and conversation with my wife is one of my very favorite things.

After dinner, we sauntered upstairs, checked our e-mail, made our individual plans for the following day and then collapsed on the couch in front of a roaring fireplace to watch TV for the day's dying hours.

As I always do, I had cranked up the electric blanket ahead of time so the bed was a blazing toaster by the time we crawled in it — another of my favorite things to do on a cold winter's night.

The all-glass back of our bedroom overlooks Lake Erie, and we often just lay in bed marveling at the moon over the water or the sky's zillions of stars winking back at us.

This night was not so placid.

I'm a stomach-sleeper, and my lovely wife is the best back-scratcher in the world. Her scratching slowly and successfully had lulled me off on my overnight journey, but the howling woke me up.

It was the wind, and, in a short time, the whole house began to groan from the gale into which it had grown.

I opened my eyes and viewed the surreal scene. My flag light illuminated the dark of night as snow blew by the window so quickly that it looked like steady streams of white light. From my perpendicular position, it looked like it was coming straight down.

The house groaned again, and, for some reason, in my mind's

eye, I saw the flimsy, cardboard houses of the poverty-stricken people Renee and I had witnessed during a visit to Venezuela. Storms of this magnitude smash their shelters like foam cups under foot.

"We are so blessed!" I whispered to Renee after sharing my vision.

"Compared to those people and the people we saw in Vietnam, every American is blessed, even the ones who think they are living in poverty here," she said. "They just don't know it."

She was right. We take so much for granted living in this country.

I've always contended that each American should have to go live in a third-world country for a year, a month or even a week. As Renee and I found out, they would come home with an entirely different attitude and appreciation for the privilege of living in the United States of America.

But what do I know?

ROOM FOR ONLY ONE FLAG!

A P R I L   1 0 ,   2 0 0 6

From what I understand, I'm Irish. Somewhere along the line, the name was O'Treece before one of my grandfathers dropped the "O" and the apostrophe, which means that I, like you, came from immigrant ancestors - that is, of course, unless one of your grandfather's names was something like Sitting Bull.

How sad it is that to see the only true original Americans, one must travel to a reservation somewhere. It's almost like going to the zoo.

There's no doubt immigrants helped make America the great country it is today, and I appreciate anyone who stands with open arms to embrace less fortunate souls in order to make a difference in their lives.

I remember my father taking in a fellow separated from his family. He fed and clothed him, warmed him by our fire and treated him like one of his own in spite of our family already bulging at the seams in our house.

There was one thing made perfectly clear, however. This was his house, he made the rules and the instant the fellow didn't want to follow those rules, he'd have been shown the door unceremoniously.

I don't mind a bit telling you how incensed I was watching protests on TV last week staged mostly by Hispanics in this country illegally. They carried signs suggesting America had stolen the Southwest from Mexico and they burned American flags while waving the Mexican. They demanded their "rights."

Huh? What rights? They sneaked into our country illegally and now demand rights? They need to be shown the door like my father would have done.

How about if I sneak into your home and demand that you feed and clothe me, pay for my health care and hospitalization, get me a driver's license and find me a job? I expect you would do the same as my father.

I am not insensitive. What I am is a believer that we are a nation of laws, and the only way it works is when everyone obeys them.

There are rules where you could adopt me, and - once those rules are followed - you could welcome me into your home and then offer me all the aforementioned amenities.

We read every day how the rest of our world hates America. If that's so, why does everyone want to come here?

I also think the World Trade Centers - and the thousands who died inside - still would be standing today if immigration laws had some teeth.

Blanket amnesty for the 11 million illegal immigrants in this country only will send the signal to millions more that the coast is clear. And, while the Christian in me desires to be accommodating to anyone who needs help getting pulled out of their hole, I still have locks on the inside of my doors for a reason!

In 1907, President Teddy Roosevelt said, "We have room for but one flag, the American flag. We have room for but one language, the English language, and we have room for but one sole loyalty, and that is loyalty to the American people."

As we cautiously try to help others in a world awash in evil, I also heartily endorse another quote from the old Rough Rider - the one that says, "Speak softly, but carry a big stick!"

But what do I know?

TEAMMATE CATCHES MORE THAN WILD PITCH

A P R I L   1 7 ,   2 0 0 6

I love hearing from old friends and reminiscing about old times - especially when those times were unique, one-of-a-kind times.

I recently received a call from an old friend, Kenny Moore, who had moved north some time ago. He asked how Renee and I were doing and shared that friends had been cutting out and sending my column to him on occasion.

During our conversation, I remembered something Kenny had done years ago that was, shall we say, out of the ordinary. We were teammates on a softball team. I played third base; Kenny was our catcher.

In order to get the gist of the story, you need to know that Kenny was a big man. I can't recall whether he played football, but he would have made a great middle linebacker. Let's just say there were no winners among base runners who tried to score on close plays at the plate whether safe or out. Hitting a brick wall might have been more pleasant.

Kenny also could belt the ball with the best, and more than a few times he came up big for us with the game on the line. The Vietnam veteran also was a tough City of Monroe police detective extremely dedicated to his job.

One hot summer night, we were playing at the old ball field no longer there at Hellenberg Park on the city's east side.

It was slow-pitch "Blooper Ball," as we used to call it. The pitcher could put a 13-foot arc on the pitch in an attempt to make it more difficult for the batter to hit. Unfortunately, it also made pitches that fell short of the plate more difficult for the catcher to catch because the ball usually would take a big bounce over the catcher's head and roll to the backstop.

On one such occasion, the ball did exactly that, and Kenny

bounded up out of his crouch and ran back to retrieve the ball. What happened next I have never seen happen - previously or since - in my 50-some years of watching or playing ball.

As he was about to pick up the ball, he noticed a man standing behind the backstop. He stopped, crammed his hand down the crotch of his uniform, pulled out a pistol and screamed, "Don't move!" and pointed it at the man.

Needless to say, spectators and players from both teams stood speechless as the game came to a screeching halt while catcher - and detective - Kenny Moore captured an escaped convict from Jackson prison who made the mistake of attending the game.

Soon, a squad car came to take the prisoner away. Kenny tucked his pistol back in his pants, the game resumed and the first pitch from our pitcher hit a good six inches off the plate.

"Uh...STRIKE!" called the umpire. The batter jerked his head around and gave the umpire a "You gotta be kidding!" look before glancing at Kenny and then saying, "Yes sir, definitely a strike."

The game went pretty quickly after that, and, yes, we won.

All those years we played together, I never knew he was carrying a gun. And, while he certainly was a dedicated employee, he probably would have changed his tune had that gun ever gone off in his shorts.

But what do I know?

LOVE ONE ANOTHER

A P R I L 2 4 , 2 0 0 6

Father used to say, "No matter how bad you think you have it, somebody has it worse!"

Father and Mother both bathed me in old sayings like this during my childhood. The purpose was to impress upon me that whatever problem I was having actually was trivial compared to what others might be going through at the same time.

Last week, Renee and I celebrated three months of life since her January brain surgery. Everywhere I go, concerned friends and strangers inquire as to her condition, so allow me this moment to update.

The most amazing woman on the planet is as sharp and beautiful as ever. Her hair has grown enough to start covering the tops of her ears, and her spirit is inextinguishable.

I take her to therapy three days a week in her quest to learn to walk all over again, and - amazingly - not once have I heard, "Why me?" or "Why God?" or "Poor, poor, pitiful me!"

Although she does have some feeling, her right leg from the knee down still is mostly paralyzed - along with the ring and pinky fingers of her right hand - and she can walk with the aid of a leg brace and a four-pronged cane. Trips up or down the stairs that used to take 15 minutes have been reduced to five, and we are grateful to God for His healing touch on her life.

I have lived the majority of my life on overdrive; I want to do it all, see it all, smell it all, taste it all and feel it all because I know it will all be gone in what seems like a blink of an eye. And, while I still endorse that mentality, another of Mom and Dad's sayings - "Take time to smell the flowers!" - suddenly is prevalent as the result of our situation with Renee.

Unfortunately, I must admit that, unlike her, back in January, I did ask God, "Why me?" I will detail His amazing answer somewhere down the line. But, for today, I want to note that it was this week's tragedy newspaper headline that got me thinking about that opening statement.

Tuesday's head-on automobile crash instantly had killed the beautiful young wife and mother and had critically injured her two infant children riding with her, the youngest of which died two days later.

I remember the gripping terror of thinking I might have only the day and a half left with the woman of my dreams before surgery that could take her life or leave her paraplegic.

Father was right! As bad as I thought I had/have it, my problem is actually trivial compared to the young father who undoubtedly kissed and said goodbye to his wife and children that day with no idea that he never would have that same opportunity again.

Would you join me in praying for comfort and healing for this young father, Matt Thompson, and especially for his son, Nathen? Although I don't know him, I can't even imagine trying to deal with the horror life dealt him last week.

I hope we will all "love one another" a little more this week than last because we never know when it will be our last opportunity to do so.

But what do I know?

PATIENCE AND PRAYER

M A Y 1 , 2 0 0 6

Patience and prayer
"1: Bearing pain or trials without complaint
2: showing self-control"
Instructions along the way directed me to "abide in faith, hope and love;" I have found that advice to be extremely important, especially when adding, "But the greatest of these is love."

I love love! It is the greatest of all emotions, fruits of the spirit or acts of character. One thing I know about myself; I definitely have love in my heart.

I also have faith - not only in unquestioned belief in my Heavenly Father but that good will ultimately triumph over evil - and hope, belief in a desire that gives promise for the future.

Another thing I know is that it takes all these for me to counter the fruit described in the opening paragraph: patience!

I am not well-schooled in patience; never have been, sorry to say. I don't like waiting in line and have difficulty remaining calm when someone cuts me off in traffic or with people whose only concern is their personal agenda.

It is a difficult time to have patience, in our world and in Monroe County.

Locally, perhaps the most difficult is exercising patience while trying to navigate travel anywhere in the county, especially on the north side. It would probably be a good idea for the genius who made the decision to institute simultaneous major construction on all three main north-and-south routes to not show up to take credit for it.

As I sat "dead in the water" in traffic last week I kept telling myself, "Patience!" but it wasn't working. All I could think about was my tight schedule - programmed months before all this mess began - crumbling as my gas gauge - and wallet - were emptying, all the while going nowhere.

And then there's government recalls everywhere. We elect ones to conduct our business and the first time they do something we don't like or is not conducive to our personal agenda, the lynch mob comes out.

That is all elementary, however, when it comes to some of the other news competing for headlines: babies suspected of being beaten to death or scalded for discipline? Genocide in Darfur? Suicide bombings everywhere? Lawbreaking immigrants flying the American flag upside down under the Mexican flag while demanding rights? Iran developing nuclear weapons as they call for Israel to be blown off the map?

I have faith, love and hope and am working on patience, but the one thing I have for which I am most grateful, is prayer! No matter what the rest of the world thinks of me or what they may do to me, I know that at any moment I can speak to the Creator of the Universe and know He hears my deepest and innermost concerns.

And, as I witness a world more out of control than ever, I find myself more in intercession for it.

The One in whom I believe has promised that if His people will humble themselves, pray, seek His face and turn from wicked ways, He will hear from Heaven, forgive their sin and heal their land.

Thursday is National Day of Prayer. I'll be asking God to be patient with us as I ask Him to deliver on that promise. I think it's our only hope.

But what do I know?

DR. DOUGLAS: DEDICATED

M A Y   8 ,   2 0 0 6

A few years out of high school - while attending our wonderful Monroe Community College and trying to figure out where I was going in life - I answered a Mercy Memorial Hospital advertisement for on-the-job-training to become a scrub nurse. For those not familiar with the term, the proper name is operating room technician, or O.R. tech for short.

I studied to learn all the job requirements, including the technical names of all the instruments used in surgery. Soon I was dressed in a mask and gown, standing alongside doctors slapping such things as Kellys, hemostats and tenaculums into the palms of their gloved hands during daily surgeries.

I also was in charge of sterilizing those instruments after use. After returning from lunch one day, I walked into the back room and past the sink to unload the sterilizer.

I glanced into the sink and took another step before freezing in my tracks.

Had I seen what I thought I had seen?

Another glance confirmed it. On a bed of ice in the sink lay a man's hand and arm.

Soon my supervisor was sharing details; the man had gotten his hand caught in paper rollers at Consolidated Paper Co. The rollers had pulled his hand and forearm through and then taken his arm off at the bicep.

Called on to try and reattach the arm was one of the finest men I ever had the privilege to work with, Dr. Dale Douglas.

"Are you ready for a marathon?" he asked as we stood lathered to our elbows, scrubbing together in preparation for the task at hand.

He was right. I don't remember exactly how long we took trying to reattach the unfortunate man's arm, but I remember nurses (whom we honor this week) swabbing sweat from our foreheads as sunlight streaming through the window slowly switched to darkness. Unfortunately, we were not successful.

Instead - after realizing there was no way to save the detached arm - we grafted skin from his legs to cover what was left of his arm. I remember being amazed at the good doctor's dedication to detail. I also wondered how he could hold up so well for those eight or nine hours under such intense pressure.

Dr. Douglas was a soft-spoken, gentle soul, very articulate in his work, and, obviously, very dedicated.

"The poor man is going to wake up tomorrow with no arm," he said almost apologetically near the end of the surgery. "The least we can do is make what he has left look as good as possible."

Years later - long after leaving the medical profession - I occasionally would see the aging doctor. He always would say, "Remember that marathon surgery we did?" Then we would rehash the operation all over again, and he would add, "We did the very best we could do for him, didn't we?"

Yes, we did.

Dr. Douglas was the kind of man who always did the very best he could do for each of his patients, no matter what.

Even today, all these years later, Dr. Douglas is a measuring stick for me. I think it important to do the very best I can do - for me and for those around me for whom I have an ongoing desire to help.

But what do I know?

TAKING MOTHERS FOR GRANTED

MAY 15, 2006

I think I've taken Mother's Day for granted all these years.

What a celebration yesterday was! No matter who you are, Mother's Day can humble even the coldest of hearts.

I sat and basked in the warm glow of remembrance as I thought of all the blessings bestowed on me simply by the good fortune of having had Pearl as my mother. What a special woman she was. And even though she's been gone eight years, I rejoice in the honor of being a son of this "virtuous woman whose worth (was) far more precious than rubies."

I also rejoiced in the unequaled blessing of having my wife, the mother of our sons, alive and recovering from her recent neurosurgery and basking in the love we poured over her during dinner. God truly has blessed me.

Unfortunately, deep inside my heart, I couldn't shake off the wet blanket of sorrow that clung to it. I couldn't get Nathen Thompson - the only survivor from an April automobile crash that killed his mother and little sister - out of my mind.

Driving down Monroe St., I thought of him as I saw flower shop parking lots jammed with cars of those buying bouquets for their mothers and again in the restaurant as each table - like ours - ceremoniously serenaded that one special woman.

I thought of him when I remembered all the times my mother came running through the night to my bedside when monsters had invaded my dreams and my weeping had awakened her.

I thought of him when I remembered how many times mother had prayed for me - from asking God to guide me after graduation to protecting me in the Vietnam jungle to helping me find my way back to Him after a broken life of heartbreak and wrong decisions. My heart hurt for the 4-year-old when I realized he never will have that special one in his life again, ever.

What he does have, however, is a father, Matt, who loves him dearly, and I pray that in God's perfect timing He will bring Matt a new helpmate - someone who will develop a deep love for both and meet each of their needs.

After my initial column on the tragedy, Matt wrote to thank us for our prayers for Nathen and said, "They are definitely helping; I can see everyday when I return to his room. He is scared and unsure and covers his face when the doctors enter his room, but once he realizes they are the good guys, he might open up a little."

Continuing, Matt said, "During this rough time, God has touched my heart and opened my eyes to the wonderful things in life that often go unnoticed or unappreciated. We will get through this ... no matter what it takes."

I'm comforted by his words.

Please, continue to pray for Matt and, especially, Nathen. I know with God's guidance and Matt's attitude, they will make it.

Still, my heart is sorrowful knowing that for the rest of his life - even though I trust there will be a replacement - Nathen never will know the wonderful, unique relationship and memories that can only be created with the one who gave you birth. I also realize I've taken mine for granted.

But what do I know?

HELICOPTERS

M A Y   2 2 ,   2 0 0 6

I couldn't help myself. The first quality sunshine in almost two weeks kept screaming at me to come and bathe in it. Despite the waiting workload, the weakness took control, and I relented.

"Just for a short minute," I disciplined myself.

Soon that sun was searing my uncovered skin and the rest started crying, "Me, too!"

I stripped off the T-shirt and immediately felt that wonderful sensation of heat baking my belly and chest. I rested my head on the back of a chair and actually relaxed for the first time in months.

That short minute expanded dramatically into a time warp as I sat sprawled in crumpled fashion and simply soaked up the sun as my mind wandered away.

It was the blades of the helicopter slicing through the air that caught my attention. It came out of the sky and dropped closer to the ground before lifting its cargo up and over the break wall of the lake and landing on the beach.

Another helicopter dropped out of the sky and followed the other as a stiff breeze appeared and pushed itself in off the lake.

Suddenly the sky was full of helicopters, and, in that instant, I was whisked away to the jungle on the other side of the planet.

Suddenly I was a hundred pounds lighter, and sweat produced by the 100-degree days facilitated the black, horn-rimmed glasses' easy slide down the ridge of my nose. There was no fancy fedora but instead a heavy, steel pot that strained my neck muscles in order to keep it balanced.

Suddenly I heard the distant-but-unmistakable sound of rotor-driven blades cutting through the Southeast Asian air and echoing through the central highlands. Mentally I turned to face the sound in anticipation of seeing what looked like a giant formation of mosquitoes lifting themselves up and over the ridges of the mountain range to swarm down and force us to evacuate.

Suddenly I saw the helicopter dropping from the sky to land and the skinny 20-year-old ducking under the blades as he dashed to unload boxes of C-Rations he soon would be sifting through in hopes of finding beans and franks instead of powdered eggs.

Suddenly the wind was trying to pull the skin off my face as I hung out the door of the Huey flying 200 mph and 10 feet off the ground up Highway One.

Suddenly I was tossing my duffel bag into the bay of the bird as I caught a skid to Chu Lai one last time in order to catch a C-130 to Cam Rahn Bay where I would catch a big, blue Braniff 727 that would bring me back to "the world" and ultimately … here on this back porch to watch God's incredible plan of propagation for the maple tree.

Have you ever sat and watched those seeds break free from the womb of the buds that have been sprouting slowly these last few months? When I was a kid, we called them helicopters because they spin themselves out of the maple and whirl off on the wind to land away from the tree to wait for the sun and rain to awaken the life waiting within them.

Big Bang Theory? Please!

But what do I know?

ROLLING THUNDER

JUNE 5, 2006

Only when looking at where the floor and walls met could you tell we were moving.

One moment I was staring down from my unique vantage point on the incredible shape and size of the Pentagon. Ten minutes later, my view of the Potomac made me wonder whether somewhere along here might have been where the man for whom this city was named tossed across that famous dollar.

The revolving, circular restaurant atop Washington, D.C.'s Doubletree Hotel gave a spectacular view of perhaps the most historical skyline in the world. I could have sat there for hours.

In my mind, I imagined sitting here enjoying the view when the huge, terrorist-hijacked aircraft suddenly came streaking out of the sky to ground level in order to broadside the historical structure housing our nation's military brain trust. Five years later, one strains to find any hint as to where that tragedy even occurred.

I surveyed the huge, now-empty parking lot that would cram thousands upon thousands of motorcycles massing for the mission of Rolling Thunder, a ritual that has become as much a rite of spring as a tribute to our war dead.

In the distance a Blackhawk helicopter inched across the skyline, stopped at a specific location and then proceeded to hover motionless for the next half hour like a dragonfly on a hot summer day; security for Memorial Day celebrations already were underway.

Also in the distance, the Washington Monument towered above everything like a white lightning rod defiantly pointing into the summer sky daring anyone to come near it or the nearby Capitol and White House.

Other than making trips to doctor's offices, Renee - who had never visited our nation's capital - had not been out of town since surgery five months ago left her unable to walk. So, with some trepidation for her ability to withstand such a rigid trip, I had agreed to come and be part of Memorial Day ceremonies at the Vietnam Veterans Memorial.

I borrowed a wheelchair, and, over the weekend, pushed my honey from one end of D.C. to the other, taking in every honored memorial there was to see. What a grand time it was.

Just as seedling "helicopters" propagating off my back yard maple tree had triggered my memories of war a few weeks ago, so did four straight hours of tattooed motorcyclists' machines blasting down Constitution Ave. I stood on the hill overlooking the parade of people patiently passing the 58,000-plus names on The Wall and closed my eyes to be reminded of why this motorcycle parade got its name.

Suddenly I was sitting on a mountaintop watching what looked like thousands of little shots of lightning lighting up the night as each bomb from the massive B-52s flying overhead impacted with the ground. And the sound … just was like thunder rolling across that Southeast Asian's summer sky.

I reopened my eyes to reality as Rolling Thunder reverberated through the hills, hallowed halls and historical markers around me.

I kissed my bride and stole Forrest Gump's line to his Jenny and said, "I'm glad we could be here together in our nation's capital."

It was an honor to be there honoring so many fallen American patriots alongside the love of my life … and those riding by creating the thunder.

But what do I know?

FLYING RED HORSE

J U N E   1 2 ,   2 0 0 6

It's amazing how an opinion of someone can change over a lifetime.

I remember many mornings waking to find him staring out the window at nothing. His face drawn with pain, he would be sweating and somewhat disoriented and, occasionally, weeping.

"What's wrong, daddy?" I would ask.

Sometimes he was so choked in emotion that he couldn't talk, but, when he could, he would say, "I dreamed of the flying red horse." Mother immediately would begin packing for our trip to Tennessee.

It's been 50-some years, but, as best as I remember, it was a magnificent white stallion, 18 hands high, with a flowing mane, flaring nostrils and rippling muscles. I never saw it, but he described it so many times that I still see the image in my mind.

It was the same each time. He was on the floor of a box canyon just as the sun was setting at the other end. The stallion would leave him and begin to climb the canyon wall. Slowly, the beautiful animal - that stands in the same historical line ahead of the automobile and computer - would pick its way from one ledge to another, dislodging rocks and struggling to maintain balance to make the crest.

This time, it would spread the wings it had sprouted and begin to fly. Suddenly it would tuck the wings and dive straight at him - scaring him - before veering away at the last moment to soar back into the heavens and then fly off down the canyon wall.

When the flying white horse got to the end of the canyon, it would turn and fly across the canyon. As soon as it flew between his line of vision and the setting sun, the horse turned red, melted and fell to the canyon floor as drops of blood. At that very moment of each dream, he would wake up.

I still can remember trying to reassure him that it was only a dream; he would have none of it. I also remember that eventually the old rotary phone would ring and he would begin to weep openly because he already knew.

Mother would answer the call. On the other end of the line was a member of his family he had left behind in Tennessee to come north looking for work in the automobile industry to inform us that one of the family members had died. Usually already packed, we loaded the car and headed south for the funeral.

Sometimes the horse would leap from the floor to the top of the canyon; in each case, that family member died instantly. Every now and then he would see the person on the back of the horse, so he not only knew that someone had died but also who died.

Prophetic dreamers run rampant in our family, and I've shared many of them with you through this column. The granddaddy dream of them all, however, belonged to my father, Homer Treece, who always told me that, even now - just like it is recorded over and over in the Bible - God speaks to man through dreams.

Sunday, I'll honor the memory of the strict disciplinarian who cut me no slack in life while covering me in unconditional love ... and who, unfortunately, it took me a lifetime to realize how visionary and brilliant he really was.

But what do I know?

"PUT 'EM OUT!"

J U N E   2 6 ,   2 0 0 6

The cold January wind stung my freshly shaven face as I stood in the company street outside my Fort Knox, Ky., barracks and dragged on the Marlboro dangling from my lips. As fingers warmed crammed deep in pockets of my fatigues, the last thing on my mind was discipline.

The single stripe on the blue arm band adorned the left sleeve of my field jacket identifying the tall skinny kid from Monroe as a squad leader.

Only weeks into a new life as a member of the United States Army, I stood in the company street among hundreds of other recruits and draftees and awaited the officer of the day to make his way to the elevated viewing stand where he addressed us each morning regarding the day's training activities.

Sgt. Carlisle, no more than 120 pounds dripping wet, surely suffered from "Napoleon's Syndrome." Just back from a year of Vietnam combat duty with the Big Red One Infantry, the last thing he wanted to do was deal with us "bunch of sissies;" that's what he called us most of the time.

The "spit and polish" from head to toe platoon leader wore a Smokey the Bear drill instructor's hat and a uniform so starched it probably stood by itself in his locker.

He crossed the compound looking every bit like a Bantam rooster trying to impress hens in the barnyard and bounded up the steps of the viewing stand and simply barked, "PUT 'EM OUT!"

I pulled hands from my pockets and grabbed the cigarette in my mouth and took one last, long drag off it before taking it in my right hand, pinching it just past the filter and rolled the cigarette between my thumb and forefinger to squeeze the fire and tobacco out and onto the ground.

I continued the process of "field stripping" the butt by rolling the filter into a little ball and depositing it into my pocket for later disposal.

I glanced back at the viewing stand only to see Sgt. Carlisle eyeballing me. Suddenly his index finger was curling at me in the, "come here!" motion.

I looked around to see who he was talking to; there was nobody behind me.

I stepped out of the now-formed platoon and walked briskly to the reviewing stand where I stood before the little sergeant; even though I was on the ground we stood eyeball to eyeball.

"Yes sir?" I inquired timidly before he loudly began.

"Look you little scumbag, my job is to try to keep you alive in the jungle."

Slowly, intentionally, he continued berating me in front of the others; "People who stay alive are ones who learn to take orders."

As he continued the tirade he methodically calmed, lowered his voice and leaned into my face until finally, with his Smokey-hat's felt bill poking my forehead, whispered, "So the next time I say, 'Put 'em out,' that doesn't mean 'take one more drag,' it means ...

Suddenly his face exploded and he screamed in my face, "PUT 'EM OUT!"

Instantly I thought one of two things would happen; either my heart was going to explode or I would need a change of underwear. What I got was a quick lesson in what I think is something sorely lacking in today's world: discipline!

But what do I know?

ANSWERING THE CALL

JUNE 29, 2006

"Why the suit?" funny, fellow columnist Ray Kisonas asked during my Monroe News visit.

"I sang today for Commissioner Mell's funeral," I responded.

"Good friends?" he probed.

"Not really," I answered before divulging details of the strange story.

While visiting a friend in Mercy Memorial Hospital Saturday I had unknowingly lost my cell phone. Sunday, my honey, Renee, used our land-line to call the cell while I walked through our home - hoping to find it by hearing it ring - when the 2nd Floor Nurses Station answered. Renee told them we'd be right over to pick it up.

After retrieving the phone we started to leave when I remembered running into a gentleman in the elevator the previous day that recognized me from my News picture. Monroe County Commissioner Tom Mell's brother, Don, informed me Tom was "upstairs, terminal with cancer."

Already late for a Saturday appointment, I told Don I would pray for Tom and left, but on this day felt a strong urge to visit Tom.

I summoned a nurse after finding his room door closed and asked if she would check to see if we could visit; she entered, then returned and motioned us in.

Once inside we found the commissioner subconscious and nearing the end of his life's journey. Beside him was whom I would come to know as his wife, Lucille; beside her ... four, close, comforting friends.

I introduced myself and my wife and informed them I had felt the urge to visit after being told of Tom's condition, of which I had not previously been aware.

Miss Lucille looked strangely at me and then at her friends. For a moment there was an uneasy silence in the room and I wondered what was happening as again she looked at me and then again at her friends.

I was afraid I had interrupted something when she said, "Just a little while ago I told my friends that I wished Tom Treece would walk through the door and sing, "I Can Only Imagine," for Tom one more time before he leaves; we heard you sing that on the We Care Telethon."

A bit shocked to hear that story but quickly recognizing I was in a divine appointment - for which I had obviously felt the urge to visit and lost the cell phone - I reached down, grabbed her husband's hand and began to sing, "I can only imagine what it will be like when I walk by your side."

After the song Renee and I expressed our sympathies and left; later, I expect the commissioner found out what he had only imagined as he passed from this life.

The following day Miss Lucille e-mailed asking if I would honor Tom by singing, "God Bless the USA," at his funeral, because, "He was a proud American!"

She was right. The nine-year Marine veteran with 21 years of service in the Michigan National Guard had served his country in Okinawa and Vietnam before serving 21 more years in local government; it was my honor to sing for such a patriot.

It was also satisfying to realize I had been obedient to the urge to go to that hospital room, and in so doing honored yet another who also gave His life for the freedoms we enjoy.

But what do I know?

JUNGLE BOOTS

J U L Y 3 , 2 0 0 6

It was hotter than blazes and cars were bumper-to-bumper as thousands of bargain hunters choked Luna Pier's 15th Annual Freedom Celebration Saturday. Featured were hundreds of garage sales, including mine.

He was still quite a ways off when I picked him out of the crowd. The sight of him triggered my ear-to-ear grin as well as memories of taking shoes needing repair down the little alleyway that led to his shop - Nat's Shoe Repair - in the old Monroe Shopping Center before it burned down.

And, of course, the boots!

It was my first day back in The Land of the Free and the Home of the Brave and they were like the dead skunk in the middle of the road, "stinking to high heaven." For 13 months I had worn them through mud, monsoons and marathons of mega-sweat with the 11th Infantry in the Vietnam War.

As I processed out of the Army and prepared to resume my interrupted civilian life, I was issued the dress-green uniform that still hangs in my closet, the footwear of which were "low quarters," regular dress shoes.

I remember putting them on and then ceremoniously dumping those boots in the trash. I also remember three hours later racing back and rifling through that can to retrieve them, as in that short time those new shoes had already blistered my feet. With my dress uniform, I wore those smelly, ratty, funky old boots home.

Once home I tossed them aside and only wore them for dirty work; I had no idea they would one day become one of my most prized possessions.

They were canvas jungle boots made with leather soles, toes, heels and laces and by the time they finally became important to me the toes and heels had rotted, along with the stitches holding the canvas together. I had taken them to Nat over and over for repair, but, finally, it looked like the end of the road for them. Again, however, I couldn't bring myself to pitching them, again.

"Can you do anything to save them?" I asked Nat one last time.

"Let me see what I can do," the consummate cobbler replied and took the boots.

Cobbler friend Nat Battistone rescues my jungle boots, 2002.

The next time I saw them I couldn't believe my eyes. He had cut out the toe and the heel and replaced them with shiny new leather, and had heavy-duty re-stitched every seam of the canvas.

The pittance he charged was irrelevant to both of us. The importance to me: I had my priceless boots back; to him: pride in having done an impeccable piece of work, coupled with the joy I expressed in the bear hug I gave him.

"I'm 90 now you know!" he shared proudly before walking on down the street with his dear wife at his side.

As I watched "Nat" Battistone walk away I realized I didn't even know his real name; he's always just been Nat to me.

I also realized that simple things - like 38-year-old boots worn during war and repaired by a simple man of great skill and integrity - can sometimes be the tool that stitches hearts together in order to weave friendships to last a lifetime. It is important to have - and recognize - such simple things in one's life.

But what do I know?

SAVED FROM SUICIDE

JULY 10, 2006

Before next week's column I need to share my experience of January 16, 1991, a story I've told bits of pieces of along the way. Hopefully it will also help readers - like the friend Friday who shared she loves my column "in spite of all the religious stuff" - try to understand why I regularly write about my faith.

On the dark, destructive edge of life emanating from divorce, substance abuse and extremely bad choices, I quit my management job at a Toledo radio station that morning and slowly drove home with one thought in mind: suicide. In one last call to a friend for help I was told to go home, get on my knees and ask God to take over my life; she only irritated me more.

Always a happy guy, I loved life and lived it to the fullest but was always searching. I went to the Grand Canyon and had to descend it; at Diamond Head, I had to climb it; Niagara gorge, I had to rappel it. I wanted to fly so I jumped out of airplanes.

I tasted success in career aspirations, business, popularity, relationships and thought I had it all, but something was dreadfully missing: happiness.

I think most people in life just want to be happy, but, in spite of successes, I wasn't. There seemed to be a hole in my heart that gave an emptiness I could not plug. Until that day, that is.

No one was home when I arrived that morning; I chose my basement office for the suicide. I remember thinking of the mess I would make and how I hated leaving that for another. I considered driving to a remote spot in the country but decided to just do it.

I remember contemplating the shotgun in the closet. The only weapon I hadn't sold upon my return from war was a gift from my father; the thought of his disappointment at me using it to do what I had come to do slowed me, but only temporarily. I reached for the gun.

As I leaned forward the chair slid from under my butt and I found myself on the floor on my knees! Instantly my friend's words reverberated through my mind and I did exactly as she had suggested; with a mustard seed of faith I cried out, "God, if you're really there, take over my life and teach me how to live!" and that's exactly what He did.

I started reading the Bible, learning of Him, speaking and listening to Him, following His guidance and have been blessed beyond measure. He has given me the desires of my heart, just as promised!

Unfortunately, people who don't know Him don't want to hear of Him and tire of me talking about Him. Fact is, He simply saved my life that day and I feel a great need to reciprocate by trying to reflect Him in all I do.

I can't imagine missing the unequaled happiness I've found since He plugged that hole in my heart that day and filled it with joy I've never known. And while I have no desire to cram my beliefs down anyone's throat, I believe one of my purposes in life is to share that joy.

But what do I know?

ABRAHAM'S ALTAR

JULY 17, 2006

"Why?" I cried out, tears streaming down my face. "Am I not serving you good enough?"

That was my plea six months ago today. The day before, Renee and I had been devastated hearing she had brain tumors that must be excised immediately. Surgery was two days later.

Although optimistic, her neurosurgeon gave little hope sharing that he'd never seen anything like what her MRI showed in his 30-some years of experience. One look for me was all I needed to form my opinion: If she lived, she would be paraplegic at best. I didn't think she had a prayer!

But, of course, she did! One who places trust in The God of Abraham always has hope, especially when others pray for you.

I remembered hearing TV evangelist Joyce Meyer ask, "When trouble comes, do you run to the phone or to The Throne?" Weeping uncontrollably, I ran to The Throne and called out to God.

After "Why me?" questions, in a vision I found myself on my knees in front of Abraham's altar, only it wasn't his son, Isaac, on that altar (Genesis 22), it was Renee!

I wailed all the more as I realized God was asking me the same question He asked Abraham: Am I really first in your life? I knew I had to give her up for any hope of keeping her.

I composed myself and responded, "Lord, I am Your man, today, tomorrow during surgery and the day after. No matter the outcome, I will still be your man!"

The vision changed. Now Jesus was kneeling in the garden asking God to "Take this cup from me; nevertheless, Your will, not Mine."

It was then I heard God speak to me and say, "Look what I did for Him. You think I can't do the same for her? Trust me." And I did. Then I ran to the phone to call every believer I knew to intercede on her behalf.

It's easy - now - to look back calmly at that time, but, at that moment, letting go and giving her to Him was the most difficult thing I ever had done as He gave me nothing but the simple opportunity to trust Him. Yet, I believe that because I did not only do I still have the love of my life alive and well beside me but I also watch her walk (with help) and talk almost as if nothing ever happened.

Last week I told you about the day I gave a last-minute rejection to suicide and asked God to take over my life. Ironically, that was exactly 15 years to the day and hour we heard those devastating words: brain tumors. It was also Renee's 50th birthday.

Six months ago tomorrow, Renee lay paralyzed from the neck down. Yesterday, she walked into church, no walker, no cane, just me to hang on to. Hidden was the leg brace she must wear but not her joy in knowing God had spared her life.

If you ask her how, she'll share, "Faith in God and the prayers of His people."

Although some may think this a fable, that's exactly what happened six months ago today. When it happens to you and you know it's the truth, it never matters what anyone else thinks

But what do I know?

PATRIOTIC PRIDE

JULY 24, 2006

"I was planning on wearing a coat and tie, but when I saw this T-shirt, I knew this was what I needed to wear today," emcee Gary Vancena said. Pointing to the inscription on the shirt, Mr. Vancena, AKA DJ Daddy G. Knight, read aloud, "If you love your freedom, thank a vet."

I turned to scan the full house gathered Sunday in the banquet hall of Monroe Post 1138, Veterans of Foreign Wars, for which ribbon cutting ceremonies had taken place moments earlier.

A who's who of Monroe dignitaries was there, but mostly it was veterans with spouses and family members at their sides. Most wore significant items - specifically hats - identifying them with their branch of service.

There seemed to be one underlying theme linking each and every person in that room together: pride.

Pride beamed like a beacon from within as veterans leapt - or struggled - to their feet when Mr. Vancena played theme music from their branch of service. All around them pounded hands together in appreciation.

It was pride I saw as the state VFW Color Guard precision-marched into the building to present "The Colors" of these United States, and it was pride I saw as one with a prosthetic right arm respectfully rested it over his heart as those colors passed.

It was patriotic pride that formed the lump in the back of my throat as that flag so many have defended and died for during the past 230 years passed, and it was pride I felt in the squeeze of my hand by the woman I love.

It was pride I felt - along with missing fingers - in the aging Korean War veteran's handshake and pride I saw in the heart of the Vietnam vet struggling to keep steady the unsteady hand identifying his neurological disorder as it perched at his brow during his salute to that same flag.

It was pride I heard in the faithful voice of U.S. Rep. John Dingell - himself a proud veteran - promising that not only would we all be waiting to welcome home those now serving our country in hostile, foreign lands but also that he would ensure legislation also at the ready to meet their needs.

Pride and appreciation generated our applause as each who worked so hard to make this magnificent facility a reality stood when introduced, and it was pride driving one aging vet to stoop and retrieve litter from that new floor at the end of the service.

Unfortunately, it was sadness I felt when hearing that fundraising for this facility - now open and ready to meet the needs of its proud, patriot members - was bogged down at 50 percent.

Suddenly I felt air leaking from the balloon of pride I had carried all day. There is something so important in knowing others appreciate the sacrifices you make, especially sacrifices that allow them to live as they choose - in freedom.

I would like to ask each of you reading this to consider Gary's shirt. And, if you love the freedom you and your family are afforded in this great country, why not send a donation to Post 1138, 400 Jones Ave., Monroe 48161 in order to "thank a vet." It will give you something your money cannot buy: pride.

But what do I know?

PITCHING PRIZE

J U L Y 3 1 , 2 0 0 6

The baseball had to be thrown almost perfectly in order to pass through the hole the size of a softball. But there was no way a sports nut and competitor could walk on by, so I pulled out a hard-earned quarter from summer savings from my Monroe News paper route and paid for three balls.

I had no idea what I could win. I just wanted to prove I could throw a baseball through that little hole in the middle of the bull's-eye some 40 feet in front of me.

I remember thinking it strange seeing a children's slide next to the hole that extended almost to where I stood. Atop that slide was a wooden box with a door in front.

I wound up and threw. The ball banged against the plywood, missing the hole into which it had been drilled.

I fired the second; missed again.

Determined, I concentrated and let the last ball fly. The sound changed this time as the ball flew cleanly through the hole and into a canvas hung behind the plywood.

A bell began ringing, and I raised my arms in triumph at the successful shot. Suddenly the door opened and down the slide came this huge, white duck, squawking its displeasure at being utilized in such a manner.

"A duck?" I exclaimed to the carney operating the game.

"Feathers and all!" he replied.

"What am I going to do with a duck?" I asked.

"That's your problem."

It already was late, so I tucked the duck under my arm and made my way off the Monroe County Fairgrounds to where I had parked my father's car. Each friend I encountered along the way looked at me like I was some kind of moron and said, "What are you doing with a duck at the fair?"

When I got to the car, I made a stupid move: I put the duck in the back seat where he sat silently - until I started the car and pulled onto M-50.

Suddenly he decided he didn't like riding in the back, and, since freedom appeared to be out the front windshield, over the seat he came screeching and flapping flailing wings in my face.

Panicked, I pulled to the roadside and stopped. The duck was screaming to high heaven, but I finally pinned him, tucked him again under my arm and did what I should have done first. I got out, went to the rear of the car and deposited Donald in the trunk.

When I walked back and opened the driver's door, the interior light came on and I noticed white stuff all over the back seat. Donald had done some depositing of his own. I quickly learned you should let that stuff dry first as I simply smeared it all over the seat.

Once home, Donald decided to wake mom and dad and all the neighbors. We stuck him in the garage and the next day took him to a friend's farm where he waddled away the rest of his life.

The Monroe County Fair is a great place to create great memories. Don't let anyone tell you it's not all it's quacked up to be!

But what do I know?

CATCHING DEAD FISH

A U G U S T   7 ,   2 0 0 6

It's interesting how seeing someone triggers memories.

I watched him as I sat waiting for the funeral of our cousin to begin. He was now tall, dark and handsome, and I was proud of the loving husband and father into whom he had grown. His father - already gone on to eternal rest himself - also would have been proud.

In spite of the somber mood, I couldn't help the grin that sneaked onto my face as I remembered running into him one sunny afternoon many years ago. He was just a boy.

I had decided to take my stepson fishing. We lived near the River Raisin, and one of our favorite fishing holes was under downtown Monroe's Macomb Street Bridge.

We loaded our poles, hit the bait shop for minnows, found a parking place and made our way to the river.

Our favorite hole was obviously one of his favorites, too, as I recognized cousin Jeff Treece already there fishing when we arrived.

"Doing any good?" I asked.

"Haven't had a hit!" he exclaimed.

Jeff was bait-casting artificial lures just below the dam, so we moved past him to a spot under the bridge to give him room.

We sat down, and I reached into the minnow bucket, grabbed a wiggly one, baited Aaron's hook, set the bobber, tossed the line into the water and handed him the pole.

"I got one!" he screamed almost instantly and reeled in a nice bass.

Without having time to bait my own hook, I was unhooking his and placing the fish on our stringer. I remember Jeff noticing.

I re-baited Aaron's hook and again tossed it in the water. Again, almost instantly, he had another fish, and I repeated the process.

I finally baited my own, and, in the next half hour, we had at least 20 fish on our stringer. All the while, I kept noticing Jeff noticing us as he diligently continued bait casting. Each time we caught a fish, he longingly looked our way and occasionally said, "Nice fish!" before reeling in his line and fishing a different lure out of his tackle box in hopes of finding the one that would get him in on some of our hot action.

Suddenly I felt something heavy on the end of my rod and began reeling the line. There was no fight from a fish, so I assumed I had snagged a stick or something.

What I pulled from the water was a dead fish. Someone had hooked him earlier, but the line somehow snagged something submerged and had broken, leaving the fish confined where he eventually died. I had snagged that line and reeled in the dead fish.

As soon as I pulled it from the water, cousin Jeff reeled his line, closed his tackle box and started to leave.

"Giving up?" I called.

"You know," he began, "I didn't mind sharing the fishing hole, and I must say it was tough watching you walk up and start catching fish right and left just a few feet away while I caught nothing. But when you start catching dead fish, too, it's time for me to leave."

My pastor says the ability to remember is one of the greatest gifts God gives us. I think he's right.

But what do I know?

SHOW STOPPERS

AUGUST 14, 2006

"Contestant No. 4 ... Nichole Elizabeth Hall!"

The already-beautiful smile of my beautiful friend went ear-to-ear as Monroe County Community College President Dr. David Nixon - serving as master of ceremonies at Saturday's Miss Monroe County Scholarship Pageant - announced her name as the third of five finalists for the contest's final round. Her huge contingency of fans went wild.

It had been my honor - as it has been for the past 13 years - to be called on to honor our great country by offering my rendition of our beloved national anthem for the pageant. How proud I was to stand alongside my fellow brothers-in-arms from Monroe County Chapter 142, Vietnam Veterans of America, to sing as they gave the official presentation of the colors.

With that task completed, I settled in with my sweet wife to enjoy the show.

Dr. Nixon, taking his first stint at hosting the pageant, called upon his tremendous communication skills and broadcast experience to create a flow that kept the program progressing with profound professionalism. The 16 hometown beauties did the rest.

Perhaps the most talented group to ever compete in a local pageant delighted the audience in the splendor of the college's exquisite showcase, the Meyer Theater. Renee and I stayed glued to our seats.

As Nichole's name was called, she strolled forward to join the first two of the five finalists called - two more good friends, Jenna Catherine McCormick and Melissa Kaye Cousino, who wore the crown home.

The exciting moment was the culmination of months of preparation. The girls had competed in swimsuit, talent, evening wear, on-stage question and private interview, and now the crowning moment was at hand.

Nichole walked to the front of the stage, waved to the crowd and then hugged Jenna before turning to hug Melissa.

As she turned, we noticed Jenna's arm suddenly going with her. Just as sudden, Nichole stopped and grabbed the front of her dress. As it turned out, Jenna's bracelet had gotten hung in the back of Nichole's evening gown, and, for a moment, there was a fear the show was about to get unintentionally risque.

Melissa raced to help Jenna try to untangle the bracelet from the gown while Nichole laughed and tried to keep her composure in the delicate, candid moment.

Dr. Nixon never broke stride in keeping the already amused audience in stitches by narrating with lines like, "I told you you were going to get more than you bargained for!" before finally sending out the question, "Does anyone have any duct tape?"

With the dress finally freed, Dr. Nixon crowned the moment by accurately announcing what the audience had seen first hand: These girls loved each other and even had stopped the show to help each other in time of need.

And, in so doing, they created a memory they not only will laugh about for the rest of their lives but will tell their children's children about someday while slowly rocking them to sleep.

As I mentioned last week, memories are one of God's greatest gifts, and we get the opportunity to create them every day of our lives. I trust you are taking advantage of your opportunities. If you aren't, you should be.

But what do I know?

SAVIORS

A U G U S T   2 1 ,   2 0 0 6

I squinted into the sun to get a better look at the patch on his T-shirt and started to ask about it but didn't want to interrupt the flow of the worship service I was helping lead.

The sun was beaming and the mood festive as hundreds from our church gathered at Sterling State Park to conduct a public baptizing. My sidekick - Bobby James Ferraiuolo - and I sang for a half hour before Pastor Roy Southerland spoke on the significance - and importance - of baptism in our faith. He then led 18 baptismal candidates into and under the refreshing - and renewing - waters of Lake Erie on this hot summer day.

I noticed him drive up, park his motorcycle, stroll into the worship service and take a seat near the stage. I didn't recognize him but did recognize the patch on his shirt. For some reason it kept calling to me until I finally asked from the stage, "Brother, is that a 1st Cav patch?"

I expect he was startled to realize I was speaking to him and he glanced around at hundreds now staring his way before looking back at me and nodding yes.

It was bright yellow with a horse head in the upper right corner and it transposed me 38 years in the blink of an eye.

I love hugging my honey but I never hugged her harder than I hugged the ground that 1968 morning as I lay prostrate, pinned down by a Viet Cong sniper trying to kill me.

In the instant I recognized that patch, in my mind's ear I again heard a clacking sound from behind me, and as a flare lit up the midnight Vietnam sky I ever so carefully turned my head to see an APC (armored personnel carrier) advancing toward my position. As it passed I jumped up behind it and we captured the enemy soldier. The APC was from the 1st Cavalry Unit and from the stage I told the biker how his unit had undoubtedly saved my life that morning.

After Pastor Roy concluded his sermon he called for the baptismal candidates to prepare to enter the lake. As I put my guitar away I noticed the biker sitting in the same position; he seemed in deep thought.

I strolled over, introduced myself and told him I hoped he hadn't minded me bringing attention to him from the stage. He never answered but instead just looked at me before finally asking, "What must I do to be baptized?"

I called Pastor Roy who counseled him that those who believe in Christ allow themselves to be immersed in water to signify they will one day die, but then be resurrected - as Christ was - into eternal life.

The next thing I knew the biker - just like the eunuch in the 8th Chapter of Acts - was wading into the water and Pastor Roy baptized him, boots, pants, wallet, T-shirt, 1st Cavalry patch and all.

When he re-emerged, with the biggest smile he looked toward Heaven, pumped his fists in victory and looked like a completely different man. He was.

Later, I thought about how his unit saved my life that day in the jungle; then I thought about how my unit had perhaps helped saved his.

But what do I know?

MOM TIME

AUGUST 28, 2006

Could there possibly be another job in the world more important than that of mother? I think not!

I ran into old friend Sparky Swanson last week during dinner at Erie's Frog Leg Inn, where my wonderful wife, Renee, had taken me.

In spite of the wonderful wife he has at home, Sparky's hot date for the night was his mother, and, as she is a reader and fan of this column, he brought her over for introductions and greetings after they had spent several hours over their meal.

I had stolen occasional glances at them, and the love for each other I saw emanating from their space warmed my heart. I also must admit feeling a twinge of emptiness and jealousy knowing I'll never again have that same opportunity - at least not on this planet.

I've always admired Sparky, but my esteem for him screamed skyward as I felt the fire of his obvious love and admiration for his mother, which got me thinking about how important moms are to our world.

Today's pressure on mothers to perform is incredible. They must be everything to everybody. And, while I appreciate and applaud anyone's desire to have a personal career, still, once one bears a child, raising that child becomes life's priority, in my opinion. The future of our world depends upon how our children are molded and taught by mothers.

Yes, dads, you are critical, too, but, by recognition of our chains of attachments - from inception's life-giving umbilical cord through apron strings to heart strings I saw attached from Sparky to his elderly mother - mom breaks all barriers.

I thought of two "show-biz" mothers recently. The first was Britney Spears, whom the media crams down our throats by keeping cameras trained on her every move. We see her driving with baby on her lap and label her a "bad mom."

The other is Lisa Whelchel - a former Mouseketeer whom many of you have never heard of - who is coming to Monroe Missionary Baptist Church Sept. 29-30 to specifically talk to moms at her "Mom Time Getaways" event.

Ms. Whelchel, best known as "Blair" on NBC's long-running series "The Facts of Life," is now a home-schooling mother of three and a best-selling author of many books - including parenting books "Creative Correction" and "Taking Care of the Me in Mommy."

During "Mom Time Getaway," women will have opportunities to meet Ms. Whelchel, ask questions and hear her ideas about the rigors of being a wife and mother - and the importance of recognizing those jobs as being more important than being a TV star. I appreciate that.

I struggled with writing this column as I try not to use this space to promote "my" church, etc. But, after reading excerpts from Ms. Whelchel's books and advice columns she writes for various magazines, I thought this is important, no matter where it is held.

The clincher, however, was seeing that special glow of love between Sparky and his mom - a love that our world desperately needs, an exclusive and important love that can only come from mother.

But what do I know?

SEEING DOUBLE

SEPTEMBER 4, 2006

As I stood facing the congregation of the old country church, I had the strangest sensation of seeing double. There was nothing wrong with my vision; rather, it was a time warp of sorts that I have experienced more often as the older I grow. Today was perhaps the most extreme yet.

I glanced at the modern windows but instead saw old-time glass so curved and smoky it was difficult to see out and I could still hear them rattle and reverberate from the power of Uncle Arnold Patterson's singing from the men's "Amen Corner."

I looked up at the modern lighting and fixtures but instead saw the single strand of electric wire running the ceiling with one glowing light bulb in the middle of the room.

Although it was smoldering outside on this 90-degree August day and I was cool as a cucumber in the air conditioned church, I could still see the old pot-bellied stove in the middle of the room. Chunks of coal bulged from the bucket sitting at its base, waiting their turn to be tossed in to fuel the fire and warm the flock already warm in spirit.

While the pews were new and comfortable I saw the old, hard, hand-hewn benches that used to cause my butt to go to sleep after sitting on them for hours. In those pews were a handful of friends and relatives I remembered from those days of long ago whose youthful faces were now stenciled with age; most were rank strangers.

I shared those childhood visions with those attending the morning worship service at Speedwell, Tennessee's Red Hill Baptist Church last week as I had been invited by my former pastor - the Rev. Damon Patterson - to sing for Homecoming at my father's boyhood church.

I also saw the scared, skinny kid - who sang in public for the very first time at the request of his grandfather - standing in the exact spot I now stood 53 years later.

Moses Treece - a.k.a. "The Old Rat from the Barn" for longtime column readers - was feeble and virtually bedridden but had asked me to sing for him that Sunday even though he couldn't attend; I was 6 years old.

I still remember all those sights and sensations as I stood in front of all those old saints and belted out, "O Come Angel Band" that day for "Grampaw." I had no idea it would be the first of thousands of public appearances I would ultimately make.

I have a plan to record a new CD that Renee has decided we should call, "Coming Full Circle." Included on that CD will be that very first song I sang in public as well as the very latest one I have written and recorded.

What a wonderful experience Renee and I had traveling back to those Tennessee hills where I played as a boy. There truly is something wonderfully refreshing in revisiting the places and people who make up the roots of your life.

And, while my eyesight has failed somewhat over the years, seeing double last weekend was perhaps the sweetest treat I have tasted in quite some time as it gave me a fresh, new perspective on who I am and where I am going in this life.

But what do I know?

STINGRAYS

SEPTEMBER 7, 2006

I filled my lungs with air and slowly slipped under the surface to search the underworld with my eyes. The warm water of the Caribbean was a welcome from the searing sun above. I glanced at the shrimp in my right hand and wondered if they really could smell under water.

Movement in the distance caught my attention, and I strained to see the source. The water was crystal clear with nothing but a sandy bottom in sight, yet I couldn't decipher the image racing through the water in my direction.

No matter what the tour guide had told us about how docile these characters were, a rush flooded my body in that moment and I began to panic.

I remember thinking that it looked like a Volkswagen flapping its wings, flying through the water straight at me. I collected myself and decided I was in for the duration, come what may.

Now the giant creature was in plain view, and I wondered why I had allowed my wife and myself to get into this compromising position of potential danger. The safety of the boat was a moot point because Renee and I had ventured too far for quick retreat.

Never in my life had I seen a stranger creature than the one that cruised by me that day. It now looked like a giant mattress with eyes protruding from a mound on top that eyeballed and investigated me as it passed and circled.

Remembering my instructions, I stood up in the waist-deep water and held my hand out in front of me. There was no doubt about his smeller as the creature came straight for me and then sucked the shrimp out of my hand and into his mouth that was located on his underside, where I expected his belly should be.

Soon there were hundreds of the creatures swimming among us, drawn to the smell of the shrimp. I never will forget their velvety skin and what a sensation it was to run my hands across it. I also remember getting an up-close-and-personal inspection of their tails and the barbs that has been the center of attention the past few days.

Hearing the unexpected news of Steve (The Crocodile Hunter) Irwin being killed by a stingray reminded me of our thrilling adventure of several years ago during a vacation visit to Stingray City on Grand Cayman Island.

Other than that original panic, not once did I think I was in any danger. In fact, we were so comfortable I eventually lay back in the water and lured one up onto my chest, where he politely gave me a hickey when he sucked the shrimp off my belly.

I'm sorry to see Steve go because he was quite the entertaining bloke. I also heard a fellow countryman giving tribute on a recent newscast, sharing his view that Steve had done more for Australia than all the continent's prime ministers combined. After thinking about it, I realized he might be right. I couldn't name even one.

Rest in peace, Steve, and thanks for the thrills. Even though I've called you "crazy" many times, I do recognize - and appreciate - the fever associated with dancing out there on the edge of life.

But what do I know?

Tom feeds a stingray, Grand Cayman Island, 2003.

WAS 9-11 A WAKEUP CALL?

SEPTEMBER 11, 2006

I expect he spoke to many of "us" that day, perhaps even shaking hands before a broken English uttering of "Good morning!" or "How are you?"

I wonder if he was cool and calm and made conversation to the unsuspecting souls sitting beside him on the airplane, or, was he nervously looking around and sweating as he contemplated his moments-away murderous mission.

I wonder what Mohammed Atta's last thoughts were as he zeroed that 747 in on the first tower?

I wonder about many aspects of what caused us to mark today's fifth anniversary of one of our country's greatest tragedies, but the one thing that continuously causes me to wonder most of all is, how?

How did 19 young, Arab, Muslim extremists waltz into our country with one of history's greatest military strategies in hand, hijack four fuel and passenger laden aircraft and use them as weapons to murder thousands of our citizens, and - more importantly to them philosophically - bring this country to its knees - from which it has still not recovered - and change our way of life?

That they did is almost unbelievable for me, unless I consider similar stories from the book in which I believe.

The Holy Bible's Old Testament shares similar stories of incredible feats, such as David defeating Goliath with a slingshot, Gideon's 300 defeating Midian's 50,000 or the entire saga of Moses leading the Children of Israel out of Pharaoh's tyrannical grip.

There is an opposite aspect, however, that makes me wonder if God's hand was in 9-11 as also many times in the Bible God uses whom we consider "bad guys" - or, enemies - to punish or teach His people lessons.

For most of my 59 years America pledged as "One nation under God." We proclaimed it on our money, swore "So help me God" to measure truth of testimony, begged His favor and blessing in every state's constitutional preamble and based our legal system on 10 Commandments He gave to guide us. That's all changed now.

We took prayer out of schools and now suffer multiple mass murders. We scoff at the sanctity of marriage and butcher unborn babies like they are tumors instead of the most precious gift of life, and we screw or try to get ahead of our neighbor instead of lending him a helping hand.

We glorify the glitter and the rouge of Hollywood but vilify anyone who dares to even mention the name of The One who created it all.

So I wonder.

As foreign as it is to even think God may have blessed 9-11, I wonder if He may have "allowed" it as a simple wakeup call. Or, perhaps, as we methodically kick Him out of our country, He is simply withdrawing His hand of protection and prosperity we have so obviously been under since first qualifying our existence by acknowledging "inalienable rights endowed by our Creator."

I've shared my belief many times that everybody in life thinks they are right; I'm no different, in spite of the fact I can't undeniably, categorically prove I am.

Mohammed Atta thought he was right too. And, if somehow it turns out he was, then it will be the first time in life I will be thrilled and honored ... to be wrong!

But what do I know?

"SEEBEE SOBEE"

SEPTEMBER 25, 2006

She would put a blanket over my head and say, "Trust me!" before inevitably walking me into a tree in order to get a good laugh.

Then she would say, "I promise I won't do it again," before throwing the blanket back over my head to walk me back into the tree.

She was a pretty tough character for a girl and took crap from nobody - except, of course, our father. And, being four years older than me, she beat the crap out of me whenever she felt like it.

However, if others in the neighborhood tried it, they had to answer to her - not a good thing! You see, beating the crap out of me was a right reserved exclusively for her. She could do it, but woe unto anyone else that did.

In my early days, I never understood why my parents named my big sister Janet Face until they assured me her middle name was actually Faye.

I had my own name for her.

Also in those "BT" years - before television - Mom would make a big bowl of popcorn each day at 7 p.m., and Dad would sit me on his knee and flick on the knob of the old upright radio that was the showpiece of our living room. Together we would listen to that day's episode of "The Lone Ranger."

Not distracted by someone else's vision of what was happening, I remember imagining what the Lone Ranger and Tonto looked like. My own mind constructed the set and events described by the narrator (a sad lament to how we allow TV to construct it for us today).

I loved the relationship the two completely different action heroes had for each other, and, in my youthful mind's theater, I injected Janet and myself into their situations.

The ranger referred to his sidekick as "Kemo Sabe," a term I understand to mean "trusty scout." I couldn't say it phonetically; what came out instead was "Seebee Sobee," and I call her that to this day.

Years later, she would prove her faithfulness to her sidekick by taking the time to sit down and write me the proverbial "letter from home" every one of the more than 400 days I spent in the Vietnam jungle - an incredible feat and act of love for which I shall be eternally grateful.

I thought of Janet last week after hearing the Nancy Pelosi's and Charles Rangel's of our political world stand in defense of President Bush after we allowed Hugo Chavez - the bombastic buffoon from Venezuela - to come into our living rooms and onto the front pages of our newspapers to belittle our president and call him names.

The fact that they can call him derogatory names but wouldn't let the South American doltish dictator do so without firing back at his own character bodes well for our country. Perhaps we're not as divided as it appears.

To me, no matter whom our president is or what your opinion of him might be, anyone who agrees with this cretin - who has openly called for America's destruction - is an enemy of this country ... and of mine. It wouldn't take me long to send my big sister to beat the crap out of them!

But what do I know?

YOUNG LIONS

OCTOBER 2, 2006

Wipers whacked wildly at the windshield in feeble attempts to clear a path for me to see. With the black, northern sky serving as the perfect paint for the afternoon canvas, the western sky suddenly exploded with a blasting beam from the day's dying sun to create the most vivid rainbow I've ever beheld.

"Will they cancel the show?" asked my sweetheart.

"It'll clear and be a great night!" I answered and squinted on through the combination of rain pouring from the sky and spray spewing from tires on I-75.

And a great night it was as we enjoyed yet another fun night of food and music Saturday night in Monroe as the Downtown Development Authority presented Downtown Hoedown in Loranger Square.

After a fabulous dinner of Gai Kow at the Lichee Gardens Chinese restaurant, Renee and I strolled into Cafe Classics to sip cappuccino while listening to the personalized song stylings of good friend the Rev. Louie Barnett.

The cafe is one of many downtown venues offering music on weekends.

As time neared for the hoedown headliner to take the stage, we said goodbyes to friends in the packed house and strolled hand-in-hand down the street toward the square, stopping to marvel the beautiful window displays of the latest fashions in "Jones For Men" and the new "Me & Mrs. Jones" boutiques next door to each other.

With the sounds of local rocker Hunter Brucks echoing through the historic buildings, we sauntered on, stopping again to examine the exquisite lighting helping showcase the spectacular new Monroe Bank & Trust building.

"Downtown Monroe has been rejuvenated," remarked Renee.

She was right. Not since the days of the old Floral City Festival has downtown Monroe seen such a successful surge of activity as this past summer.

At the heart of that success - in addition to bold, innovative investments from various business owners - is the methodical marketing mind of John Patterson, president and chief executive officer of the Monroe County Convention & Tourism Bureau whose brainchild, the River Raisin Jazz Festival, helped jump start the rejuvenation.

My love affair with downtown started more than 50 years ago when mother would bring me for clothes at Kline's and lunch at Kresge's before current Downtown Monroe Business Network Chairman Gabe Martin's grandfather fitted me for footwear at the century-old Martin's Shoe House.

I also remembered my 1980's downtown days as general manager of Tower 98 radio when storefronts started emptying as businesses made mad dashes for spots at the malls. How quaint it is that the malls now look skeletal while downtowns revitalize.

Seats were scattered in the square as throngs of faithful refused to allow a little rain and cold to keep them from the fun, free for the taking.

As the sultry sounds of country-blues rocker Lee Roy Parnell's searing slide guitar sliced the evening air, I noticed the county courthouse's illuminated steeple stretching toward a haunting half-moon hinting of Halloween.

This pride of young lions surely will have something to entice me back downtown then, too, as they have obviously figured out the old adage, "You can get anything you want by giving other people what they want."

But what do I know?

PARTY LIKE IT'S 1968

OCTOBER 9, 2006

As I watched Tiger pitcher Kenny Rogers pour champagne over the head of one of the Michigan State Police's finest Saturday night, my mind drifted to a similar celebration long ago.

I squeezed the handset to activate the radio before barking, "Six Niner Alpha, Six Niner Yankee."

"Six Niner Alpha," was the response.

"Yeah, Treece on Bunker 47; wanted to warn you about something I hope will happen tomorrow morning."

The handset squawked the command bunker's reply: "What might that be?"

"The Detroit Tigers and St. Louis Cardinals are playing Game 7 of the World Series. If the Tigers win, I'm gonna light this place up and didn't want you to think we were being invaded!"

In the early morning darkness of Oct. 11, 1968, I sat atop a fortified bunker near the village of Duc Pho, South Vietnam, glued to the game being played live the night before in St. Louis' Busch Stadium on the other side of the planet.

The tiny transistor radio crammed against my ear garnered all my attention. I was a proverbial sitting duck for any Viet Cong sniper in the area. Worrying about the enemy was the last thing on my mind as my beloved Tigers were moments away from winning their first world championship during my lifetime.

Across my lap lay an M-16 automatic rifle. On my right lay 10 magazines for the weapon, each carefully loaded with tracers, 7.62-mm shells dipped in "Willie Peter," or white phosphorus. When fired, the incendiary material - that even water won't extinguish - ignites, allowing the rifleman to watch each round's flight in the dark.

On my left was a board to which I had fastened six plungers, each with wires running 30 yards in front of my bunker to blasting caps anchored inside the explosive C-4 substance that make Claymore Mines go boom.

With other goodies such as hand grenades to light up the night, the moment Curt Gowdy announced the Tigers were World Champions, I did as promised.

It resembled red, strobe-like streaks of blood as I repeatedly emptied my M-16 skyward, spraying the heavens with tracers before systematically plunging the Claymore triggers. Next were the grenades. the time I depleted my ordnance, the Tiger championship undoubtedly had cost the government thousands of dollars.

Who'd have believed these current Tigers - just three years after being baseball's laughingstock - could rebound to dominate their division and then cap it by smoking who TV commentator Joe Morgan called "the best hitting lineup in baseball history."

While they've only qualified to play for the American League championship and, if they win, the World Series, somehow I can't imagine a more intense celebration than Saturday night's.

If they do win, I'll have to dream up a new celebration because I won't be able to "light the place up" like 1968. And I don't think I have Mr. Roger's courage to drench a cop with champagne ... in spite of how much fun I expect that would be.

But what do I know?

"HOW CAN I THANK THEM?"

O C T O B E R   1 6 ,   2 0 0 6

I pulled into the garage, hit the opener to close the door behind me, got out, entered our home and called out, "Hello!"

No response.

"Perhaps she's upstairs and can't hear me," I thought to myself and bounded up the stairs to find her.

As I entered our great room, my heart leaped from my chest. There - prostrate with her face on the floor - was my beloved wife.

"Renee!" I screamed and raced to her side.

Regular readers of this column know that on her 50th birthday - nine months ago today - our world was rocked when we discovered Renee had three brain tumors that had to be excised.

The grace of God, prayers of faithful family and friends and an incredibly talented surgeon, they were. Renee, however, was left paralyzed from the neck down. But, again with God's grace, the prayers of many and her faithfulness to rehabilitation, she has since regained many of her faculties. Due to continuing paralysis of both her right leg from the knee down and right hand and forearm, she cannot drive or walk unaided.

She takes daily heavy doses of anti-seizure medicine, and, at this moment, my fears of what that medicine was combating were realized. Or so I thought.

Just as I reached her side, she raised her tear-streaked face up to me.

"What's wrong?" I screamed.

"Nothing," she assured me. "I'm just praying over the cards."

My heart slid back into its cage and resumed regular rhythm as I then realized not only that she was okay but also what she was doing.

Following her surgery and during these nine months, Renee received more than 500 get-well and encouragement cards. We were - and still are - humbled by the outpouring of love and support.

I plastered her hospital room walls with them to remind her of the many who loved her and were praying for her, then boxed and brought them along when it was time to bring her home.

Later, I noticed her arranging them in like-sized bunches then lovingly wrapping fancy ribbons around each before placing them in a basket by our fireplace. She then shared a revelation with me.

"During my prayers, I always thank God for all the people who prayed for me and sent cards," she said. "I asked Him how I could ever thank them for their love and concern, and He told me to pray for them.

"So," she continued, "every morning, after you go to work, I kneel here and pray over the basket of cards."

I hope you don't get sick of hearing me rave about this wonderful woman God gave me to share my life with; if you do, you'll just have to stop reading. Surely you know what it's like to have a son or daughter, husband or wife about whom you are so proud that you want to tell everyone.

In spite of losing her career, watching her world change forever and having to drag a virtual ball and chain everywhere she goes, not once have I heard, "Why me?" "Why, God?" or "Poor, pitiful me!" Instead, she is grateful and prays for others.

What a joy to have the woman of your dreams also be the hero of your heart.

But what do I know?

"H-E-E-E-L-P!"

For a guy, he had perhaps the prettiest hair I had ever seen - long to his shoulders and shiny. You'll notice I said "had." There isn't much of it left anymore.

And, like me then, he was skinny as a bean pole. It's obvious neither of us learned to push away from the table.

I buy cars from him now at Monroe's Friendly Ford dealership because he's an honest man of God I know I can trust. He's also one of my oldest friends, and I remember holding him when he was a baby. I was a mere boy myself.

We met at church. His family - minus his father - would come regularly to our house for Sunday dinner. I never knew his father; neither did he because his father was critically wounded in World War II and died not long after he was born.

My father - a great man of faith - was obedient to Scripture that instructs us to care for "the fatherless and the widows," and he and mom tried to help them whenever possible.

His mother, Lorraine, is one of the sweetest people on the planet. I call her my "second mom" as she has always "mothered" me as well.

His brother, Roger - another of my oldest and best friends - and I share quite a history together, including spending years on the road playing in a rock 'n' roll band as well as getting arrested for toilet papering General Custer's statue. Right now, I'm helping him record a CD of his original songs.

After one Sunday dinner, we three kids decided to play hide and seek in a wooded area near my house. We took turns being "it" and had fun finding each other. When caught, you had to help find others still hiding.

Once while I was "it," Roger and I searched everywhere for him to no avail. He couldn't have been more than six or seven, so we began to worry.

Suddenly, we heard this long and pronounced cry ringing through the pine trees: "H-E-L-P!" We ran to the sound but still couldn't find him.

Then we heard, "I'm up here," and looked to find him perched a good 30 feet up in a pine tree, standing on one limb while holding on to another over his head.

As fate would have it, just then we heard a loud crack. The limb on which he was standing broke, leaving him temporarily hanging from the top one.

Within seconds, it snapped, too, and he came crashing down the side of that tree.

I swear he bounced when he hit the ground, and Roger and I ran to him fearing the worst.

"Are you okay?" we asked.

Scared, scratched and bruised all over, he whimpered a bit and then said, "I think so," before pointing to the tree and saying, "Look!"

We looked up and saw that every branch of that side of the pine tree was broken off, which undoubtedly was a good thing as each one had broken his fall and probably saved his life.

I love my friends and love getting together to laugh about old memories we've created together. Perhaps none are finer than those created with my dear friend, David Manning.

But what do I know?

UFO

OCTOBER 30, 2006

"Uh, Kerry?" I stammered.

"I know," he responded, "I've been watching it too."

We had spent the previous night in Winnipeg watching the final game of the classic World Series between Boston and Cincinnati on TV; what a classic it was.

Most undoubtedly remember Carlton Fisk "waving" his home run fair. For me it was watching perhaps the best baseball lineup ever assembled in Cincy's Rose, Perez, Bench, Foster, Griffey, Concepcion and the rest.

Winnipeg was the last stop on the Canadian tour of our rock 'n' roll band. And, as fate would have it, our equipment truck twisted a rear axle and wasn't going anywhere until repaired.

Our roadie - Kerry Stewart - and I were left behind to have the truck fixed and drive home while the rest of the band drove on in a separate vehicle.

The grueling tour started in Thunder Bay, Ontario, and took us west to Vancouver and then back to that final stop in Winnipeg.

We left the hotel around midnight and drove south to the border and spent the next few hours under the microscope of American customs agents who were sure these two hippies - with hair spilling over their shoulders and beards to match - were undoubtedly drug runners or subversive agents.

After they unloaded our truck and inspected every orifice we were finally cleared and we continued south across the desolate North Dakota prairie.

We talked awhile before fading into a tired tolerance of quietly watching the miles go by. Ours was the only vehicle on the road.

Around 4 a.m. I noticed the lights of Fargo ahead in the distance. I remember how strange it looked, there under the big sky with its concentration of lights in this small area and not another light in sight for as far as the eye could see.

Suddenly I noticed another light that caught my eye. It was brighter than any of the city lights and seemed to be fixed high in the air, stationary over the city. At first I thought it was on a huge flagpole or water tower but it was much too high.

It never moved for the longest time and as we got closer to it I wondered if Kerry saw it; finally I shared my inquisition and he answered immediately.

"What do you suppose that is?" I continued.

"No idea but it sure is strange," was his response.

We drove on, watching in silence until we neared the Fargo outskirts.

Suddenly the light began to move, upward and slowly gaining momentum before finally rocketing straight up and disappearing into the early morning sky. We were stunned!

I slammed the brakes and asked, "Did you see that?"

Kerry confirmed what we had both seen even though we had no idea what it was.

"Nobody will ever believe us!" I lamented.

"Doesn't matter," was his reply of wisdom.

And, of course, he was right. I've always been an open-minded guy who can accept and deal with almost anything as long as it makes sense to me. And, even though this didn't particularly make sense, I know what I saw.

Do you believe in UFO's? Kerry Stewart and I do as I'm sure we saw one visit and take off that morning in Fargo, North Dakota.

But what do I know?

NOT JUST A RIGHT...

N O V E M B E R 6 , 2 0 0 6

What an honor it is to have the privilege to vote!

As I sit sifting through thoughts on election eve I think about all the people in the world who don't have that privilege. I also think about how recent that neither women nor blacks had that privilege in America. My how times change; we've rocketed to the opposite end of the spectrum as there are now those in authority campaigning for even illegal immigrants to have that privilege, among others.

I think about other changes in this time-honored tradition during my lifetime, specifically, attitudes. Campaigning used to be spirited contests where honorable men and women respectfully and discreetly engaged each other to gain position before ultimately amalgamating to move our country forward; those times appear gone.

I've grown weary of simply seeing the political season approach and am downright ashamed of current attitudes and methods used to gain those positions. I've never seen so much trash and outright lies - from both parties - being tossed at each other. Character, honor, integrity, veracity; none of those matter anymore, only winning.

I wonder why anyone would want to subject themselves to this kind of scrutiny. I'm sure we all have something in our past we wouldn't want paraded in tomorrow's headlines. But the instant someone steps forward to try to lead and make a difference in the lives of those they govern, adversaries insert the proverbial microscope digging for dirt in their storied past with which to smear them. It doesn't matter if they've changed or how much good they've done, only the bad.

I can't wait for tomorrow! Unfortunately, it's not because I'm excited to see who wins what election but because tomorrow feels like trash day; I get to set all this garbage at the curb and Wednesday, it's gone. Sad lament!

Another sad lament is the excitement generated by the projection that "maybe" 40 percent of Michigan's citizens will actually vote. How pathetic.

Still, the simple essence of what will happen tomorrow clangs like a church bell echoing through the valley, calling me - and, I hope, you - to the responsibility of making your voice heard.

And, no matter what the water cooler talk or pollsters project, what I am proud to have is the privilege to peruse the personal platforms of the people participating in the election process and then make my selections based on what I think is best.

Then, I hope we can come together as truly united states seeking a more perfect union in which to better seek life, liberty and the pursuit of happiness as intended by the framers of our republic.

Somehow I don't see that happening as with each passing day we seem to be more divided than united. Somehow I perceive that anyone opposing whoever in power would quickly side with external enemies to justify or advance their personal positions or agendas.

Somehow I see anarchy hovering like vultures over an anticipated carcass.

If nothing more than for my grandchildren's sake, I can't tell you how much I hope I am wrong.

In the meantime, I hope to see you at the polls tomorrow and I hope you join me in the belief that voting is not only a right but a responsibility as well as a privilege!

But what do I know?

B E N N Y

N O V E M B E R   1 3 ,   2 0 0 6

I can't remember the last time I had so much fun at a funeral. Come to think of it, I don't know that I've ever had fun at a funeral - that is until a few weeks ago at Second Missionary Baptist Church.

I was saddened to read in the paper that an old friend had passed away. I sometimes called him Mr. Rhythm, but he was mostly just Benny to me.

I attended school with his brother, Willie, one of Monroe's greatest athletes ever, and sister, Geraldine, who is still a knockout. I perhaps was even better friends with two other brothers, Colton and Robert Lee.

I don't remember meeting Benny Jones; he always just seemed to be there. Most people would see him coming and notice lifeless legs swinging between strides of crutches. What I always saw was the ear-to-ear smile tattooed to his face.

The man was a style maven routinely outfitted in the finest threads, but the smile was Benny Jones' magnet.

Those who know me know I love to sing. Doesn't matter if I'm any good. I just love to sing. The instruction book from which I try to fashion my life teaches us to "make a joyful noise," but before I sincerely sought counsel in that book, it was Benny who helped me unleash that love.

Not long after returning from war and laboring through simple jobs trying to reclaim who I was before temporarily losing him in Vietnam, I turned to an old friend to help with that reclamation process: my guitar.

Old friend Jack Campbell allowed me to sing and play that guitar in his downtown matchbox establishment. My remuneration was the 50 cent cover charge. One who regularly paid that admission was one of the finest percussionists Monroe ever produced: Benny Jones.

One night during a late performance break, Benny called me to his side and dispensed words of wisdom.

"Treece, dig," he began. "You got a nice voice, but you ain't lettin' go. Man, stop worryin' what people think and just throw your head back and sing from your soul!"

When I climbed back on stage, I did exactly as Benny instructed and haven't looked back since. And because of that great inspiration given me by one who deserved to be a recipient himself, I knew I had to pay my respects at his "home-going" - and what a home-going it was.

Because Benny had accepted Christ as his Savior, the funeral was nothing but a celebration featuring speakers and singers simply doing what Benny had told me to do all those years ago.

My treat was having my old school chum - Grammy-nominated favorite son, Rance Allen - eulogizing Benny and honoring him and our Lord in song before my "Brotherman," the Rev. Al Overstreet, lit us all up with a sermon.

I still can't decide if the fried chicken or black-eyed peas won my taste test during dinner that followed, but I can tell you this: Black folk definitely know how to worship and how to eat.

What a thrill to honor the sojourn of my dear, departed friend along with The One with whom he now resides - and to leave a funeral feeling like I just had one of the best times of my life.

But what do I know?

"THE WRECK OF THE EDMUND FITZGERALD"

N O V E M B E R 2 0 , 2 0 0 6

With his hand he made motions as if it was a ship rolling up and down on heavy seas. Then he stopped his hand on top of the "wave" and looked at me and said, "Personally, I think she went up on one wave and when she came down," - he stopped talking and plunged his hand down before adding - "she went straight down and broke apart when she hit the bottom."

He took a swig from his gin bottle before tossing the Time magazine on the table and saying, "I wrote the song after reading about it in there."

In the winter of 1976 I was standing on the doorstep of my lifelong dream of recording an album. In a musical group and having written several songs to be included on it, I was as excited as I had ever been.

Eastern Sound was the recording studio that sat in the heart of downtown Toronto, Ontario; I was in awe when given the tour.

I became fast friends with the man who would produce our album and he invited me to the studio late one night a few days before we began our recording session. Little did I know of the historical evening I was about to witness.

Also in the studio that evening putting final touches on his "Summertime Dream" LP was the great Canadian folk singer/ songwriter, Gordon Lightfoot.

There was a side room to the studio and as fate would have it for me, I had the unique opportunity to sit silently in that room's darkness to watch this fabled artist record his now legendary epic, "Wreck of the Edmund Fitzgerald."

I remember the haunting sound his guitarist produced by playing through a new device called a synthesizer, and how - when he recorded the vocal - Lightfoot cleared the studio and killed all the lights save the one illuminating his parchment of scribbled words. For a fledgling singer/songwriter, I was in heaven.

Trying to overcome being steamrolled by the magnitude of his persona, I talked with him later and shared how moved I was by the song's lyrics.

"I'm having a party at my house to celebrate finishing the record," he told me before continuing with, "Wanna come?"

What a dumb question to ask a star-struck kid.

To give you an indication of the grandeur of his "house," as we walked in the back door his lady-friend said, "They called and offered $3.4 million!" to which he replied, "Do they only want the bottom floor?"

That bottom floor was magnificent. Gold albums adorned decorated walls and three grand pianos were scattered throughout elegant rooms.

He steered me to a separate room where he picked up the Time magazine and gin bottle and told me the story of how he wrote a simple song that would, in time, turn what was actually just another one of the estimated 6,000 Great Lakes commercial shipwrecks into one of the most fabled tragedies in history.

I thought of him last week and our special time together as I paused to remember the 29 men still entombed in that watery grave 31 years after "the gales of November came early."

I am also in awe of the power lying behind the ability to fashion simple words.

But what do I know?

"I'VE CREATED A MONSTER"

NOVEMBER 27, 2006

After finishing a follow-up interview with my friend, Charles Slat, *Monroe Evening News* staff writer, about a project my wife and I unveiled a year ago, I started thinking about a saying I once heard.

"I've created a monster!" is usually used when someone starts or creates something that takes on a life of its own or turns into something much larger than EVER anticipated.

I expect that in today's paper you'll read Charlie's story about, "The Ghost Closet: Return to Vietnam on the Wings of DOVE," a book I wrote about a 2001 mission trip Renee and I took to the country in which I served as a soldier in the late 1960's. DOVE is an acronym for "Development of Vietnam Endeavors;" we build schools and hospitals in that Asian nation.

Before I left (and before I began writing for them) The Monroe News asked me to keep a journal of the trip. We were so busy I had no time to write, so upon our return I sat down at the computer and wrote a story simply to follow through on my word.

I began writing at 6:00 a.m. and wrote, and wrote, and wrote! It was as if I had mentally marinated the meat of the trip with the maturity 35 years affords and the more I wrote the more the mission melded with the memories and exploded in flavor on the screen. Finally, at 10 p.m. I told Renee, "I've created a monster!"

I couldn't seem to turn it off but finally forced myself to finish. It was so lengthy I thought The News would never print it; still, my word was my bond so I delivered it. I was shocked when they printed the entire story.

I was more shocked when a week later checks started arriving in my mailbox from folks wanting to support what we were doing; that's when Renee and I decided to turn the story into a book and build a school in Vietnam with the proceeds. I returned to the computer.

One year ago the hardbound books arrived and we began our

"Organ Grinder & Monkey" show: I sing and tell about the project and Renee sells the books and takes the money.

Money goes a long way in Vietnam compared to America. Our original plan was to build a simple, modest school but as the book began to sell and donations began rolling in we kept upgrading larger and larger; finally a benefactor - moved after reading the book - vaulted us over the $32,000 mark.

A spring typhoon that hit the village where I served left a dire need for a primary school; unfortunately, we need another $13,000 to reach its $50,000 price tag.

All that means, however, is that the organ grinder and his monkey must make more appearances, sing more songs and trust that more people will agree that the only way we are going to survive on this planet is to figure out a way to get along with each other. We believe that educating children - no matter their nationality - and amplifying the Fruits of the Spirit - love, joy, peace, patience, kindness, goodness, faithfulness, gentleness and self-control - is the way it can happen.

We've created a monster, but this is a good one!

But what do I know?

THE ORGAN GRINDER
AND HIS MONKEY

D E C E M B E R 4 , 2 0 0 6

"Hey, who are you calling a monkey?" Renee kidded me.

In last week's column I shared the story of how my wife and I hatched a plan to build a school in Vietnam by using the profits from a book I wrote about our recent trip to that Asian country.

In that column I referred to us as like an "organ grinder and his monkey" because in the last year we have appeared in every church, service club, coffee house or anywhere welcomed to tell our story.

Long time column readers will remember that Renee was left disabled after having three brain tumors excised last January. Initially paralyzed from the neck down, you wouldn't know it to look at her as her hair has returned along with feeling in most of her body, and - as long as she's wearing the special louvered brace on her still partially paralyzed leg - one will only notice an exaggerated limp when she walks.

We had to close the door on her life's profession - running our beauty salon - but she has dived into new ventures, the primary one of which is handling everything that leads to "the cup."

There is a chapter in my book - "The Ghost Closet" - called, "The Organ Grinder and His Monkey," about two former ARVN (Army of the Republic of Viet Nam) soldiers we met in a marketplace in the Vietnam city of Hue.

The "organ grinder" had a homemade, wooden prosthesis where his left leg used to be; closer observation revealed eyes that saw no more. Wired around his neck was a microphone and slung from his shoulder was a dry-rotted electric guitar powered by a portable battery pack slung from his other shoulder.

The "monkey" had also been an ARVN and war's cost for him was both legs below the groin. He had fashioned wheels onto a flat piece of wood for ease as he knuckled what was left of himself around and dragged the organ grinder's amplifier.

But, his most important job was handling the cup!

As soon as he saw the smile on my face telling him that his organ grinder's musical lure had hooked me, all he had to do was reel me in; he lifted the cup in my direction.

I had been hearing the fabulous, haunting music of the organ grinder drifting through the marketplace and had commented to Renee that I must find and purchase a CD of that music; I was shocked discovering it was live and coming from former comrades of war. I filled the cup with cash.

When researching for last week's column I thought of the correlation Renee and I now have with the organ grinder and his monkey. With the guitar slung from my shoulder I sing and tell the story of our school plans while Renee extends the cup to people who are moved to help us.

The major difference between them and us, of course, is we are simply trying to help the Vietnamese people while they are simply trying to find something to eat!

Last week a friend said, "Great work you guys are doing, and I must tell you Tom, you've got the most beautiful monkey I've ever seen!"

Surely Renee won't mind being called a beautiful monkey!

But what do I know?

CYCLES

DECEMBER 11, 2006

I've come to realize that most everything in life is cyclic, from the complexities of the universe to the mundane.

When I was a boy and asked about war, my father simply quoted scripture predicting there would "always be war and rumors of war" and that nations (ethnic groups) would rise against nations and kingdoms (countries) against kingdoms (Matthew 21:6-7).

While I was a baby-boomer born just after World War II and hardly remember Korea, I was in the front row for Vietnam and remember well the attitudes prevalent of that age.

Many Americans were extremely vocal with, "Kill the Commies!" attitudes in the early years of that war, which, in the later were just as vociferous with, "I always knew this was a bad idea." They are "fence-sitters" who simply reflect the overall mood of the country; when it's popular, they're for it; when it isn't, they're against it.

It's sadly humorous to watch this whimsical re-run being played out on today's stage - specifically in Washington - as the Iraq War begins its cyclic descent. Voters spoke loud and clear in the last election; they are, rightly so, sick of this war. Me too!

However, Thursday I stood once again - mentally - perched atop the concrete observation bunker on the crest of Oahu's Diamond Head volcano and looked down on the Honolulu harbor where 65 years earlier the sneak attack on Pearl Harbor plunged us into World War II after killing nearly 3,000 American soldiers.

Instantly the channel changed in my mind and I was gasping after watching the second sneak attack airplane plow into the World Trade Center's tower two, ultimately helping kill another 3,000 innocent, unsuspecting Americans.

While there was no clearly identifiable "kingdom," there certainly was an identifiable "nation" responsible: Islamic militancy.

Just as predecessor Roosevelt did, President Bush went after the aggressors; unfortunately, they weren't as clearly defined as the Japanese. He knew the Taliban stronghold was in Afghanistan and began there.

I questioned the president extending it to Iraq but justified it believing Saddam was a mass murderer who needed to be removed. Watching his own people celebrate his falling statue only confirmed that justification.

"Mission Accomplished" turned out to be only the photo-op for which it was intended and then we sat and watched - and watched - each day's news filled with sectarian violence that not only killed large numbers of Iraqi civilians but American soldiers as well.

I expect few of you hate war more than me, but my hesitation to jump on the new cyclic bandwagon is ... this whole Islamic militancy thing was emboldened after President Carter's pathetic response to the 1979 Iran hostage crisis. Since that time militants methodically bombed United States interests abroad until they got bold enough to stroll onto American soil to do their evil deeds.

Here's the thing. In the five years since 9/11 there hasn't been one attack on American interests outside of the war zone. My fear is that when we pull out of Iraq to please the cyclic masses, those attacks will recommence, here! I hope I'm wrong.

Unfortunately, I worry that the wild celebration over Democrats cyclic return to power (Clinton over Bush I.) will give the green light for terrorists to once again bring their cycle of death to a street corner near you.

But what do I know?

CHICHEN ITZA

D E C E M B E R   1 8 ,   2 0 0 6

I did something yesterday I don't do much anymore: saw a movie at the cinema. While I enjoy the big screen experience it doesn't circumvent the ease of pausing the DVD when I need to hit the bathroom or make popcorn for my sweetheart.

I was intrigued by reviews of the new Mel Gibson movie, "Apocalyto," and didn't want to wait for the DVD. I had heard it was violent - it was - as were the multiple previews preceding it.

My intrigue came from the subject people: ancient Mayan Indians.

Years ago Renee and I traveled to one of our favorite vacation destinations, Mexico's Yucatan Peninsula. From Isle de Cozumel we rented a van and drove four hours across the jungle to a place called "Chichen Itza," an ancient Mayan city that is without doubt one of the most interesting places I have ever been.

The Maya - without the wheel, sophisticated tools or beasts of burden - carved incredible architecture throughout the Yucatan during the turn of the BC-AD time period. All these years later their stone temples and pyramids still stand as testaments to their architectural skills.

The Maya were incredible mathematicians as well, giving us the calendar concept we use today.

The main pyramid at Chichen Itza - El Castillo (the castle) - stands some 80 feet in the air. Each of four stairways has 91 steps - equaling the number of days separating the four phases of the annual solar cycle: winter solstice, spring equinox, summer solstice and fall equinox - for a total of 364 steps. The 365th step for all is the top floor, equaling, of course, the number of days in our solar year.

The Maya mapped the heavens and knew the seasons intricately. A phenomenon of El Castillo is its construction in such a location that each year - at the spring and fall Equinox - as the sun slowly sets it

Tom and Renee at Mexico's Chichen Itza Mayan Ruins, 2003.

sends a slinking shadow illuminating the silhouette of a giant stone snake slithering down the stairway to the snake's colossal carved head at the base of the pyramid; thousands come to watch each year.

A concave room at the top allowed high priests to stand inside out of sight and speak to people gathered below who thought the gods were speaking to them. Incredibly, I stood at the top and in a normal voice coaxed Renee to make the climb to the top. (Afraid of heights, she walked up but went back down on her butt).

Another amazing construction is the Ball Court, a stadium-like structure where a strange game was played. On a field longer than that used for football, two teams tried to kick a ball through stone-carved, perpendicular hoops 20 feet off the ground. The captain of the winning team then presented himself to the king who then decapitated him and drained his blood to be used as a sacrifice to the gods for fertile farmland. To sports buffs it gives greater meaning to "giving yourself up for the team!"

No one knows what caused the Mayans to decline and give up their cities. Perhaps it was odd beliefs like this, as well as like the human brutality featured in Apocalyto. Or, perhaps, simply, no one arrived in time to tell them what Christmas is really all about.

But what do I know?

TIME WAITS FOR NO ONE …
ESPECIALLY ON DEADLINE

J A N U A R Y   2 ,   2 0 0 7

Time - and our perception of it - is amazing. It definitely marches on, with or without you. Some have all the time in the world; others never have enough. I am of the latter.

Sunday night, the world counted down the final hours, minutes and seconds of 2006. Times Square was jammed with the largest New Year's Eve crowd ever. People were there to celebrate time - the end of one year and the beginning of another.

I, on the other hand, could not have cared less what day or year it was as my wife and I were on our third consecutive day of misery from being in bed with the flu.

How sick was I? Here are two hints:

First, who but a very sick guy would complain about spending three days in bed with the sexiest woman on the planet?

Second, we were so sick we even missed our oldest grandson's birthday party, something Nonnie and Poppy never would do unless they were really sick.

I had so anticipated these days off. I had many things on my "to do" list, none of which were accomplished.

Even as I write, I keep glancing at the clock as I have just about an hour to get this column written and e-mailed to the newspaper; I guess I am going through my own different sort of personal countdown.

It was amazing to watch the response of people during the weekend coverage of three completely different men for whom time ran out.

The honorable, dignified respect given by the thousands who quietly filed by the flag-draped casket of President Gerald Ford was light-years away compared to the party thrown to celebrate the life of soul singer, James Brown.

Then, even more extreme opposites came from different ones affected by the violent end of time for Saddam Hussein. One video showed overjoyed Iraqis dancing wildly in the streets while the next showed traumatized followers grieving over his grave and vowing revenge for his death.

I thought about my life and how it seems to have flown by despite the snail's pace I remember while waiting to become a teenager and then during each day of war.

It doesn't seem that long ago that I was listening to Prince sing about how "we're going to party like it's 1999" and wondering what it would be like when that year finally did come. Now it seems like only yesterday we were worried about "Y2K." Could that actually have been seven years ago?

On the mantle of my fireplace sits my father's wedding gift to my mother 70 years ago, an old, wind-up Seth Thomas clock that just chimed eight times to tell me today's *Monroe Evening News* will be going on without me if I don't get this column to them pronto.

I've discovered a lot of truth in my life - perhaps none more accurate than the statement, "Life is like a roll of toilet paper; the closer you get to the end, the faster it goes."

And speaking of toilet paper, while I hate being sick and hate wasting time even more, I celebrate that at least I am still king of my world as I was able to sit on my throne all weekend without any interruptions.

But what do I know?

CRUCIFIED WITH CHRIST

JANUARY 8, 2007

It seems as though I've been somewhat at odds with the rest of society for most of my life. I was never a troublemaker though some may have thought so in younger days.

Raised in a strict Southern Baptist home, we were in church virtually every time the doors were open and on our knees every night before bedtime in front of our living room couch, which served as our family altar. Later I remember resenting being "forced" to go to church.

I remember "religious wars" of our society; most everyone believed in God but was adamant that their religion was the right one.

After returning from spending my 20th year of life at war I was sure I had come of age and nobody was going to tell me what I could or couldn't do anymore. I hit the road with my guitar "seeking my fame and fortune, looking for a pot of gold," as John Fogerty shared in his song, "Lodi." There was no fame, no fortune and no pot of gold.

There was, however, anger and resentment for having arbitrarily been plucked from the life I knew and sent 14,000 miles to the other side of the planet, handed an automatic weapon and told to kill people I didn't know or have anything against while life went on as normal back here in the States.

After my service I was in no-man's-land; I felt abandoned by my government while simultaneously being labeled by the left as a warmonger for simply serving. I became liberally anti-war after 15 years and 55,000+ lost lives then had my patriotism questioned. I took solace knowing that when my country called on me, I responded.

At the same time my spirituality - or lack of it - was also being questioned as the entire country was a God-fearing nation and the mere thought of atheism was virtually unheard of or tolerated. It wasn't that I didn't believe, I just felt I couldn't take anyone else's opinion or word anymore (as I had done all my life in church, school and home);

I had to find out for myself. Again I found myself out of step with the mood of the country.

I now see my lifelong search for truth as a gradual nosedive. Og Mandino once said, "Everything you find in life that is false only leads you to what is true." As I've shared, that nosedive took me to the edge of suicide where - instead of pulling the trigger - I asked God to come into my heart and take over my life, and He did. He changed my life so radically I can hardly believe I'm the same person. And, I guess I'm not.

My truth - since - is that I have never known such joy. I never knew what being one with my wife was all about. I never knew about "the peace that passes all understanding."

Yesterday I read a scathing attack blaming all of America's troubles on God, and specifically, Christianity, and I realized that once again I seem to be out of step with the mood of the country.

I also believe it won't be long before Christians will have a much greater understanding of what it truly means to be "crucified with Christ."

But what do I know?

"Y O U R L O V E A M A Z E S M E"

J A N U A R Y 1 5, 2 0 0 7

My dear Renee,

What a blessed man I am! Other than accepting the free gift of God's amazing grace in my life, nothing I ever have done has been deserving of the tremendous blessings I have been given. And I know that because of my decision to accept that grace, God sent me you.

Tomorrow is your birthday, but I feel like the one who's been given the gift. It's hard to fathom that a year already has gone by since our lives were turned upside down by Dr. K's words: brain tumors.

After seeing your MRI, I thought our wonderful life together was over and I undoubtedly was having my last intelligent conversations with you. Instantly I realized the true depth of my love for you as all I wanted at that moment was to be able to have those tumors in my head instead of yours.

I hope you won't mind me sharing this personal letter with my readers, but, as you know, so very many of them have helped us bear this burden from the start. I don't think a day has gone by that someone hasn't called, written or personally told us they have been praying for you. How blessed we are! And how blessed I am to have this avenue of communication to thank them all at once.

I want you to know how proud I am of you. I get a hangnail and complain. You have three tumors removed from your brain - leaving you paralyzed from the neck down and in a struggle for life and a return of your faculties - and never once complained. Through surgery, ICU and all those months of grueling acute rehabilitation, not once did I hear, "Why me?" "Poor me!" or "Why God?"

And, speaking of God, He, of course, gets all the credit. Never will I forget "seeing" you on Abraham's altar and realizing I also was being asked if I was willing to give you up. That perhaps was the most difficult day of my life. But how grateful I am to have made the right choice. He said He would use this for His glory, and has He ever. I can't believe how many have come inquiring about our miracle and how reassuring it is to point them to the Miracle Worker.

And, now, a year later, I'm amazed at your attitude. Your determination to march on - whether you overcome the continuing paralysis in your arm, hand and leg or whether it will be the "thorn in your side" - is simply remarkable.

I also must tell you of the joy in my heart each time I watch you work your magic with Drake and Gaige. Grandchildren have no concept of disability as they race around exploring their new world with "Nonnie" in hot pursuit, leg brace and all. They also have no idea yet of the incredible treasure that is theirs in you. Their day will come, as has mine.

How grateful I am that God brought you to me, and I hope you know how very much I cherish you.

Happy birthday, baby!

With all my love,

Tommy

PS: Can't wait to see what God has in store for us this year. It's gonna be great!

But what do I know?

BEACH GLASS

JANUARY 23, 2007

The icy blast that finally gripped southeastern Michigan last weekend had not only turned the Lake Erie liquid into slush but also had angered the loch enough to cause it to pound the shoreline, reminding me that one man's trash is another man's treasure.

Even though I've tried hard not to express my disdain for winter over the past few years to you column-wise, I couldn't rob my heart of that personal joy as the motion of the waves captured my stare almost as easily as crackling campfires of summer. I sadly relented to the reality that months would yet pass before I once again would stroll barefoot on that beach in search of treasure.

Mind you, in fear of waking the sleeping winter lion by gloating, I dare not complain, considering what we've faced so far has been a loving lamb compared to fierce roars of winters past.

And yet, while I must wait out the sun's sojourn before it once again warms and soothes those angry waves, I bask in the knowledge that their very action is what makes my treasures my treasures.

What be those, you ask?

Trash! Not to me, of course, but certainly to those who set them in motion.

Specifically, I speak of glass - beach glass, it's called. The ironic comparison to life is what lures me to value it.

Glass is blown or formed in various shapes, colors and sizes for various purposes - the most common of which is for holding liquid. The most glaring example of the treasure's beginning is when it becomes trash in the mind of the owner - perhaps a fisherman - and, once empty, is unceremoniously dumped overboard into the lake.

Like a bottle fresh from the factory, people are created shiny and new and mostly without blemish. Eventually - purposely or not - through mistrust, reckless behavior, carelessness or downright evil intent, those closest to us eventually trash us, leaving us broken and in pieces like the fisherman's bottle that breaks on the bottom leaving sharp, cutting edges to slice anyone who comes near. For a while ...

Time, however - like God - slowly, methodically heals all wounds. The glass is tumbled by time and tide as wave action imitates life by gradually grinding the pieces across the lake bottom. Ultimately, the formerly razor-sharp edges are slowly sandblasted and smoothed until they are no longer even capable of cutting.

Eventually, the glass, now virtually unrecognizable, is transformed into a new entity and gets spit out of the sea and onto the beach. Here, a character strange to his neighbors comes along - who himself having been broken with sharp, cutting edges that God, like time and the sea, smoothed and polished into a new being - picks them up, wipes away the sand and surf and transports them home to a new place of honor in shiny, new containers.

These containers are scattered throughout our home as constant reminders of how broken lives can be transformed. And, when I think about that transformation - be it in broken glass or human lives - I believe transformation's key is in allowing one's self to relent to a superior force or power.

But what do I know?

AT THE FOOT OF THE CROSS

JANUARY 29, 2007

The recent 10-year anniversary of the day Comair Flight 3272 - its wings iced and malfunctioning - nosedived out of a sky full of blizzard to crash and explode with 29 precious lives inside, got me thinking of that fateful day.

Knowing it was a news story of major proportions for our sleepy community, the Tower 98 radio station general manager ordered his news team into action to detail the tragedy for our listeners.

Also knowing the plane had crashed in a park owned by my church - ironically near the base of a large, wooden cross that had been erected - was helpful as I knew who to call.

Longtime friend Danny Connor, the park's caretaker, lived a stone's throw from the crash site; I made the call and spoke with his daughter, Cathy, who had seen the crash. The newsman in me wanted a live interview; the humanitarian recognizing the trauma she had just witnessed, didn't.

I saw Cathy last week and we talked again about that fateful day; I asked if she would now consider sharing her story; she agreed.

The 14 year-old Dundee High School freshman had exited the school bus and was hurrying her pace as snow and cold nipped at her nose. Suddenly a strange sound stopped her in her tracks.

"It sounded like a loud whistle coming from above me," she began. "It sounded heavy, or at least like it was produced by some heavy object. When I looked up there was a fast-falling white streak, a loud explosion, a ball of fire, and then, nothing; it was totally silent. I could hear my heart beating and told myself I should move, run, do something."

Cathy ran the rest of the way to her house where she met her father heading to the site to see if there was anything he could do.

"I'll never forget the look on his face," she said, "To this day it makes me uneasy as I've never seen my dad - who handles difficult situations with ease and always knows what to do - so scared or unsure. That day he was completely beside himself."

After Cathy's mother called 911, confusion reigned the rest of the night as the family guided authorities to the crash site through their snow-caked yard and answered a barrage of phone calls from concerned family and friends, as well as media hounds - like me - from all over the country.

"I'm still not sure how they knew I'd seen the crash," she continued, "but they did, and they knew my number."

What the sensitive Cathy remembers most from the following days was, "the firemen and police officers who had the unfortunate task of gathering what was left from the small commuter flight and its passengers. I never thanked them in person, but I most certainly thank God for what they did!"

In closing she shared, "I've never been back there and don't think I ever will as I saw all I needed to see January 9th, 1997!"

Cathy's was one of the few first-hand accounts from that tragic day. I appreciated her time and especially her remembrance of the rescue personnel's heroic efforts and I find it highly ironic that those 29 passengers died at the foot of a cross.

But what do I know?

BIRDS OF A FEATHER

F E B R U A R Y 5 , 2 0 0 7

Mother quoted old sayings or Bible verses for everything that happened in life; it was one of the ways she taught us kids.

One such saying was, "Birds of a feather flock together," meaning similar people always find it easy to relate to each other in life.

I thought about that yesterday after telling a story to friends discussing the current music tour of Ann Arbor native and veteran rock 'n' roller Bob Seger and how our lives came together as teenagers on S. Telegraph Rd. in Monroe.

Unless you skated in the '50s at the Floral City Roller Rink or danced the night away in the '60s at Monroe's first and only wildly successful teen hangout - The Club - you'd have no idea anything ever existed there except the tree and weed-choked land found on the site today.

In the '60s, however, it was the place to be - especially if you wanted to see rising rock stars such as Seger, who with his band, The Last Heard, headlined weekend shows the first two weeks of every month.

It was my pleasure to share the stage with this budding star as part of one of the house bands, Caesar and the Romans. (And, yes, sometimes we even wore togas on stage to complete the motif.)

I remember simultaneous hurt and happiness a few years later upon hearing his hit "Heavy Music" played on AFVN - Armed Forces Vietnam Radio - and longed once again to have a guitar in my hands instead of an automatic weapon.

Finally back in the states and back on stage, I ran into him on the road occasionally while performing in like locations, most recently in Vancouver, British Columbia, in the mid-'70s. His "Beautiful Loser" album was months away from making him a major star.

One such night - at Detroit's "Rock & Roll Farm" - he told me, "It's not about how good you are, it's about how long can you hold out."

the mid-'80s, I could hold out no longer and gave up dreams of a music career for a steady job in radio.

Oddly enough, radio reunited us again in the '90s as our local station was romanced by Capitol Records, Seger's record label. Once the representative heard of my history with his label's star, he provided Renee and me tickets and backstage passes for Bob's upcoming Savage Hall performance in Toledo.

I showed the representative pictures of our early years together. His comment was, "He'll freak when he sees that Beatle haircut!" I responded, "No, he'll freak when he sees that Gibson Firebird guitar he undoubtedly sold years ago!"

After the show, we waited backstage; finally, in walked Bob. After introducing Renee, I shared the pictures. He laughed then stopped and pined, "Oh man, my old Gibson Firebird!" I looked at the representative and said, "Told ya!"

I knew, as I had a similar reaction after seeing my old Les Paul guitar in another's hands 30 years after selling it for a $200 truck payment.

Mom was right; birds of a feather do flock together.

I'm thrilled for my high-flying friend's great success, and I think it's true that some birds are born to soar while others are destined to stay on the ground.

But what do I know?

ONE MAN WITH COURAGE

FEBRUARY 12, 2007

With immeasurable wisdom he undoubtedly was the right man for the right time.

The cost, however, was also immeasurable, yet he lived the advice of former President Andrew Jackson: "One man with courage makes a majority."

Reading some of his quotes gives great insight into the man and I wonder how he would be treated today.

He said, "A child is a person who is going to carry on what you have started. He is going to sit where you are sitting, and when you are gone attend to those things which you think are important. You may adopt all the policies you please, but how they are carried out depends on him. He will assume control of your cities, states, and nations. He is going to move in and take over your churches, schools, universities and corporations; the fate of humanity is in his hands."

He was concerned about those who would promote themselves into authoritative positions and warned, "Nearly all men can stand adversity, but if you want to test a man's character, give him power."

As he himself became a lynchpin with power in time of war he spoke out against others who gained but abused that power and said, "Congressmen who willfully take actions during wartime that damage morale and undermine the military are saboteurs and should be arrested, exiled, or hanged."

Yet, with the softest of hearts he gave hope to a bereaved mother whose son had been killed at war by personally writing to say, "In this sad world of ours, sorrow comes to all, and to the young it comes with bitterest agony because it takes them unaware ... perfect relief is not possible, except with time. You cannot realize that you will ever feel better ... you are sure to be happy again. To know this, which is certainly true, will make you some less miserable now. I have had experience enough to know what I say and you need only to believe it to feel better."

Openly and boldly he acknowledged the source from which he drew his strength and guidance with quotes like, "I have been driven many times upon my knees by the overwhelming conviction that I had nowhere else to go," and, "Without the assistance of the Divine Being who ever attended him, I cannot succeed. With that assistance I cannot fail."

Over 150 years ago he reflected my concerns for America today when he said, "In sincerity and truth, let us then rest humbly in the hope, authorized by the Divine teachings, that the united cry of the Nation will be heard on high, and answered with blessings, no less the pardon of our national sins, and the restoration of our now divided and suffering Country, to its former happy condition of unity and peace."

I expect that if asked to list the five greatest presidents of all time, most Americans would include the name of the man who was born 198 years ago today.

What's tragic is to think that if he walked into an American school today and again said, "I know there is a God, and that He hates injustice and slavery. I see the storm coming, and I know that His hand is in it," he would probably be sued or arrested!

But what do I know?

MADAMOISELLE SHARED
OLE JOHNNY-BOY

FEBRUARY 19, 2007

A recent TV program featuring extremes of parental pride reminded me of an episode from my honeymoon.

I was never much of a shopper, so I simply wandered through the store while my new bride did the serious shopping - or so I thought. Although we only had been married for days, we had dated for years, so I instantly knew the sound of her scream and bolted for the area of the store from where it had come.

We were downtown Philipsburg, the capital of Dutch St. Maarten in the Lesser Antilles and having the time of our lives, as honeymooners should.

The previous day, with trolling lines trailing, we stretched out and soaked the searing sun of the Caribbean as we sailed a Catamaran south to the French island of St. Barthelemy.

The yellowfin tuna also were hungry that day, and we grilled them on the spot for one of the finest, freshest meals in memory.

Back on St. Maarten, we rented a car and circumnavigated the island, the northern side of which also is a French territory. We climbed the island's highest peak and gazed over Simpson Bay from historic Fort Louis and imagined what it must have been like when Christopher Columbus anchored here on his way to discover the country from which we had flown days earlier.

Once back in Philipsburg, we strolled the street hand-in-hand amid throngs of cruise ship tourists searching for trinkets to take home to loved ones while locals went about their daily routines of hawking them.

One such local sat by the roadway intricately weaving palm tree leaves into the beautiful basket out of which Renee and I serve bread today.

When she screamed in that store, I thought someone was trying to steal my new bride and I - the gallant knight in white armor - raced off

Renee with Mademoiselle
magazine featuring son, John,
Phillipsburg, St. Maarten, 1998.

to her rescue. Instead, I found her standing in front of a magazine rack with tears streaming down her face.

"What's wrong?" I screamed.

"Look!" she cried back holding open the pages of Mademoiselle. As it was printed in French, I couldn't read a word but suddenly saw the reason for her outburst. Staring back from a full-page color advertisement was our oldest son, John, who had left us a year earlier to seek his fortune as a model in New York City.

John had told us of a Candies Shoes ad he shot featuring contemporary folk singer, Lisa Loeb. After finding the magazine, Renee leafed through on the chance it might be there.

"My boy is a star in New York!" she called out to all who would hear.

I wiped the tears of joy from the proud mother's eyes and ushered her to the checkout counter where we purchased the magazine.

For the rest of the afternoon - and honeymoon - Renee opened the magazine to anyone who even looked her, shoved the ad in his or her face and said, "That's my son!" Unfortunately, most were German or French tourists who had no idea what she was saying, and a few thought she was pointing at Lisa Loeb and obviously had her genders mixed up.

Parental pride is a good thing, but had the ad featured our sons as ditch diggers, I'm sure Renee would have done the same.

But what do I know?

"TURN THE PAGE"

FEBRUARY 26, 2007

Every time I sing Bob Seger's road anthem, "Turn the Page," I think about that day.

Perhaps "tired from the trip" was a more fitting description than "strung out from the road" as lifelong friend David Strunk wheeled the Volkswagen Beetle bus into the restaurant parking lot and we shuffled inside for rest and nourishment.

The VW engine groaned a sigh of relief when the ignition disengaged as it also got to take a break from the last few hours of laboring to pull us and our heavy load over the West Virginia mountaintops.

The previous day, I sang in the legendary downtown Monroe hole-in-the-wall establishment known as Campbell's Bar, where admission for the night was two cans of food or a box of clothing. David and I then packed and re-packed until we had all the donated goods loaded and then headed for the Mason-Dixon line and site of the tragedy.

Thirty-five years ago today, a coal slurry dam - constructed on a mountaintop by the Pittston Coal Co. - burst after days of rain and sent 132 million gallons of chalky, black water and waste cascading down the Buffalo Creek valley, virtually destroying 16 unsuspecting coal-mining communities below. Of the more than 5,000 living in the wall of water's path, 125 were killed, 1,121 were injured and 4,000-plus were left homeless.

Answering the call for assistance, David and I approached Jack Campbell with the fundraising plan. Astounded by the response, we joyfully headed deep into the Appalachians to represent the giving spirit of our Monroe compatriots.

The word "redneck" surfaces when I think about the ones waiting when we walked into that restaurant. I remember the deafening roar of silence slicing through the table chatter as they got their first glimpse of us.

The three years since returning from war was just enough time for my hair and beard to grow to unacceptable 1972 societal lengths, and they were not happy to see these "hippies" encroaching on one of their favorite haunts.

We heard all those same old cliches that Seger sang of - including "Is that a woman or a man?" and "I don't know whether to kiss him or shoot him!" - as we grabbed a corner table and tried to blend in.

While the locals became more emboldened with their harassments, we were certainly "outnumbered" and didn't dare "take a stand," so we wolfed down our food and I nervously watched the rear-view mirror long into the miles ahead as we made our getaway.

Hours later, after inching our way through the line of similar vehicles, we unloaded our supplies onto a railway dock and were back on our way home.

"Is that a woman or a man?" Tom, 1972

After getting my first firsthand look at social intolerance, I was shocked and dismayed we were treated with such disregard considering our mercy mission was only to help their stricken neighbors. And it was all because of our hair length.

Although male hair length no longer seems an issue, social intolerance continues with some people hating others who don't see things as they do.

And, although moral intolerance continues to be a concern, I think old age has mellowed me. I'm no longer up in arms over social issues. Instead, I take Seger's advice and simply "turn the page."

But what do I know?

MAKING LOVE NOT WAR

M A R C H   5 ,   2 0 0 7

HUE, Vietnam - Staring out the porthole I couldn't stop my mind from wandering back to the first time I made this trip; just as then there was nothing but ocean for miles, hours. I thought about the lonely, desperate 20-year old soldier scared out of his skin crammed into that tin can like a sardine; at 6-foot-5, the trip was tormenting.

Thank God this one was different!

The first leg of our 25,000 plus-mile journey was another sardine can to Dallas followed by still another to San Francisco where we switched from the U.S. airline I'll not mention to the fabulous Chinese airline, EVA Air. I've flown everything from military to commercial to private in my life, EVA is the best!

From cramped quarters in the American airliners I felt lucky just getting a cranberry juice and tiny bag of pretzels; a while ago the impeccably groomed EVA stewardess started me with a steaming towel to freshen myself and then delivered dinner: baby shrimp louie salad, chicken with lemons and rosemary, Mongolian beef, fresh fruit, ice cream sandwich plus coffee, tea and snack.

Later, breakfast was stir-fried, nappa cabbage with dried Shrimp, Taiwanese sausage, savory porridge with baby seafood, fresh fruit, ham with cole slaw, yogurt and a cheese omelette with hash brown potatoes. Best of all, complimentary. I wondered what they could possibly be serving in first class!

After dinner I reclined my seat and stretched the same frame (that has unfortunately added 100 pounds since that 1968 trip) out to enjoy the 16-hour flight.

Renee asked, "How can they do this and American airlines can't?" I told her it probably has something to do with multi-million dollar CEO bonuses about which we've read lately.

After changing planes in Taipei, we arrived safely in Saigon - formerly Ho Chi Minh City - and bused to our hotel.

Then, after a quick shower, Renee and I strolled downtown taking in the sights and sounds and marveling at the incredible changes that have taken place during this city and country's last 40 years. Perhaps more incredible for me was the fact that I was strolling these same streets holding the hand of the woman I love instead of an automatic weapon.

Tomorrow our D.O.V.E. Fund contingent of 14 will fly north to Phu Bai and motorcade up Highway 1 to Hue to begin our work in Quang Tri Province. Since forming in 2000 we have raised more than $1 million to build over 30 schools, three medical clinics, five water projects and have dug over 300 fresh-water wells.

What Renee and I are thrilled about, however, is the school we will build in the village near where I served as a soldier 40 years ago. Our original goal was to build a $6,000 nursery school with proceeds from my book, "The Ghost Closet." But, after the incredible generosity of those of you who not only bought the book but - more importantly - also bought into our project's mission of love, next week we will begin construction on a $65,000 school in the village near where I served as a soldier after that very first trip!

What a thrill to be here this time winning the hearts and minds of the Vietnamese people by making love, not war!

But what do I know?

SEEDS SCATTERED BY
WAR'S WHIRLWIND

M A R C H   1 2 ,   2 0 0 7

HOI ANN, Vietnam - Gazing out over the South China Sea, I'm reminded of the many times the 20-year-old soldier sat and gazed in that same direction longing for home. I couldn't wait to leave then; now, I don't want to.

It's been a whirlwind trip so far traveling the country inspecting schools our group, The DOVE Fund, previously built, dedicating ones just completed and searching for new areas of need for future projects. Needs glare at us from every turn.

Speaking of whirlwinds ... Wisdom comes with time, and I realize now that God uses whirlwinds in our lives to scatter His seeds of love - if we let Him.

Being drafted and sent to war with an Army infantry unit was the most traumatic thing that had ever happened to me. I was not a willing participant; I served because I believed in fulfilling the duty to my country and I did not want to disgrace my family name or go to jail.

Thirty-nine years later, I'm back in the land I swore never again would feel the weight of my footsteps and realize God was scattering my seeds then through that whirlwind of war in preparation to use me now to make a difference in the lives of these less-fortunate souls I walk among today.

Saturday, Renee and I returned to the village where I served during war - only this time with a message of peace and love. We visited the children in their current school, part of which a spring typhoon had destroyed. Conditions - by American standards - were pathetic, yet they were thrilled simply to have a place to learn.

We took shovels and ceremoniously turned dirt for the new school we are building with proceeds from my book, "The Ghost Closet," and we danced with them in the courtyard during exercise time. Renee would not be denied the opportunity in spite of her physical handicap, and rivers of tears from the moment's emotional joy drenched her. It was rivers of sweat drenching me as I once again felt the searing equatorial heat.

We brought 150 pounds of pencils, crayons, coloring books, etc., graciously given by local churches and friends, including Monroe Bank & Trust, La-Z-Boy, Tenneco, Fifth Third Bank and Monroe County Convention & Tourism Bureau. The children were ecstatic.

Pouring over details and blueprints with the contractor, we were shocked to discover only one bathroom was planned to meet the needs of the 780 students who will attend split-day sessions. Unacceptable!

He gave us the cost for an additional "water closet" (as they call them here). As a result, watch for Renee and me back in our community to hawk more books and share our vision in order to continue to help these people who have nothing but the desire to learn, enjoy their families and be happy.

I am so very grateful for the opportunity to make a difference in the lives of the Vietnamese people who were victimized and virtually devastated from being pawns of war.

I also thank God for allowing me to live long enough to realize that the storms we encounter along life's way are actually blessings in disguise that scatter our seeds and allow us to bloom gloriously where we ultimately are planted.

Tom and Renee, building our school in Duc Pho, Vietnam, 2007.

WHAT PRICE HAPPINESS?

MARCH 19, 2007

NHA TRANG, Vietnam - As the sun strolls onto the morning stage to illuminate this Southeast Asian section of the world, I sip morning coffee so strong the spoon stands almost vertically and watch the world below me. I've parachuted from planes flying lower than the height of the top floor of this hotel - in other words, the view is spectacular.

It's 5:30 a.m. and the beautiful beach below is teeming with Vietnamese, as are the bath-like waters of gorgeous Nha Trang Bay. No one is frolicking and having fun; they are exercising; Vietnamese do this every morning.

As I continue to observe the Vietnamese people, I'm amazed at their work ethic, resourcefulness, veracity, disposition, discipline and pride, to name a few of the many applicable phrases.

I'm reminded of two brothers. One has everything Americans think they need for happiness - wife, kids, home, job, money and a fine car; the other has none of those, yet he is happy while the other constantly seems miserable.

I make the correlation with American and Vietnamese people. The Vietnamese have virtually nothing, yet they seem to be the happiest, friendliest people I've ever been around. Each child - if lucky - has an antique bicycle and a few clothes. American children probably get more during one Christmas than Vietnamese do their entire childhood, but you'd never know it.

We've visited more than 20 schools during this mission trip, and I'm amazed how well-mannered and disciplined schoolchildren are. Not once have I seen inappropriate behavior. Not once have I seen women - students or adults - dressed or acting indecent.

Wearing controversial T-shirts is no problem as dress code is a moot point. All students wear uniforms from nursery school through high school.

Attendance isn't a problem, either, as students must pay to attend school. They can't wait to get there. Many American kids seem to hate school and only go because they have to.

I haven't seen much need for police here. No one locks their doors. Actually, most homes - or huts - don't even have doors, but the people have such integrity that they wouldn't think of ripping off anyone.

Their work ethic is impeccable, and most perform back-breaking work from daylight till dark. They turn the soil using water buffalo pulling a single plow and then harrow the ground - with hand hoes not high-performance tractors.

I remember as a soldier how they took every piece of trash we discarded and used it for something. Nothing has changed. They throw nothing away and don't waste anything - from space to time to trash.

My parents and most people from days of my youth had similar attitudes and work ethics, but I just don't see much of that anymore. Instead, I see defiance and outrageousness and everyone's concern over their rights instead of what is right.

Perhaps I'm not looking hard enough, but I don't think that's it. I see a completely different America than the one I was introduced to 59 years ago.

It's a bit odd for me to see all these people who - like so many others in the world - would love to come to America. Somehow I find myself wanting to warn them that freedom and prosperity very well could exact a heavy price: the happiness they already possess.

But what do I know?

CENSORSHIP

A P R I L   2 ,   2 0 0 7

I didn't attend last week's "Freedom Forum" concert at the Meyer Theater but read with great interest its coverage in *The Monroe Evening News*. More so was my interest piqued by Editor Deb Saul's Saturday column celebrating America's lack of censorship by highlighting a few of the show's song examples that had historically pushed people of authority to its edge.

Specifically she asked if it mattered that past outcries over whether or not "Puff, The Magic Dragon" was about marijuana use or "Louie, Louie" was about sexual immorality as both are now featured as telephone on-hold music.

Deb suggests our "First Amendment is a safety valve that allows protest and powerful emotions to vent without resorting to violence or censorship," and that "the country that allows its citizens that kind of freedom should be a model for the whole world."

While I desperately want to agree I can't help thinking - and being more concerned - about where we're headed than where we've been. I mean, how far should First Amendment rights go?

I agree that "Puff" and "Louie" are pretty elementary now, but what about some of the songs playing on radios, iPods and CD's today? Songs with lyrics about the joys of raping women or killing cops are already five to 10 years old; should we expect them to be elevator music in a few more years? Will they be no big deal?

I wonder if today's parents really know the content of some of the lyrics going directly from earphones into their children's brains. We all know that being outrageous is what gets you noticed these days, not content of character or quality of talent - consider Sanjaya!

I guarantee you this: There's no way *The Monroe Evening News* would print some of the explicit lyrics most children have access to these days!

Yesterday I went online to Google some of these lyrics; I must tell you even this salty old paratrooper was shocked by what he read, so much so there's no way I could clean them up enough to pass along to you.

I acknowledge dismay over my parents' concerns about the Beach Boys and Beatles lyrics I sang, but my point is, where does it end? My concern is that First Amendment rights are heading in the "anything goes" direction.

Friday's Toledo Blade reported that of 920 Toledo teachers surveyed, 20 percent (184) acknowledged "they had been assaulted or physically threatened last school year by students." Unbelievable, but more so, unacceptable! Could these statistics have anything to do with amplification and celebration of these rights?

While I know that America's freedoms are the "model for the world" and the lure that keeps immigrants flooding our borders, I can't help but think about the model students I found during my visits to over 20 schools during our recent trip to Vietnam. As I reported, the children - kindergarten through college - showed us nothing but class and dignity; their government won't tolerate anything less!

I believe in the First Amendment but wonder how far we will let the interpretation of its boundaries - if there are any - go. Unfortunately, I also think the lack of some sort of censorship is part of the reason we have so much American violence, as well as teachers fearing for their lives each time they go to work.

But what do I know?

"IT TAKES MONEY TO RIDE THE TRAIN"

APRIL 8, 2007

"Son, it takes money to ride the train!"

Mother scolded me with that statement in my younger days for not being more concerned about finances. I never was one to worry about money as long as I had enough. The issue, of course, is always, "How much is enough?"

For me, a bologna sandwich and glass of water was enough sustenance, a guitar and quiet space enough diversion and shelter. Like most parents, she wanted more for me. While she loved my father's blind determination to provide for his family, he was a dirt-poor laborer who struggled just to get by while she fantasized of more - hence the prodding.

Truth is, in a capitalistic society, it does take money to get by. The more you have, the finer the quality of life you can have - if that is what you seek. What disturbs me is when money determines whether one lives, dies or is rescued from tragedy. Our work with We Care and other relief organizations has shown us how money makes the difference for those with no insurance or enough coverage for their child's life-saving treatment. How tragic!

On a less grievous level, how sad it is that some children with talent never develop it because their families cannot afford the needed instrument or tool. Yet, as long as the drive to succeed is there, the human spirit finds a way to break through. Consider Rembrandt, who had no money for brushes yet ultimately painted some of history's greatest masterpieces.

For me, everything in life comes down to attitude - why you do what you do or what you do with what you have.

The Bible warns more about money than it does about the ultimate endings of heaven and hell. I believe that's because our Creator knew that by giving us free will, man naturally would gravitate to the one materialistic thing that could advance him over others: money.

Mom was right; a capitalistic society dictates that everything comes down to money: fixing roads, repairing infrastructures, heating homes, educating children, choosing presidents ...

Huh? Yes, especially choosing presidents and legislative leaders.

Recent fundraising declarations by presidential hopefuls got me thinking about money. Those with the highest totals grabbed frontrunner headlines (Mitt Romney?) Those with puny showings - regardless of whether they might be the perfect person to lead our country from these difficult times - are probably out of the race before it even begins.

Virtually all of these hopefuls, along with Washington's elect, are millionaires, and it's difficult to think they can relate to little people struggling to make ends meet.

In successive campaigns, New York Mayor Michael Bloomberg spent nearly $200 million of his own money to win a job paying less than $100,000 annually, which proves it's all about buying power and position. (When you're worth $5.5 billion, what's $200 million compared to being the most powerful man in America's most powerful state?)

The opportunity to shape the future of our great country - built by sweat of brow and the quest for inalienable rights endowed by our Creator - now is available to the highest bidder.

I believe this philosophy is accurate, and it causes me great concern for our future - especially as I continue to empty my wallet filling my tank with Arab oil.

But what do I know?

FOUNDED ON FAITH

APRIL 9, 2007

What a treat to read last week's letters to the editor responding to the gentleman proclaiming his belief that there is no God. I was impressed by each!

I used to get upset when reading such proclamations as I always want to defend The One who unmistakably rescued me from taking my own life during desperate times some 16 years ago.

And, while it still stings when I hear someone disrespect or speak negatively about the most important person in my world, my faith has grown to where I don't get upset anymore. In fact, last week I joyfully anticipated those letters after reading his diatribe.

Christians must speak out with even greater frequency if we intend to protect the way of life for which our forefathers fought and died as it is in real danger.

Prayer was banned from schools and what we now reap from allowing that seed to be sown is monotonous multiple mass murders that we hardly stop to notice anymore.

Prior to that era America prevailed in every world conflict threatening our way of life and I believe the reason was because we called to God and asked Him to guide and guard us through those conflicts.

It saddened me to visit the new World Wars Monument in Washington, D.C., last Memorial Day and discover the last four words of President Roosevelt's famous war declaration - "so help us God" - were not included when that speech was chiseled into a memorial wall, obviously as not to offend. I was offended!

I believe American prosperity came because the nation proudly proclaimed on its money that "In God We Trust." How ironic to read that the new American quarter was struck with that phrase noticeably missing and then reading last week that for the first time in history, General Motors has taken a back seat in automobile production to tiny

Japan's Toyota Corporation.

Whether anyone likes or believes it, our country was founded on faith in God. Founders qualified their declaration of independence with belief that rights of freedom are "endowed by our Creator" and they too cried out to God for support of their venture by pledging their all when they ended it with, "And for the support of this Declaration, with a firm reliance on the protection of Divine Providence we mutually pledge to each other our Lives, our Fortunes and our sacred Honor."

Constitution preambles of every state begin with a similar reference or plea to God, yet, we have allowed a liberal minority to slowly push Him out of the picture and change the very purpose for which early Pilgrims flocked to these shores.

"Freedom OF Religion" was the issue, not freedom FROM religion. I believe Pilgrims came searching for a new nation where they could have freedom of religion in order not to have one specific religion crammed down their throats. I think they all believed in God but didn't want to be "pigeonholed" into being a Methodist, Catholic or Lutheran, etc.

Thursday is National Day of Prayer and I'll be praying that more Christians will take a stand for what they believe, just as those letter writers did last week. Otherwise I worry the day will come when one will be incarcerated or killed for so doing.

But what do I know?

DESERVING HIS MONIKER

APRIL 16, 2007

You'd have to be living in a cave not to know of the continuing furor over New York radio host Don Imus calling the Rutgers women's basketball team "nappy-headed hos," which led to his firing.

How ironic this comes on the heels of my recent column about the need for censorship. Perhaps more important was the ensuing column about how everything comes down to money that also considered why we do what we do.

While I have no love lost for shock-jock Imus, I feel a bit sorry for him as he has been transposed from the furor focus to a simple pawn as the power behind money rears its ugly head in this matter.

Imus has spewed his insulting brand of humor for decades without consequences. Suddenly by using a phrase hatched in the black community, he is winnowed and vilified in the media fire fueled by the likes of Al Sharpton and Jesse Jackson until ultimately fired by his employer.

You'll notice I didn't dignify Sharpton and Jackson by using the moniker "the Rev." before their names; that was no accident. While I have great fear of The One who instructs in His book to "touch not my anointed," (Psalm 105:15) I have difficulty accepting that someone is anointed by God when all I ever hear them talk about is bigotry, racism and hatred instead of His love and teachings. That makes me consider the old aphorism about "the pot calling the kettle black." (No pun intended!)

Sharpton expects us to forget about his false accusations and embellishments in the Tawana Brawley case (in which he was accused of "playing the race card," which he always does). Jackson ignores his love-child hush money and New York City Jewish reference of "Himey-Town."

For my censorship column reference (where race never was mentioned), I downloaded lyrics from the top 10 rap/hip-hop songs where the n, mf, b, c and ho words were used constantly. Of course, I must abbreviate these filthy words for you, yet your children hear them daily in explicit terms I wouldn't even dare share with you, their parents.

Turn on Black Entertainment Television (BET) videos where women are demeaned as "hos" in virtually every video, then tell me why Sharpton and Jackson aren't all over the news screaming about this travesty?

Here's part of the irony: Kids weren't listening to Imus, adults were; adults aren't listening to or watching rap and hip-hop, kids are. Yet Imus pays the price.

Here's the other - and most important - part: money. The "courageous" stand CBS and MSNBC took in firing Imus came only after the major advertisers pulled their money. Imus has ranted similarly for years, but, without public outcry, he was darling of the set making millions. Thus, firing him wasn't a moral or ethics decision; it was, as it always is in America these days, all about money!

This column isn't about race, as censorship and morals are needed on both sides of the aisle. Instead, it reverberates words of the man who said, "There comes a time when one must take a position that's neither safe, nor political, nor popular, but he must take it because his conscience tells him that it's right."

The Rev. Dr. Martin Luther King deserved his moniker.

But what do I know?

DEAR GAIGE: "POPPY LOVES YOU!"

M A Y 2 1 , 2 0 0 7

Dear Gaige,

Been wondering when I would get around to writing you a letter like I did to your big brother, Drake, when he was your age? My inspiration came yesterday.

I'm glad you whimpered softly when I took you to the church nursery. It was obvious you didn't want to stay. Your brother is just the opposite; he can't wait to get there to play with his friends. So while he stayed, I carried you into the sanctuary, and we sat with your mom and Nonnie.

Last week, I told my readers how you love to cuddle. Anyone in sight of us yesterday saw what I meant. You buried your head into my shoulder and were so content just to let me hold you. I felt your little heart beating and heard the tiny breaths of air you drew in and out of your lungs.

I cradled you into my arms and watched your eyelids get sluggish as sleep slowly claimed you. Those moments were precious.

As I looked into your eyes, I wondered what they would see in the next 50 years. I wondered how they would change from how they light up now when you see an ice cream cone to the day they see the woman of your dreams coming down the aisle to join you at the altar.

"Poppy loves you!"
Gaige Braxton Carr, 2006

I wondered how they might illuminate when they see your son or grandson for the first time, and I remembered mine when they first saw you.

Looking at your ears, I wondered what they might hear in years to come. I wondered how you would feel when you heard "Gaige Braxton Carr" announced just before you march across the stage in a cap and gown.

As I looked at your lips, I wondered how that little heart might flutter the moment you taste your first real kiss. And as I listened to Pastor Roy, I wondered what words would come from your mouth - perhaps even as a pastor, a teacher or even a great singer.

I looked at your nose and saw you in my mind's eye calling to your wife at the end of a hard day's work, "Something sure smells good!" before sitting down to dinner with your family.

I looked at your forehead and hoped it never would become creased and wrinkled from worry as the result of storms of life that undoubtedly will come slashing at your door.

While there in God's presence, I asked Him to keep His hedge of protection around you always. I asked if I could have but one wish for your life, it would be that you would come to know Him as Lord of your life, too.

Once you were sound asleep, I moved you back to my shoulder and felt a bonding between us that was priceless. I told your mom and Nonnie there was no other place on Earth I'd rather have been at that moment.

I hope God allows me to live long enough to personally see and hear the things about which I've wondered about today. If not, I hope your mom scrapbooks this column for you so when you get old enough to read and understand, you always will know how very much your grandfather loved you. I love you buddy!

Love,

Poppy

REST IN PEACE, MY BROTHERS

MAY 29, 2007

As long as I live, I won't forget the little-boy grin on the face of my dear friend, Rodney Vore, as we stood alongside a "No Fishing" sign at a Georgia lake edge awaiting our turn to train inside an Army armored personnel carrier. Grabbing a stick resembling a fishing pole, he said, "Take my picture!" I cherish that picture today.

Bandmate Lenny Liparato could play any instrument you put into his hands. We'd skip study hall and meet another friend, Rance Allen, in the Monroe High School music room to wail on the piano and rock 'n' roll till the bell rang us back to class.

Last time I saw Lenny, we sat on his living room couch days before he deployed to Vietnam. He said, "I got a bad feeling about this, Tom. I don't think I'm coming back."

He wasn't wrong.

A letter postmarked May 14, 1968, from my lifelong friend, Richard Gilbert, had inside a picture of him with his arms around two Vietnamese friends. His words, "It's not so bad over here," were attempts to calm my fears as he knew I would be joining him in the Vietnam War a month later. Two weeks later, I learned that he had been killed ... May 14, 1968.

Days ago, I was telling a friend of the great Summerfield High School sports teams from the late '60s and of the spark plug that made them go, Vince LaRocca. Mighty Mite was his fitting nickname as he was certainly one of the best athletes I ever saw. I think of Vince each time I pass the cemetery on the last curve before getting to the City of Petersburg.

I remember being so proud of Sammy Bosenbark for learning how to fly a Huey helicopter, and I also remember that far-away look in his father's eyes each time I ran into him years later and mentioned Sammy's name.

I remember quiet and shy Dicky Dusseau at Custer School and the years of Memorial Day visits I made to his LaSalle Cemetery grave.

I remember the picture of another Custer schoolmate, Melvin Duty, on the front page of *The Monroe Evening News* after he had captured a Cayman in one of the local creeks.

I never knew Ed Munson, but got a thumbnail sketch of his life after stopping at a LaSalle garage sale years ago and engaging in conversation with the nice lady running it. Once his mother found out I was a Vietnam War veteran, she told me all about her wonderful son and how she missed him.

Dear Friend, Lenny Liparato, KIA Vietnam, 1968.

I miss my friends - these American heroes - this Memorial Day, and I take this moment to honor their memories as I continue to wonder, "Why them and not me?"

I also miss days of my youth when mother loaded us kids into the car, along with flats of flowers and buckets of water and headed to the cemetery to decorate graves of our loved ones and those who had given the ultimate sacrifice in defense of our great country.

The tradition of collectively honoring our war dead on Decoration Day has faded along with the name. The way things are going, I expect Memorial Day will soon fade into Barbecue Day.

But what do I know?

LONGING FOR A LIFE
OF SATURDAYS

JUNE 4, 2007

I love Saturdays!

Saturday is MY day. Weekdays belong to my employer and Sunday belongs to my Lord, but Saturday is my day.

This Saturday was especially wonderful as I had a relaxed morning of coffee and prayer time without having to race off to work.

I'd been trying to find time to watch a friend - Monroe High School senior pitching sensation Jessica Irwin - perform. With the win-or-go-home district finals Saturday, I feared this might be my last chance.

At the softball diamond, I sat behind home plate to better see her "stuff." I squinted through the blazing sun and studied her eyes as she balanced the chartreuse ball against her hip and spun it continuously while studying her catcher's signs.

With one motion she began her windup, whipping her arm circularly to deliver the inappropriately named sphere underarm to the plate 40 short feet away at approximately 60 to 70 mph. The sun wasn't the only thing blazing.

If you've ever been hit by a softball, you'll know why it's inappropriately named. I assure you I wouldn't want to grab a bat and step in against her. She fanned 13 with relative ease and knocked in the winning runs with her bat. The only hit off her was a "seeing-eye" single up the middle.

Jessica holds most MHS pitching records, including strikeouts in a season and career, and is undecided as to where she will continue her brilliant career next year.

As dominating as she is, what impresses me most is her persona. We attend church together, and I know her as the most humble, sweet girl you'd ever want to meet. One of her coaches told me later, "She's the kind of girl you want your daughter to be like."

I hated to leave - as she later would lead MHS to the District championship by tossing yet another 1-hitter - but I was working our family booth at the annual Relay for Life at the fairgrounds.

What an incredible event that has turned into. In spite of the heat, everyone was in a great mood and the festive atmosphere was infectious. While I love the annual fair, the relay is more fun because of why we do what we do. Everyone is there for one purpose: eliminating cancer in our lifetime.

It was great seeing so many friends and checking out new, innovative fundraising methods teams had devised since last year. Dear friend and disc jockey Daddy G. Knight, who annually donates his time and equipment, kept us dancing to the music.

One of the best booths was constructed by the wonderful staff of my dentist, Dr. David Yentz. I don't think anyone had more fun than him - other than me. Finally, after three years, I beat him in our annual basketball shoot and dropped him repeatedly in the dunk tank.

On the way home, Renee and I picked up our grandsons and then built castles in the sand and skipped stones on the lake before baths, bedtime stories, prayers and sleep.

It was a great day to be alive, and it made me long for retirement when I can turn every day into Saturday - which I'm sure is one of the few advantages of growing old.

But what do I know?

LIFE IS ALL ABOUT ME

J U N E   1 8 ,   2 0 0 7

At the time, it seemed the least important thing He told me - probably because He was talking about Himself while I only was thinking of her, and ultimately me.

Jan. 17, 2006, I was on my face before God. The previous morning, the brilliant neurosurgeon gave the woman of my dreams - and me - virtually no hope for her to recover from surgery to remove three tumors the MRI had exposed hiding in her brain.

I had called everyone I knew, asking them to intercede for her to our Heavenly Father; now it was my time for a true heart-to-heart with Him.

I could write a book about the three days during which those tumors were found and removed because many miraculous things happened ... and still are happening.

Recently, the ringing phone had Renee's lifelong friend from Ann Arbor on the line saying, "My son's fiancé's aunt just had brain surgery similar to yours and is paralyzed like you were. Will you and Tom please pray for her?"

Renee answered, "How about if we visit her, too?"

The friend ecstatically encouraged us to do so.

The next day, we loaded into our vehicle and drove the familiar path to Toledo's St. Vincent Mercy Medical Center, where memories of the most traumatic time of my life rushed through my brain.

The elevator opened, and I led Renee through what virtually had been my home for a month. Pushing the button on the wall opened the ICU doors, and once again we were inside the trauma unit with which I had grown so accustomed.

After the joy of nurses recognizing their former patient doing so well, we were ushered to the aunt, who, oddly enough, was in the same bed in the same room with the same nurse as Renee had.

I gently knuckled the glass door, on the other side of which sat the husband and father tenderly holding the hand of the woman of his dreams. Behind them stood their children. All had desperation on their faces.

The husband gave me a look as if to say, "We don't know you; can't you see we have an intense family situation here?"

I opened the door and helped Renee into the room.

"I'm Tom Treece. This is my wife, Renee," I began. "Seventeen months ago, she lay in this very same bed in this very same room, and it was me sitting there holding my wife's hand as she lay paralyzed after brain surgery. We came to share hope with you."

They looked at my beautiful Renee - standing, smiling, with long, glistening hair hiding the ugly scar on top of her head - and listened as she shared how God had given us a healing miracle. I watched as faces segued from desperation to hope.

Suddenly I remembered His words that day - "Life is about Me, and I will use this for My glory!" - and realized I was witnessing it firsthand.

During the past 17 months, they've called, e-mailed, rang our doorbell late at night to say, "My son, husband, wife, neighbor, cousin has a brain tumor. Can you tell us about your miracle?"

We just point them to the Miracle Worker because I believe what He told me - that life is all about Him.

But what do I know?

ROAD RAGE

J U N E 2 5 , 2 0 0 7

He couldn't have hurt me worse had he reached through the window and smacked me!

I started to leave when Renee called, "Hey, I need a kiss before you leave; you never know what might happen!"

"You're right," I responded, "I might get killed on the expressway and never get another!"

"Don't even talk like that!" she scolded before planting a wet one on me and pushing me out the door.

Rushing to make a recording session on time, I was in the passing lane cruising 80 on I-75 when I noticed his white Lincoln entering the freeway from LaPlaisance Rd.'s northbound entrance ramp.

Two semis - a car length apart - occupied the inside lane.

As I passed the first semi the Lincoln came from nowhere, slicing across both lanes through the opening to cut me off. I smoked the tires slamming the brakes and fortunately was able to avoid rear-ending him.

The tires weren't the only thing smoking as I immediately thought of how close I had come to making Renee prophetic; sadly, I couldn't let it go at that.

As soon as the Lincoln passed the semi and pulled back into the middle lane I raced alongside until I was door-to-door and then screamed at him through the passenger window, "You almost got us both killed, you idiot!"

Unfortunately, his two-word response - beginning with an "F" and ending with a "You" - smoked me worse than the brakes did the tires. Instantly furious, I screamed back at him, "Pull over and I'll close that filthy mouth of yours, you _____!"

I called him a name I'm too ashamed to repeat; let's just say it's a slang term for the backside of the human body.

That's when he smacked me; not with his fist but with his words: "Ah, yes, Mr. Christian!"

I was shocked; he had recognized me.

"Sure, I know who you are," he screamed back, "I see your picture in the paper," before again derogatorily addressing me, "Mr. Christian!"

I felt an emotional knife plunge into my heart and for one of the few times in my life I was speechless. In that moment I had lost control; road rage had transformed me into just another like him and anyone else who treat others with reckless abandon.

Recognizing he had stunned me he finally said, "Sorry I cut you off!"

With my heart crushed I exited the E-way, pulled off the road and immediately tried to pray. I couldn't.

Lyrics of a song I sing asks God "Make me a reflection of Your Light." Instead, I had disgraced Him.

I don't mind being called "Jesus Freak," but "Holier Than Thou," or, "Mr. Self Righteous" stings. Truth is I'm just another sinner scratching and clawing through life trying to get it right. Unfortunately, regularly, I don't, and openly proclaiming my faith with my picture in the paper weekly only makes it worse.

Mr. Lincoln, whoever you are, please accept my apology, and please don't judge The One I desire to emulate by my inexcusable behavior. I've asked Him to forgive me; I hope you can too.

Also, I hope you know that it's because of guys like us He had to come to earth in the first place.

But what do I know?

SOMEDAY FIREWORKS
MIGHT NOT BE FUN

J U L Y 2 , 2 0 0 7

What a great weekend to celebrate freedom; I only can hope there are many more.

I came home from work Friday, stripped my clothes and donned shorts and T-shirt to prepare for a garage sale Renee and I had Saturday.

The strong, brisk breeze billowing off the lake into my bedroom was the finest air conditioning for which one could hope. It was then I noticed them.

I never had seen a grouping like this before, so I grabbed binoculars and carefully eased onto the upstairs porch for a closer view. Having impeccable eyesight, they spook at the slightest movement. This time, however, they were unconcerned with me as they obviously were in the midst of a great school of fish.

They reminded me of children jockeying for position on a playground, each pushing past the others in order to be first in line. I raised the binoculars and squinted for a more magnified look.

With scrawny stick-like legs, five Great Blue Herons eased through the shoals searching for dinner. Their long necks reminded me of a herd of giraffes, and it was amazing to watch them lock sight on a fish, cock that neck and then rocket bright-yellow bills into the water to spear and gulp their meal. Fascinating!

With work to be done, I sadly bid them adieu and headed to the garage to help Renee sort through our junk, err, stuff, with which we were determined to part.

Once a year, the City of Luna Pier lures the outside world to come and scour our trash and treasures during citywide garage sales. Saturday, the city was choked with bargain hunters as God blessed us with a gorgeous day.

I enjoyed chatting with various visitors throughout the day and watching our stuff being carted away to the tune of our pockets jingling.

As the day's shadows stretched longer, we regretfully hauled what was left back inside perhaps to await a moving sale in the near future before I headed for our famous pier to facilitate the night's festivities.

Disc jockey Daddy G. Knight had everyone's favorite tunes blasting across our shoreline and echoing throughout downtown as the city was alive with the beginnings of our annual Freedom Celebration. Our wonderful mayor, Todd Deal, welcomed the crowd and local singing phenom Ashley Greer belted out a heart-wrenching version of our national anthem.

We rewarded longtime, behind-the-scenes worker Art Lutz with our Citizen of the Year award before turning our attention skyward for "the rocket's red glare and bombs bursting in air." And, once again, the Luna Pier Volunteer Fire Department's spectacular fireworks show thrilled all in attendance.

With my honey home in bed after overworking herself at our sale, I made a hasty exit to join her. It had been a fun, fabulous day, and I faded into sleep to the sounds of whistling skyrockets and intermittent explosions.

On Sunday, I narrated our church's patriotic service and was overcome with emotion as we paid tribute to fallen comrades who paid the tab for the rest of us to live in peace and enjoy our freedoms.

Later, watching coverage of defused London car bombings, I wondered how long before we hear those explosions in America instead of simple, celebratory ones. Sadly, I don't expect it will be long.

But what do I know?

JOBLESS, BUT AT PEACE

JULY 9, 2007

What a wonderful weekend!

I love the dog days of summer. And while it can get a bit uncomfortable, it's never too hot for me. I've always wondered whether my 13 months spent on the Asian Equator permanently put me in that mode because, now, the hotter the better for me.

On Friday night, my sweetheart made reservations at one of our favorite places, the Frog Leg Inn, for 7 p.m. - the same time the Luna Pier City Council would be voting to decide my job fate.

"What's the occasion?" I asked.

"It's a wherever-God's-taking-us-next celebration dinner," she replied.

We already knew I would not be reappointed to my position because the gentleman missing from last week's deadlocked 3-3 vote meeting had voted against rehiring me last year. Dinner and my job ended at about the same time.

On Saturday - for the first time all year - I stretched out on the back porch and soaked up some sun and realized I was relaxing for the first time in a long time. I watched boats skipping across the lake, terns diving for dinner and Canadian honkers guiding their newborns into the shallows to feed.

On Saturday night, I had the honor of singing at the wedding of my former secretary from my days as GM at Monroe's Tower 98 radio station. Tracee Bodell married Dan Fortinberry, the man of her dreams. My heart was full of joy to see hers in the same condition.

On Sunday, after my musical group, Cross Point, led a morning worship service at the Covered Wagon Camp Resort in Ottawa Lake, Renee and I attended the heartwarming dedication service of two new Luna Pier homes miraculously built in a few short weeks by Habitat for Humanity. They are beautiful.

Even more beautiful was the spirit that flowed from the young lady whose family will occupy one of the sites as she stepped to the microphone. She poured out her thanks to the many who helped her family finally realize the American dream of owning their own home. Then, in closing moments, she was frozen with that rare but wonderful characteristic of being humbled and overcome with emotion and thanks.

What a wonderful organization Habitat for Humanity is. It's such a throwback to days of old when people truly helped each other. When one in the community had a problem, all came running to help - whether it was to plant their garden because they couldn't or rebuild barns destroyed by weather or fire. It's a dying characteristic.

Near the end of the day, Renee and I received fresh pictures of the school we are building in Vietnam. Finishing touches are being applied, and the rush is on to get it completed in time for the first day of school Aug. 15.

It was a heart-warming weekend.

There are uncertainties as we look down the road, but our faith is strong - as is our love for each other and those around us who share our world. And, yes, that includes those who decided my fate Friday; they're only doing what they believe is right.

How wonderful to feel such peace in my heart in spite of being jobless at 60. Only the love of God could give that to me.

But what do I know?

CIRCLE THE WAGONS

J U L Y   1 6 ,   2 0 0 7

As a boy, my perception was that America was indeed "one nation under God" and virtually everyone believed in Him - and if you didn't, you suffered persecution.

It wasn't that long after the Joseph McCarthy fear-mongering era of labeling anyone that didn't share your political or religious viewpoint a Communist.

It also was a time of "religious wars," in which denominations verbally combated each other. My own parents told me, "Whatever you do, don't marry a Catholic!" I heard similar stories from Catholics about Baptists, Lutherans, Pentecostals, etc.

There now seems to be all-out war on religion in general, and persecution is targeted for anyone who does believe in God and, specifically, Jesus.

Our entire culture and way of life heretofore is under microscopic scrutiny, and anything that might offend anyone must be eliminated.

Nothing has been more controversial than the recent resignation of Monroe County Community College chorale director John Tyner over changes made without his input after complaints about the commencement music's religious references.

I know both him and MCCC President Dr. David Nixon and feel for each.

After the community outpouring of support for him, Mr. Tyner needs no extra push from me, although I, too, would walk through fire for this great motivational man of integrity, faith and talent.

At the same time, although I didn't like his decision, Dr. Nixon has been unjustly hammered for his actions regarding this issue.

As former general manager of Monroe's Tower 98 radio, my job was to run the day-to-day operations of the station. In truth, I only had one job, and that was to protect the station's license - for without the license, we couldn't even turn the power on, let alone make money.

Dr. Nixon has done the same. He, too, is a man of great integrity who did what he did to protect the college, specifically from lawsuits.

Perhaps another day's column should examine lawsuits because decisions are daily made in business, industry and government to avoid them instead of doing what is right.

I hear often from those who hate that I regularly refer to God in my writing. I've explained it's because He saved me from suicide and gave me never-before-experienced peace and joy. It is my culture. It's the rock on which I now stand. Everything I think, say and do relates to that. I can't help talking about it.

At the same time, America is trying to decide if we are - or want to continue to be - "one nation under God." Most don't want to talk about it, but I don't think we have a choice because I believe the cultural base of our country was founded on it and our laws fashioned accordingly. And the MCCC controversy confirms it.

I also believe true freedom allows each of us to think, worship and live as we choose as long as it conforms to laws governing our land. I wouldn't want someone dictating to me a religion in which I must believe.

How quaint it is that those warring denominations from youth are now much more tolerant of each other. What they need to do is circle the wagons because current attacks and persecutions are nothing compared to ones that are on the way.

But what do I know?

PRIORITIES

JULY 30, 2007

I was thinking about priorities and how we each differ regarding their placement in our lives. What's important to some is irrelevant to others.

Having spent a great deal of my life associated with the media, it's been easy see how radio, TV and newspapers give us what they believe we want to hear, see and read.

I think we all secretly desire to slow down and gawk at the tragic accident on the highway even though we know it impedes rescue efforts, resumption of traffic flow, etc. We also yawn while reading of multiple millions made by those able to slap a baseball regularly into the seats, yet gasp when we learn the wages of doctors saving our lives.

A few years ago this newspaper ran two stories on the same day that left me thinking about priorities. I purposely waited this long to write about it as I wanted to ensure no negative light be cast upon the young lady in one of the stories.

The first of those two stories featured bold headlines and a picture of the girl on the front page of the sports section above the fold. It gave her name and told the story of how she came off the bench in the closing moments of a tightly contested basketball game to score four points and help her team win the contest. It was a great story and even quoted her on how she felt about her great success.

The other story was no more than one or two paragraphs and was "buried" deep inside the paper; certainly not prominently displayed. I expect I wouldn't have noticed it had it not been for the fact that it was about the daughter of my physician.

I had been following her short but stellar career mainly due to my relationship with her father. Still in high school, she was a champion equestrian as well as an award-winning writer who displayed wisdom and composition far beyond her years.

The story was short and sweet and simply told that she had become a National Merit Scholar.

One girl scored four points in a local basketball game and got her picture on the front page and name in bold headlines. The other won countrywide honors as a National Merit Scholar and had her success story buried in the dead zone of the newspaper.

I am not minimizing the young basketball player's effort - hers was important, for herself and for the success of her team. Neither do I criticize the sports editor or writers; they simply give us what we want to read. The point I wish to make is about us; most people don't want to read about an outstanding scholar, but because of our emphasis on sports and athletic ability, relatively minimal effort garners headlines.

It's the same for the Boy Scout who helps the elderly lady across the street; who cares! However, let that same boy use a gun and kill a cop and suddenly he's front page news for weeks.

Unfortunately, most of us prioritize for the sensational stuff. And, while these two stories are hardly of that magnitude they still hint of an also unfortunate indication of which side is winning in the ongoing, overall battle between good and evil.

But what do I know?

GREEN BEANS

A U G U S T   6 ,   2 0 0 7

"Just one more stop!" I told Renee and steered her toward the Monroe County Fair building's first display.

My eyes scanned the shelves of jars until stopping on one full of green beans that specifically captured my attention. A smile slowly came to my lips as my mind began to drift.

Suddenly I was a boy again, sitting in the kitchen watching mother examine each section of the broken green beans.

Her Master Gardener husband - my father - grew the beans in our garden, and, along with my siblings, Hal and Janet, we had picked and then broken them.

Breaking beans always was an interesting chore. We sat for hours in the cool of the breezeway talking about whatever was happening in our lives while snapping off the pointed little ends of the beans and pulling the "string" off one side before doing the same to the other and then breaking them into sections.

Mother then washed them thoroughly and began the canning process.

"Canning is a dying art!" Renee interrupted my precious memory.

"Yes it is," I responded before drifting back to mother.

To prepare each of the jars, she would send me to retrieve jars from our old, damp, dingy, scary, Michigan basement throughout winter. She would simply yet lovingly pour the beans into pint or quart Mason jars.

But for ones she intended to bring to this same Monroe County Fair for display and judging, she strategically placed each bean section exactly where and how she wanted it to be seen. Once satisfied with "the look" of the jar, she would place it into the pressure cooker and begin the cooking process.

I never thought much about it as a boy, but Saturday it had a different meaning. I remembered wondering why she would take such painstaking care to make sure each jar she entered for judging was perfect. It was evident in that same moment, as I then remembered that after mother left us for heaven, we found a tattered cardboard box full of all the blue ribbons she won each year.

My mind drifted to nights when mother would make a big pot of soup beans and a pan of cornbread and then send me to that basement dungeon to bring a fresh can of beets to the table. She would proudly eye those beautiful red beets and then listen carefully for the sound upon opening, telling her the seal was good and that she had canned them properly.

I thought of Dolly Parton's masterpiece song "Coat of Many Colors" and how she told of "the love my momma sewed in every stitch" in describing a coat her mother made her from "a box of rags someone gave us" when she was just a girl.

As I stared at that jar of green beans, I felt the love of mother along with the emotion of tears trying to seep into my eyes. Remembering how much love and attention mother gave a simple jar of canned green beans only made me realize how much more love and attention she gave us kids.

Is your mother still here? If so, now would be a great time to call and thank her for all that love she gave you!

But what do I know?

"NOBODY WAS LOOKING AT YOUR SHOES!"

A U G U S T   1 3 ,   2 0 0 7

"Can we take it slow tonight?" Renee asked. "I'd like to wear my dress shoes."

That question caused me to think this weekend about some of the many differences between men and women. Perhaps the most obvious - at least to me - is the difference in the perception of importance.

I am a simple man and admit to not being concerned about things most others are. I don't really care what color something is; all I am concerned about is whether it works.

I feel similarly toward food; when my stomach starts grumbling and distracts me from my work, all I care about is getting it to stop grumbling so I can return to work. I don't think or dream about food, and, other than going out for a fine dinner with her, I could care less about what I eat, as long as it works.

Renee has a place for everything and everything in its place. I must adhere to that philosophy with my personal belongings, otherwise she finds a place for them and I search forever until finally asking where she put them.

I'm not overly concerned with clutter, as out of sight is out of mind to me. Renee, on the other hand, is just the opposite; everything needs a place to hide. If you are a husband, you know what they say about keeping momma happy.

I'd probably look like a refugee if it weren't for Renee. When we are getting dressed for an occasion, I come out of the closet and show myself to her and she says, "Nope, black belt with black shoes!" and sends me to change.

Don't get me wrong, I don't want to look like a dweeb any more than I normally do, but my mind is just not geared toward being concerned about whether my belt matches my shoes; the only thing I'm concerned about is whether it works.

Not so with women. They aren't nearly as concerned with how something works as they are about how it looks.

After Renee's brain surgery left her paralyzed from the right knee down, we had to order special men's shoes large enough to accommodate the brace she must wear in order to walk. I love them because they work; she hates them because they look like something her dweeb husband would wear if she weren't around to keep him straight.

We attended the wonderful Miss Monroe County Scholarship Pageant on Saturday night at the Meyer Theater where the audience, along with the stage, was packed with drop-dead-gorgeous women. I felt so blessed because the most gorgeous one of all was on my arm.

Wearing dress shoes, however, meant wearing no brace, which dictated a snail's pace with constant fear of falling, which, for her 6-foot-5 husband, was quite nerve-racking. Yet, what a minute sacrifice.

I promised God before her surgery that if He would let her live, I would meet her needs forever. I'd feed her if she couldn't eat, carry her if she couldn't walk and speak for her if she couldn't talk.

Saturday night, everyone marveled at not only Renee's beauty but the incredible miracle God gave us with her recovery. And while I'm no fashion plate, I feel pretty confident in saying, "Baby, nobody was looking at your shoes!"

But what do I know?

FAITHFULNESS

A U G U S T   2 0 ,   2 0 0 7

"Faithfulness" came to mind as I contemplated what to write about today; what also came to mind was a rock-hard birthday cake!

Being faithful to write this column weekly has been difficult as sometimes the brain just draws a blank. Fortunately, God has been faithful as I seek His guidance before I write and He always gives me something.

I want to be faithful in life, to my wife, our children, grandchildren, to you, to God. I want friends to know I will be there when and if I'm needed.

One of the greatest feats of faithfulness in my life was orchestrated by my sister, Janet. She had an opportunity unwittingly placed before her and chose to respond.

In addition to personal trauma, being drafted into the Army and sent to war in Vietnam had a traumatic effect on my tight-knit family and for the next two years they were smothered by a blanket of worry and sorrow for my safety.

Finding myself on the other side of the planet 14,000 miles away from everything I knew and loved was difficult at best; knowing I was there to kill people and try to keep them from killing me was virtually unthinkable.

"Seebee Sobee:" Faithful sister Janet, 2006.

Other than precious memories that drove me to complete my mission in order to return home, there wasn't much light at the end of the tunnel. That is, had it not been for Janet.

She made a decision to be faithful to her little brother, and, as a result, in the next 13 months I received over 400 letters as she wrote me at least once every day I was at war! To me, Barry Bonds' recent home run record is nothing compared to that.

After recently writing my 200th column for *The Monroe Evening News* I think about how I've struggled to come up with something to write about once a week; I can't imagine trying to write something positive and happy to cheer a sibling once per day. Truthfully, those letters were some of the most boring, sterile letters anyone has ever received, and, yet, they undoubtedly were extremely important elements of my survival.

Each day during "mail call" I heard my name and while the guys with whom I served were happy for me they were simultaneously jealous I had so many loved ones flooding me with mail from home.

Sometimes we wouldn't get mail for weeks so when we did they had to endure hearing, "Treece, Treece, and Treece" repeatedly. They also assumed these letters were from a girlfriend; I never told them different.

One day during mail a heavy box came; inside was a birthday cake Janet had made and sent a month before. Needless to say it was hard as a rock and the guys kidded that all I had to do now was hit the Viet Cong in the head with it. Laughing about it years later she would say, "I just wanted you to have a cake for your birthday."

I will be forever grateful to Janet for the great love - and faithfulness - she gave me during the most difficult time of my life.

I believe faithfulness, like so many other positive human characteristics, is just another by-product of the most important element in life: love!

But what do I know?

FROM FEAR TO FRUITION— WITH HIS PLAN

A U G U S T   2 7 ,   2 0 0 7

It's so amazing to me how - when you let Him - God guides and directs our lives.

The whole concept of God is so outrageously wonderful that most people believe He's nothing more than a fairy tale - until they meet Him personally and He begins His amazing work in their lives.

One such instance for Renee and me came in January, 2000. Ohio Congresswoman Marcy Kaptur requested I attend a meeting of local Vietnam veterans and Rotarians to discuss possibilities of helping the war-torn people of Vietnam.

We organized as The D.O.V.E. Fund (Development of Vietnam Endeavors) and began fundraising work, concentrating on developing educational and medical facilities for these poverty-stricken people - and especially the children.

And, as all true leaders-by-example do, our board of trustees agreed we couldn't ask others to give if we weren't individual givers ourselves. We set a specific, annual financial trustee requirement above and beyond the value of our time.

Having previously downsized from a six-figure job to one paying a quarter of that, this requirement was a burden for Renee and me, and we didn't know if I could afford to stay with the organization.

On suicide's doorstep after a life of trouble, I had made a decision to follow Jesus Christ and He led me out of the darkness I was in for so many years. I learned not to become anxious about anything and simply give whatever trouble I was having to Him. And He always worked it our for my good - even when there seemed no way possible.

Renee and I asked Him to show us a way we could meet my financial requirement for D.O.V.E.

Not long after He gave me the idea of writing a book about a trip back to Vietnam, we dedicated the original five schools we had built there. That trip proved to be a tremendous healing for this veteran who had lived 30-plus years with ghosts of war in his mental closet.

We also decided we would use all profits from the book to personally build a $6,000 nursery school in the village where I served as a soldier during the war. We decided to donate the initial $5,000 - that way, if the book bombed, we figured we could always pawn off $1,000 worth of books to our families and friends.

God blessed those "barley loaves and fish" and, on Sept. 5, the $65,000 Pho Phong Elementary School will open for its first day of classes for 783 children of the village of Duc Pho in the Quang Ngai Province of the Republic of Vietnam.

We are excited!

Yet as exciting as it is to see such a tiny seed blossom into such a magnificent entity, it's just another blessed event in the lives of those who have learned to trust God to meet their needs.

God replaced our fear that we could not meet financial requirements to stay in this group with a plan (our book, "The Ghost Closet") that has become the largest single contributor to the $1.3 million the D.O.V.E. Fund has collected to date.

His amazing guidance and grace really isn't amazing at all; rather, it's everyday stuff for the believer. What's amazing is that more people don't believe it.

But what do I know?

PHO PHONG: A REALITY

S E P T E M B E R 4 , 2 0 0 7

My how things change!

All I could think of 39 years ago was getting away from where I was at the time; today all I can think about is wishing I was back there tomorrow.

During prayer time this morning I again saw in my mind's eye the little girl from the "Beauty and the Beast" picture about whom I wrote in my book, "The Ghost Closet."

I saw the mud squishing up between her toes and the look in the eye of the two-ton water buffalo she commanded with soft whispers and gentle tugs on the string tied to the ring in his nose.

I saw the longing look in her eyes as she gazed past me at the frolicking children playing happily across the street in the courtyard of the school us foreigners had just dedicated in her hamlet.

She had no chance for an education despite being close enough to hit the school with a rock pulled from the ground her family hand-hoed that day; one must pay for children to attend schools; that is, if there is one.

She was needed in the rice fields as growing food dominates life for the poverty-stricken people of Vietnam.

In April, 2001, the humanitarian group to which I belong - Development of Vietnam Endeavors (D.O.V.E.) - dedicated the first of five schools we had funded in the land where most of us served as soldiers during the war.

So moved by the little girl and the entire experience of returning with peace and love to the land where I previously carried weapons of war, I wrote the book about that experience. Renee and I then decided to use all the book's profits to build a $6,000 nursery school in the village where I had served.

Then, you came into the equation. You bought into our vision by purchasing the book as she and I took our dog and pony show on the road to local churches, service clubs and anywhere invited to tell our story.

Soon we had enough to build that school, but, you kept buying and donating so we upgraded plans for a bigger school and more students. Next thing we knew we were adding a second story to the blueprints as our humble, $6,000 project turned into a $65,000 venture!

Last March, after God had blessed us with Renee recovering from her brain surgery enough to travel again to Vietnam, we broke ground and helped pour the Pho Phong Elementary School's foundation.

We were kept apprised of construction progress and are thrilled to share that Wednesday morning (which will actually be this evening on the other side of the planet), 783 children from the Village of Duc Pho, Vietnam, will have a brand, spanking new school to attend and receive an education.

Renee and I thank you for your love, prayers and financial support for our school without which it couldn't have happened.

We also thank God for the vision that has given so many the opportunities for education they wouldn't have had. Also, for turning a terrible time in history into such glorious healing that would make even me want to return to the place I once swore I would never; I'm sure only He could have done that for me.

But what do I know?

Tom and Renee with children of Pho Phong School, Vietnam, 2007.

OBSESSED WITH 9-11

S E P T E M B E R   1 0 ,   2 0 0 7

I read an article last week suggesting America is obsessed with 9/11 and that we should de-emphasize its anniversary.

I've always been of the opposite opinion. I've wanted to see TV coverage of those planes flying into the World Trade Towers and exploding to kill more than 2,500 of our citizens - not because I'm an ambulance chaser or love violence but because I believe those who fail to learn lessons from the past are prone to repeat them. Although I'd rather not talk or think about it, the truth is I don't ever want to forget it despite wanting it just to go away.

After reading the text from the latest Osama bin laden video, I realize he and they are not going away and must be addressed.

How poignant as we sit in this stagnant Michigan economy - with the closing of our local automobile factory forecasting dire consequences - that he speak to America about capitalism, democracy and our way of life.

His plan for our defeat is to bleed us into bankruptcy as they did the Russians in Afghanistan by causing us to pour billions into the war efforts. Is it working? Time will tell.

The bottom line of his rhetoric is pure and simple: Democracy is not working and the only thing that will save America is submission to Islam.

Oddly, his philosophy and mine are somewhat similar. We both believe in a supreme being - he calls Him Allah, I call Him God.

The differences come from the different books in which we believe - his, the Quran; mine, the Bible.

The greatest difference is in the response we expect from sharing their religion. Osama believes Allah sent the prophet Mohammed with the Quran, and, ultimately, those who reject him and Islam must die here on Earth.

I, as a Christian, believe God sent Jesus and the Bible, and the choice is yours whether to accept Him. Unbelief simply causes one to be eternally separated from Him.

Each way of life - capitalism versus Islam - has extremisms. After trying my best to watch last night's MTV Awards in order to try to keep a pulse on what America's young people are into, I understand why many in the world think America is paving the way to ruin.

On the other hand, after watching the brutal beheadings of Nicholas Berg and others in the name of Allah, as well as extensive coverage of the suppression of women in the Islamic culture via such things as burkas and public beatings, I don't think too many American women will be interested in moving in that direction either.

I must admit that the face of democracy and capitalism has changed dramatically in my lifetime. It used to be that Americans gave a fair day's work for a fair day's pay. And while there always have been pockets of impurity, most Americans were loving, giving and concerned for their neighbors - at home and abroad. The love of money and all it can acquire seems to have changed all that.

I still believe in democracy and capitalism but believe we must return to endorsing the foundations on which it was built; otherwise, bin Laden is right and America is doomed, and it won't have anything to do with religion.

But what do I know?

GRAND CANYON

S E P T E M B E R 1 7 , 2 0 0 7

Whoever named it knew what they were doing.

I've been around the world a few times, but unquestionably this was one of the most incredible things I ever had seen - so much so that I couldn't just say, "Wow!" and get back in the car and drive away. Instead, I headed for the local store and bought a backpack and food for three days.

I had quite the advantage over two friends who had invited me to join them for the proverbial "trip to California." I still was in great shape from my Army days. I would need that stamina for the down-and-up 35-mile trek upon which we were about to embark.

Like crazy, adventuresome youth, we had quit our jobs and headed West, visiting friends in Madison, Wis., before crossing the mighty Mississippi and South Dakota's Badlands and then heading south to Wyoming and Colorado.

After a week in Denver, we continued southwest across New Mexico to Arizona, where we spent another week with my dear friend, Wayne Snyder, who was attending Arizona State University.

Continuing on, our intent was just to stop for a quick glance as we drove north to see what turned out to be the site of sites: the Grand Canyon.

It literally took my breath away, and I remember just standing there and staring at what is still one of the most incredible scenes I ever have seen.

The canyon is 277 miles long, averages 5,000 feet in depth and spans 18 miles at its widest point. Trust me, you have to see it to believe it.

I remember standing on the south rim and watching a huge storm of black, boiling clouds - complete with lightning bolts and thunder - move down the canyon while I stood in pleasant   above it all.

After we had driven the entire rim and stopped at each vantage point, it was time to leave. The problem for me was that I couldn't.

Tom on his way to the bottom of the Grand Canyon, 1971.

"Let's go to the bottom!" I challenged my buddies. And that's exactly what we did.

We rested at a ranger station halfway down before finally crossing the Navaho Bridge traversing the raging Colorado River and turned in for the night. I stared up at millions of stars from the belly of the Canyon and felt so terribly tiny and insignificant.

The next morning, we ventured further up the north rim, and I sat on a vantage point wondering how long it took to carve the canyon and where that excess rock had gone.

We headed back the next day, recrossing the bridge and beginning the long, arduous climb out of the canyon.

Like I said, having only recently returned from the Vietnam War, I was in great shape and knew the importance of rationing food and water, unlike my exhausted compatriots.

I also advised them that signs along streams warning against drinking the water meant exactly that. Unfortunately, they paid the caveat no heed and got sick as dogs.

Back at the ranger station I traded my pocketknife for two cans of Campbell's bean with bacon soup, heated it and got enough nourishment in them to finally get them out of the canyon.

Those three days were three of the most memorable of my life. Kudos to whoever named it, because it certainly was grand!

But what do I know?

HE'S THE BEST
SEPTEMBER 24, 2007

I know that people who don't know Him tire of hearing me talk about my relationship with God. But when you watch Him repeatedly do incredible things in your life, it's difficult not to talk about Him.

You've heard my stories crediting Him for bringing me through war, divorce, drugs, alcohol and numerous other life-changing events - the most traumatic of which was Renee's brain surgery of a year ago. More recently was my sudden and unexpected loss of employment just days ahead of my 60th birthday.

It was amazing how neither of us panicked. Instead, Renee and I were excited as we have learned to trust Him, knowing He is in charge of our lives and knows our needs before we even ask.

Truth is, it was time for us to leave the City of Luna Pier. Perhaps we'll talk more about that at another time.

Our big problem with leaving Luna Pier was the same problem that has dominated headlines of this and other newspapers lately: the stagnant housing market resulting from a depressed economy (that undoubtedly only will get worse when our local Ford plant closes).

Instead of pining, we got on our knees and asked the God of Abraham to send us a buyer for our home. There is a Scripture (Romans 8:28) that promises, "All things work together for good to those who love God and are called according to His purpose." We consistently claim that promise.

The Scripture's key is qualification: We love God and proclaim it openly and also believe we are called according to His purpose. I believe it was His purpose that put me on Page 3 of this newspaper despite minimal education and experience. And I didn't scream and moan when I recently lost my job because I believed He was moving me.

Despite leafing nightly through pages of pictures of homes on the market in *The Monroe News* and seeing a sea of "For Sale" signs along every street we drove, we continued to believe in that promise and trust God to meet our need.

Five weeks after calling a Realtor, the first couple to look at our home said, "We love it; we'll take it!" and the deal was virtually done.

There was a small glitch involving title work, but we didn't panic. We just gave the problem to Him, and He worked it out like He always does.

I hate leaving the lake, but we've been talking about downsizing for some time, so we have purchased a beautiful new Townes on Front condo and will be moving back to Monroe before the week is out.

I didn't want to write this column as I worried about possibly offending those who have not had success selling their homes. However, I had a greater urge to share our success in hopes that others might be encouraged to "believe and not doubt" as He instructs.

Unbelievers who hate reading about my and Renee's joy should just not bother reading this column. Alternatively, if you are a believer and need some encouragement, know that God loves you and wants to give you the desires of your heart as He has us.

Also, if you're looking for a Realtor, He's the best!

But what do I know?

PICTURE PERFECT

O C T O B E R 1 , 2 0 0 7

"It's the perfect picture for the cover!" I told Jim Dombrowski, creative services manager for the Monroe Publishing Co.; "It shows me down on one knee with my arm around a little Vietnamese boy and my M-16 automatic weapon is subdued and slung under my arm."

It was a few years ago and we were discussing what picture to use for the cover of my recent book, "The Ghost Closet," that was being published by The Monroe Evening News parent company.

Jim is a computer wizard at graphic arts and has since done not only that cover but the cover of my CD single, "The Wide Road," as well as the cover of my new book soon to be available, "But What Do I Know, Volume I."

"So where's the picture?" he asked.

"I'm sure I put it in a safe place so I wouldn't lose it," was my answer. The problem was that I had virtually torn my house apart looking for that safe place to no avail.

"Personally I recommend we use the picture of the little girl waving from doorway of her home in the village, but, it's your book," he continued before sending me home to continue looking for the picture.

Those who have worked with me through the years will undoubtedly testify they have no idea how I ever find anything on my desk. I call it "organized chaos" while I'm sure they would call it, "chaos!" It may not look like it but I usually know exactly where everything is; it just takes me time to find it. However, no matter how hard I looked I could not find the picture.

Mr. Dombrowski is a consummate professional whom I have not only learned to like immensely over the years but to also implicitly trust. When deadline arrived and a decision had to be made for the book's cover, I had no choice but to use the picture of the little girl waving.

Recently, while preparing for a moving sale, Renee came across an old scanner we had discarded and planned to sell. When she opened it to clean the glass, out popped the missing picture of me with the little boy.

It had faded quite a bit in the 39 years since it was taken but it's one of my favorite pictures from my past. Behind us in the picture is the Duc Pho village orphanage where I used to visit regularly to play with the kids and give money to the nuns running it. Fittingly, a cross stands above the sign that reads, "Love."

I expect that any success I enjoyed in my management career has been directly related to something I learned a long time ago; that was to always pick the best person for the job, tell them what I want them to do and then get out of their way and let them do it.

Now that I have both pictures in front of me, and despite how much I love the one of me and the little boy, the picture Jim picked was unquestionably the right one for the cover.

Thank God for professionals who in turn make the rest of us look good. And thank you, Jim Dombrowski, for your professionalism, patience and persistence in doing what you knew all along was right. You're the best!

But what do I know?

Village boy selling ice cold Coke to Tom in Duc Pho, 1968.

TRUST

With this final chapter I would like to make a special dedication of this book to the board of directors, officers, stockholders and employees of my hometown bank, Monroe Bank & Trust, and especially to a special friend there; you know who you are!

I can still remember as a boy holding mother's hand as she would lead me inside what was then their only office, located on Front Street in downtown Monroe, Michigan, to do our family's banking.

I remember staring up at the vaulted ceiling and feeling so small in such a huge place. I also remember tiptoeing to try to see who was behind the teller's window that my mother trusted to take our money.

I remember her taking me through the mouth of the cavernous vault where she trusted our valuables to their safety deposit box.

"Trust" is an important word in our language. One of my favorite definitions from Webster is, "something entrusted to one to be cared for in the interest of another."

Some 60 years later and now with a family of my own, we continue to trust MBT with our banking needs.

However, Monroe Bank & Trust realized long ago the need to be more than just a trusted place to save, invest and grow your money, so they in turn invested back in our communities.

No matter where you look around Monroe County you will see that investment; in our families, farms, factories and fairs as well as our downtowns and community developments. Monroe Bank & Trust stimulated business by backing thousands of businesses through the years and they stood strong even after sometimes being left "holding the bag" when some of those businesses failed.

From that local office that awed this pup all those years ago they now have invested 26 branch offices and scattered numerous ATM's across our county.

Further commitment to our communities is witnessed each time one of our many humanitarian or non-profit agencies have a fair or fundraiser as MBT sends their Enlist volunteers to help staff the events, rewarding those employees with time off from work.

You have read in this book about the school my wife, Renee, and I built in the village where I served as a soldier during the Vietnam War. That school was mostly financed by the sale of my book, "The Ghost Closet." When it came time to kick off that campaign with a book release party, it was Monroe Bank & Trust who stepped forward to promote that event which was, in turn, critical to the project's success.

The joy Renee and I have in the relationship of our marriage is based on the trust we jointly have in and for each other.

The joy we have in the relationship with our Heavenly Father is based on the trust we have in His promise to never leave or forsake us.

The joy we have in the relationship with Monroe Bank & Trust is knowing that for over 150 years, through a Civil War and The Great Depression to the current dismal state of our economy, and as numerous other pretenders have come and gone, our hometown bank has remained not only locally-owned but strong and faithful to the trust their name promises to each and every one of us.

In this day and time one doesn't find just anywhere the track record of trust one will always find when they do their banking at Monroe Bank & Trust!

But what do I know?

Printed in the United States
200374BV00001B/61-210/A